CONTENTS

INTRODUCTION

The 2003 Dwight D. Eisenhower National Security Conference was held September 25–26, 2003. Conference participants worked to accomplish several objectives:

- "...help promote...a common knowledge and understanding of the critical issues of our time."—Dwight D. Eisenhower, July 1948 (broadcast entitled "The Veteran Wants to Know");

- provide a broad and unique forum to discuss and debate contemporary and future national security issues;

- examine and advance ways to more effectively focus the instruments of national power; and

- contribute to the ongoing national security dialogue while broadening the experience of mid-level and senior Army leaders through exposure to diverse issues, institutions, and perspectives.

The co-sponsors of this conference were the Woodrow Wilson International Center for Scholars; the Medill School of Journalism, Northwestern University; the Center for International Security and Cooperation (CISAC), Stanford University; the International Crisis Group; the Director of Net Assessment, Office of the Secretary of Defense; and the U.S. Army. This two-day conference was held in the Ronald Reagan Building and International Trade Center, Washington, D.C.

Five addresses and four panel discussions challenged the more than 500 who attended. Joseph Nye, Ph.D., dean of the John F. Kennedy School of Government at Harvard University; Philip Merrill, chairman of the Export-Import Bank of the United States; Secretary of Defense Donald Rumsfeld; Honeywell Chief Executive Officer (CEO) David Cote; and Ambassador Richard Armitage, deputy secretary of state, all addressed the conference.

Panels were as diverse as they were lively and engaging.

The first panel covered the topic of state failure. The Woodrow Wilson International Center for Scholars sponsored the panel, and its director of international studies, Robert Litwak, Ph.D., moderated. Panelists included Dr. Charles Krauthammer, syndicated columnist, the *Washington Post*; Chester Crocker, Ph.D., James R. Schlesinger professor of strategic studies at Georgetown University; David Gordon, Ph.D., director of transnational issues at the CIA; and Ambassador Wendy Sherman, principal, the Albright Group.

The second panel explored the topic of the media's role in reporting and influencing world events. The Medill School of Journalism sponsored the panel and Professor Roy Gutman moderated. Panelists included Doug Farah, the *Washington Post*; Dan Murphy, the *Christian Science Monitor*; Steve LeVine, the *Wall Street Journal*; and Hisham Melhem, the Lebanese daily, *As-Safir*, and Dubai-based Al-Arabiya television.

The third panel attempted to draw predictive lessons from three case studies of recent nuclear proliferation. The Center for International Security and Cooperation sponsored the panel and CISAC's Scott D. Sagan, Ph.D., moderated. Panelists were George Perkovich, Ph.D., vice president for studies at the Carnegie Endowment for International Peace; Polly (Mary) Nayak, senior advisor, Abraxas Corporation; and Daniel B. Poneman, principal, the Scowcroft Group.

The final panel explored the timely subject of political and military challenges in Iraq. The International Crisis Group sponsored the panel and Ambassador Nancy E. Soderberg moderated. Panelists included Barham Salih, Ph.D., regional administrator, Sulaimania, Iraq; Rafeeuddin Ahmed, former special advisor to the UN secretary-general on Iraq; Fareed Yasseen, Ph.D., advisor to Adnan Pachachi, member of the Iraqi Governing Council; and Ambassador James Dobbins, director of the International Security and Defense Policy Center, RAND Corporation.

SUMMARY

NATIONAL POWER IN AN UNPREDICTABLE WORLD

At the 2003 conference, discussions among the participants centered on the theme, *National Security for the 21st Century—National Power in an Unpredictable World*. Dialogue began with a theoretical analysis of the concept of "soft power" and its potential application to assuage unpredictability and continued through topics ranging from the media to business, to intelligence, and to diplomacy. The conference closed with a heated, though thoughtful, discussion of the challenges posed by American involvement in Iraq.

Day One

Joseph Nye, Jr., Ph.D., dean of the John F. Kennedy School of Government, Harvard University, opened the conference by arguing that "power distribution today is like a three-dimensional chess board," with classic military issues on the top, economic issues in the middle, events and issues that cross state boundaries on the bottom board. With this concept he intimated that military strength is a necessary condition of power, but not a sufficient condition. On the other hand, he also agreed with the underlying basis of current policy, stating "the privatization of war represents a dramatic change in world politics, the U.S. was correct in altering the National Security Strategy in September 2002 to focus on terrorism and weapons of mass destruction."

In the opening panel discussion, Robert Litwak, Ph.D., moderated a lively discussion of divergent views about failed or failing states. On one end, Ambassador Wendy Sherman felt, in most circumstances, failed or failing states warrant U.S. strategies for support. On the other, Dr. Charles Krauthammer argued that only our direct national interests should command direct, national actions. In his opinion, most failed states and humanitarian crises, though sad, do not necessarily jeopardize our national security.

President and chairman of the Export-Import Bank of the United States, Philip Merrill, spoke eloquently about the power of our nation's economy and how the economy could be better used as an instrument of national power. He argued that we have yet to make sufficient use of our economic assets and wealth to advance national interest and ease the burden on our military. Supporting this claim he said, "It is worth noting that the military power of the U.S. pales in comparison to our economic power."

In what may be a first for a national security conference of this caliber, the afternoon panel brought together four distinguished field reporters to provide a fresh and independent view of items that are high on the national agenda, as well as information that the public did not expect on matters they should want to be aware. Professor Roy Gutman moderated this panel of journalists whose travels have covered most of the world. Gutman laid out the basis for discussion by hypothesizing that "Since the end of the Cold War, states that used to be on the periphery are no longer. There is no periphery in the new world disorder." His panelists agreed or disagreed to varying degrees, while each highlighted challenges in his region of expertise.

Introduced by Army Chief of Staff General Peter Schoomaker, Secretary of Defense Donald Rumsfeld delivered the conference keynote address and fielded nearly 20 questions from the audience. He lauded the administration's handling of the Iraq war and the ongoing reconstruction. He argued that there is no comparable experience in history, even in postwar Germany, postwar Japan, Kosovo, or Bosnia, where things have moved so rapidly. In the question-and-answer session, he fielded queries ranging from civil service reform to our strained relationship with European allies, to the size of our military force.

Day Two

The second day of the Eisenhower National Security Conference further explored different facets of national power. It opened with an address by Honeywell CEO David Cote. His presentation covered three major points: how he runs such a large and diverse company, his perspective of how business should fit into a well-functioning society, and how the world is evolving (from a business standpoint) and its implications for national security. Much of his thought centered on the leadership dimension of changing a large organization and its parallel to the military transformation. He said the challenge for high-level leaders is to "figure out what decisions should be made locally and what decisions should be driven centrally. Too much local is anarchy, too much central is paralysis." He also focused a portion of his address on our growing economic interconnectedness with the European Union.

Later that morning, Scott Sagan, Ph.D., moderated a panel of experts that covered four case studies of nuclear proliferation and what lesson we should draw to help diminish the "proliferation prediction problem." The panel argued that there may be no more important and daunting a question for our national security than how well we understand the status of current and potential nuclear weapons programs in other states. George Perkovich, Ph.D., argued that our desire for "tactical intelligence" (What do they have now? How soon can they bomb us?) hinders what is truly important: "strategic intelligence" (Why do they want nukes? What are the reasons a country feels the desire to proliferate?). All seemed to agree that we need to be respectful of the fact that the behavior and tactics of intelligence officials and analysts will always influence the behavior of what is being studied.

No national security conference held in this era could be complete without a discussion of the current operation in Iraq. Ambassador Nancy Soderberg assembled the final panel to do just that. She focused her panel's discussion on specific political and military challenges facing the United States and the world. Although the panelists did not arrive at a common consensus, the discussion was both enlightening and thoughtful. Barham Salih and Fareed Yasseen, both from Iraq, argued that life in Iraq is much better than what the TV news shows and that progress is being made daily. Ambassador James Dobbins argued that all the discussion boils down to two issues: how quickly and how substantially to share power with the world and how quickly and how substantially to transfer power to the Iraqi people. On one point, all seemed to agree with one of the panelists who stated that the terrorists and the antidemocratic forces understand that the fight in Iraq will redefine the future of the Middle East. The stakes are very high. Do not be surprised if it gets worse before it gets better.

It is a testament to the military organizers of the 2003 Dwight D. Eisenhower National Security Conference that the final event of the conference was an address by a State Department official. Deputy Secretary of State Richard Armitage gave a powerful closing speech to wrap up the conference and tie in all aspects of our national power. He stated, "The power of a nation has never resided—and never will reside—solely in military might. After all, a soldier can only stand there . . . for so long, particularly when he or she comes from the all-volunteer force of a democratic society." Armitage brought the conference to a close with a linkage to Nye's opening remarks. He said, "At the end of the day, that American soldier, standing there with tenure on the land, has to stand for more than the power of a magnificent gun; the soldier also has to stand for the power of our ideals."

Full transcripts and video and audio presentations from the conference can be found at *http://www.eisenhowerseries.com*. Themes and schedules for future events also are located at this web site.

Conference Charter

National Security for the 21st Century— National Power in an Unpredictable World

The definition of national power continues to evolve and change. The United States possesses unchallenged dominance, yet its actions are constrained by an increasingly interconnected world. Elsewhere, the evolution of international and regional organizations continues to erode the Westphalian definition of national power. Global interdependence constricts all nations alike. Some view this environment as lacking structure and, therefore, unpredictable. Is it? Or, must we identify the emerging trends of this new, unnamed era?

The end of the Cold War, the explosion of information technology, and the expansion of the global economy provide unprecedented challenges for national security. National security organizations, policies, and relationships must transform to meet these challenges and exploit emerging opportunities. A continuing, open dialogue among these organizations is essential. The Dwight D. Eisenhower National Security Series and Conference strive to contribute substantively to this dialogue.

The conference is the culmination of the annual Dwight D. Eisenhower National Security Series, a year of programs and activities that addresses the critical security issues of our time. Participants and audiences include a wide range of current and former national security policy makers, senior military officials, congressional leaders, internationally recognized security specialists, corporate and industry leaders, and the media.

OPENING ADDRESS

THE CHANGING ROLE OF NATIONAL POWER

Joseph S. Nye, Jr., Ph.D., Dean, John F. Kennedy School of Government, Harvard University

Introduction by: Susan Eisenhower, President and Chief Executive Officer, The Eisenhower Institute

Summary

Susan Eisenhower, President and CEO, The Eisenhower Institute

- The theme of *National Power in an Unpredictable World* is similar to the debate that faced President Dwight D. Eisenhower and his own policy team a half century ago.

1. Just like then, now we question what role the United States should play in assuring not only our own national security, but also international security and stability. We also question what means of national power could or should be applied to achieve U.S. policy goals in that role. Then, as now, policy makers were aware that the nature of national power was shifting and new approaches for its applications were necessary.

2. During the early Eisenhower years, the battle hand-off of the task of maintaining international security and stability passed from Great Britain to the United States. Domestically, a bitter debate raged over whether this was an appropriate role for the United States.

3. Even as the United States discussed what its role should be, it discovered a fundamental change of national power was under way. The advent of nuclear power called into question the ability of great powers to apply their habitual measures and political powers—including military force. Then, as now, the United States grappled with the difference between power and capability.

- The group that has been brought together for this conference merges the worlds between which Dwight Eisenhower moved so comfortably—that of civilian life, military life, and academia.

Joseph S. Nye, Jr., Ph.D., Dean, John F. Kennedy School of
        Government, Harvard University

• What is power? The dictionary definition says it is the capacity to do things. Basically, it is the ability to get the outcomes you want. More specifically, it is the ability to influence the behavior of others to get the outcomes you want. There are several ways to do this: coerce with threats, induce with payments, or attract and co-opt.

1. Behavior can be affected without coercion. People may follow a movement or teachings because they believe in the legitimacy of the objective or out of respect for the moral authority of an individual.

2. Practical politicians and ordinary people often find it difficult to sort out the motivations behind behavior and, thus, often turn to a shortcut, which simply says power is the possession of capabilities or resources that can influence outcomes. These resources may include a relatively large population, territory, natural resources, economic strength, or social stability, to name a few. The virtue of looking at power in terms of resources rather than behavior is that it is concrete, measurable, and predictable. Power in this sense means holding the high cards in a card game. The problem with this approach is that sometimes we do not get the outcomes that the resources seem to demand.

3. There is a paradox of unrealized power when one defines it in terms of resources. In more tangible examples, Vietnam was weaker by many measures than the United States; the United States was the world's only superpower on September 11.

4. Converting resources into realized power to obtain desired outcomes requires strategy and leadership. Yet inadequate strategies and poor leadership often emerge, such as the examples of Japan before World War II or Saddam Hussein in 1990.

5. Measuring power is difficult. Measuring power in terms of resources is imperfect, although useful. It helps to know not only who has the high cards, but one must understand the context and the game being played and that the value of the cards may change.

6. The classical definition of power places a great deal of emphasis on military power. Renowned British historian A.J.P. Taylor argued that the traditional test of a great power in international politics was its strength for war—war, the ultimate game where cards are laid out on the table and one can see who really has what. But technologies change over time, and this changes the sources of strength for war.

• Looking at the world in the context of today's global information age, the distribution of power is far more complex than in the past because the contexts are so variable. It can be described in terms of a three-dimensional chess game.

1. On the top board of classic military issues, there is a unipolar distribution of power. The United States is the only superpower and will likely remain this way for several decades.

2. On the middle board of state economics, the distribution of power is already multipolar. As the talks in Cancun demonstrated, the United States cannot get a trade agreement, which is the outcome that it wants, without the agreement of the European Union, China, and developing countries.

3. The bottom board consists of transnational issues that cross borders outside the control of governments, such as international crime, terrorism, and the spread of infectious diseases. Here, power is widely distributed and chaotically organized among state and nonstate actors. It does not make sense to speak of unipolarity or an American empire at this level.

• It is a mistake to focus only on military strength on the top board—to mistake what is necessary for what is sufficient. Although military power is essential, if one is playing three-dimensional chess in a single dimension, eventually everyone will lose.

• Science and technology have added dimensions to military resources. In the nuclear age, the United States and the Soviet Union possessed similar might in the past age of the superpowers. Science and technology and the information revolution helped the United States surge ahead as the world's only military superpower. Although the progress of science and technology strengthened the United States in one dimension, it also had contradictory effects. Technological changes have increased the political and social cost of using military force in conquest.

• Modern technologies and communications have led to the rise and spread of nationalism, and social changes within the great powers have raised the cost of military force. Contemporary analyst Robert Kagan has pointed out how these social changes have gone even further in Europe than in the United States.

• In a global economy, the United States must consider how the use of force might jeopardize its economic objectives. During the 19th century, when the United States wanted to force Japan to open its markets, Commodore Matthew C. Perry threatened the use of military force. That idea today is clearly unthinkable. In another example, during the 1930s, Japan worked to colonize its neighbors as a way to increased power. It is difficult to imagine Japan today trying to use military force to conquer its neighbors.

• Military power does play some role in world politics today, but the context in which it is used is different. Technology has allowed the use of force by nonstate actors in a way that has not been used in the past. This is seen with the rise of a new terrorism, defined as the deliberate attack on noncombatants with the objective of spreading fear and intimidation, like the attacks September 11.

1. Two developments have made terrorism more lethal and difficult to manage. First, at home, our highly technological, modern civilizations have much more complex and efficient, yet fragile and vulnerable, systems. Second, the democratization of technology makes it inexpensive and more accessible and allows terrorists to organize and communicate, particularly with the Internet.

2. These technological challenges are not limited to Islamic terrorists. They put destructive capabilities that once were limited to governments and armies into the hands of deviant groups and other individuals.

3. A destructive individual like Hitler required the apparatus of a totalitarian government. Now it is done without the instruments of government. This is the privatization of war and represents a dramatic change in world politics.

• The United States was correct to alter its national security strategy to focus on terrorism and weapons of mass destruction. However, the Bush administration has focused too heavily on hard power and not enough on soft power.

1. Hard power is the ability to get others to do what you want by threatening them with inducements. It is quite tangible.

2. The second face of power rests on the ability to co-opt people rather than coerce people. Soft power is not the same as influence; it is one source of influence. It is attractive power.

3. Soft power rests on mainly three resources of a nation: its culture, in places that culture is attractive to others; its political values, when it lives up to them at home and abroad; and its foreign policies, when they are seen as legitimate and having moral authority.

4. American policies and culture may not be attractive to different groups at the same time.

5. Skeptics object to soft power because they think of power narrowly in terms of command or as an act of control. This ignores the structural phase of power. Soft power is not weakness. Governments need to ensure that their own actions and policies reinforce rather than undercut soft power to make it effective. All power depends on context, and that means there will be more soft power where there are willing interpreters and receivers.

6. When American policies lose legitimacy in the eyes of others, attitudes of distrust tend to fester and further reduce our leverage.

• Beneath the surface structure of world politics, there have been profound changes. September 11 was like a flash of lightning on a summer evening that illuminated those changes brought about by globalization and the democratization of technology.

• We have been far more successful in the domain of hard power, where we've invested more and trained more, and we have a clearer idea of what we're doing. We have been less successful in the areas of soft power, where our public diplomacy has been inadequate and our neglect of allies and institutions has created a sense of illegitimacy that has squandered our attractiveness. America's success will depend upon our deeper understanding of the role of soft power and developing a better strategy to use hard and soft power to reinforce each other.

Analysis

In his remarks, Joseph Nye discussed the evolution of national power in today's changing world and how methods of applying that power must also change. Specifically, he encouraged the greater use of what he calls soft power: the elements of national power that produce desired change through persuasion and example, not those elements that force change through coercion or monetary inducement.

Nye provided two arguments for more emphasis on soft power. He first stated that using hard power—especially military force—is fraught with disadvantages, the most obvious of which are human and economic costs. In today's complex, technology-dependent, and multipolar world, the use of hard power increasingly may produce broad, adverse consequences, even for the "victor." His complementary second argument was that soft power can produce many of the same effects, but without all of the disadvantages. According to Nye, this approach has proved effective in many situations for some countries and could be effective for the United States. More than ever, Nye claimed, soft power is the more effective answer to threats posed by democratization of technology, which has led to privatization of war by increasingly lethal, nonstate actors.

Nye finished by grounding his points in current policies designed by the Bush administration to win the war on terrorism. Though applauding the shift in national security strategy, he believed that current overdependence on hard power to implement that strategy—though successful in achieving short-term goals—has squandered America's influence with much of the world. For optimal success, Nye would have the United States draw upon traditions of diplomacy and rebalance the mix of soft and hard power in favor of the former.

Nye is renowned as both an analyst of and proponent for soft power. Indeed, some give him credit for coining the term, at least in its most common, modern usage. At a minimum, he has been an avid supporter of the concept for well over a decade. In some ways, his address during the Eisenhower Conference simply represented an adaptation of his central argument to fit the current strategic environment. However, the argument for soft power's value does not depend on the changes in the world since September 11, 2001. In the face of conventional wisdom that "everything has changed" since that terrible day, though, few question the emphasis on change. Nye wisely has been calling for the more effective use of soft power for more than a decade; the fact that policy makers are now giving further consideration to his argument because of the new strategic realities may not be entirely logical, but, nonetheless, may produce some positive results.

He called for a mix of hard and soft power and would likely agree that as a diplomatic situation changes, so, too, would the temporary ascendancy of one type of power. In the most violent and critical regions of the world, balancing the two is especially crucial. By its very nature, effective application of hard power creates dramatic results, some positive and some negative, some intended and some unintended. Soft power is no different, though often more subtle. When selecting the political tools of choice, care should be given to consider the outcomes and interactions of both.

Finally, Nye noted that in the Middle East, hard power is a necessary response to the committed terrorists, but soft power is necessary to remove their recruitment base. His optimism is based on indications that there is broad-based attraction to U.S. and Western culture. There also are confirmed modernists and traditionalists in the region and, most important, as a target of our soft power, many between the two poles. The Middle East is much like nearly all cases of cultural diffusion: The receiving members of a culture disagree about how selectively to adapt invasive cultural artifacts, usually with preference toward material rather than nonmaterial opportunities. The very attractiveness of Western culture creates polarization in traditional societies. By being successful at spreading our culture to many, we guarantee at least short-term success for terrorist recruiters during transitional periods, when traditionalists can be expected to fiercely defend what they correctly perceive as a threatened way of life. All we can do is balance hard and soft power, increasing soft power when and where it becomes prudent to do so.

Transcript

ANNOUNCER: Ladies and Gentlemen. Welcome to the 2003 Eisenhower National Security Conference. Please welcome Dr. Janne Nolan, adjunct professor, Security Studies Program, Georgetown University.

JANNE E. NOLAN, Ph.D: Thank you very much. Welcome to the 2003 Eisenhower National Security Conference. It's a great honor to be here to participate in this great event. And to be part of this culmination of a yearlong effort sponsored by the U.S. Army along with a number of co-sponsoring institutions, which I'll identify in a minute. All of us here today owe a very great tribute to the U.S. Army and its leadership for conducting this discourse that brings in such a great diversity of expertise and backgrounds through its planning process. Represented today are the Woodrow Wilson International Center for Scholars; the Medill School of Journalism from Northwestern University; the Center for International Security and Arms Control, Center for International Security and Cooperation—forgive me, I went to Stanford and was part of that program; it used to be called the Center for International Security and Arms Control—the International Crisis Group; and the Director for Net Assessment, the Secretary of Defense. This eclectic array of scholars and practitioners represents truly the Army's ability to see forward and to provide a vision to the kinds of challenges that we all face as Americans.

To see the synergy among the media, business leaders, journalists, the scholarly community, and especially the military community, as we face a world that is shifting in paradigms, the United States has obviously dominant power but faces increasing risks and evermore fractionation in the international system. Before I move to introduce our Army chief of staff and to go on with administrative comments, I'd like to take a second to recognize the people who are not here because they are overseas serving our interests and defending security all over the world—if we could just take a moment of silence.

Thank you.

[moment of silence]

Janne E. Nolan

Thank you.

One of the key features of the Eisenhower Series and Conference is the fact that it has an annual theme. And as you'll see from your conference material, the annual theme this year is *National Security for the 21st Century— National Power in an Unpredictable World*. This conference series has brought together the kind of people who can help us to think through these very complex challenges.

I need to make a couple of administrative announcements before I move to the formal introduction. First of all, our success in today's event depends on your participation. In turn, that means that while all questions are welcome, please wait until someone comes to you with the microphone before you start to speak. Please identify yourself. Please speak up, as I have been told to do. And please turn off your cell phones.

Let me now turn to introduction of General Pete Schoomaker. As I'm sure you all know, General Schoomaker became the 35th Army chief of staff in August of 2003. He is hardly new to any of the members of this audience or to the military leadership and to the U.S. Army after 31 years of distinguished service. He came back at the request of the secretary of defense. He is an outstanding leader, an outstanding commander, an outstanding visionary. And he's known particularly for his unprecedented experience in joint operations. In Special Forces, but elsewhere, a kind of jointness and joint perspective that is uniquely suited to the security challenges of the 21st century.

Please join me in welcoming General Schoomaker.

GENERAL PETER J. SCHOOMAKER: Well, thank you and good morning, everyone. And welcome. Thank you, Dr. Nolan for those kind words and your generous introduction.

The Army is proud about its continued association with the Dwight David Eisenhower National Security Series, and we are glad to co-sponsor this capstone event of the series, the Eisenhower Conference. The quality of our distinguished speakers and guests underlines the importance of the conference. And it's good to see all of you here.

I understand that we have a greater than average turnout this year. I appreciate everyone taking the time out of his or her busy schedules to attend because I think you will find it both rewarding and important. We are

General Peter J. Schoomaker

indebted to each of the partners for their continued dedication to the broadening of the national security dialogue and helping to redefine or refine our understanding of the tremendous challenges our country faces. Our strength as a nation is a product of the democratic, economic, cultural, military, and other accomplishments of past leaders, who have invested their time and energy into our great nation. Our charter for this series is to perpetuate President Eisenhower's enduring legacy of leadership and to help promote a common knowledge and understanding of the critical issues of our time. We are especially grateful to the Eisenhower family for their continued involvement and gracious support. We appreciate their consent in naming this conference in honor of the 34th president of the United States.

It is now my great pleasure and honor to introduce Ms. Susan Eisenhower, a well-recognized and widely consulted scholar of United States–Russian relations, a best-selling author, and a much sought-after speaker for insights across many disciplines. She is well respected as an expert, and we are privileged to have her join us here today. Ladies and gentlemen, please join me in a warm welcome for Ms. Susan Eisenhower.

SUSAN EISENHOWER: Thank you, General Schoomaker. Honored guests. It's a great pleasure for me to be here and a privilege. This is the second Eisenhower National Security Conference, and I must say last year's was a tremendous success. And this year promises to surpass all our expectations. I'm

Susan Eisenhower

a great believer in the importance of bringing together practitioners and theorists for a reasoned debate on critical issues. The series has done just that and more. Once again, the Army has brought together leaders from industry, government, academia, and the media to tackle the key questions in our national security debate. And this promises to be an invigorating two days of discussion. My family and I are deeply proud that the Army has chosen to name this distinguished series after my grandfather, for it encourages exactly the kind of independent thinking and respectful discussion he would champion as the best foundation for sound decision making. As you know, this year is the 50th anniversary of Dwight Eisenhower's inauguration and I think the theme of this year's series is especially appropriate. Its theme on *National Power in an Unpredictable World* would sound tremendously familiar to the policy makers of my grandfather's generation.

In many ways, the current debate on the role of the United States and its application of power and contemporary world affairs is similar to the debate that faced President Eisenhower and his own policy team a half century ago. Then, as now, the overriding issue was what role should the United States play in assuring not only our own national security, but international security and stability as well. And by what means of national power could or should be applied to achieve U.S. policy goals in that role? Then, as now, policy makers were aware that the nature of national power was shifting and new approaches for its applications were necessary.

In the early Eisenhower years, the battle hand-off, as my Army host might call it, of the task of maintaining international security stability passed from Britain to the United States, a process which had started in the late 1940s, but was still under way. Domestically, and especially within the Republican Party, a bitter debate raged over whether this was even a proper role for the United States. Yet, even then, as we debated what our role should be, we discovered that a fundamental change in the nature of national power was also under way. The advent and spread of atomic and then nuclear weapons, with their fearsome destructive capacities, called into question the ability of great powers to apply their habitual measures and applications of power including military force.

Then as now, the United States grappled with the difference between power and capability. And in the Eisenhower era, the shift had already begun toward finding effective applications for a range of measures—economic, political, and even cultural—in pursuit of these goals. That's why I think it's particularly appropriate that we are focusing on this topic today. And I think we will move into some extraordinary discussions as the next two days unfold. I think the Eisenhower Series has already made its mark for its critical contribution to the national debate. And today and tomorrow, we have a special opportunity to carry that forward. Indeed, the group that has been brought together merges the worlds that Dwight Eisenhower moved so comfortably between, that of civilian life, military life, and academia.

So now it is my personal pleasure to introduce another man who has moved with ease between more than two worlds, our keynote speaker, Dr. Joseph S. Nye, Jr. I have to say it is a personal pleasure for me to introduce Joe, if I may call him that, since I had the wonderful opportunity to spend the fall semester of 1998 as a fellow at the Institute of Politics at the Kennedy School of Government where Joe was dean and still is. All of us who worked in that environment understand his very special style that was forged by keen intellect, a sense of humor, and his capacity for leadership. Dr. Nye has been dean of the Kennedy School of Government since 1995 after returning to Harvard from government service. In 1993 and 1994, he was chairman of the National Intelligence Council, which coordinates intelligence estimates for the president, and from 1994 and 1995, he served as assistant secretary of defense for international security affairs. In both capacities, he was awarded for his distinguished service.

Joe was no stranger to Washington when he came in the 1990s. During the Carter years, he left his successful tenure as a Harvard professor to serve as deputy under secretary of state for security assistance, science and technology, and chaired the National Security Council Group on Nonproliferation of Nuclear Weapons. In recognition of the service, he received the highest Department of State commendation, the Distinguished Honor Award. Dr. Nye, a Princeton graduate with a postgraduate degree from Oxford University and Harvard University, is a fellow of the American Academy of Arts and Sciences and of the Academy of Diplomacy. And he serves on many distinguished boards and is a regular commentator for television and radio.

Somehow in the midst of his extraordinarily busy schedule, he's managed to publish extensively. His most recent books being *The Paradox of American Power*, which came out in 2002, and two other editions of his book, *Understanding International Conflicts and Power and Interdependence*. And also, he recently co-edited *Governance in a Globalizing World*. Well, after reading that list of these extraordinary publications, I think that there can be no doubt that with his work in the scholarly area, as well as that which he has contributed by his service to the United States government, that he is an ideal individual to open our conference. Thank you very much.

JOSEPH S. NYE, JR., Ph.D: Thank you very much, Susan, for that kind introduction. Whenever I hear a nice introduction like that, I'm always reminded, though, of my children. Because when somebody calls our house and asks, "Is Dr. Nye there?" They always say, "Yes, but he's not the useful kind."

My job this morning is to launch us on the question of the changing role of national power, and I think the topic couldn't be more appropriate. I mean, we are told now that the United States has more power than any country since the days of Rome. Indeed, some people even talk about a U.S. empire. Well, I think there are great problems with these approaches to power. And so I'd like to lead you through some of those problems before bringing us back in my conclusion to the role of the United States in the world today.

Joseph S. Nye, Jr.

First of all, what is power? Well, we look in the dictionary; it tells us that it's the capacity to do things, basically the ability to get the outcomes you want. And more specifically, it's the ability to influence behavior of others to get the outcomes you want. And there are several ways to do that. You can coerce them with threats, you can induce them with payments, or you can attract them and co-opt them. Sometimes I can affect your behavior without commanding it. If you believe that my objectives are legitimate, I may be able to persuade you without using threats or inducements. For example, loyal Catholics may follow the pope's teachings on capital punishment, not because of a threat of excommunication, but out of respect for his moral authority. And some radical Muslims, or radical Islamists, may be attracted to support Osama bin Laden's actions, not because of payments or threats, but because they believe in the legitimacy of his objectives.

Practical politicians and ordinary people often find it hard to sort out this question of what are the motivations behind behavior. And they often turn to a second way of defining power, a shortcut, which simply says that power is the possession of the capabilities or resources that can influence outcomes, so we look at countries and their resources. We look at a relatively large population or territory or natural resources or economic strength, military force, social stability, and so forth. And the virtue of looking at power in terms of resources, rather than behavior—it's concrete, measurable, and it's predictable. And power in this sense means holding the high cards in a card game. But the problem with this approach is that we sometimes don't get the outcomes that the resources seem to demand. There's the paradox of unrealized power when you define it in terms of resources. In other words, if you're showing the high cards in a poker game, others are likely to fold their hands rather than to challenge you.

But power resources are not as fungible as money and what wins in one game may not help at all in another. You can hold a wonderful poker hand, but it doesn't help if the game is bridge. Even if the game is poker, you can still play your hand poorly or fall victim to bluff and deception and lose. So having the resources of power doesn't guarantee that you'll always get the outcomes you want. For example, Vietnam was weaker by many measures than the United States. And the United States was the world's only superpower on September 11. So converting resources into realized power, in a sense of obtaining desired outcomes, requires well-designed strategies and skillful leadership. Yet inadequate strategies and poor leadership often emerges. Witness Japan or Germany in 1941 or Saddam Hussein in 1990.

So measuring power is difficult. If we measure it in terms of resources, that's an imperfect, but useful, shorthand. It always helps if you're playing a card game to know who has the high cards. But you also have to realize the importance of context, being able to understand the game you're playing. Oil was not a very impressive power resource before the industrial age. And uranium was not a significant power resource before the nuclear age. In earlier periods, the classical definition of power tended to place a great deal of emphasis on military power. And A.J.P. Taylor, the great British historian, for example, argued that the traditional test of a great power in international politics was strength for war, that war was the ultimate game in which the cards were laid out on the table and you could see who really had what. But the trouble is that technologies change over time and they change the sources of strength for war.

Take an example of the 18th century, where you have agrarian technologies in Europe, and the key resource there was essentially territory because it gave you a base for taxes and for recruitment of infantry, which was mostly mercenaries. And so at the end of the Napoleonic Wars (the Congress of Vienna), Prussia presented its fellow victors with a precise plan for its own reconstruction—which territories and populations should be transferred from France to Prussia to make sure that there was a balance of power. And in the pre-nationalist period, it didn't matter that many of the people transferred in those provinces didn't speak a word of German. However, within half a century, the context changed. And popular sentiments of nationalism had grown greatly, so that when Germany seized Alsace Lorraine from France in 1870, it became one of the underlying causes of World War I. And instead of being assets, those transferred provinces became liabilities, in the changed context of nationalism. Though, there are power resources that cannot be judged without knowing the context. Before you judge who is holding the high cards, you have to understand what game you're playing and the value of the cards may be changing. If you look at the world today, which I sometimes call a "global information age," the distribution of powers is far more complex than in the past because the contexts are so variable.

I made the metaphor or used the metaphor of power distribution today being like a three-dimensional chess game. On the top board of classic military issues, there is a unipolar distribution of power. The United States is the only superpower. And I expect it will remain that way for several decades. But if you look at the middle board of interstate economic issues, the distribution of power is already multipolar. As the talks in Cancun a few weeks ago demonstrated, the U.S. can't get a trade agreement, can't get the outcomes it wants, without the cooperation of not only the European Union, but also China, Japan, developing countries. If you look at something like antitrust or financial regulation, again, we can't do it alone. So it makes little sense to call this a unipolar world in this realm of economic issues. And on the bottom board of transnational relations, things that cross borders outside the control of government, whether it be international crime, terrorism, spread of infectious diseases, and so forth, power is widely distributed and chaotically organized. In fact, it's organized among both state and nonstate actors. And it makes no sense at all to call this bottom board of transnational relations a unipolar world, or American hegemony, or American empire. And yet this is the set of issues that is now intruding into the world of grand strategy. Many political leaders still focus almost entirely on military assets on the top board of military solutions. They mistake what is necessary for what is sufficient. They are one-dimensional players in a three-dimensional game. And if you're playing three-dimensional chess on one board only, in the long run, you will lose.

Let's look for a moment at the changing role of military power. Military power remains absolutely essential, as I said a minute ago, a necessary condition. But it's also worth noticing how science and technology have added dramatic new dimensions to military power resources. In the nuclear age, the United States and the Soviet Union possessed not only industrial might, but also nuclear arsenals and intercontinental missiles. That was the age of the superpowers. Subsequently, the leading role of the United States in the information revolution, civilian-driven, near the end of the century, allowed it to create a revolution in military affairs. And that ability to use information technology to create precision weapons, real-time intelligence, broad surveillance of regional battlefields, and improved command and control allowed the United States to surge ahead as the world's only military superpower.

But the progress of science and technology, while it strengthened us in one dimension, also had contradictory effects. And this has been true for more than a century. On the one hand, the United States is the only superpower with unmatched military might. But at the same time, these technological changes have increased the political and social costs of using military force in conquest. Take nuclear weapons. Paradoxically, they prove so awesome and destructive that they are muscle-bound—good for deterrence but too costly for use, except theoretical in the most extreme circumstances. And thus nonnuclear North Vietnam prevailed over nuclear America. And nonnuclear Argentina was not deterred from attacking the British Balkan Islands, despite Britain's nuclear status.

A second important technological change was the way that modern communications technology fomented the rise and spread of nationalism, which made it more difficult for empires to rule over socially awakened populations. In the 19th century, Britain ruled a quarter of the world with a tiny fraction of the world's population. In an age of widespread nationalism though, colonial rule has become too expensive. Formal empires such as Europe exercised in the 19th and 20th centuries are simply too costly for the 21st century. In addition to nuclear and communications technology, social changes inside the great powers have also raised the cost of using military force. Postindustrial democracies are focused on welfare more than glory. This doesn't mean they will not use force, even when casualties are expected. Witness Britain, France, and the United States in the 1991 Gulf War. But the absence of a prevailing warrior ethic in modern democracy means that the use of force requires an elaborate moral justification. For advanced democracies, war remains possible, but less acceptable than it was a half century or a century ago. As Robert Cooper has put it, the most powerful states have lost much of their lust to conquer.

Robert Kagan, a contemporary analyst, has correctly pointed out that these social changes have gone further in Europe than the United States. His clever phrase that Americans are from Mars and Europeans from Venus oversimplifies the differences. After all, Europeans joined in pressing for the use of force in Kosovo in 1999. And the situation in Europe—it's true that the resolution of creating a peaceful island, which has made the prospects of another Franco-German war look impossible, does predispose the Europeans somewhat more toward peaceful solutions of conflict. However, in a global economy, even the United States must consider how the use of force might jeopardize its economic objectives.

Think for a minute of the difference in terms of use of power between this century and a century earlier. When we wanted to force Japan to open its markets in the 19th century, Commodore Perry threatened bombardment, and it worked. The idea that we could force open Japanese markets or change the value of the yen by a threat of force today is clearly unthinkable. Nor can one imagine the United States using force to resolve disputes with Canada or Europe. Unlike earlier periods, islands of peace, where the use of force is no longer an option in relations among states, have come to characterize relations among almost all the modern liberal democracies, and not just in Europe. And in their relations with each other, all advanced democracies are from Venus. Even nondemocratic countries that feel fewer popular moral constraints on the use of force have to consider the effects on their economic objectives. War risks deterring investors that control flows of capital in a globalized economy. A century ago, it may have been easier to seize another state's territory by force than to develop one's own internal economy. But it's a difficult scenario to imagine today. For example, Japan in the 1930s developed a Greater East Asia Co-Prosperity Sphere as a way to augment its power. It's quite difficult to imagine Japan succeeding or trying to use military force to colonize its neighbors today.

Now none of this suggests that military force plays no role in world politics today. Of course it does. Civil wars are rife in many parts of the world where collapsed empires have left failed states and power vacuums. Even more important is the way in which the democratization of technology is leading to the privatization of war. Technology is a double-edged sword. And what we're seeing today is that force still remains tremendously important, but it's distributed differently and the context in which it is used differs. In particular, I think it's worth noticing that technology has empowered the use of force by nonstate actors in a way that's never been true in the past. And that, of course, we see with the rise of the new terrorism.

Terrorism is not new. And I am defining it as the deliberate attack on noncombatants with the objective of spreading fear and intimidation. September 11 was a dramatic escalation of an age-old phenomenon. Yet two developments have made terrorism more lethal and more difficult to manage in the 21st century. One of these grows out of the progress of science and technology at home. Our highly technological modern civilizations have much more complex and fragile basic systems. Market forces and openness have combined to increase the efficiency of many of our vital systems, such as those that provide transportation, information, energy, and health care. But some systems may become more vulnerable and fragile as they become more complex and efficient. At the same time, the other factor that's occurring as a result of technology is what I call the democratization of technology, making the instruments of mass destruction smaller, cheaper, and more readily available to a wider range of individuals and groups. Where bombs and timers were once heavy and expensive, plastic explosives and digital timers are light and cheap. The costs of hijacking an airplane are sometimes little more than the price of a ticket. In addition, the success of the information revolution is providing inexpensive means of communication and organization that allows groups once restricted to local and national police jurisdictions to become global in their scope.

Thirty years ago, instantaneous global communication was sufficiently extensive that it was the prerogative only of large entities with large budgets like governments, multinational corporations, or perhaps the Roman Catholic Church. But today, the Internet has made instantaneous global communications virtually free for anyone with access to a modem. Similarly, the Internet has reduced the cost of searching for information—making contacts related to instruments of wide-scale destruction. Terrorists depend on getting their message out quickly to a broad audience through mass media and the Internet. Witness the widespread dissemination of bin Laden's television interviews and videotapes after September 11. Terrorism also depends crucially on its ability to attract support from the crowd at least as much as the ability to destroy the enemy's will to fight. These technological trends have created a new set of conditions that have increased the lethality and difficulty of managing terrorism.

Because of September 11 and the unprecedented scale of al Qaeda, the current focus is properly on terrorism associated with Islamic extremists. But it would be a mistake to limit our attention or responses simply to Islamic terrorists for that would ignore the wider effects of the democratization of technology and the broader set of challenges that must be met. Technological progress is putting into the hands of deviant groups and individuals destructive capabilities that were once limited primarily to governments and armies. Every large group of people has some members who deviate from the norm. And some of those are bent on mass destruction. It is worth remembering that the worst case of terrorism in the United States before September 11 was Timothy McVeigh, a purely homegrown antigovernment fanatic. Similarly, the Aum Shinrikyo cult that spread sarin in the Tokyo subway system in 1995 had nothing to do with Islam. And even if the current wave of Islamic terrorism turns out to be generational or cyclical, as terrorist waves in the past have been, the world will still have to confront the long-term secular dangers that arise out of the democratization of technology. I think you could make an argument that the lethality of terrorism has been increasing. In the '70s, events like the killing of the Israeli athletes at the Munich Olympics took lives in the tens. In the '80s, Sikh extremists who bombed an Air India flight caused something over 300 deaths. And of course September 11 was several thousand.

It's not at all science fiction to extrapolate this curve and imagine terrorists getting hold of weapons of mass destruction and being able to kill in the area of millions. To kill millions of people in the 20th century, a destructive individual like Hitler or Stalin required the apparatus of a totalitarian government. Unfortunately, it's now all too easy to envision extremist groups and individuals killing millions without the instruments of government. This is truly the privatization of war and it represents a dramatic change in world politics.

The United States was correct in altering its national security strategy in September 2002, to focus on terrorism and weapons of mass destruction. But the means that the Bush administration has chosen focused too heavily on simply hard power and have not taken enough account of soft power, another dimension. And that's a mistake because terrorists stand to gain recruits and popular support if we underestimate the importance of soft power.

Now, what do I mean by soft power? Hard power is easy to understand. It's quite tangible. Hard power is the ability to get others to do what you want through threatening them with inducements, tariffs, or threats, sticks. But sometimes you can get the outcomes you want without tangible threats or payoffs. The indirect way to get what you want has sometimes been called the second face of power. A country may obtain the outcomes it wants in world politics because others want to follow it, admiring its values, emulating its examples, aspiring to its level of prosperity and openness. And in this sense, it's also important to set the agenda and attract others in world politics, not only to force them to change through military or economic instruments. This soft power, getting others to want the outcomes that we want, co-opts people, rather than coerces them. Soft power rests on the ability to shape the preferences of others. At the personal level, we all know the power of attraction and seduction. Power in a relationship or a marriage does not necessarily reside with the larger partner. And modern executives running large corporations know that leadership is not just a matter of issuing commands, but also involves leading by example and attracting others to do what you want. In fact, the new corporate management strategies argue that it's difficult to run a large organization by commands alone, unless you can get buy-in to your values from others.

Soft power is not simply the same as influence, though it's one source of influence. After all, influence can rest on the hard power of threats and payments. And soft power is more than just persuasion or the ability to move people to buy the argument, though that's an important part of it. It's also the ability to entice and attract. And attraction often leads to acquiescence in the outcomes that we want. Simply put, in behavioral terms, soft power is attractive power. It uses a different type of currency, not the currency of force or money to engender cooperation. Its attraction to shared values and the justness of duty are contributing to the achievement of those values. Of course in many real-world situations, people's motives are mixed. And the distinction between hard and soft power is one of degree. Nonetheless, it is an important dimension, which we ignore at our risk. Sometimes the same power resources can affect the entire spectrum of behavior from coercion to attraction. A country that suffers economic and military decline, for example, will lose not only its hard power, but also its ability to attract others in soft power.

But soft power is not simply the reflection of hard power. The Vatican has soft power, despite Stalin's mocking question of how many divisions does the pope have. Conversely, the Kremlin lost much of its soft power after the Soviet Union invaded Hungary and Czechoslovakia. Even though by classical military measures, Soviet power continued to increase. So its hard power increased while its soft power declined. Some countries such as Canada, Netherlands, Scandinavian states, for example, have political clout that's far greater than their military and economic weight would indicate because of the incorporation of attractive causes such as economic aid or peacemaking in their definitions of their national interest. And Britain in the 19th century and America in the second half of the 20th century enhanced their soft power by creating a structure of international rules and institutions. They were consistent with the liberal and democratic nature of British and American capitalism, free trade, the gold standard in the 19th century, the International Monetary Fund, the World Trade Organization, and the UN [United Nations], in the case of the United States.

If a country can make its power legitimate in the eyes of others, it will encounter less resistance to its wishes. If a country can support institutions that encourage others to channel and limit their activities in ways it prefers, it will not need to spend as much on costly carrots and sticks as it otherwise would. The soft power of a country rests primarily on three resources: its culture, in places where that's attractive to others; its political values when it lives up to them at home and abroad; and its foreign policies when they're seen as legitimate and having moral authority. Some analysts make the mistake of treating soft power simply as popular cultural power. They basically say, well, it's just Coke or McDonald's, but, in fact, it's not. The effectiveness of any power resource depends on its context. And in some context, the American policies or American culture will not be attractive or attract different groups at the same time. If you look at Iran today, American culture may produce rejection, at least among the ruling Mullahs, and yet Hollywood images that repel the ruling Mullahs are attractive to younger generations who watch our videocassettes in the privacy of their homes.

In other cases like Argentina, American human rights policies that were rejected by the military government in the 1970s, produced considerable soft power for the United States two decades later when many of those jailed in the 70s rose to power. And there's more to cultural resources than just pop culture. The half-million students who study in the United States' universities every year or the Asian entrepreneurs who return home after succeeding in Silicon Valley tend to reach a lease with power in their own countries.

Government policies at home and abroad can enhance or destroy our soft power. For example, President Eisenhower in the 1950s pointed out that racial segregation at home was undercutting American soft power in newly emerging African countries. Indeed, foreign policy strongly affects soft power. Jimmy Carter's human rights policies are a case in point as well as the government's efforts to promote democracy in the Reagan and Clinton administrations. And conversely, foreign policies that appear arrogant or illegitimate in the eyes of others diminished American soft powers, as polls have shown in the early part of the 20th century. So soft power is extremely important, but we don't always use it as well as we should. Some skeptics object to the idea of soft power because they think of power narrowly in terms of command or act of control. In their view, imitation and attraction are simply that, not power. But the trouble with this is that it ignores the structural face or second face of power. Your dinner speaker tonight has said one of Rumsfeld's rules is that weakness is provocative. True, but soft power is not weakness; it's a form of power. Similarly, others object to the idea of soft power because governments are not in full control of it. Firms, universities, foundations, churches, other nongovernmental groups can develop soft power of their own, [which] may reinforce or be at odds with official foreign policy goals. And that's all the more reason for governments to make sure that their own actions and policies reinforce rather than undercut soft power.

Now I said earlier that all power depends on context. And that means we'll have more soft power where there are willing interpreters and receivers. And in situations when you have democracies and parliaments, soft power is increasingly important. Thus it was impossible, for example, for the Turkish government to allow the transport of American troops across the country in 2003 because of the unpopularity of American policy. In contrast, it was easier for us to obtain bases in authoritarian Uzbekistan for operations in Afghanistan. But clearly in the first case, our soft power had a negative effect—or our absence of soft power had a negative effect on our hard power.

Soft power is probably more effective in the areas that are more difficult to measure. But if one considers various American national interests, soft power may be less relevant than hard power in preventing attacks, policing our borders, and protecting allies. But it is a crucial role to play in promoting democracy, human rights, and open markets. The fact that soft power effectiveness varies by context does not make it irrelevant, any more than the facts that bombs and bayonets are ineffective resources when we seek to prevent the spread of infectious diseases, slow global warming, or create democracy. Now in conclusion, what does this mean for American foreign policy? Anti-Americanism has been increasing for the last few years. A widespread and fashionable view is that the Americans are developing a classical empire. A Gallop international poll found that pluralities in 29 countries around the world said that American foreign policies had a negative effect on their attitudes toward the U.S. Skeptics about soft power say not to worry, as Fouad Ajami wrote, "The United States need not worry about the hearts and minds in foreign lands." Foreigners may grumble, but they have little choice because we are so strong. Moreover, the United States has been unpopular in the past, yet managed to recover. We do not need permanent allies and institutions; we can always pick up the coalition of the willing, as we need. As Secretary Rumsfeld has said, "the issue should determine the coalitions, not vice versa." But it would be a mistake to dismiss the recent decline of our attractiveness so lightly.

It's true that the United States has recovered from unpopular policies in the past. But that was against the backdrop of the Cold War in which other countries faced and feared a Soviet Union as a greater evil. Moreover, while American size and association with disruptive modernity is constant and will always lead to some degree of concern and resentment about the United States, wise policies can soften the sharp edges of the reality and reduce the resentments they engender. And that's what the United States did after World War II. We used our soft power resources and co-opted others into a set of alliances and institutions that lasted for 60 years. We won the Cold War against the Soviet Union with a mixed strategy—military force for effective containment and soft power for domestic transformation inside the Soviet bloc. So it's a mistake to discount soft power as just an image. When we discount it, we realize that we will pay a price. Most important, if the United States is so unpopular in a country that being pro-American is the kiss of death in their domestic politics, political leaders are unlikely to make concessions to help us. Turkey, Mexico, and Chile were prime examples in March of 2003. When American policies lose their legitimacy and credibility in the eyes of others, attitudes of distrust tend to fester and further reduce our leverage.

Beneath the surface structure of world politics, there have been profound changes. September 11 was like a flash of lightning on a summer evening that illuminated those changes brought about by globalization and democratization of technology. The Bush administration has correctly identified the new challenges and has reoriented American strategy accordingly. But the administration, like the Congress and the public, has been torn between different approaches to the implementation of the new strategy. The result has been a mixture of both successes and failures. We have been far more successful in the domain of hard power, where we've invested more and trained more and have a clearer idea of what we're doing. We have been less successful in the areas of soft power, where our public diplomacy has been inadequate and our neglect of allies and institutions has created a sense of illegitimacy that has squandered our attractiveness. Yet this is ironic because the United States is the country that built some of the longest lasting alliances and institutions that the modern world has ever seen. These institutions have been central to our policy and they helped us to win the Cold War.

Essentially, it is time for us now to draw upon our traditions in foreign policies in a different way. We need more Jefferson and much less Jackson. Wilsonians are correct about the importance of democratic transformation of world politics over the long run, but they need to temper their impatience with more Hamiltonian realism. In short, America's success will depend upon our deeper understanding of the role of soft power and developing a better strategy to use hard and soft power to reinforce each other. We've done it before, and I believe we can do it again. Thank you very much.

JANNE E. NOLAN, Ph.D.: Thank you very, very much, Joe. As always, the voice of reason, dispassion, and extreme profundity of thought as well as extremely relevant analysis. We have about 10–12 minutes for questions. Maybe 15. If you could stand when you raise your hand and I will recognize you. If I could see through these lights, which are very bright—someone will bring you a microphone. I see no hands out there. If you could please stand up. Could you identify yourself, please?

AUDIENCE MEMBER: Hi. Captain Rizetti. One of my colleagues I know, Dr. Tom Barnett, has published and talked extensively. Dr. Barnett is focused more on predictability [inaudible] versus the gap of nonfunctioning [inaudible]. The world is less unpredictable if you frame it in terms of globalization and interdependencies. Your comments regarding soft power, it seems to me, works by functioning members [inaudible]. What we struggle with is the predictability [inaudible].

NYE: It's a very good point, which is when we think about the use of power in today's world it varies in different areas, depending on whether you have functioning states. And I think this is something that the National Security Strategy stated very well, which it said we have more to fear from failed states than from other great powers. When you look at the condition of Sierra Leone, Somalia, and Afghanistan, there is a great danger that there is nobody at the other end of the line in terms of effective governments. And in cases like that, obviously you need to use hard power. Nothing I said about soft power was designed to undercut the significance of hard power. It was to say that our great mistake is to think that hard power is sufficient. It's not. It's necessary, but it's not sufficient. What we need to do is use hard power military force as we did in Afghanistan and hard power of economic assistance, inducements, to try to create structures in places like Afghanistan or Sierra Leone or Liberia. But we also have to remember that the reason we're doing this is to prevent these areas from becoming breeding grounds for terrorism. And we need to get them integrated into the globalization systems.

For example, if you look at the Middle East, most Middle Eastern economies have fallen badly behind in terms of economic growth and modernization. And we need to use our capacity, our hard capacities, both to police the area and to attract them—I'm sorry, to get them into the system of these other areas of economic growth. But we also need to attract them, in particularly the moderate elements there. In other words, the great danger in terrorism is you need hard power to kill people like bin Laden. You're never going to attract him, but you need soft power to attract the moderates so that he can't recruit them. And we have spent a lot more effort and been a lot more successful on the killing part than on the attracting part of it. So I think the basic diagnosis—that we have to focus on these areas, which is identified in the National Security Strategy, which is correct. But I think we haven't put enough resources into developing a strategy for the attracting part of it. I must just say, if you look at American public diplomacy, it's very interesting as just a matter of resources. The United States public diplomacy is about one quarter of the 1 percent of the resources we spend on the military. And at the end of the Cold War, if we cut it back by 30 percent, thinking it didn't matter, that's a mistaken allocation of resources—not that we should cut the military but that we should add the other.

NOLAN: I cannot believe that this is a shy crowd.

NYE: Well, there's someone on the right, Janne, I can see. The lights really are impossible.

NOLAN: I see a question here. Sir, over here. And a question over here. So let's take you first—a little easier to reach.

AUDIENCE MEMBER: There's another power besides hard and soft. And that is domestic power. Staying in office. Does this corrupt the pursuit of hard and soft power?

NYE: Well, certainly maintaining your power base at home is essential if you're going to be effective in wielding hard or soft power. And, of course, there are efforts that you have to make that you do at home which may undercut either your hard or your soft power. I was looking at Tom Friedman's column in the *New York Times* today, in which he pointed out the enormous inconsistency between the domestic politics, which lead us to subsidize farmers and at the same time drive out producers of cotton in poor countries, and at the same time, talk about the fact that these countries should follow free market principles. And Friedman points out that as you bankrupt Pakistani farmers, and at the same time have gas guzzlers which increase the consumption of oil, which puts more money in Saudi Arabia, which transfers the money to madrassas in Pakistan, where the sons of the bankrupt farmers get only a Koranic education in fundamentalist terms, and then later we wonder why we are seeing more terrorists arising; there is an inconsistency there. But getting a coherent strategy in that case is thwarted by the power of domestic-politics and agricultural lobbies. And that's a nonpartisan comment because it cuts across the aisle. But it is a good example, I think, of where the need to maintain domestic power prevents us from implementing a coherent strategy in an area we have said is a top priority, countering terrorism.

AUDIENCE MEMBER: Nick Frazier from the BBC. I was very struck by the honesty with which you allude to the loss of American prestige and the unpopularity of America in much of the world. It's evident every week in Europe, increasingly. I wonder if you could be a bit more specific about how dangerous you think this is and what sort of resources could be deployed to change it? I mean, do you have hopes that it can be reversed rapidly? Or what exactly would America have to do?

NYE: Well I think if you look at the polls, the evidence is pretty clear. In Europe, on average, we've lost about 30 points in countries, including those friendly to us that helped us in the war, such as Spain and Italy, in the last year. And if you look at Indonesia, the largest Islamic country, in 2000, 75 percent of Indonesians said they were attracted to the United States. This year that's gone down to 15 percent. That's a big loss.

Now, the people who say it doesn't matter say, you know, we're big and we're tough, and they'll just have to take their lumps and follow us. The trouble with that is if you go to an example such as I gave of Turkey, when we wanted to get the 4th Infantry Division across Turkey, the fact that we had become wildly unpopular in Turkish public opinion meant that the Turkish parliament would not vote to allow that to occur. So our loss of soft power definitely hurt our hard power.

Now, it's been true that in the past, for example after the Vietnam War, the United States has been unattractive. But we recovered. But as I mentioned in my talk, we recovered in the context of a Cold War in which there was a greater evil of the Soviet Union. The question is whether we can recover that well and that quickly now. Certainly, what you hear from these polls when you read them carefully, and the subservient questions, is a bit more bowed to the institutions. A bit less arrogance, a bit more feeling that we're taking into our national interest the interests of others would do a good deal to restore some of that soft power. And I think that question of the style of foreign policy actually makes a huge difference. And we have been relatively inattentive to the costs of the style of foreign policy. And I think that it won't turn things around overnight, but it will make a difference.

Sometimes people say, well, don't worry about it. We're the big kid on the block. We're so big that we're bound to be resented. You know, we should just take our lumps and that's it. Trouble with that argument is there is a little bit in it, which is there's always some resentment of the big kid on the block. But that power, America's relative size, hasn't changed in the last three years. But our popularity has changed dramatically in the downward direction. And since you can't explain change with a constant, then you have a problem, which you can't just explain away by saying it's a function of American size. Most of the polls show it's a function of American policies. I mean if you ask the question of people, you'll get that answer. And I think that does often have a lot to do with the style as well as the substance of policies.

NOLAN: We can take about two more questions. Over here. Please wait for the mic, and is there another question?

NYE: He has a mic, Janne.

AUDIENCE MEMBER: Good morning, Doctor. Commander Burke from the U.S. Navy. My question deals with how do we get out of the trap of continuing to have to use hard power, when especially with Islam and Muslims? It's an ideological disagreement or hatred of the soft power, the politics, the economic achievements, the perceived ethical issues?

NYE: Well, it's a very important question. And I think the premise, though, has to be that they don't all hate us. In fact, when you look again at the polls carefully, most of them actually admire us and admire American people. And if you look at the Pew polls, for example, great dislike for American policies, but an admiration for American science and technology, even for American popular culture. Many people in the Middle East, which is only a part of the Islamic world, are worried about modernity, worried about change, feel that their societies have not adapted properly, but, nonetheless, they're not turning their back on that. They still want the things of democracy and human rights and a higher standard of living that we stand for. And I think the important thing is for us to have policies which identify with the aspirations of that moderate middle.

You're never going to cure the bin Ladens or the al-Zawahiris. Only force, I think, will solve that. But you can prevent them from recruiting widely. And I think, if you look at the policies of the Bush administration, when the president talks about increasing money for aid, increasing our support for campaigns against HIV/AIDS his remarks at the UN the other day about trade traffic and people for prostitution and so forth, those are good investments in our soft power. We want to show that we are aligned with the aspirations of these people. Economic assistance is not going to remove terrorism. For one thing, it takes decades to make a difference. And we don't have decades. But economic assistance can show that we are aligned with the aspirations of those people, and that makes it harder for bin Laden and his recruiting from them. So I think what we need to be doing is asking, how well are we putting forward that positive side of the United States in the Middle East? And are there ways in which we can put forward our hard power, which doesn't have quite the sense and ring of arrogance that turns people off. If we can adjust our strategy to dial up a bit more of the soft attractiveness and to smooth off some of the edges that create a sense of arrogance of when we use hard power, I think we will be able to attract a middle. The middle has not gone over to the other side yet. And that's the critical strategy for this war against terrorism is to make sure that you're walking on two legs. Not just one.

NOLAN: We have time for a final question. A hand over there.

AUDIENCE MEMBER: Sir, I'm Col. George Topic, from the Industrial College of the Armed Forces. And I'm interested in the application of military instrument to the development and use of soft power and any comments you might have about the implications of such on force design or even transformation?

NYE: Well, I think the United States attracts certain people and has certain attractiveness because of the effectiveness of our military. I mean, our military is admired, and that enhances our attractiveness. So in addition to its hard dimensions, an effective military has a certain soft dimension, which is attractiveness. Another aspect of it, which is often not paid attention to, is the importance of military-to-military contacts. One of the things that struck me when I was in the Pentagon was how extraordinarily useful it was to have these frequent contacts between American officers and their counterparts in many other countries because it basically was a way to have others come to see what we were really like, that the American military consisted of human beings who had values that were important; and those military-to-military programs were extraordinarily important in terms of American soft power, just like education and universities are. And any time people talk about cutting back on these programs, IMET [International Military Education and Training], and others, I think it's just a terrible mistake because its main job is hard power. But the military can also produce soft power for this country.

NOLAN: Thank you very, very much, Joe Nye, for your extremely provocative and interesting kickoff to this series. And thank you all for your questions. We are now going to take a 30-minute break. The Army recognizes the need for networking in this kind of situation. And there will be an announcement to bring you back for the following sessions.

Again, please join me in thanking Dean Joe Nye. Thank you.

PANEL 1

WHEN STATES FAIL: THREATS TO INTERNATIONAL ORDER AND STABILITY

Co-sponsor: Woodrow Wilson International Center for Scholars

Moderator: Robert S. Litwak, Ph.D., Director of International Studies, Woodrow Wilson International Center for Scholars

David Gordon, Ph.D., Director, Office of Transnational Issues, Central Intelligence Agency

Chester A. Crocker, Ph.D., James R. Schlesinger Professor of Strategic Studies, Georgetown University

Ambassador Wendy R. Sherman, Principal, The Albright Group

Dr. Charles Krauthammer, Syndicated Columnist, The *Washington Post*

Panel Charter

In its April 2001 report, the U.S. Commission on National Security/21st Century, also known as the Hart-Rudman Commission, identified failed or failing states as one of the principal threats to international order that the United States will face in the coming decades. As with the other major challenges of American foreign policy, the context in which this issue is currently addressed was transformed in the wake of the September 11 terrorist attacks, which were mounted by a transnational terrorist group, al Qaeda, from the sanctuary of a failed state, Afghanistan.

The term "failed state" entered the U.S. diplomatic lexicon and gained wide currency in the aftermath of the Cold War. The Clinton administration identified failed states as one of four categories in its typology of countries comprising the post–Cold War international system—the other three being advanced industrial democracies, emerging democracies with market economies, and "rogue states." The administration established the State Failure Task Force in 1994 to examine the causes of state failure, as well as measures to ameliorate its consequences and forestall its occurrence. While each case presents its own unique circumstances—historical experience, geography, and natural resources—the burgeoning litera-

Left to right, *Robert S. Litwak, David Gordon, Chester A. Crocker,*
Wendy R. Sherman, and Charles Krauthammer.

ture in the policy community on state failure has identified key indicators of this
phenomenon. Prominent among these are a rapid deterioration in living standards and the economy, the monopolization of political and economic power by
a corrupt elite, and the collapse of governmental institutions. Failing and failed
states vary significantly in degree. At the extreme end of the state capacity continuum are instances of total collapse, such as Somalia in 1991.

Somalia was the first instance in the post–Cold War era of U.S. military intervention in a failed state—one initiated as a humanitarian mission, but which later
was expanded into nation building. During the 1990s, the use of American military power in failed states such as Haiti, as well as in other instances involving
ethnic strife, was criticized by some as "social work" in places where vital U.S.
national interests were not at stake. The analytical distinction between the 1990s
categories—that is, between rogue states that threatened U.S. interests and failed
states that did not—was called into question by September 11. Afghanistan, where
the attacks were planned by Osama bin Laden's terrorist organization, was both a
failed state and, in one commentator's play on State Department terminology, "a
terrorist-sponsored state." Weak state capacity in Afghanistan had permitted al
Qaeda to virtually take over a country. In the aftermath of September 11, the argument was increasingly made that the failed state issue could no longer be ignored
or dismissed because, in the interconnected age of globalization, any such state
could become a staging ground for a horrific, mass casualty attack on U.S. soil.

This panel will examine the future challenge posed by failed states for U.S. national security.

Discussion Points

• What is a failed state? What are the major factors that distinguish a strong state from a weak one, and a weak or failing country from a failed state?

• What are the criteria for determining U.S. involvement? Do all failed states affect U.S. national interests? Do some countries matter more than others because of their strategic location? Should the United States become engaged in cases where there is a humanitarian crisis, but U.S. national interests are not visibly or immediately at stake?

• What are the strategies and tools that can be used to address the failed state challenge? Can prevention strategies, effectively employed early, stop a failing state from slipping into the failed category? What is the role of other actors, such as the United Nations, regional organizations, or other capable states, notably the European Union and Japan? Under what conditions should the U.S. military intervene to stabilize a failing or failed state?

Summary

David Gordon, Ph.D., Director, Office of Transnational Issues, Central
Intelligence Agency

• The CIA established the State Failure Task Force almost a decade ago to determine why states fail and to better understand the failure continuum that ranges from extreme examples like Somalia to more common instances of weak and failing, but not yet failed, states. Failed and failing states often have much in common: internal wars, sharp retreats from democracy, human rights violations, ungoverned zones that can harbor terrorists, general humanitarian crises, drug trafficking, and the spillover of domestic instability to infect other states in the region.

• The task force has identified four pivotal types of events linked to state failure that present useful subjects of analysis: revolutionary war, which involves an organized, armed challenge to state authority and often produces mass casualties; ethnic war, which also involves such an armed challenge; adverse regime change, where there is a weakening of democracy or a wider collapse of authority structures within the state; and genocide or politicide, which constitutes deliberate efforts by the state or other organized political agents to destroy a particular group.

• The instabilities involved in state failure are consistent and recurrent, complicating efforts at conflict resolution, though there are only a few outbreaks of severe, acute political instability each year. Such instability tends to persist, so the number of states threatened by failure at any given time is much higher, totaling an average of 17 or 18 in recent years. Additionally, those states that are able to emerge from failure remain vulnerable to significant crises, as Haiti's and Liberia's attempts at democracy have demonstrated.

• The most important factor in determining a state's risk of severe instability and failure is the state's patterns of political behavior. Along these lines, partial democracies are the most vulnerable to failure and instability. Countries like Iran and Nigeria, which combine free elections with elements of autocracy, are more at risk than their fully autocratic counterparts. In such countries, intense, dysfunctional, factional competition can lead to state failure, especially given the absence of strong checks on the executive. Thus, while it may be a positive, long-term trend that one in three regimes in the world today falls into the "partial democracy" category, this situation presents enormous instability problems in the short term.

• Poverty and economic indicators generally do not directly correlate with rates of state failure and severe instability, but economic factors are important in the sense that they shape a state's ability to sustain democracy. Thus, impoverished countries that are poorly integrated into the world economy are more likely to be failed or failing states than countries that do not fit this description; but such economic problems, in themselves, are not useful predictors of state failure or severe instability.

• States that discriminate against particular ethnic or communal groups are at greater risk, as discrimination increases the likelihood of ethnic or other internal wars, which in turn bring other forms of instability.

• Countries in "bad neighborhoods" are particularly at risk since political conflict in one failed or failing state can spill across borders to drag a contiguous state down into severe instability as well. Soldiers, refugees, and weapons have all easily crossed borders in such bad neighborhoods as Africa's Great Lakes region and the South Asian subcontinent.

• Analysis of these causes of state failure yields specific foreign policy strategies for fighting state failure. It will be necessary to strengthen checks and balances across branches of government in countries identified as at risk of becoming failed or failing states, as well as discourage at-risk states from enacting the sort of discriminatory policies that can foster extreme factionalism and even internal war. Furthermore, it will be necessary to employ regional strategies, in addition to country-specific ones, to address the threat of failed-state and failing-state spillover to contiguous states in regions identified as bad neighborhoods.

Chester A. Crocker, Ph.D., James R. Schlesinger Professor of Strategic
          Studies, Georgetown University

• Failed states may be the most dangerous, long-term security challenge facing policy makers today. They pose a variety of hard and soft security challenges that cannot be ignored: They can become breeding grounds for terrorism and extremist or fundamentalist politics, tend to produce humanitarian crises, including the recruitment of child soldiers, the abuse of women and children and health pandemics; host drug-trafficking networks, gun-running networks, warlord economies, and other criminal business threats; and infect nearby states and, thus, bring regional conflict and destabilization.

• Failed states can transition into rogue states, and the analytic distinction between the two categories has broken down in many ways. North Korea, for example, may be both a failed state and a rogue state.

• Indicators of state failure include international disengagement and abandonment of a state that was previously engaged in and supported by the international system, a shift in the balance of power on the ground from civilians to young men with guns, the alignment of elites with criminal business enterprises, and dominance of actual state leadership by those who are effectively warlords and heads of criminal business enterprises. Another indicator is the abandonment of whole provinces or regions of the state to lawlessness in order to facilitate business opportunities for criminal business enterprises.

• Policy makers cannot afford to look at threats in a single dimension by focusing exclusively on homeland security. They also must consider threats to American forces deployed overseas, American allies, American norms and values, and American political interests in general.

• Specific criteria for American intervention in failed and failing states include whether or not the state poses a risk of terrorist buildup or rogue-state development, is inherently important as a regional anchor state or American security partner, threatens to export its instability across borders to neighboring states, poses a humanitarian crisis and a political imperative for involvement, and presents the United States with certain diplomatic obligations by virtue of international expectations of what America should do.

• While there are not that many states that are fully failed states, there are many failing states and potential failing states. Given the expense and difficulty of dealing with failed states, it is important that policy makers deal with failing and potential failing states before they slide into the failed-state category. Indeed, as we are learning in Iraq, post-conflict reconstruction can prove the most expensive way of all of dealing with failed states, and we must work to prevent current and future failing states from reaching this stage.

• Policy makers should inventory the relevant institutions, coalitions, alliances, and informal friendships that might share the burden of dealing with the some 50 to 60 failed, failing, and potential failing states that threaten the international community.

• We should break state failure into well-defined phases and develop differentiated strategies for addressing each stage. A strategy for addressing early-stage failing states might include diplomatic coordination and intelligence sharing with allies who have the ability to influence the failing state's leadership. It could also include concerted efforts to discredit problematic actors and undermine whatever foreign support bases they have. A strategy for addressing later-stage states in imminent danger of failure might include coercive diplomacy and an internationalized peace process to ease a new regime into power before it is too late.

- Efforts to combat state failure also may be differentiated between state-specific strategies and more general strategies that are geared at reforming the international environment.

- The challenge we face in addressing state failure is nothing less than state building. It will be necessary to strengthen these countries' judicial systems, police systems, free press, and other domestic institutions.

Ambassador Wendy R. Sherman, Principal, The Albright Group

- George W. Bush argued in his presidential campaign that the Clinton administration had been hyperactive in the world and that foreign policy should be predicated on national interest, not on the "interest of the illusory international community."

- In contrast, the Clinton administration saw American interests and security as inextricable from the interests of the international community and argued that if we turn away from the developing world, we invite more poverty, more failed states, more civil wars, and more terrorism. The Clinton-Atwood approach to security policy saw it as imperative to attack the root causes of conflict within fragile states, promote collective security with an emphasis on preventive diplomacy, and engage in preventive defense. This approach to security policy admittedly had a rough and tragic start in Somalia.

- A RAND study on American nation-building efforts offered some important lessons from our own experience that might be applied to policy toward failed and failing states. Our continuing experiences in rebuilding Iraq reinforce these lessons.

1. National building objectives should be scaled to available forces, resources, and staying power.

2. Military forces must be complemented by civilian law enforcement, economic reconstruction, and political development efforts.

3. Unity of command is often as important in peacetime nation-building exercises as it is in war prosecution.

4. There can be no economic or political development without security.

- In efforts at both prevention and more traditional intervention, multilateralism can be complex and time-consuming but, ultimately, proves less expensive and even more effective at helping transformation and regional stability. Of course, multilateralism is only feasible if the United States' potential coalition partners share American interests.

- Though President Bush initially saw himself as a realist opposed to Clinton's more Wilsonian approach to foreign affairs, September 11 has reshaped the Bush administration's foreign policy doctrine to a focus on defending, preserving, and extending the peace by efforts to fight terrorists and tyrants, with an emphasis on preemption, building good relations among the great powers, and encouraging free and open societies on every continent.

- Bush sees the current nation-building efforts in Iraq as an opportunity to fundamentally change the Middle East. While many argue that this is not colonialism in that it is not about acquiring territory, it is a sort of "postcolonial colonialism," a strategy of dealing with failed states through an imperialism of ideas.

• The Pew Global Attitudes Project surveyed 38,000 people in 44 countries during fall 2002. After the spring 2003 Iraq war, it surveyed another 16,000 people in 20 countries and in the Palestinian National Authority. The survey found several things:

1. People in states that are often considered failing or weak see globalization as a positive force but are worried about the pace of the modern world.

2. People in such states want freedom of association, a modern democracy, and, most of all, better judicial systems.

3. Those surveyed increasingly view the United Nations as a failing institution.

4. The populations of seven out of the eight Muslim states surveyed believe they will face an American military attack in the near future.

5. Those surveyed generally like American values but see the United States as an arrogant power that is increasingly weakening international institutions and exacerbating the gap between rich and poor.

6. In short, the survey found how we work with the world impacts how world populations see us and, in turn, how well we are able to achieve what we need to achieve.

• The Cancun trade talks were a disaster, and future Cancuns must be avoided if we want to prevent an increase in the number of failed and failing states in the world. Poverty does not cause terrorism but, nonetheless, remains a factor in its development. Poverty offers an environment ripe for the exploitation of those who are looking to move in and encourage the forces behind terrorist activity.

• The United States cannot be all things to all people. However, even if future U.S. security policies are not perfectly legal in terms of compliance with international law, we must ensure that we maintain credibility and legitimacy on the world stage.

Dr. Charles Krauthammer, Syndicated Columnist, The *Washington Post*

• It is tempting to define "failed and failing states" in terms of hostility, chaos, and disorder, but this poses analytic problems. To be sure, Liberia and Somalia are classic failed states, but others are often mentioned that are less clear-cut. Haiti, for instance, has been a state for 200 years; though it has failed in serving its people, analytically, it may not belong in the failed-state category. With North Korea, another country frequently mentioned as a failed state, the international community faces a problem of "hyperstability"; Pyongyang may have failed in that its people are starving and suffering, but the state itself has by no means been a failure in achieving its own priorities. Finally, though Afghanistan did not control all of its territory and may have failed when viewed through the prism of our own values, the Taliban state did control 80 to 90 percent of its territory and proved somewhat successful in implementing its own values. Additionally, the

United States intervened in Afghanistan not because of the areas that the Afghan state could not control, but because, in the areas the state did control, the state had decided to harbor terrorists. Looking at countries with functioning institutions as failed states muddies the waters. Still, the impulse to do so and the analytic difficulty that results highlight the fact that the main geopolitical criterion we consider must continue to be hostility to the United States and to American values.

• Realists are not necessarily opposed to nation building; no realist would deny the necessity of the American-led nation-building efforts in Japan and Germany after World War II. Thus, the difference between realists and Wilsonians on this issue does not hinge on whether or not the United States should nation build, but rather on where the United States should nation build. Realists argue that the United States should only commit soldiers to nation-building efforts in places like Afghanistan where American security is in jeopardy.

• In places like Haiti, where the United States has a human imperative to ease the suffering, but American security interests are not at stake, policy makers must employ economic aid and other tools that do not risk the lives of American soldiers.

• Policy makers also must have a sense of the limits of American power. Indeed, it would be arrogant to think that any American effort, including one that involves American soldiers, could create a functioning state in a place like Somalia. Thus, as American power cannot achieve everything everywhere, we must discriminate in where we apply it. The terrorist attacks of September 11, 2001, have made such discrimination simpler by making it easier to identify the places where instability poses an existential threat to American security.

• The realist preferences of the American public pose a final constraint on American policy makers with respect to intervention in failed states that are not of strategic importance to the United States. The majority of Americans oppose the $87 billion spending proposal for rebuilding Iraq, a country where failure to rebuild would be catastrophic to American strategic interests. It is unrealistic to think that the American public would back intervention in places far less crucial to American security.

Analysis

Despite the title, the panel examined "The Challenge Posed by Failed States for U.S. National Security." In that context, the panel explored four key issues: what constitutes a failed state, why states fail, why state failure matters, and what kind of response to failed states is best. Underlying all the commentary, another issue was addressed: Although the challenges of state failure are both significant and meaningful enough to justify high-level attention, the term itself fails to adequately address the nature of the problem that the United States and the rest of the global community face.

What is a failed state? First, state failure represents one point in a process, not an absolute outcome. It generally is the point in the process of governance where the state loses the capacity and/or the will to perform its essential governance and security functions. For some states, the process of governance has been so inhibited that the state never developed those capabilities in the first place. The logic behind this distinction is simply that it is impossible to lose that which never existed.

However, if we focus only on the capacity to govern, we may lose sight of the fact that the state and its institutions may lack effective legitimacy, such as in Haiti, North Korea, Taliban Afghanistan, and Saddam Hussein's Iraq. History demonstrates that individuals and groups can frequently prop up the capacity of the state to govern through the use of sheer force and "state terrorism." Over time, however, the weaknesses inherent in the lack of government legitimacy will likely lead to the eventual erosion of its authority and a certain kind of state failure.

A tendency resulting from the focus on state failure has been to concentrate attention on state collapse—the so-called failed state. To be effective, however, we must address the causes of state failure early in the process, not simply after they have already run their courses and have achieved crisis proportions. Thus, we need to understand some of the more specific causes and consequences of state failure.

Why do states fail? The CIA's State Failure Task Force has developed a list of circumstances under which states fail. Those circumstances center on legitimate governance functions. That is, if the state does not fairly and adequately provide security, meet basic human needs, allow for socioeconomic development, provide general freedoms under the rule of law, and promote trust and cooperation between communal groups, there are both motive and opportunity for instability and violence. In turn, that instability fuels a vicious cycle in which already weak states succumb to widespread civil violence that further erodes socioeconomic and political justice, generates distrust among various sectors of the society, and progressively diminishes the ability and will of the government to conduct the business of the state. Failure to achieve or maintain legitimacy and deal effectively with progressively worsening internal social, economic, political, and security problems results in virtually complete turmoil and generally ineffective institutions. In many cases where these processes are at work, governments are waging war on their citizens, fighting to survive assaults from their citizens, or have become a mere faction among competing forces claiming the right to govern all or part of a disputed national territory. Thus, the result is state failure.

Additionally, and within this context, states fail for two other reasons. First, pressures to liberalize political and economic systems quickly and radically may result in the collapse of governmental authority and the rule of law. Simply holding "free" elections for national leaders without attending to other patterns of political authority and "responsible democracy" risks creating weak and vulnerable institutions. In this immature "democratic" situation, security and law and order are often progressively replaced by "irresponsible" democracy and corruption, at best, or criminal anarchy and armed factional violence, at worst. In any case, the state collapses under the weight of irresponsible, misguided, insensitive, inept, and/or corrupt leadership. Second, other states collapse as a result of the conscious efforts of certain actors to bring them down or control them for their own nefarious purposes. As an example, the forces of technology, such as information and communications, and the easy availability of numerous weapons have greatly empowered and equipped those self-proclaimed leaders who wish to challenge governmental authority and replace it with their own. Clearly, there are different paths toward state failure.

The panelists listed several reasons why failed states matter and why they deserve a place at the top of the list of global challenges. The argument was, generally, that failing or failed states comprise the most dangerous, long-term security challenge facing the global community today. More specifically, failed states become breeding zones for instability and terrorism. They breed massive humanitarian disasters and major refugee flows. They can host "evil" networks of all kinds, whether they involve criminal business enterprise, narco-trafficking, or some form of ideological crusade. They spawn all kinds of things we do not like, such as human rights violations; torture, poverty, starvation, and disease; the recruitment and use of child soldiers; illegal drug trafficking; trafficking in women and body parts; trafficking and proliferation of conventional weapons systems and weapons of mass destruction; genocide and ethnic cleansing; and warlordism, criminal anarchy, and insurgency. At the same time, they usually are unconfined and spill over into regional syndromes of destabilization and conflict.

Additionally, failing and failed states simply do not go away. Failing and failed states become dysfunctional states, rogue states, criminal states, narco-states, or new "people's democracies." In short, they linger and they generally go from bad to worse. The longer they persist, the more they and their problems endanger global peace and security. As a consequence, if the United States, its allies, and the rest of the international community wait to deal with failed states, they will be dealing with the hardest and the most expensive cases. The relevant questions, then, ask where and when to attempt these efforts. The realist's answer to the first question is that attempts must be undertaken where it matters most, not just wherever a failed or failing state presents itself. Whether limiting oneself to only "important" failed or failing states or attempting to address all of them, the answer to the second question is that heading off the problems of a failing state must be attempted as early as possible in the state failure process.

The panelists also discussed responses to failing and failed states. Logically, the realist's questions and answers above imply that the first option in considering a response is whether to respond at all. "Doing nothing" is not necessarily the strategically vacuous counterpart of "doing something." The presumption is that one chooses to do nothing or something as a result of having weighed the various costs and benefits of specific courses of action. In that connection, not all individual cases of potential or actual state failure matter equally. Some states matter more than others. Even so, the costs in terms of time, treasure, and blood may be prohibitive. Thus, the United States should be extremely circumspect in deciding where we go, what we do, and how we spend the resources we have.

The primary implication was that the United States should consider a grand strategy that adopts state failure as a core focus and combines it with a "pivotal states" approach to the world. The concept of pivotal states plays in this approach in three different ways.

First, the strategic imperative of failing or failed states requires that the United States makes a close examination of the contemporary security environment, go beyond a unilateral military approach, and employ a much broader set of strategic-political ways and means in dealing with it.

Second, we should examine the world and key regions with an eye toward determining which cases of state failure would potentially threaten us and our allies most. Those are the cases for which we should be prepared to undertake the most consistent and long-term efforts to prevent or deal with state failure.

Third, the United States should look within various regions for other key actors who can play larger roles in monitoring, preventing, and addressing the challenges of state failure. An international and multilaterally coordinated, regionally based, multidimensional framework for action—rather than a unilateralist military approach—is essential for strategic success now and for the future.

Transcript

JANNE E. NOLAN, Ph.D.: Good morning. Welcome back. I'm here to introduce our first panel discussion, which you can see from the video will focus on this critical issue of failed states, an issue that could hardly have been imagined to become the preeminent security concern as recently as 15 years ago. Even the formidable Soviet Union would move to become an issue as much of failing governments and chaos as any kind of military, traditional military threat. It's a great pleasure to introduce the panel chairman today, Dr. Robert Litwak, who's the director of international studies at the Woodrow Wilson Center. As you can see from his bio, he has published many books. His most recent, *Rogue States and U.S. Foreign Policy*, is directly relevant to this topic, and this is a very distinguished panel of speakers. Rob has a Ph.D. from the London School of Economics; he's also held fellowships at Harvard University, at the International Institute for Strategic Studies, at the Russian Academy of Sciences, and at the U.S. Institute of Peace. He, in turn, will introduce the panel members, and I ask you to join me in welcoming Robert Litwak. Thank you.

ROBERT S. LITWAK, Ph.D.: Thank you, and good morning, ladies and gentlemen.

The Woodrow Wilson Center is honored to be partnering with the Army and the other distinguished co-sponsors of this conference. It's particularly apt that a conference that memorializes Dwight Eisenhower's legacy is being held in a building honoring Ronald Reagan, a wing of which houses the Woodrow Wilson Center. As Dr. Nolan stated, the Woodrow Wilson Center's mission is to improve the quality of the public policy debate on the most pressing issues facing our nation through dialogue such as we're engaged in here today and tomorrow. The Bush administration's National Security Strategy declared, "America is now threatened less by conquering states than by failing states."

Robert S. Litwak

The term "failed state" entered the U.S. diplomatic lexicon and gained wide currency in the aftermath of the Cold War. During the 1990s, the use of American military power in failed states such as Haiti and Somalia was criticized by some as social work, in places where vital U.S. national interests were not at stake. As with the other major challenges in American foreign policy, the context in which this issue was addressed was transformed in the aftermath of 9/11. A transnational terrorist group, al Qaeda, mounted those terrorist attacks from the sanctuary of a failed state, Afghanistan. The argument was increasingly made that the failed state issue could no longer be ignored or dismissed because, in the interconnected age of globalization, any such state could become a staging area for a horrific mass casualty attack on U.S. soil. As the *New York Times'* Tom Friedman puts it, if you don't visit a bad neighborhood, it will visit you.

This panel will examine the future challenge posed by failed states for U.S. national security. We'll explore three key issues.

First, what is a failed state? What factors distinguish a strong state from a weak one and a weak or failing country from a failed state?

Second, what are the criteria for determining U.S. involvement? Do all failed states affect U.S. national interests? Do some countries matter more than others because of their strategic location? Should the United States become involved in cases where there is a humanitarian crisis but where U.S. national interests are not visibly or immediately at stake?

And third, what are the strategies and tools the U.S. policy makers can use to address the failed state challenge? Can early preventive action involving the United States and others stop a failing state from slipping into the failed category? Under what conditions should the United States militarily intervene to stabilize the failed state?

To address these questions, we're fortunate to have four distinguished specialists on this panel.

David Gordon is director of the Office of Transnational Issues at the Central Intelligence Agency. Prior to joining the CIA he was national intelligence officer for economic and global issues on the National Intelligence Council, where he directed the council's seminal *Global Trends 2015* report. Before entering government service he was a professor at the University of Michigan and Michigan State University.

Charles Krauthammer is a Pulitzer Prize winning writer whose syndicated columns appear in the *Washington Post* and the *Washington Times*. After the 1991 Gulf War, Dr. Krauthammer authored a widely discussed article in the *Journal of Foreign Affairs*—"The Unipolar Moment," which made an unequivocal case for American unilateralism. Since 9/11, he's continued to make this case. His columns include the following titles: "U.N., RIP," and "We Don't Peacekeep." Earlier in his career, Dr. Krauthammer, who received an M.D. from Harvard Medical School, was a practicing psychiatrist.

Chester Crocker is the James R. Schlesinger professor of strategic studies at Georgetown University's School of Foreign Service and is chairman of the board of the United States Institute of Peace. As assistant secretary of state in the Reagan administration, he led the diplomacy that produced treaties resulting in the independence of Namibia and the withdrawal of Cuban and South African forces from Angola. He's written widely on post–Cold War security issues, including an article relevant to this panel in the current issue of *Foreign Affairs*: "Engaging Failing States."

Finally, Wendy Sherman is a principal of the Albright Group, an international advisory firm. In the second Clinton administration, she was the counselor of the Department of State with the rank of ambassador. She previously served as assistant secretary of state for legislative affairs. Ambassador Sherman has also worked in a variety of positions in the nonprofit sector, including as president and CEO of the Fannie Mae Foundation.

The panelists will each speak for approximately 15 minutes in the order that I introduce them. We'll give them an opportunity after the presentations to react to each other and then entertain comments and questions from the floor. Now it's my pleasure to turn the floor over to our first speaker, Chester Crocker. Excuse me, David Gordon.

DAVID GORDON, Ph.D.: Thank you, Rob. It's a great honor for me to be here at the Eisenhower Conference, and I want to thank the organizers, and it's a particular pleasure to participate with such distinguished colleagues on this panel.

The Central Intelligence Agency established the State Failure Task Force nearly a decade ago to look at why states fail. The task force has defined political instability broadly, viewing true failed states, like Somalia or Afghanistan, as extreme cases on a continuum that includes more common forms of crisis, such as internal wars and sharp retreats from democracy, that afflict weak states or failing states, but not necessarily failed states. We did so because, as Chet Crocker reminds us in his *Foreign Affairs* piece, state failure is a gradual process: before total collapse occurs, states become embroiled in other kinds of political crises that they're unable or unwilling to resolve. Even more important, many of the consequences of state collapse—human rights violations, ungoverned zones that become potential terrorist havens, humanitarian crises, drug trafficking, and regional spillover—occur in failing as well as failed states. So from a policy maker's perspective, the ability to assess vulnerability to these lesser crises is important.

David Gordon

The task force has chosen to analyze four types of events. Two of these: revolutionary war and ethnic war, involve organized armed challenges to state authority that result in thousands of deaths. A third type, adverse regime change, entails either a sharp decline in the degree of democracy or a wider collapse of authority within a state. The fourth type of event is genocide or politicide, which we define as a deliberate effort by the state or by organized political agents to destroy in whole or in part, particular ethnic, communal, religious, or political groups. By looking at several hundred historic crises since 1955 and testing hundreds of political, social, demographic, economic, and environmental variables, the task force has developed quantitative models that identify risk factors and underlying conditions that typically precede the onset of severe instability or state failure.

What I want to do today is focus on five important findings, particularly recent findings, from this effort to help us understand the dynamics of the state failure process and tease out some policy implications—several policy implications—for tactically responding to failing states and failed states.

The first point is that instabilities in state failure are persistent and recurrent and that complicates efforts of conflict resolution. Although outbreaks of severe and acute political instability are relatively rare, only perhaps two or three per year on average, such events tend to persist, and so the number of states experiencing serious political instability at any one time is much higher. In recent years, roughly 17 or 18 countries are so afflicted. Basically, acute political instability fuels a vicious circle in which already weak states succumb to widespread violence that further erodes the economy, cripples the machinery of government, and sows distrust between communal groups, creating both motive and opportunity for further violence and disorder. For these same reasons, states that emerge from failure tend to be very vulnerable to renewed crises for several years. Recent examples include Haiti, which has seen lawlessness in a series of failed democratization attempts over the last 15–20 years; and Liberia, where repeated bouts of civil war over the last 13 years have produced a series of brittle regimes, the latest of which collapsed this year. Moreover, one type of instability leads to another. Civil wars, either revolutionary or ethnic, tend to spark adverse regime transitions, additional internal wars, or genocidal incidents nearly 40 percent of the time. In fact, genocides and politicides almost always occur in the wake of other forms of instability. So as a result of this, states with recent history of upheaval are very likely to experience future crises. This pattern, which is exemplified by the conflicts in Kosovo and Rwanda, reflects the role that insecurity, fear, and hatred play in these tragedies.

What are the main causes and sources of severe political instability and state failure? A country's political institution and patterns of political behavior are the most important determinants of its risk of severe instability or state failures, with partial democracies being the most vulnerable. While autocracies that allow some political competition, like Haiti or Yemen, appear to be more vulnerable to crises than their more repressive counterparts, the most vulnerable kinds of regimes are partial democracies, countries that have started a process of democratization that combine at least partially free elections with elements of autocratic rule, including a largely unchecked chief executive. Such countries in the current world include both Iran, for instance, and Nigeria. Particularly important here, in which partial democracies get on pathways to failure, is the presence of very, very intense factional competition. When groups engage in uncompromising and violent struggles over political authority in the context of partial democracy, such as what has been happening in the 1990s in Sierra Leone, an outbreak of internal war or adverse regime change, other forms of state failure are highly likely to occur. The absence of strong checks on the executive also compounds the effects of dysfunctional competition in these kinds of societies. So countries like Albania in the 1990s or Cote d'Ivoire prior to last year's civil war were particularly vulnerable because of the combination of intense factional competition and a largely unchecked chief executive.

There are increasing numbers of partial democracies in the world, perhaps one in three regimes in the world today is a partial democracy. That, in the long term, may be a positive trend if these countries evolve into full democracies. In the short term, however, the increased number of partial democracies suggests the possibility of a heightened risk of serious instability, often presaging a return to authoritarian rule, as has occurred in many fledgling democracies, including

Belarus and Congo-Brazzaville, or internal war and state collapse, as has occurred in African states of Sierra Leone and Cote d'Ivoire.

The second substantial determinant of state failure in countries is the fact that countries with large swaths of poverty and overall poor quality of life with economies that are internally focused and are not integrated into the world economy are more likely to experience a political crisis. Let me emphasize that there are many, many, many countries in the world that fit these criteria. Among those countries, the political variables that I spoke of earlier are much more determinative than is relative level of poverty. While failed states do tend to be poor countries, poverty in and of itself is not the major determination of state failure.

Now, economic factors do play something of a role in shaping the odds that a country will be able to sustain democracy. Reinforcing other studies' findings, the State Failure Task Force has found that democracies in impoverished countries are more likely to backslide into autocracy than are democracies in richer countries.

Fourth point is that states that formally discriminate against or violently repress particular ethnic or communal groups are more likely to experience severe political crises. This is not a surprising finding. Discrimination increases the risk of ethnic war, in particular, but the tendency of internal wars to spark other forms of instability suggests that discrimination heightens the risk of other types of crises as well.

And the final point, analytically, is that countries in bad neighborhoods, neighborhoods where other countries are embroiled in violence, internal conflicts, are more likely to experience political instability. Conflict spills across borders in many ways: soldiers and guerrillas cross borders to attack targets or to seek refuge; refugees cross borders placing economic burdens on their countries of destination; conflicts in neighboring states make guns and other weapons available across borders; concern for the plight of ethnic kin encourages violence as well. In recent years we've seen these bad neighborhood effects most strongly expressed in sub-Saharan Africa, where clusters of conflicts have occurred in West Africa, in the Great Lakes region, and in northeast Africa. But we also have examples of this in South Asia, where conflicts in Afghanistan and India heavily influence the domestic politics and regional relations for several surrounding countries.

Let me talk very, very briefly and conclude by looking at the implications of these findings for efforts to try to prevent and mitigate the impact of state failure. The first point is that institutional design may be an important component of preventive action. Simply holding free elections for chief executive without attending to other patterns of political authority risks creating weak democracies with, in fact, continued vulnerability to political violence. Addressing the design of the electoral system by incorporating rules that favor coalition building and encouraging parties to reach across communal lines or regional lines might help avert the kind of factionalism that tends to challenge new democracies. Strengthening systems of checks and balances between branches of governments could also be an important element of this.

Secondly, to directly discourage states from discriminating or violently repressing communal groups is another potential conflict prevention strategy. In many instances, the state's behavior is probably more of an emblem of the regime's underlying weakness and a sign that violence and intolerance are important elements of the local political currency. It raises an important diplomatic opportunity for the United States and others who wish to avoid a final slide into state failure.

Finally, I think the effects of conflicts on neighboring states imply that, particularly in bad neighborhoods, efforts to address the challenge of state failure are likely to require regional as well as country-specific strategies. To prevent a crisis from emerging in one state, it may be necessary to help end a conflict in another.

Let me end with that point, and again, thank you very, very much for inviting me here this morning.

LITWAK: Thank you very much, David. Our next speaker is Charles Krauthammer.

DR. CHARLES KRAUTHAMMER: In your absence in the waiting room, we had a mutiny and decided to change the order. I think I'm going last, if that's all right? A polite mutiny.

LITWAK: Okay. Then we will turn to Chester Crocker.

CHESTER A. CROCKER, Ph.D.: Thank you very much for this opportunity to address some comments on an important theme, which we have with us today. Our chairman has given us a clear mandate to discuss definitions of failed states, criteria for U.S. involvement, and strategies and tools for dealing with the challenge or the threat of state failure.

I'm going to add one element to that mix, which is: Why are they so important? Because I think it's central that we start with a clear understanding of that issue of the importance and why failed states deserve a place right up at the top of our list of global challenges as perhaps the most dangerous long-term security challenge facing us in the world today. I say that because I think there are two points that need to be clarified. One is that, sometimes, failed states become a hard security challenge. They aren't a soft security challenge; they can become a hard security challenge. And that point needs to be understood analytically, so that warrants putting failed states right up there with the threat of WMD [weapons of mass destruction] and terrorism as a potential hard security challenge. But the second point, which is equally important, is that soft security challenges are very important too. And so we shouldn't be put in the position analytically, as we look down the road 10, 20 years, of deciding that we only have time for the hard security challenges, which obviously terrorism and WMD states, rogue states, are. We

must be able to address all the most
important challenges out there, if we're
to be the global leader that we believe
ourselves to be.

That's one reason why it was right
to do what we did 13 years too late in
Liberia recently. And it still would be
good if we did a bit more of it. Why?
Because failed states really matter, and
I'm going to run down a brief list of
arguments why they really matter, just
to refresh that discussion. We saw some
of that in preambular material. Because
they can become breeding zones for
terrorism, that's pretty obvious. They
can also breed massive humanitarian
disasters, which require some form of
response, not necessarily for strategic
reasons, but for political reasons in all
democratic countries. Thirdly, because
they can host evil networks of all kinds,

Chester A. Crocker

whether they're involved in criminal business enterprise or narco-trafficking and
so forth. Fourthly, as David Gordon had said, because they spill so often into
regional syndromes of conflict and destabilization. So we're not just talking really
about whether we should have done something in Rwanda because Rwanda was
important in a human sense. Of course, it was the worst genocide since World
War II, but because Rwanda led to Congo and Congo led to Burundi, and the rest
of them led to other problems, and Congo-Brazzaville—before you know it, you
have a huge area, larger than mainland China, which is in some degree of upheaval.
So there's that argument.

And then fifth, because these kinds of situations tend to spawn a whole
series of things we don't like. When you have state failure, you have a vacuum.
You have the absence of public services provided to the population by
government, and that very absence is a vacuum which all too often is filled not
only by criminal mafias, but also by Islamic fundamentalism in states where
that's an issue. So let's face it, some of the things we're seeing. We're seeing a
rivalry between different kinds of service providers to the populous, and that
battle, that competition is not necessarily being won by legitimate governments
in lots of places. We see all kinds of things that we really do not like in zones of
state failure. The recruitment of child soldiers, trafficking in women, economies
that get wrecked, extremist policies, as I've suggested, health pandemics, and
so forth. So, I argue that, in fact, this syndrome of state failure deserves a place
right up there at the top of the list, and that furthermore, as our chairman has

indicated in his framing comments, the analytical distinction between failed states and rogue states has effectively broken down. In fact, there are a few examples out there where you see both. You see, for example, North Korea which is both a rogue state and a failed state.

Some definitions—I think the previous speaker has covered that ground. I'll be very brief in talking about it. But I do think it's interesting to ask ourselves, not only what is a failed state, but more important, how do we see failure as it's occurring along that spectrum—along that entire spectrum of behavior patterns—so you know it when you see it. It's a little bit like trying to define pornography, I realize, but here is the way I see it and how I recognize it. I recognize state failure when I see international disengagement and abandonment of countries that previously were very closely linked to the international system, and they've lost their external support structure and their external networks, and then, "Watch out, Katy, bar the door." That is precisely what happened historically in Liberia, in Somalia, in Afghanistan, Congo, and the list goes on.

I see state failure coming when I see the balance of power on the ground shifting against civilians of all kinds and in favor of young men with guns. That's a long list of countries we're talking about. I see state failure when elites begin to align themselves to criminal business enterprises, and you can see it and you can watch it; you can read it in your intel reports and you can see it in good journalism. Liberia is another case; former Yugoslavia is a case. I see it when the rulers themselves become the criminal business enterprise, as we have seen in Burma and we have seen in Nigeria. Or when entire provinces become ungoverned in order to facilitate good business opportunities for bad guys, as we have seen in Georgia, in parts of Congo, and in Colombia.

So that's just an idea to supplement somewhat what David Gordon has very usefully laid out about definitions. Now, when should the U.S. become involved? Again, in my view, we don't need to think only about direct physical threats to our own homeland security, we need to think about threats to American forces overseas, to our allies overseas, to American norms and values, and, in a general sense, to our political interests. If we are the great nation that we say we are—and I certainly believe we intend to stay that way—we have a longer list of very important interests than just the most immediate and most direct physical threats.

So where is the zone of state failure and how do we make some choices? How does America choose? The zone of state failure, and of failing states, is huge. It goes from Senegal to Sarawak. It goes from Dushanbe to Durban. Clearly we need to make some choices; they have to have some criteria. Mine are as follows. Places are at risk of a terrorist buildup or rogue state developing, which is why, of course, we take so seriously the South Asian dynamic between India and Pakistan, because one of those could potentially become big, big trouble for us for all kinds of reasons. I don't think I need to mention which. That's also why we're focusing on Sudan with a serious set of diplomatic and political initiatives today. It's why we in the Reagan administration, for which I'm not speaking here this morning—nor am I speaking officially for the U.S. Institute of Peace, a little disclaimer—why we focused on South Africa during the 1980s, because we did not want to see it head down that path to some form of roguedom, either because of WMD or other things that it might be doing. So that is certainly one set of criteria.

The second set of criteria involves the country's inherent regional importance as an anchor state or security partner of ours. Quite obviously, by any definition Turkey is a very important country and we'd better never let Turkey become a failed state.

The issue, thirdly, of regional contagion I think has been discussed and developed already, so I won't expand on that. The issue of humanitarian and political stakes I think is pretty clear. When things get to a certain point, you are compelled to act. I am informed that our president today, our current president, has indeed read the story of Samantha Powers' account of what happened in Rwanda, and been very moved by it, and has uttered the phrase, "Not on my watch will we see a Rwanda." Well, we'll see if he means that. But in any case, that's what I'm talking about when I say humanitarian.

And then finally, there are the American diplomatic stakes. A great nation cannot always control and manipulate the perception that others have of what we should do. And that is why we reluctantly, but eventually, did put some boots on the ground in a limited, token way in Liberia recently.

All right, what strategies and tools make sense? Those are my criteria. They're very broad and crude—obviously, they need to be refined. But what strategies and tools make sense for addressing the failing state challenge? Because, as I have said before, and I want to underscore the distinction, the number of failed states is a short list. And if you wait until you are just dealing with failed states, you're dealing with the hardest cases and you're dealing with the most expensive cases, picking up all the pieces and starting over again. And we're much better off to try to head off failure when we can see it coming.

There are three points I want to make here about strategies and tools. The first, the sensible place to start is to identify who else is in this struggle with us, to identify the institutions, the coalitions, the alliances, the partnerships, and the friendships which we can work with in order to share this huge burden because the number of potential failing states is probably somewhere like 50 or 60. And we clearly need to do a lot of systematic burden sharing if we're to be serious, if we're to walk the walk on failed states and not just talk the talk. So we need a serious inventory of the assets and the interests—a very quick illustration of what I mean by that: A lot of people have commented that what we need more of right now in Iraq are light infantry or paramilitary or constabulary and less heavy ground forces of the kind that we have a lot of. Where do we look around the world for other people who have lots of those kinds of things? We know where to look and we should be working with them to see who's going to take the lead on Civ-Pol [International Civilian Police Program], who's going to take the lead on *gendarmerie*- and *carabiniere*-type forces. Who's going to really provide the on-the-ground light infantry people, which we need more of? So that's just an example. The inventory needs to include intangible as well as tangible assets for figuring out who is going to work with us on these things. We'll never get on top of this challenge if we don't have a good strong inventory of legitimate partners and institutions to work with.

The second thing we need to do is to break down state failure into phases, which is a pretty obvious point. Early-stage failure that you see, where you want to nip it in the bud, as distinguished from late-stage failure, where it risks falling over the edge of the abyss and becoming another Liberia, if you like. And then, of course, there is the stage of post-conflict reconstruction, which is the most expensive part of all, as we're finding out in Iraq. Again, I can give examples, depending on how much time we have, but when you are talking about early-stage actions among the things we can do, working with allies, is to devise plans for influencing, persuading, and even coercing local rulers before it's too late, before they head down those negative paths that David Gordon so clearly outlined for us. Combine decisive action on a number of fronts, which could include such things as intelligence sharing with key allies, concerted measures to deal with bad guys who are beginning to get entrenched, to rip up their local and foreign support bases, to discredit them, to name them, to shame them, and to impose sanctions on them. There's a lot you can do. There's a lot we are doing but very selectively. So that's a little different than a late-stage case, where you really have to keep a country or a society from going right over the edge, where you may need to get involved in coercive diplomacy and militarily backed international peace processes designed to create a transition to a new regime.

The third distinction I think is useful to make is between specific failed-state strategies—that is, where you're taking on a specific case of a Nigeria, let's say, or a Pakistan, or an Indonesia, and these are all obviously potential cases—or whether we're taking on the overall phenomenon that David Gordon was talking about, of state failure, and dealing with the international environment in which societies tend to fail. Let me be very clear about what I'm saying: The generic approach is to do things like the G-8 meeting in Evian last June recently did—to adopt a much more rigorous sounding code of transparency for dealing with the extractive industries of mining and hydrocarbons in some of these countries and to get governments and companies to publish what they pay and actually hold up a higher standard of transparency in these kinds of societies. That obviously is not a Nigerian strategy, that's a global strategy, so I call it generic.

Another thing we can do is to talk much more openly than I think we have about what the real challenge is in many of these countries. It's not just democracy building—it is state building. These countries have weak institutions or no institutions; they need the systematic help of the international community in strengthening their judiciary systems, strengthening their police systems, strengthening their own free press, and those kinds of things which make a big, big difference. When it gets to dealing with specific cases, there are so many things that we can do, and they range from assistance bilaterally to the role of our political leaders in trying to get local rulers to get off the wagon when they're developing bad habits and that kind of thing. Let me give a conflict management illustration very quickly here. Quite recently, the president of the Philippines visited our president here in Washington and the two leaders agreed at the end of their discussions that it would be useful for a U.S. quasi-official organization, whose board I happen to chair, the U.S. Institute of Peace, to get involved in trying to open up the channels of discussion between the central government of Manila and the moral Islamic Liberation Front in Mindanao. That is precisely the kind of thing we should be doing and doing more of. That's just a specific illustration of the point. I think I probably covered the ground here, and I'm told that I'm about to get the hook. So let me just make one final comment. Our strategy cannot be only or even primarily military. It cannot be aimed only at destroying immediate threats to our security. It is not a burden primarily or only for DOD [Department of Defense], and it cannot be done by the U.S. by itself.

Thank you very much.

LITWAK: Thank you very much, Chet. Wendy Sherman?

AMBASSADOR WENDY R. SHERMAN: Good morning, glad to be here. I thought that Charles was going to be a setup for me, but I'm going to be a setup for him instead. We're here to talk about failed and weak states, how to cope with them, support them, to become something other than that, undo them, or otherwise deal with them. And let me say at the outset, this is one hell of a difficult job.

The analytics that both David and Chester put forward were quite critical in thinking about this, but doing something about it is very, very difficult. How to prevent failed states, how to intervene in failed states, neither are easy tasks. When President Bush ran for office, he basically said that the Clinton administration had been hyperactive around engagement in the world—hyperactive in terms of humanitarian intervention, seeking approval everywhere, that there was no place that we didn't want to go into. Though as both my colleagues pointed out, we did not intervene in Rwanda. We could not get the international community to intervene in Rwanda, much to, I think all of our regret, who were part of those choices and those decisions. But President Bush, when he was campaigning, said that there would be no Rwanda, there would be no Haiti, there would be no Bosnia, there would be no nation building. And, in fact, many people thought it was sort of a campaign tactic, "A-B-C,"—"Anything But Clinton." National Security Advisor Rice outlined a policy of no foreign policy of social work, which I take some personal offense at being not a lawyer, as many believe I am, but a social worker who believes that much of life needs good use of clinical skills and community organizing. Rice said that foreign policy will proceed from the firm

ground of national interests, not from
the interests of the illusory international
community. And I think many people
were glad for sort of a more robust
national interest, national security
focused foreign policy.

The Clinton policy, which was, I
think, well-described by Brian Atwood,
the head of AID, our international aid
organization, who said America's
security and prosperity are interwoven
with that of the entire world. This era
offers countless opportunities for
progress and, very prophetically, this
was in 1994. But if we turn away from
the developing world, we invite more
world poverty, more failed nations,
more civil war, and more terrorism.
The Clinton/Atwood approach really
for failed states sat on three pillars as
described by the Stohls in the 2001

Wendy R. Sherman

paper, "Failed and Failing States": attack the root causes of conflict within fragile
states, promote collective security with respect to responses to needs, and engage
in preventive diplomacy (and, Bill Perry and Ash Carter would say, engage in
preventive defense). Needless to say, the Clinton administration had a very rough
start to their policy as we all know from the tragic consequences in Somalia in
October of 1993, when we lost 18 members of our military and had one of our
military captured alive and humiliated across CNN all over the world.

The RAND study on America's role in nation building taught us some
important lessons to be learned from our own experience, and among those
lessons were that nation building objectives should be scaled to available forces,
resources, and staying power. Military forces need to be complemented by civil
capabilities for law enforcement, economic reconstruction, and political
development. Unity of command can be as important in peace operations as in
war, and there can be no economic or political development without security—
much of which I think we're all seeing being replayed again now in Iraq. Overall,
the RAND study gave us a lot of very good and useful lessons learned about
how to deal with failed states, both preventively and through military
intervention. Many factors are involved in being successful, but key determinants
are the level of effort, time, manpower and money, whether that's in prevention
or intervention. Multilateral prevention-intervention is complex and time-
consuming but ultimately less expensive. And multilateral intervention can
produce greater transformation and regional reconciliation than unilateral efforts

can. Unity of command, whether in peacetime or wartime, and broad participation are compatible if there is a common vision.

There is an inverse correlation between the size of the stabilization force, as we are finding out now, and the level of risk. Neighboring states, as has been said by Chester and by David, can exert significant influence. Accountability for past injustices can be very powerful, though difficult. And very importantly, there is no quick route in either prevention or military intervention, and the aftermath of nation building by year seems to be about the minimum staying power that we often, neither the United States nor the international community, have.

When President Bush came in, he set out a set of objectives that were very different than the Clinton administration. He saw himself as a realist, as opposed to the Clinton Wilsonians. It was quite different than the first Bush administration doctrine, where President Bush "One" said we have a vision of a new partnership of nations based on consultation, cooperation, and collective action, whose goals are to increase democracy, increase prosperity, increase peace, and reduce arms. But, as has been pointed out by Robert Litwak, 9/11 and the commitment to finish the job in Iraq has reshaped the second Bush administration's doctrine. Now objectives are to defend, preserve, and extend the peace as is said in the national security doctrine, and the United States will accomplish these three goals by fighting terrorists and tyrants, building good relations among great powers, and encouraging free and open societies on every continent. Quite a different agenda, quite an acknowledgment of the importance and character of failed and weak states than on the campaign trail. And to be perfectly fair here, most candidates say one thing on the campaign trail and quite another when they become president.

The Bush national security doctrine has raised terrorism to a first order and says our forces must be dominant for the foreseeable future. Much of this is in the great CFR document, and a new National Security Strategy, which I think is quite useful, and emphasizes cooperation of great powers under American leadership. It also calls for removing root causes of terrorism and tyranny. Obviously one of the tools for doing this in the Bush agenda is a doctrine of preemption. Iraq and the circumstances we now find ourselves in have created cause for rethinking by critics; although the president is quite steadfast in the framework, although he has now taken to very extensive and expensive nation building in Iraq and state building, I quite agree. He seeks fundamental change in the Middle East through Iraq and in fact is really stating a very, very bold vision that goes beyond the Clinton vision. To in fact say by state building and nation building in Iraq, we will change the states and the nations of the entire Middle East. Most people say that this is not colonialism because the United States has never been about territorial acquisition, and indeed we have not. But in fact the Bush administration in many ways has gone beyond the Clinton administration to what I would call "postcolonial colonialism," an imperialism of ideas to deal with failed states—bold but hard as hell to do alone, and hard to do without the other great powers and without international institutions.

So briefly, in the few moments I have left, let me tell you what I think all of this has meant in terms of where we are in the world. I've been very fortunate to be a consultant to the Pew Global Attitudes Project, a data research study that has talked with 38,000 people in 44 countries in the fall of 2002, and then another 16,000 people in 20 countries, and the Palestinian authority, after the Iraq war in May 2003. And the results of that data, which you can see on the Pew web site if you want to look for yourself, are quite stunning. On the one hand, all over the world, in states that we would consider failing and certainly weak states, globalization is seen as a very positive force, but people are worried about the pace of modern life. They want Western-style democracy, freedom of expression, a strong judiciary is probably what people want more than anything, freedom of association, freedom of religion, but most people don't believe they have it. There is staggering, staggering loss of favorability of the United States in the world. And in the Muslim world, it is absolutely off the cliff. The United Nations is seen more and more as a failing institution, which I think is not helpful in this huge job we have to do with failed and weak states. And in the Muslim world, in seven out of eight countries that were looked at, they believe the United States will militarily attack them in the near future. The data show that, although people want our values, seek our values, they see the United States as arrogant and moving away from helping them and supporting them through institutional—international institutions—and of exacerbating the gap between the rich and the poor.

Why does this matter to the first part of my presentation, about where we head with failed and weak states and what we ought to do? It is because how we position ourselves in the world, how we work with the world, has an impact on how people see us, which has an impact on our ultimate national security interests, which is the safety and security of our people. Recently, we saw this played out, and I actually wrote these notes before Tom Friedman's I thought useful column this morning. What we just saw happen at the World Trade Organization in Cancun is part of what we must not do if, in fact, we don't want to face more and more failed and weak states around the world. We have to work on ending the gap between the rich and the poor, not because poverty in itself creates terrorism—I quite agree, it does not. It is not a direct link. But it is so that it is a factor, and it is so that it can create a breeding ground for those who are looking for a place to move in and create and strengthen the forces of terrorism, and so, just as Tom pointed out this morning, when Benin, Burkina Faso, Chad, and Mali—not countries that we would all think of as strong and free and on their way to all of the great things we would hope for people around the world—look for a breakthrough on cotton and wonder why the United States, which gives $3 billion to 25,000 cotton farmers, does not intervene. We, in fact, are sowing a seed that we could otherwise prevent in the potential for a failed or weak state among them.

We have to do things about the transnational issues and the soft power issues that Chester mentioned, like HIV/AIDS. And the United States cannot be all things to all people everywhere. So if President Bush is to move forward with his bold vision of not only change, but transformation, it will take working and playing well with others and making sure we have the credibility and the legitimacy, even if not the perfect legality, to move forward in intervening either to prevent or to end a terrible situation. Thank you.

LITWAK: Turn now, finally, to Charles Krauthammer.

KRAUTHAMMER: Thank you, Robert, it's a pleasure to be here. I was here last year. We had a rather spirited discussion about unilateralism, and I think we're going to have a spirited discussion here today about failed states.

Let me begin by trying to address Robert's framework of questions in order. The first has to do with an analytical question of what is a failed state and how do we define it? Because if we're going to have any coherence in discussing how we approach it, we need to know what the subject matter is. I think it's rather difficult because we may have different criteria. The possible criteria are instability, hostility, chaos, disorder; and the classic examples of failed states that we talk about are countries like Liberia or Somalia. But we've heard others mentioned, and I think it does raise some analytic questions—Haiti and North Korea, for example. While Haiti has had statehood for 200 years, it certainly has failed in terms of serving its people, but I'm not sure how it would fit our criteria of failure in terms of stability if we use, for example, as the model, Liberia and Somalia. North Korea is an even odder example, because if anything, it's a place where their problem is hyperstability. It's run, as Karen Elliott House wrote rather acutely the other day, as an anthill; it's a failed state in the sense that its people are starving and suffering, of course, but it certainly is a state of remarkable efficiency, given its own goals. Afghanistan was also mentioned as a failed state, and I think that's an interesting question. Clearly, it did not have control of all of its territory; it had a kind of simmering and rather static civil war. It controlled very much of its territory—the overwhelming majority—but I'm not sure we would categorize it as a failed state in the sense that, within the territory that it controls, which was 80 or 90 percent of Afghanistan, it had pretty good control. It may have failed in terms of our values, but in terms of its values, it was rather quite successful.

And one of the problems of failed states, we all agree upon, is that if it does not exert control over its territory, those wild, wild West areas can become the locus of terrorism transnational criminality, et cetera, but it seems to me that the reason that we intervened in Afghanistan was not because of difficulties with terrorism and the hostility coming from the areas out of the control of the central government, it was because of the terrorism coming out of the areas under the control of the central government. In other words, it was a rather coherent entity in terms of its hostility to the United States. Thus, I'm not sure how it fits into the category of failure. So when we talk about failed states, I think it's an interesting sociological and anthropological question, and I think it does raise the example of Rwanda, of moral issues. But in terms of political, diplomatic, and foreign policy, and ultimately military questions facing us, I think the major criterion has to be hostility—hostility to us, our allies, and our values. And that gets us into the issue that Wendy Sherman raised about two different visions of how the United States ought to respond to these failed hostile states, which is how I would categorize them, around the world. Do we nation build or do we not? I think it's a mistake to interpret either what the president said in his campaign, or what I might call the realist view of nation building, by saying that realists are against nation building in principle, and Clintonian-Wilsonian idealists believe it has to be

Charles Krauthammer

done. I think that's a false distinction. After all, there is no reasonable, realist American who would deny that nation building in Germany and Japan after the Second World War was not only a necessity, but one of the great successes of American foreign policy in our history. The question with nation building is not do you do it or do you not, which is, I think, a question of almost no interest, because it's much too broad. The question is where do you do it? And the realist answer is that you do it where it matters. You're either cynical, I might say, in answering that question, but some places in the world matter to the United States very acutely, and to the West. And I would include Afghanistan in that category. And some places, for all of the human suffering, do not matter to us as national security, foreign policy, or military issues, and I would categorize, for example, Haiti there. That's not to say you don't do anything for Haiti, we are human beings, we have moral obligations, but I think that a president has a great moral obligation in committing soldiers who must answer his commands and risk their lives and die, if necessary. Before he commits them, I think the president has to be acting, thinking that he's acting in the national security interest of the country. We certainly have other tools and other means to help suffering peoples in failed states, such as Liberia. We have economic means, diplomatic means; we can provide logistics; we have great expertise with disaster relief; and I think most Americans would agree that we can and should commit our tax revenues to those kinds of enterprises to aid suffering people in failed states.

But for a president to take the step of committing American soldiers and risking their lives, I think the criterion has to be higher. The bar has to be higher. And that is, it has to be a serious, important threat to the national security of the United States. Which is why Robert in his introduction talked about people who criticize the Clinton administration for social work. I was the one who coined that term regarding our activity, our intervention in Haiti and also in other places, when we tried to escalate our involvement in Somalia, from pure humanitarian relief to nation building, which became the Clinton administration policy later in our involvement. There are some places in the world where, for all of our strength and all of our power and all of our wealth, we are not going to succeed in creating what the conditions on the ground will not allow the creation of. I mean, there's a certain arrogance; the realists and conservatives are accused of arrogance. I can't think of anything more arrogant than the belief that the United States is able to create in a place like Somalia a functioning state that requires all kinds of ingredients—social, economic, historical—that are not in place and that we may try enormous efforts and our efforts will be written on sand as we saw it in a place like that. And look at Haiti today after our intervention; I think it's extremely hard to argue that we had advanced the cause of nation building in Haiti as a result of our intervention.

First of all, we have to have a sense of limits. What can we do given our power? And secondly, we have to have a sense of discrimination because of our limits, we do not have unlimited resources. We are not god-like in our power in the world. We have to choose, therefore, those areas that are of extreme importance to us. Germany and Japan are the classic examples. And as a result of 9/11, we can identify those areas in the world which are extremely important to us because we now know the nature of the existential threat that we face in the early part of this century—the successor, if you will, to the Soviet threat in the Cold War and to the fascist threat before it. And therefore, I think, we are interested in certain specific failed states, where we will invest our resources and blood, as well as the treasure of our country—and those are places like Afghanistan and Iraq, which are in very important regions—precisely because of our recent history. And that's why I'm very reluctant, and rather opposed to any military intervention of the United States in a place like Liberia. Not that as a human being I wouldn't want to see that suffering relieved, but where do you draw the line? Why are we, therefore, not intervening in Congo, where far more people are dying every day? The places where we could intervene and make a difference are almost infinite, and unless we apply strict criteria having to do with our national security, we will spend ourselves into oblivion, both in blood and in treasure, in rectifying all the evils and the suffering of the world. We do not do social work. I did not know that Wendy was a social worker. I'm a former psychiatrist—actually, a psychiatrist in remission—and there are places in the world where I think would benefit from the absence of psychiatry, if not social work. So I'm not sure I want to be an evangelist with our notions of therapy. And I certainly don't want to use the U.S. military as an agent of therapy. This is a very deadly serious issue, the commitment of American troops, and it ought to be; we ought to have extremely stringent criteria.

So what I'm left with, I think, is to say that analytically we have a difficult issue in defining the failed states because there are all kinds of criteria that one could apply. I think it's most useful to apply to a state that is living in a situation of chaos and disorder because if you consider states like North Korea, Haiti, and others that actually have functioning institutions or, in the case of Pyongyang, hyper-functioning institutions, I think you muddy the waters. And I think in looking at failed states and in deciding how America ought to approach it, I think clearly we ought to do what we can as a great and wealthy power to alleviate suffering.

As a military power, as the leader of the free world, I think we ought to be extremely stringent in applying the military and the vast resources that we have to places that are absolutely critical to our national security because if you look today at what is the central focus of our efforts, Afghanistan and Iraq, we have had enormous criticism of this administration for its commitment of $87 billion, which is a lot of money, but relative to an $11 trillion economy. Relative to the unbelievable destruction of 9/11, which was in the hundreds of billions of dollars, and probably to the greater destruction that will be suffered for the next 9/11, particularly if it involves weapons of mass destruction, it is a relatively modest sum. And yet, this administration is being seriously attacked from all corners for its extravagance in nation building in Iraq. I looked at the public opinion polls yesterday, the majority of Americans oppose spending the $87 billion. And here is a place where, were we to fail, were we to withdraw, leaving a failed state behind, it would be catastrophic for our national security. Given the reluctance, very understandable, of hardworking Americans to commit their resources and their sons and daughters to building other countries and to rescuing other people, and given that resistance, even in a place of central strategic importance like Iraq, I think it is entirely unrealistic to expect that we're going to have the support of the American people for spending our blood and treasure in places of far less importance and far less interest. Given those circumstances, I think we should be extremely circumspect in deciding where we go, what we do, and how we spend what we have. Thank you very much.

LITWAK: Thank you very much, Charles. Before turning to the audience for comments and questions from the floor, I'd like to give the panelists an opportunity, if they wish to exercise it, an opportunity to react to what they've heard. We've had a very rich menu of views on the three issues that are the charter of this panel, the analytical criteria of trying to put some analytical rigor on the concepts of failed state, and the process of state failure. Secondly, trying to flesh out some criteria on conditions under which the United States, alone or with others, should get involved. And thirdly, what are the effective strategies to ameliorate causes of state failure and prevent its occurrence?

We've had some, particularly in the last two presentations, sharply contrasting views on the policy prescription side, as well as on the analytical side, in our initial two presentations. If the panelists would wish to comment, we'll have a round of that and then return to the floor. So Wendy, then Chet, then David.

SHERMAN: There's probably more ground of common agreement that Charles and I have than meets the eye. I, too, believe we ought to be very careful when we commit the men and women of this country and use the treasure of their lives and our budget in what we do around the world. And I'm interested, in fact, in how, Charles, you would define hostility. If hostility is the prime criteria for when we do military intervention, I would say that makes Afghanistan pretty clear. Because we know that Osama bin Laden was behind the 9/11 tragedy, and our committing our troops to root him out and root out al Qaeda was very clear, and the hostility was very clear. In Iraq, Iraq's imminent threat to the United States, in my view, is still of some question.

I'm very supportive of committing funds now, if we get a number of questions answered, because I agree that we cannot allow failure in Iraq. It's too devastating, now that we are there. But if one looks at hostility, as someone who spends an enormous amount of time on the North Korea issue, their potential of being an imminent threat is probably phenomenally greater than that of Iraq. And yet I would be the last person to say that we ought to commit our military to an immediate intervention in North Korea. So I would be curious as to how one defines, and how you define, and how the people in the audience would define my colleagues' hostility, and how imminent the threat has to be or whether the threat has to have occurred?

KRAUTHAMMER: Well, I'm rather surprised that you seem to require imminence to be an essential feature of the threat before it requires a response. Your entire presentation was talking about how we have to anticipate hostility to prevent the seeds of terrorism.

SHERMAN: Not necessarily with armed military intervention

KRAUTHAMMER: I understand. But you offered us the longer perspective, and then you demand that, in order to respond militarily, we have to have an imminent threat. First of all, and I don't want to sidetrack us into an argument about Iraq, although I suspect it's inevitable these days, especially if you put Wendy and I up here; but Mr. Chairman, I didn't start it, but I intend to finish it.

The claim by this administration was never made that the threat from Iraq was imminent. When the president made his presentation to the nation in the State of the Union address earlier this year, he specifically said, "There are those who say we must wait until the threat is imminent." And he specifically said, "This administration does not agree with that approach, that the lesson of 9/11 is that we live in a world where the stealth of our enemies, the potential for destruction that they have, and the margin for error is so small, that we cannot have the traditional luxury of waiting for imminence." The French and the British could watch the Germans mobilize and start their trains and bring out their troops in August of 1914; they had time; they made the wrong decision. That is not how we're going to be attacked in the future. That is not how we were attacked on 9/11, and thus in the world we live in today, post 9/11, imminence cannot be the criteria. It's the potential for destruction and the level of hostility, and I think that is why the president was correct in identifying three countries working on weapons of mass destruction—Iraq, Iran, and North Korea—as the threats to our nation. So I think it's very important to make that distinction.

Hostility, I think, is pretty obvious: Afghanistan, Iraq, Iran, North Korea. Do you use the military in all instances? Of course not; you have to decide what's doable or what's not. But I think hostility has to be the essential criterion of any intervention, otherwise, we are going to intervene in places as the Clinton administration did, like Haiti and Somalia, and—I would even argue—in the Balkans, which end up spreading ourselves thin, spending our resources, and leaving us less prepared for the real threat and issue which is today, terrorism and emanating from the Middle East and the Islamic world.

LITWAK: Let's get Chet and bring him into the discussion.

CROCKER: Wendy Sherman got off a wonderful line in her comments about what was troubling folks out there in the study of attitudes, and that was that a lot of people are worried about the pace of modern life, a sentiment with which I can rapidly agree and identify myself. And one of the problems with the pace of modern life is that we find in discussions like this all too often that we are reduced to bumper stickers because of the reasons of time. And one of the bumper stickers that is least helpful in a discussion of this kind is the term *nation building* because—and there's a wonderful new book out from RAND, *America's Role in Nation-Building: From Germany to Iraq*, and Jim Dobbins has done a fine job—but the trouble is that term gets entrenched when what we're talking about is not nation building. We have enough nations out there. We're not looking for more nations. What we need to do is start building states, helping countries build state institutions and helping states become sovereign so they can control their own borders, control what goes on inside their own countries. It is no good for us to be preaching at other weak states. After all, what are we doing to contribute to this and to deal with it? What are we doing to shut down the funding of diaspora mechanisms within our own shores that fuel civil wars in places like Sri Lanka and Northern Ireland? I mean let's get real. Nation building is one thing, but state building is what is necessary. So I would submit that Iraq is not a nation, it is a state that was built by the British out of three Turkish provinces, and it's got a long ways to go.

The second point that relates, in terms of bumper stickers, is the discussion we were sliding into here, not only about Iraq, but about military intervention. I don't think the primary issue is when do you commit U.S. troops. I think the primary issue is: Are we serious? Are we going to walk the walk on addressing the failed-state challenge? Which in many respects is analogous to the war on terrorism. You're using the same kind of instruments, you're using forensic accounting, you're using intelligence, you're using developmental tools, you're using diplomatic engagement, you're trying to actually get settlements. For example, what the Norwegians and others are trying to do in Sri Lanka, to get a settlement, that's great, and we're backing it. I just think we need to get the debate defined a little bit more precisely. This is not about when do we commit our people on the ground with boots. That's the last resort.

LITWAK: Thank you. Let's open it up now for questions and comments from the floor. There are individuals with microphones. First question. If speakers could please stand and identify themselves. Yes, sir.

AUDIENCE MEMBER: Petty Officer David Gault. Grad student, Joint Military Intelligence College. Dr. Gordon, would you please elaborate on foreign denial and deception programs and how it impedes or affects U.S. policy and what the U.S. is doing to curtail this?

GORDON: I'm not going to go into a lot of detail about foreign denial and deception in this unclassified context. Let me say that I think that there are denial and deception elements to our analytic challenge in identifying some of the dynamics of state failure and some of the characteristics that we've been looking at. And in formulating our models, we are engaging those elements. I don't want, in this circumstance, to talk in more particulars of that problem.

LITWAK: Other questions, comments? Yes, sir.

AUDIENCE MEMBER: Captain Mike Jason. By using the CIA State Failure Task Force criteria you briefed, Dr. Gordon—poverty, low quality of life, not fully integrated in a world economy, a discriminating government in a bad neighborhood—there are some quite obviously wealthy states, perhaps oil producing, that are on the verge of, really, state failure, by most of these criteria. How does the panel propose we deal with this state or these states, perhaps in a realist and global, international, idealist way?

LITWAK: Well, is Dr. Gordon's microphone amplified? Okay, perhaps one of the technical people can assist and if one of the other panelists wants to take a shot at that question or have a comment on it, you're welcome to. Chet?

CROCKER: A quick comment. I mentioned the recent work of the G-8 at Evian this past year. You might have a look on the web site of Evian for an example, but there is serious work being done to try and intensify the coordinating skills and the coordinating efforts of the major advanced post industrial nations on the issue of transparency, and the issue of bad governance and the issue of mining and extractive industry revenue flows which gets right to your point. If Nigeria doesn't make it and if it doesn't make it under this president, it's not going to make it. Then it will be because of a failure to address the governance challenges that exist in this very oil rich state, whose revenues are slated to go up like this, while its domestic and internal security challenges are going down like that.

SHERMAN: I think during our years, and I think the president is seeing this in his own administration as well, the transnational issues, whether they are corruption, financial flows, drug trafficking, counterfeiting, institutions of accountability in a society, are critical issues that have to get dealt with through either international regimes, economic sanctions and pressure, selectively used so they're effective, international cooperation, certainly in the war against terrorism. Without disrupting those financial networks, without going after some of the less visible elements that create these problems, you don't deal with underlying problems in any of these countries. I think that we probably wish that we had pushed harder on some of those areas. We did a lot, but wish we—in retrospect, now retrospect's a wonderful thing—we had done even more. And I think there are terribly important regimes that need to get put in place, and international cooperation that needs to be sought to increase that pressure. There are a number of tools that can be used quite effectively.

GORDON: Let me make a couple of comments analytically on these kinds of societies. I think there are elements that push these states toward being vulnerable to being failed states, but also limit the vulnerability to failure. The two that push them toward vulnerability are first, in resource-rich countries, there's much less of an incentive for government accountability. Governments need less cooperation of their citizens, they don't have to create a broad tax-base, a broad fiscal base, and I think that tends to increase the likelihood for state failure. Also, the state itself, as a major controller of resources, becomes much more of a target for political competition and for the intense factionalization that I spoke of. On the other hand, the very fact of an ongoing resource flow limits the likelihood that these kinds of societies will go fully down the path of becoming fully failed states, although there are examples—Zaire under Mobutu—where a resource-based state did become almost a fully failed state.

KRAUTHAMMER: I want to inject a note of realism, which is another way of injecting a note of pessimism, in this discussion. And that is, perhaps, there are some places that intrinsically will not be states. I mean, Wendy talked about the Bush administration's post-colonial colonialism. But the idea of the state is a very Western idea; it's a very new idea, relatively speaking. And we want to, as I understand it, make sure that it's imposed on every society or every place on the planet. I understand that makes for order, and it's probably a useful goal. But it may be, if I could be a little bit provocative, a kind of colonialism or imperialism, in deciding that a place like Somalia—places that have not had that sort of national consciousness or unity or Western-type state structures—has to have them. Now, we want a place like Somalia to be relatively peaceful and quiet and nonthreatening and humane to its own people, but I wonder whether, as anti-colonials here, we aren't being somewhat colonial in imposing this idea. And in fact, the best suggestion for places like Somalia has been a kind of soft colonialism. People have talked seriously about reviving the idea of the League of Nations, of the mandate. In fact, that's what America is doing on its own in places like Afghanistan and others, unilaterally or sometimes with or without UN approval. But that is what we're engaged in. And I think we ought to be a little bit more open and honest about how imperial and colonial this idea of statehood is, and our imposition of it on places for the stability of the world and also for our own security and convenience.

LITWAK: If I could just pick up on two of the points made in the presentations. The first is, in David Gordon's presentation, he mentioned that in his analysis, by his research and analytical team, that the most politically unstable polities are the quasi-democracies, which is a very important finding, given that the overall framework of American foreign policy, certainly in the 1990s, was sort of an engagement and enlargement—the notion that stability sort of flowed from a kind of Wilsonian view of extending democracies, and you create a more specific international system. But that process is messy, and the quasi-democracies are highly unstable, can lead to increased instability.

And Charles pointed out in his presentation that in some of the failed states, for the kind of thug regimes where we have regimes monopolizing political power, you have a kind of a hyperstability, where the character of the regime can persist and is quite durable and is able to insulate itself from the consequences of failure, despite the fact of what's happening on the societal level. So this tension, I think, is an important one in terms of making distinctions on cases.

Specifically for Charles, you've eloquently and forcefully made the case for sort of the strategic relevance argument for involvement, in the high-bar argument, et cetera. But I'd like to just push you a bit on sort of the critique of that view that's coming from the globalization school that says, in the interconnected world, you know, it's almost tautological to say we only get involved in cases where it's of strategic relevance because in the interconnected age any place can become that kind of polity. Is there one you can act on in a meaningful time frame?

KRAUTHAMMER: Well, that global perspective insight, I think, is rather useless. Of course, any place could, in theory, become important. But in that case, we ought to be investing in, I don't know, in Togo or Guinea, or I can pick you any. In other words, you throw darts at a map. That's not how you pick. You have to have a sense of priorities. You have to have a sense of order. I mean Haiti is not in the same class as Afghanistan. And Somalia is not in the same class as Iraq. Obviously, in the long run, as Keynes taught us, we're all dead by then. But nonetheless, in the long run, any place could, in theory, become unstable. The Falklands exploded on us once overnight and nobody had ever heard of it. And all of a sudden there was a war going on in the South Atlantic. So these things can happen. But you make your judgments, and I think 9/11 was a pretty loud announcement to us of what the great existential—the successor to the existential threats of the 20th century—was going to be. That is the locus of the threat today, not to say there aren't others. North Korea is not an Islamic radical state; there are, of course, others. But I think the conjunction of weapons of mass destruction and rogue states is the issue of our time. I wrote that in 1990 in the paper that you cited, and I think that is where the locus of our efforts has to be. Other places are important, but of relatively less importance, and, thus, they ought to receive relatively less attention and resources because we are not omnipotent.

LITWAK: Any comment on that as well as well as the first question I had on the tensions between failed and democratic societies?

SHERMAN: I probably agree more with Charles than he would imagine that we are not omnipotent. And I think our potential for arrogance, because we are the last remaining superpower, cannot be overstated. I hope that whoever is president in the next election believes that America is strong and great, yet humble. That it's not "A-B-C"—it's not "All Bill Clinton" or "Anything but Bill Clinton"— but it is rather a new formulation that really responds to the world that we're living in. And I agree that the existential threat is the one we saw in 9/11, which is terrorism or terrorists with weapons of mass destruction, not conventional airplanes, which is really the existential moment that none of us want to see. But if one believes that, then one must have a long enough view to know where it might come from next. And it will come from the Indonesias or the Kenyas or the other countries where, if they cannot come together as a functioning state in a globalized economy, will be breeding grounds for terrorists, that will affect our national security. So I absolutely agree one needs priorities, and one uses military intervention as a last resort. But we unfortunately, because of 9/11, do not, I believe, have the luxury to have a short and narrow view. We must have a long and broad view to know where the next threat is coming from.

LITWAK: Chet Crocker, and then Dave Gordon, and then we'll go to Janne Nolan with a question.

CROCKER: I think we're actually still getting a little tangled up analytically here. With respect to Charles' comments on Afghanistan as a failed state—under the Taliban, it was a failed state that had been taken over by a very unattractive fundamentalist dictatorship. So the point on Afghanistan is not whether the Taliban government of Afghanistan was a failed state. No, Afghanistan had become an ugly place under the control of people who had moved into a failed state, had taken it over, and in fact had become a terrorist-sponsored state, rather than state-supported terrorism. We have to get the sequence right here. I think that's really an important issue, as we think about this. The imperial challenge that Charles has put forward, I'm going to rise to that. Because what most of us who argue for doing something about failing states are arguing for is, in fact, a fairly forward-leaning approach to global engagement. Not by ourselves and not primarily militarily. I just want to leave it there, so that the points are clear. There is a difference here on the panel, but I think there is also a little distortion if the argument is reduced to, should we intervene or not? That's not what it's about.

KRAUTHAMMER: Well, should we spend our resources, diplomatic, economic, and political?

CROCKER: That's the same question.

KRAUTHAMMER: And I argue that you don't spend it equally everywhere because anywhere could potentially be a threat. I think that's not enough of an argument. You have to be extremely specific and extremely analytic in every situation and seeing whether or not it's relevant to our national security because some places are and some aren't.

CROCKER: I couldn't agree more. I would wager that Indonesia is relevant to our national security.

KRAUTHAMMER: I would argue—you argue strongly—not about Indonesia, but about Liberia. And I would challenge you to tell me how that ranks as a national security threat to the United States.

CROCKER: The place was founded by Americans, for Americans, everybody in the world except us, accepts that it's basically the 51st state of the Union. And it's a slam-dunk to do something for a few weeks, and then go on and hand it off to the UN with burden sharing and they will do it.

KRAUTHAMMER: What you're making is a moral argument, which I don't dispute. But I was trying to get you to make a national security argument, which apparently you're reluctant to do.

CROCKER: No, it's a political argument. It's not a national security argument.

LITWAK: David?

GORDON: On democracy and partial democracy, I think the point isn't that democracy is a bad or not a good thing. I think that the old saw is right. Democracy itself is stabilizing; once countries become mature democracies, the risk of severe political instability, the kinds of phenomena that we're talking about, decreases very, very dramatically to virtually nil. But the democratization process itself is destabilizing and very challenging, and that's the theme here. And it's not to say that we shouldn't support democratization but that we have to be very realistic, we have to be hardheaded in particular, in terms of institutional design, as we're engaging both bilaterally and in the institutional—and excuse me—in the international institutional context on these issues.

SHERMAN: Robert, if I can add just one thing out of the Pew data that really made David's point, which is that in those countries, which are recent democracies, when you ask people, do they want a strong economy, a strong leader, strong democratic institutions, you'll see in some of the newer democracies, they want a strong leader above all else. There is an anxiety as you look through the data that the democracy dividend they expected they don't have, that they feel a certain insecurity and instability. They don't know what the future is going to be. They think things are not as good as they once were, although they may be hopeful about the future. And so it's not enough to have an election and have this sort of what we call post-euphoria democracy. It is a long slog from here to there, and it's quite clear people acknowledge that, see it, and name it themselves.

LITWAK: Thank you. Janne Nolan.

AUDIENCE MEMBER: Thank you. I'm Janne Nolan. I have a question for, I guess, all the panelists with respect to the various criteria of how the former Soviet Union fits into the conception of level of American interests and level of American investment. It's also a question of the politics—what we have typically seen as foreign aid, which includes the whole agenda of Nunn-Lugar, nuclear disarmament, securing the materials for weapons of mass destruction. We've heard an argument here today that the $87 billion-plus for Iraq meets the criteria of necessary commitment to address what could be extremely difficult, a future security threat. We have difficulty getting close to a billion for the series of denuclearization programs in the former Soviet Union, which would be a primary source for access to weapons of mass destruction by any of these so-called failed states. I'd like some comments—especially you, Charles, and Wendy. Thank you.

KRAUTHAMMER: I endorse your support for that program or for the importance of it. I don't think there's any conflict between them. And it certainly is extremely cost-effective. Iraq is inefficient because it requires a huge investment for a very problematic outcome. But when you can spend money that is a vastly smaller sum to secure weapons of mass destruction in places where they are horribly exposed, I think we ought to do it. I'm entirely in agreement with you.

LITWAK: I mean it's striking that Saddam Hussein in 10 years, given that fissile material was the missing ingredient of his program and with hundreds of tons of inadequately secured fissile material north of the border, didn't go that covert procurement route, as far as we know. Other comments?

SHERMAN: Nunn-Lugar program is incredibly effective. I think the nuclear threat initiative that is ongoing now is very important and should be strengthened in every way it possibly can. And I continue to be concerned about loose nukes in the former Soviet Union, and I think we need to pay more attention to it than we currently are. It's a huge risk.

CROCKER: A quick comment. I thought you were going to ask initially, Janne, if the former Soviet Union was a failed state. Obviously, in a certain sense it is, and some of its parts give you pause from time to time in the broader sense we've been discussing primarily in this panel. I certainly identify with the thrust of your point.

GORDON: Let me make a final point for Janne that I think that there is an emerging, increasingly national security dimension to foreign aid having to do with failed states and state building, to take on Chet Crocker's phrase. And I think one of the places most relevant for that are some of the states of the former Soviet Union.

LITWAK: Gentlemen in the middle there.

AUDIENCE MEMBER: Jeff Clarke, Army History. I would like to have someone on the panel address the underlying economic factors, trends, and policies in producing failed states. By that I mean, when I go around to Army audiences addressing the subject, one of the things I stress is economic globalism; that is the tendency of the last 10–20 years of industrialized states to expand their service economies and move their labor-intensive manufacturing jobs, and the technology that goes with them, overseas into Third World countries, and the vast changes and instability for the participants, and those who don't participate sometimes, that often result from this over a long period of time. Thank you.

LITWAK: Thank you. Anyone wish to comment on that?

GORDON: I think, again, as I mentioned in my talk, while it is true that failed states are overwhelmingly poor states and states with a lot of impoverished people, among those states that the level of poverty in and of itself is not a particularly strong determinant of whether a state fails; I think it is the case that those states that are able to find niches of effective integration into the broader world economy are again much less vulnerable to state failure. But that the failure to do so—whether that's cause or effect—it gets back to, I think, the very good point that Chet made in his talk about sort of a signal of state failure being international abandonment and whether that is, again, cause or effect is unclear; you can see where it happens, though. So, states that are in the process or have been successful in integrating themselves into the world economy, if only at a fairly rudimentary level, are a lot less vulnerable to that. There is an economic dimension to this. But I think that the common sense or common perception out there about poverty as a direct cause of terrorism, of state failure, I'm actually quite suspicious. I don't think the data give a lot of support. I think that it is contextual, as Wendy said, and it's a signal when things are going bad economically, particularly when linkages to the international system begin to deteriorate and these illicit networks play a larger role. These are important signals that political stability is going to be at substantial risk.

SHERMAN: There are issues, however, I believe, that go back to what David said originally about emerging democracies, which are the issues of rising expectations. And I think underlying your question is—at least what I heard in your question is—jobs that get exported abroad, people begin to see there are some that can have jobs, skews the difference between the haves and the have-nots. In fact, sometimes it creates a broad middle class that then creates a need for greater accountability and transparency which helps in not creating a failed state. But it is a very complex process. And Chet has made a very important point several times that we ought not to be too reductionist here on any side of this equation. I do think, and the reason I made the comment about Cancun and why I thought Tom Friedman's piece this morning was quite useful, is I do think there is a dynamic at play in the world that doesn't go to a specific failed state or a specific creation of terrorism in a specific place, but rather a sense of whether there is such a growing gap in power between the West and the rest of the world. That is something that we need to attend to or we will create something that we do not have any control over. So I think it's important we look at the economic sector, that we deal with things like the World Trade Organization, that we have a positive trade agenda that creates positive consequences for people around the world, because of the gap and rising expectations that can fuel expectations that head in the wrong direction.

KRAUTHAMMER: But there's a serious irony here, and that is, obviously, by strengthening other countries economically through opening trade and clearly by exporting jobs. I mean we basically have spent the last 30 years exporting manufacture from the West, from the United States, to China and other places in the East. And the results in China and other places in the East have been remarkable—the greatest lifting of people out of poverty in the history of the world, certainly stabilizing a lot of those societies, new democracies, emerging strong democracies—Korea and Taiwan and elsewhere, and hopefully in China. This part of our strategy is to bring them into the global economy, as a way to stabilize them in some sense, domesticate them in terms of their international activity. And that's all to the good, and we all agree, and that's what globalization is about, and that's why everybody deplores Cancun. But the flip side is, the Democratic Party and the unions represent a lot of people in America who are losing those jobs. And they suffer. I'm with Wendy on Cancun and cotton. I think it's a scandal how we subsidize cotton, but we do have cotton farmers and they're going to be wiped out. The French are holding out because they have theirs.

So we have a dilemma, which on the one hand we're all in favor of this wonderful spreading of the wealth by sort of an Adam Smith–like specialization. We do high-tech stuff. They make toys. And it works for 10 or 20 or 30 years, but then they want to make more than toys. They want to make chips, and what you have is a huge resistance in America, largely among Democrats and the unions, to any of that. There are Democratic candidates who want to abolish NAFTA [North American Free Trade Agreement]. So it's not that—there's a flip side here, and all of our either altruism and helping others abroad or all of our foresight in thinking of bringing other countries into the world economy as a way of pacifying the world and making us more safe, comes at a cost—a domestic cost. It's a cost of real lives, real people, and politically, it's extremely hard to do because these people have a voice.

LITWAK: Thank you, Charles.

SHERMAN: I know we're at the end, but I can't leave it in that reductionist place, as Chet has said. It is not a choice between bringing this boat up and our boat falling. That is a false choice. It is complicated to lift these boats, while at the same time, making sure that our families are secure, that our workers have jobs, and have high-paying jobs, but it is possible. It can be done, and what the unions are fighting for is not so much protectionism of a particular job and a particular sector, but to make sure all of the boats rise and not that some rise and others fall.

KRAUTHAMMER: That's easy to say.

SHERMAN: Very hard to do. Very hard to do.

KRAUTHAMMER: If you're up here and you're an intellectual, that's easy to say. If you're a textile worker who's now unemployed, it's a little harder to say.

SHERMAN: I totally agree—I'm from Baltimore.

KRAUTHAMMER: And the reduction is if you're unemployed and you don't have a job.

LITWAK: Thank you both. We're really—our time is up. But I wanted to give Chet one—he's been waiting very patiently. Very briefly, if you will, Chet.

CROCKER: I think one of the things that this panel has revealed as a point of fundamental difference has to do with the question of prevention and forward look and trying to deal with the future cases that we know are coming at us, and with which tools. That's really where I think our focus probably ought to be. If we had another run at this panel, we ought to be looking at how to prevent the next ones, because—and that would lead us to the question about economics that was raised just a moment ago, using all of our tools. There really are very limited precise number of things that give you the indices of what's about to go south in some of these places. Is illegal business gaining over legal business? Is the illegal export of certain kinds of commodities beginning to take place at the expense of regular trade? Is the trade organized by people who are closely organized to the folks in power? Are they linked up with diasporas who are, in fact, sending the money to arms dealers who are, in fact, going into business locally. That set of patterns you can see. You can see it physically, daily, through your intelligence briefings, and we need to do something about it. It doesn't mean putting boots on the ground, necessarily. It means putting all of our wits together, connecting our wits to our wallets.

LITWAK: Thank you very much, Chet. Please join me in thanking our panelists for excellent presentations.

LUNCHEON ADDRESS

U.S. ECONOMIC POWER AND ITS APPLICATION IN IRAQ

Philip Merrill, President and Chairman, Export-Import Bank of the United
    States

Introduction by: Sandra L. Pack, Assistant Secretary of the Army for
    Financial Management and Comptroller

Summary

• The events of the last two years have conclusively shown that the United
States has the most powerful and most operationally versatile military in world
history. The United States is able to project devastating force around the globe in
record time and reap many significant strategic and political benefits as a result.

• The United States has the right to be proud of its military capabilities, but
they pale in comparison to U.S. economic power.

• The United States has a $10.5 trillion economy, which is almost three
times larger than its nearest competitor, Japan—and the best is yet to come. The
United States has shown an amazing capacity for productivity, growth, and economic reinvention. Within the normal business cycle, and savings, surplus, and
deficit projections, the United States will continue to have explosive growth in
the 21st century—just as it did over the last two centuries.

• Two core theses apply:

1. In the first core thesis, the central fact of the 21st century is the
enormous size of the U.S. economy compared to everyone else's economy.
Contrast this with the dominant political fact of the 20th century, which was
the growth of huge military forces in the hands of totalitarian states that were
willing to use them. This is a kind of shift that has been recognized more by
other countries than by the United States. This country realizes it is rich and
powerful but does not completely realize by how much. Taken as a whole, the
world sees the United States as a Gulliver to be tied down with Lilliputian
strings through various multilateral institutions and treaties as well as other
legal instruments.

2. According to the second core thesis, while the United States has been able to gain considerable international advantage from its military, it has yet to make sufficient strategic use of its economic assets and wealth to advance its national interests and ease the burden on its military. Just as there is no other military power that can overwhelm the United States, so there is no other economic power that can displace this country. And the United States needs to find a new way to marshal its economic assets to its advantage, just as it has used less than 4 percent of its gross domestic product to marshal military assets. The United States needs to become more comfortable with the idea of using its money for nonmilitary expenditures that advance the national interest.

• There is a sharp distinction between the responsible exercise of economic power and foreign aid. Aid is intended for humanitarian needs, and although the American people have wonderful charitable impulses, those are not the topic of discussion today.

• The United States got it wrong after World War I. It won the war but lost the peace. The United States did get it right after World War II, largely by understanding that the key to avoiding yet another world war was to put people to work. The Marshall Plan ensured peace and prosperity throughout the Western world.

• Today's threats do not emanate from large, bureaucratic military machines.

1. Weapons of mass destruction in the hands of three or four Third World rogue states is the principal threat along with the transfer of these weapons to nonstate actors who would use them mercilessly and unhesitatingly.

2. Terrorism and militant religious fundamentalism are also threats, but the United States has dealt with them and will find new ways of dealing with them through improved intelligence and related means.

3. For some threats, military resources are required. We need to be concerned about the underutilization of communication skills and a similar reluctance to use wealth to reinforce or supplant the U.S. military.

• There are three pillars to the successful reconstruction of Iraq: physical security, political stability, and economic growth.

• There are many guesses as to how much it will cost to fix Iraq. The Export-Import Bank of the United States agrees with the White House on a number of close to $100 billion over several years.

• Where will the money come from for the economic development of Iraq?

1. One answer is it will come from the American taxpayer.

2. Another is to use the proceeds from Iraqi oil—100 percent for Iraq's own benefit—in reconstructing the country. Iraq has great needs but also tremendous oil reserves. It should be able to afford a lot, but the problem is time.

3. In order to have physical security and political stability in Iraq, the United States must do something to enable Iraqis to realize their wealth more quickly. It is cheaper as well as smarter to make them relatively rich than it is for

the United States to continue on what, in time—if not already—is sure to be seen as an occupying power.

• There are several key steps to move Iraq quickly toward economic independence:

1. The first step must be to deal with the restructuring of Iraq's prewar debt. The Ex-Im (Export-Import) Bank is working on several initiatives to help Iraq move forward economically. It has approved a $500 million short-term credit line for the new Trade Bank of Iraq.

2. Additionally, the Ex-Im Bank is exploring the possibility of a multibillion dollar, unsecured, medium-term credit that will be focused solely on oil field reconstruction.

3. Although Iraq's oil reserves are great, they will not generate the money needed today to ensure Iraq's success. Pay-as-you-go likely will not cut it.

4. Iraq will need approximately $20 to $30 billion in long-term investment to move from its current 1 million barrels per day to 5 million barrels per day of sustained oil production. The request for that investment must come from the Iraqis because, in the end, it is their oil, and they can use it as they wish.

5. If this investment does not take place, the American taxpayer will end up paying most of Iraq's development bill. Ex-Im is willing and ready to play a role in supporting such investment with regard to its own exporters. Additionally, it could be a multilateral effort, as many of the 26 official Organisation for Economic Co-operation and Development (OECD) export credit agencies are willing and able to do the same.

6. Another possibility is an "Alaska Solution," meaning attract foreign investment in the oil sector and other areas that can provide dividends directly to the citizens of Iraq. It also is possible for Iraq to realize value today for future oil revenues.

• Iraqis need to realize some economic value today in order to establish the physical security, political stability, and economic development their country needs. In order for Iraqis to achieve self-sufficiency, Americans will need to marshal and deploy their economic resources as effectively as they have deployed their military resources.

Analysis

Philip Merrill advanced a powerful case for expanding U.S. economic aid for Iraqi reconstruction but could not in a short talk address all of the potential challenges or obstacles. One may want to consider some further issues:

• How much can we afford? The United States is a wealthy nation, but we have made a variety of fiscal choices that constrain resource availability. How large an increase in U.S. assistance to Iraq can be accommodated before those choices would have to be revisited?

• How do economic and political or cultural issues interact? The economically efficient approach to restoring Iraqi oil production, for example, might well be to contract with Western firms to provide the necessary technology and perform the work quickly themselves. Yet this may alienate Iraqi nationalists concerned over foreign control of Iraqi economic assets. Iraqi culture places a premium on family and kinship bonds, so many Iraqis see nepotism in a much less negative light than many Westerners. Imposition of Western business management practices in the context of reconstruction assistance may be seen by some as an inappropriate cultural intrusion under the guise of economic aid. More broadly, are there political or cultural constraints on our ability to leverage American economic power for Iraqi reconstruction?

• To what extent are the goals of Iraqi self-determination and economic efficiency in conflict with one another, and how will this affect our ability to leverage our economic power? Under Saddam, for example, much of the Iraqi economy was state-owned; establishment of free-market principles would imply a massive restructuring of the Iraqi economy and might encounter resistance from a work force and population accustomed to very different modes of commerce. If Iraqis prefer an economically inefficient ideology, will we accept this in the name of self-determination and accept the concomitant loss of performance for U.S. aid, or will we insist on small government and free markets in order to make the most of our aid, but at the expense of Iraqi autonomy?

• To what extent should economic aid precede political development and physical security? Spending money to repair pipelines only to have them destroyed by sabotage, for example, can be very inefficient. And a political system that can ensure economic accountability may be necessary for aid to have any lasting impact. On the other hand, security may be difficult to establish without the popular support that only economic reconstruction can provide, and a stable, accountable political system may be hard to create in the midst of insecurity and economic hardship. Given this, is it too soon for a massive increase in aid? Is it too late? Or must we accept inefficiency in reconstruction aid in order to overcome a downward cycle of economic/political/military interaction?

Transcript

JANNE E. NOLAN, Ph.D.: Thank you. I hope you enjoyed your lunch. And it's an enviable position not to be standing up here between you and your dessert.

It's my honor to introduce our next participant, Sandra Pack, who is the assistant secretary of the Army for financial management and the comptroller appointed to that position in 2001. I read this bio with awe and amazement at the job that is involved in this portfolio of being the person to manage all the financial issues, financial operations, all the accounting practices, all the procedures, and ultimately, balance the books for the U.S. Army. I think that is a formidable job that you, I'm sure, do extremely well. Sandra Pack was a distinguished businesswoman prior to this appointment, very active in the political processes of this country and is a very distinguished individual.

Please join me in welcoming her today.

Sandra L. Pack

SANDRA L. PACK: Thank you for those very kind words. I don't know that I'm deserving because I have a whole lot of help. But, good afternoon, everybody. While you continue your lunch, we're going to provide you with some food for thought as well.

For the last 10 months our speaker, Mr. Philip Merrill, has been the president and chairman of the U.S. Export-Import Bank, an institution that does not get a whole lot of public attention. The bank is the official export credit agency of the United States, and its mission is to help finance the export of U.S. goods and services to international markets. The Ex-Im Bank, if I can refer to it that way, does not compete with private sector lenders. It assumes credit and country risks that the private sector is unable or unwilling to take on. Given this role, you might think that Philip Merrill comes from a strict finance background. Au contraire. His professional and personal experience is extraordinarily diverse. Until his confirmation as Ex-Im Bank chief, Mr. Merrill was chairman of the board for the Capital Gazette Communications, Inc., which publishes the *Washingtonian* magazine and five newspapers, including the *Annapolis Capital*, to which I am a subscriber—have been for about 16 years; it's a good paper. Mr. Merrill has been a hands-on publisher and even a sometime reporter. His commitment to the American ideals of freedom of speech and freedom of the press is noteworthy. In 2001, Mr. Merrill donated $10 million to the University of Maryland's journalism school. Mr. Merrill also is actively involved in environmental protection. He's a trustee and a major contributor to the Chesapeake Bay Foundation. The foundation's new environmental center was built with a gift from Mr. Merrill, and it's a beautiful center. Mr. Merrill has a long history in government as well. This is the seventh presidential administration in which he has served. His previous positions include, among others, NATO assistant secretary-general, counselor to the under secretary of defense for policy, special assistant to the deputy secretary of state, and U.S. representative to the Law of the Sea Conference.

Please join me in welcoming Philip Merrill.

PHILIP MERRILL: Well, let me thank you, Sandra. Sandra and I both live near Annapolis in Arnold, Maryland. Her introduction is not only the nicest introduction I've had this day, or that I'm going to have this day, but it's the nicest that I've ever had from a resident of the neighborhood in which I live.

I also want to say that I always feel comfortable in a Defense Department atmosphere because I have so many years in and out, in several administrations and in the Department of Defense. And since I'm also an alumnus, so to speak, of the United States Army, although at a slightly different viewpoint than the chief of staff, I'm comfortable always in a military atmosphere.

Philip Merrill

I also want to say that anything that Susan Eisenhower throws or is involved in, I'm for. She's a terrific person. She called today to say she wasn't going to be here at lunch, but she's just a first-class asset to our country.

The events of the last two years have conclusively shown that the United States has the most powerful and most operationally versatile military in world history. We are able to project devastating force around the globe in record time, and we reap many significant strategic and political benefits as a result.

While we all have the right to be proud of our military capabilities—and many people in the audience today can take considerable credit for creating them, including the chief of staff who has special operations background—it is worth noting that the military power of the United States pales in comparison to our economic power.

This country has a $10-and-half-trillion economy—almost three times larger than our nearest competitor, which is Japan. As a point of comparison, our Cold War adversary, Russia, has a $350 billion economy—3 percent of ours. Put another way, Russia is one Holland, China is about three Hollands or the equivalent of a Benelux.

It is hard to exaggerate the size and growth of the U.S. economy when viewed from other countries. Brazil, for example, with 60 percent of our population, has a GDP [gross domestic product] of around $500 billion, 5 percent of ours. Fifteen or twenty years from now, our GDP will go from $10 trillion to $20 trillion; you can count on it, and one can only hope that Brazil will be striving toward $1 trillion.

And I think that for the United States the best is yet to come. The United States has shown an amazing capacity for productivity, growth, and economic reinvention. Within the normal business cycle, and savings, surplus, and deficit projections, I believe that the U.S. will continue to have explosive growth in the 21st century, just as it did over the last two centuries.

In 1962, the U.S. GDP, in today's dollars, was $586 billion. In just 40 years, we have created more than $100 trillion in new net worth. This is a level of wealth creation without historic parallel. The Spanish control of Latin America, the Dutch trade with the East Indies, and the British Raj in India all look like marginal investments by comparison.

This leads me to my two core theses for this day.

First, the central fact of the 21st century is the enormous size of the U.S. economy compared with everyone else. Contrast this with the dominant political fact of the 20th century, which was the growth of huge military forces in the hands of totalitarian states that were willing and able to use them. This is a kind of tectonic shift that has been recognized more by other countries than by Americans. Of course, we realize that we are rich and powerful, but we don't completely realize by how much.

One country that does understand this is China, which has been concentrating its efforts on growing its economy. Compared, again for example, with Russia, they have been quite successful. Russia, despite a very well-educated population with huge technological skills—their fighter pilots, our fighter pilots, their scientists, our scientists, their space program, our space program, they're pretty good—produces nothing that is competitive in world markets except for energy and other natural resources, such as gold. China has a $100 billion trade surplus with the United States and actually has Wal-Mart as its distribution agent—with $12 billion in annual sales to that one company alone.

Taken as a whole, the world sees us as a Gulliver to be tied down with Lilliputian strings through various multilateral institutions and treaties, as well as other legal instruments. Of course, we don't see ourselves this way.

My second thesis is that, while we have been able to get great international advantage from our military, we have yet to make sufficient strategic use of our economic assets and our wealth to advance our national interests and ease the burden on our military.

Just as there is no other military power that can overwhelm us, so is there no other economic power that can displace us. We need to find a new way to marshal our economic assets to our advantage just as we have used less than 4 percent of our GDP to marshal our military assets. Our overwhelming military capacity is a reflection of our wealth, not the cause of it. And this again is a historic change, if you go back over examples of Rome and so on, go back over 10,000 years; this is something new. Put another way, we should get more comfortable with the idea of using our money for nonmilitary expenditures that advance our national interests.

I wish to note clearly that I draw here a sharp distinction between the responsible exercise of economic power and foreign aid. Aid is intended for humanitarian needs. The American people have wonderful charitable impulses, but those are not the topic of which I speak this day.

Basically we got it wrong after World War I. We won the war, but lost the peace. We got it right after World War II, largely by understanding that the key to avoiding yet another world war was to put people to work. The Marshall Plan, applied at a time when we had a lot less than we have now, ensured peace and prosperity throughout the Western world through a combination of loans and grants that were offered to friends and enemies alike.

That the Russians refused it became their problem. That they prohibited Eastern Europe from accepting it became their tragedy.

More than anything else, we were able to preclude the militancy and anger of large numbers of unemployed young men with military experience and capability, the kind of men who were so instrumental in the mobilization of Nazi Germany and the original Soviet Union.

Today's threats do not emanate from large bureaucratic military machines, 20th century style. Nor is there much uncertainty for the moment about what these threats are, although there is plenty of uncertainty over how to deal with them.

I speak, of course, of weapons of mass destruction in the hands of three or four Third World rogue states as obviously the principal threat, along with the transfer of these weapons to nonstate actors, who would use them mercilessly and unhesitatingly.

And there is the corresponding threat of terrorism, per se, which now comes with the support of large numbers of what should be decent, ordinary people. Militant religious fundamentalism, however, has been with us for many centuries, and we will find new ways of dealing with it through improved intelligence and related means. A lot of people are working on that problem.

For some of these threats, military responses are required. As we have seen in Afghanistan and other places, we may be required to send troops very further afield than ever before. I don't know what is further afield than Afghanistan. The U.S. Navy surely did not expect to be involved in Afghanistan, even though this is not a Navy audience. And concepts akin to the British strategy of "find and strike" will become more relevant. We have proven that we can find and defeat nonconventional foes in difficult environments and we will get even better at it, and, in large measure, that is why General Schoomaker is here.

Yet no military officer I know believes that force is the answer to all, or even the majority, of these problems. General Keane, who asked me to speak here today, the vice chief of staff, has been especially concerned about underutilization of our communications skills, at which our country excels, in Iraq and other places, to explain our policies. And he and I are equally concerned about a similar reluctance to use our wealth to reinforce and supplant our military.

It obviously makes sense to illustrate this argument with the specific case of Iraq, which is at the top of our national agenda.

There are three pillars to the successful reconstruction of Iraq: physical security, political stability, and economic growth.

I focus here on the economic needs of Iraq and how to pay for them.

Including minimum infrastructure and energy development, how much will it cost to "fix" Iraq? There are many guesses. But in testimony in the Senate last week, the Treasury, State Department, me—Ex-Im Bank—agreed with the White House number of close to $100 billion over several years. All the numbers are the same. Everybody's basically got the same rough numbers.

Right now, we are spending $1 billion per week to maintain somewhere between 120,000 and 140,000 troops in Iraq. This is out of a 485,000-person active Army. This audience needs no education on what such a massive deployment will mean for the Army if it continues indefinitely. The military and political strain is incalculable.

So where will the money come from for the economic development of Iraq?

One answer is, of course, the American taxpayer. Another is to use the proceeds from Iraqi oil—100 percent for Iraq's own benefit—in reconstructing their country. Iraq has great needs, but also tremendous oil reserves. It should be able to afford a lot—so what is the problem? The problem is time.

It has been five months since the fall of Saddam Hussein. That is a mere blink in the 5,000-year history of Iraq. However, without adequate food, water, electricity, or a job, five months is more than a lifetime for any individual. Look at the uproar in this country over people who have been without power for six days, do you—I mean, they're tearing their hair up and down the streets of Washington.

In order to have physical security and political stability, we must do something to enable Iraqis to realize their wealth more quickly. It is cheaper, as well as smarter, to make them relatively rich than it is for the United States to continue on what, in time, if not already, is sure to make us be seen as an "occupying" power.

Keep in mind that Iran and Syria both have a vested interest in taking advantage of Iraqi popular frustration to turn Iraq into Lebanon through guerrilla-type terrorist means. And they are experts at it. Recent bombings are indicative of how many soft targets are available to dedicated terrorists of any stripe.

In order to move Iraq quickly toward economic independence, there are several key steps, the first of which must be to deal with the restructuring of Iraq's prewar debt.

A country with a prewar GDP of $26 billion, about the same as the annual sales of Lowe's or 10 percent of Wal-Mart's sales, cannot service $130 billion in debt, plus billions in reparation obligations from their own previous wars. If there is going to be any long-term investment in Iraq, this debt will have to be dealt with promptly—and not on the normal timetable for the Paris Club process. There simply isn't time.

Ex-Im Bank is working on several initiatives to help Iraq move forward economically. In particular, our board has approved a $500 million short-term credit line for the new Trade Bank of Iraq.

Further out, we are exploring the possibility of a multibillion dollar, unsecured, medium-term credit facility that will be focused solely on oil field reconstruction.

However, while Iraq's oil reserves are great—even these reserves won't generate the money needed today to ensure Iraq's success. Pay-as-you-go is not likely to cut it.

The one thing I want to convey is that Iraq will need approximately $20 billion to $30 billion in long-term investment to get from the current 1 million barrels per day to 5 million barrels per day of sustained oil production. The request for that investment must come from the Iraqis. In the end, it is their oil, and they can use it as they wish.

However, if that investment doesn't take place, the American taxpayer will end up paying most of Iraq's development bill. If it does take place, Iraq can generate for itself $20 billion to $30 billion to $40 billion-plus per year for its own development, depending on oil prices and ramping up time.

Ex-Im would be willing and ready to play a role in supporting such investment with regard to our own exporters—that's what we do, support our exporters— and we know that many of the 26 official OECD export credit agencies are willing and able to do the same—they talk to us regularly. This would therefore be a multilateral effort. I emphasize multilateral.

With or without governmental support, investors will require that the Coalition Provisional Authority [CPA] reach some understanding with the Iraqi people on the ultimate benefits of foreign direct investment. It is not a simple problem to overcome the inherent resistance to Western investment in Iraq and throughout, for that matter, the Middle East. And in this respect, Jerry Bremer, a good man, has his hands full.

One possibility is an "Alaska Solution." Attract foreign investment—in the oil sector and other areas—that can provide dividends directly to the citizens of Iraq, the way the citizens of Alaska get dividends from their oil fields. Imagine what $10 per person—a week's pay—would mean to the economic life of the average Iraqi. There are 23 million Iraqis. At $10 a head that is $230 million— more than one might think in a country where $2 a day is the average wage. And a lot more if you think of it in terms of a family of four. This is small change compared to the amounts we are spending now.

It is also possible for Iraq to get value today for future oil revenues through various forms of securitization.

Let me cite some history. I already mentioned the Marshall Plan and the enormous economic benefits that our country and the world reaped from that investment. There are some other examples from Ex-Im Bank's past that are also relevant.

When Israel was being formed, Ex-Im provided the initial provisional military administration with loans based on the idea that the future government would be supported by the United States and was therefore a good risk.

Then Ex-Im Bank Chairman William McChesney Martin said that Ex-Im believed it would have, and I quote, "reasonable assurance of repayment because the United States is going to support Israel in every reasonable way." The analogy to Iraq is directly on point.

Also, the Bank also utilized an oil and gas framework for Russia so that investment in oil infrastructure was possible as the Soviet Union evolved into the CIS [Commonwealth of Independent States] and then to Russia. I was at NATO [North Atlantic Treaty Organization] during that period. It all looks simple looking backwards; at the time, nobody I knew—I don't think anybody—and nobody I knew who knew anybody had any clue of how the Soviet Union was going to splinter, and this—what looks backwards like a very simple process would take place. Chaos understates the sense of the time.

In closing, let me emphasize that Iraqis need to realize some economic value today in order to establish the physical security, political stability, and economic development their country needs and to which the United States is fully committed.

In order for Iraq to achieve self-sufficiency, we Americans will need to marshal and deploy our economic resources as effectively as we have those of our military. Our objective is a vibrant Iraqi economy where jobs and opportunities trump terror.

Over the long run, we will need to think more conceptually about how to use our wealth, our economic resources, our communication skills, and perhaps some unconventional thinking to advance and support our national interests. I am confident and, indeed, I have no doubt that we can do this.

Thank you. And I'll be happy to take questions.

MERRILL: Either you're scared or I'm totally unstimulating. Over here, number one in the—somebody else raise their hand, because the mic guy needs to know where to go after this.

AUDIENCE MEMBER: My question concerns the export-import part of all this. It seems to me that we are an enormously powerful nation economically, but we've been running a trade imbalance, not just with China, but with everybody else for about 30 years—no end in sight. It seems to me that that's a potential fly in the ointment in terms of our being able to sustain our wealth and the growth that you forecast.

MERRILL: I've heard that question before, and real short answer, I just don't agree with it. I mean, this argument on whether you're better to import or export, import or export oil, or go your own—half of trade deficit is oil. Another is China, which is a special situation; the rest of it comes down to about $500 billion. The rest of it comes down to a relatively insignificant amount. I'm not a mercantilist. I do not think it is a key issue. That's where I'm at.

AUDIENCE MEMBER: Even if it's sustained? Certainly for a year or two, plus [inaudible]?

MERRILL: I just don't think it matters an awful lot compared to the sheer growth of the U.S. economy.

AUDIENCE MEMBER: Guy Dinmore of the *Financial Times*. Sorry, I'm over on your left.

MERRILL: Okay. That's a long way over there.

AUDIENCE MEMBER: I can see you on the screen. No, I can't.
You mentioned in your speech the possibility of the securitization of Iraqi oil. I believe this is a very controversial subject.

MERRILL: Yeah, I've gotten a lot of heat for it.

AUDIENCE MEMBER: And it appears that the CPA, for the moment, has set this aside for the future Iraqi administration to decide on, which of course by then would be rather too late. How, practically, would you do it? And, in more concrete terms, what do you have in mind?

MERRILL: The practical issue is very simple. I mean, my desk, which is quite a large desk, it was Jesse Jones' desk. It's sort of an icon. This thing is bigger than a super double bed and overlooks the White House. This desk has people pounding on it every day because it's big. There are oilmen, plus Bulgarians, Czechs, Romanians, Poles, pounding on the desk saying, "We go in there, we can fix Iraq. I got 300 guys; I'll put them in as Iraqi oil-field workers. I'll get those oil fields running. Just give me a contract." Have to lend to somebody. Who [am I] to lend to? It has to be lent to some entity of the Iraqi people. So the political issue of who to lend to, to hire the contractors, is issue number one.
But the big issue is the political issue. We do not want to be seen as having taken over Iraq in order to produce Western oil or for Western oil companies, not just United States oil companies, Western oil companies or international. The problem is to create an entity in Iraq that will be politically acceptable to Iraqis and will attract private foreign investment. I met last week in London with three of the—well, the presidents of Shell and BP and three of the 10 largest banks in the world; they all said the same thing. We're interested. We want to go. Same thing, the oilmen said. We're waiting to see what kind of commercial code they have. We'll wait and see; we'll buy things short term, up to a year, but we're not going to put in $10 or $15 billion unless we know that what we put it in for is going to be there 5, 10 years from now. That political issue is a critical issue. So the issue, like I said, I repeat it. It's a thing for the Iraqis to decide for themselves.

We hope they will decide it because it's their oil and their money. The world needs their oil. They can produce 5 or 6 million barrels a day relatively easily if they can attract the investment to produce it. It would still be their oil. But they have to want it. Political issue, not economic issue.

AUDIENCE MEMBER: Richard Sencotta, I'm a demographer and I work for a public health organization in town, Population Action International, the founder of which was Maj. Gen. William Draper, and his son was once head of the Ex-Im Bank.

MERRILL: Oh, yeah. Bill Draper, he's a friend, and there's a wonderful magazine called *American Demographics*, published in Ithaca, New York, which I happen to read regularly, and I happen to be a Cornell alumnus.

AUDIENCE MEMBER: As a matter of fact, a couple of the things you talked about, it's easy for a demographer to key in on. One of them, you talked about the large numbers of youth in some of these countries, particularly Iraq and throughout that area, and Africa as well. Secondly, you talk about a family of four. Well, in Iraq, of course, it's about a family of about seven, if you count the grandfather who's living in there. So my question is, really, how does foreign aid fit in with your types of investment? Because you want to put these young men to work, but in the meantime, the population of Iraq, if it continues to grow at the speed it is, right now, it would double in about 25 years. With a large proportion of youth, it's very difficult to employ. Particularly, I mean, even the cases in Saudi Arabia, where they've been unable to put a lot of educated people to work.

MERRILL: That fact that the Saudis have 5,000 corrupt princes is a different set of issues. I said specifically, I didn't come to talk about foreign aid. I would rather bite off the answer to this by saying, that 30 years ago we had a billion people in the First World, now we have 2 billion of 6 billion in the First World. Twenty years from now we'll have 3 billion of 7 billion in the First World. And, so we're making progress. There's still the same number of hungry, sick, and tired people out there. And I don't have a good answer for that. And if you have one, publish it somewhere and send it to me.

NOLAN: [inaudible]

MERRILL: I didn't say that, you said that, somebody said earlier—I'm willing to take questions as long as people want to ask them, but I don't want to overrun my welcome. So let people—you're in charge. Here's the chief of staff of the Army—he ought to be in charge. Are you in charge? I hope I'm in charge of the bank. They don't think I'm in charge of the bank over there, they think they're in charge of the bank.

AUDIENCE MEMBER: Good afternoon, sir. Capt. Jim Sadler. I'm currently a fellow at SAIS, Johns Hopkins, here in the city.

MERRILL: I hope you're one of my Merrill fellows there.

AUDIENCE MEMBER: Sir, my question to you is, is the United States looking at securitizing the debt of Iraq, much like we did in Mexico in 1994, in order to relieve that debt, and get that burden off their back sooner or is it more looking toward debt reduction in a multilateral sense? And my second question is, to get the direct investment that we need in Iraq, are they looking to stabilize the currency so that will attract investors much like a peg, or going to let it float for a while to get the investment quickly into Iraq?

MERRILL: Those are two pretty sophisticated questions and this is a large audience.

Let me deal with the second one first. The issue of restructuring or canceling or suspending a debt is in the process of debate within the United States government. We have a policy, the Treasury Department handles it, of sending things to what's called the Paris Club—they write the debt off in two or three years. You asked the people running the United States Army whether they think they have two or three years to get control in Iraq. I don't think we have two or three years. Therefore, my suggestions have been to move much more quickly. I take the position—not the administration's position, I want to be clear—that war cancels all debts. I think we did not indict the fighter pilots who bombed Japan for trespassing in restricted airspace. I think we did not deal with Mitsubishi or Krupt on the basis of honoring all prewar contracts. But it did take some time to work those things out. It's an interesting case; as a practical matter, no outside investor is going to invest long term in Iraq if the money is going to go to repay debt. Since they can't repay debt, what's going to happen, is any oil that's produced after, I think, 2007, it's a temporary UN moratorium, it's only two or three years, will be seized by a plague of lawyers in literally every country in the world because oil is fungible. So the answer is, restructure it now very quickly, outside the Paris Club.

With respect to the Mexican gas framework and so forth, I just think it's more complicated than we want to deal with it here and now. I'd rather just say no than start a more sophisticated discussion than I think our leaders here wish.

NOLAN: Thank you so much. I hate to interrupt you because I could listen to you all afternoon, but could you please join me in thanking Mr. Merrill for a wonderful presentation?

MERRILL: Thank you. I appreciate that. Back to you.

PANEL 2

U.S. POWER AND THE NEW WORLD DISORDER:
AN ANALYSIS BY THE NEWS MEDIA

Co-sponsor: Medill School of Journalism, Northwestern University

Moderator: Roy Gutman, Adjunct Professor, Medill School of Journalism,
      Northwestern University

Hisham Melhem, As-Safir and Al-Arabiya Television

Dan Murphy, The Christian Science Monitor

Steve LeVine, The Wall Street Journal

Douglas C. Farah, The Washington Post

Panel Charter

Journalists, when they do their job, function both as a mirror on contemporary events and a distant early-warning system. They provide a fresh and independent view of items that are high on the national agenda, as well as information that the public did not expect or seek on matters they should want to be aware. The essence of journalism is to dig out the news—a task that during the zero-sum days of the Cold War era seems, in retrospect, to have been a straight-forward endeavor. But after the fall of the Berlin Wall in 1989 and the replacement of a bipolar, competitive world system by a sole remaining superpower, the world has had to be redefined—event-by-event and story-by-story. Ironically, even as U.S. influence reached new heights and the role of the United States became indispensable in the farthest reaches, the public, as perceived by editors, began to lose interest in foreign affairs. This was all the more surprising as reporters and their audiences in the United States, thanks to education, free trade, and extensive personal travel, reached a new level of sophistication. Adding to the challenge to journalists is the obvious factor that, in a period of change, developments that eventually will have the greatest impact are not always spotted when they occur. When an empire collapses, security vacuums readily develop along the periphery and, if allowed to persist, can tempt local factions to

Left to right: *Roy Gutman, Hisham Melhem, Dan Murphy,*
Steve LeVine, and Douglas Farah

encourage nationalism and war. What had been the periphery suddenly becomes center stage.

During the early 1990s, reporters on the scene got their stories into print or
on the air during the rise of extremist nationalism that led to wars and atrocities
in the Balkans and, to a lesser extent, during the Rwandan genocide. But, with
few exceptions, nothing like that occurred in South Asia in the second part of the
decade. Kashmiri separatists and their targets were dying at the rate of 50 per
week. One atrocity too many could trigger a conventional war on the subcontinent, which could go thermonuclear, with vast repercussions. But other than
nuclear and missile tests, the underlying political developments received scant
attention in the media. In Africa, two million or more Congolese died in the past
four years as a consequence of the breakdown in public health services during the
Rwandan and Ugandan occupations of eastern Congo, but that horror story never
made it into the public consciousness in this country. Finally, after capturing Kabul
in 1996, the Taliban displaced hundreds of thousands of civilians by force and
were responsible for enormous war crimes. Osama bin Laden, seeing an opportunity to make himself indispensable, threw his resources and his loyal, trained
personnel into the war effort. But little of this was reported at the time.

The journalists on this panel are field reporters, used to navigating through
the weed patch on the lookout for the ground-level developments that will

have major impact. The emphasis in every presentation will be on the developments and trends the public should be aware of but may not have adequately appreciated.

Discussion Points

- In the Islamic world, what are the upheavals that are foreseeable and which ones are not?
- In Central Asia, is the belt of instability emerging from the post–Cold War security vacuum?
- In Afghanistan, what are the problems in establishing a political framework and a modern order after the fall of the Taliban?
- In Africa, will the pesky local wars drag the United States in, sooner or later?

Summary

- Journalists in a free society have the task of identifying the trends and developments that domestic political leaders may prefer to ignore or play down. That maxim applies more than ever in the complex international environment that the United States has faced since September 11. In the spirit of telling it like it is and presenting on-the-ground realities, four international affairs reporters gave their unvarnished reports on as many parts of the world:

    1. Hisham Melhem of the Lebanese daily, *As-Safir*, provided an overview of Arab world attitudes toward the United States.

    2. Steve LeVine of the *Wall Street Journal* described the challenges to U.S. policy in Central Asia.

    3. Dan Murphy of the *Christian Science Monitor* discussed Indonesia's small wars and how they promote the rise of terrorist groups.

    4. Douglas Farah of the *Washington Post* discussed the turmoil in West Africa, where some states have effectively become criminal enterprises and opened their gates to criminals of every type.

- There were a number of highlights in the presentations:

    1. The United States is an indispensable player in every region on Earth today, but in many places, it is not playing its role effectively. In some instances, the focus on "getting evil-doers" like Saddam Hussein, while it may have the approval of the domestic U.S. audience, is having an opposite and, indeed, counterproductive impact in Islamic countries.

    2. The situation is especially dire in Indonesia, where distrust of the United States now dominates the thinking of the educated elites. This is a complete reversal from just five years ago.

    3. From the perspective of the Arab world, the United States is reaching beyond its grasp when it sets Western-style democracy as its goal in Iraq.

4. In West Africa, America's hands-off policy has been ineffective, and the deterioration of government has provided a breeding ground for terrorist money laundering and other operations detrimental to U.S. security.

5. American policy in Central Asia is riddled by inconsistencies that greatly reduce U.S. influence, but hard bargaining over international loans and the establishment of bases could restore human rights and help those societies find equilibrium.

Roy Gutman, Adjunct Professor, Medill School of Journalism,
          Northwestern University

• Moderator Roy Gutman of Northwestern University's Medill School of Journalism opened by suggesting that states located on what used to be regarded as the periphery of the East-West confrontation have become the center of the new world disorder—there is no periphery any longer. In this context, he suggested that lumping problem areas into the category of "failed states" is no longer a useful enterprise.

• An earlier panel left no doubt that there is no clear definition of a "failed state" and as many as 50 states fall into this category or the category of "failing states." Too often when a state is designated as failed, it goes off the radar screen; what is needed is a more dynamic description that indicates the role for U.S. foreign policy intervention. As an alternative, Gutman proposed classifying trouble spots according to where there is a power vacuum—a situation that may lead to civil war, or a security vacuum—a situation that could lead to an international war. Those are the places that will present the greatest potential threats in this era because small, obscure wars can mask far greater threats: larger wars, war crimes, crimes against humanity and genocide, the drug trade, criminal enterprise, and terrorism. Those failed or failing states at war or on the brink of war are the locations where the U.S. government must develop and pursue an effective foreign policy.

Hisham Melhem, As-Safir and Al-Arabiya Television

• Hisham Melhem noted that the United States, until relatively recently, had a unique position among great powers, for it alone had no colonial legacy in the Arab or Muslim world. But today, anti-Americanism is "like a religion." There are two reasons. The first is what he perceived as unqualified U.S. support for Israel, not only for Israel's right to exist, but for Israel's conquest of Arab territory—an issue that resonates with Arabs, Muslims, and nationalists "from Casablanca to Cairo to Karachi." The second factor is American support for autocratic, repressive, and totalitarian regimes dating back half a century.

• When Washington invades Iraq in order to establish democracy, many Arabs view the aspiration with cynicism "and even worse than cynicism." In the eyes of many Arabs, the sufferings of the Iraqi people were caused by the UN sanctions; and they too easily overlook the brutality of the Saddam Hussein regime. In the negative mood that now prevails, the United States is seen as invading the region using its culture, the information revolution, its economic power as well as its military might.

- With this in mind, in the war against terror, it is vital to differentiate between two kinds of terror. Not all terrorists are alike. One type is the metaphysical, unrelenting, irrational, radical, and violent terrorist. There is "no political compromise" with this kind of terror; coercion is the only response. But the second kind of terror derives from legitimate political causes—from the Front de Liberation Nationale, or FLN, and the liberation of Algeria to the struggle against apartheid in South Africa; from Israel's founding to Chechnya today; examples of such legitimate causes abound. President Bush's assertion that Palestine should not be born out of violence is unrealistic; the United States and Israel were born out of violence. "You cannot reduce those to a core issue of terrorism," said Melhem.

- From Palestine to Kashmir, what is required is not so much the use of force, but the provision of "a political horizon"—something that has been lacking since the discourse on terror began after September 11.

- U.S. policy in Iraq would be best served by lowering the aims to a more practical level. The alternative, a U.S. failure in Iraq, would have almost unthinkable consequences. Melhem said, "I am terrified when I think of the consequences of an American debacle or failure in Iraq today. . . . This would be truly a historic disaster" in which victory would be claimed by Osama bin Laden, radicals in Iran, and terrorists the world over.

- But it is time to "lower the ceiling" and start planning more practically. A decade hence, Iraq will not be Sweden, or Switzerland, the United States, or Germany. It is naive to think that Iraq will become the model for the Arab world. "Let us not chase after Jeffersonians. Let's not be naive and think we can export our great system and make Baghdad on the Euphrates similar to Washington on the Potomac. It ain't going to happen," Melhem stated.

- Instead, the United States should focus on Arab reformers and Muslim reformers and encourage them to help redesign and rebuild their societies according to democratic models that they will have to develop.

Dan Murphy, The *Christian Science Monitor*

- Dan Murphy, who has spent the last decade in Indonesia, said the war on terror has damaged America's reputation and influence in the world's most populous Muslim country and throughout Southeast Asia. The situation has degenerated. Indonesia is in desperate need of American help as it moves toward democracy, but U.S. foreign policy, the invasion of Iraq, and the continued fighting between Israelis and Palestinians has weakened Washington's ability to lend a helping hand. "I don't have a single Indonesian Muslim friend anymore who believes America is a force for good in the world," he said.

- What is needed is a U.S. foreign policy focused on ending the ethnic conflicts that the Indonesian government and military have managed so badly.

- These small wars in obscure corners of the archipelago, such as Maluku, have become a platform providing training, sustenance, and an infrastructure to local extremist organizations affiliated with al Qaeda. In these former Spice Islands, where fighting broke out between Christians and Muslims in 1999, police and military units joined the different sides, seeming to cancel out each other. More than half-a-million people were displaced. In that turmoil, the Jemaah Islamiya (JI), which has received al Qaeda training and funding, set up shop. The JI was unknown to outsiders at the time but was a covert, disciplined group devoted to creating a theocracy uniting Islamic parts of Southeast Asia, from southern Thailand to the southern Philippines. No one really noticed them, and most observers discounted the religious overtones of the conflict and the jihadi ambitions of its fighters. "Boy, was I wrong," said Murphy. The conflict provided "fertile ground for recruiting and training operatives and will continue to have an impact for years to come."

- The war is now over, but men who served with the JI in Maluku have participated in every major terrorist attack attributed to the JI, which began with the bombing of almost 20 Christian churches on Christmas Eve 2000. JI has bombed train stations in Manila, an airport on Mindanao, killed 202 people in the attack on two Bali nightclubs, and arranged the attack in August 2003 on the Marriott Hotel in Jakarta. Maluku will function for an entire generation of Southeast Asian men as Afghanistan did for the "Afghan Arabs."

- What could the United States do? The Maluku conflict also played a key role in the development of JI's ideological framework and skills base. JI even used the occasion to put out the conspiracy theory that the United States and its allies were trying to "Christianize" Indonesia. Looking back, it can be said that JI moved in as opportunists after the conflict had spiraled out of control, trying to shape the war to its own goals. What allowed this to happen was the failure of the Indonesian state and the corruption and incompetence of Indonesian forces, which all seemed to encourage the conflict because they created economic opportunities for the JI. The answer to this crisis is to make every possible effort to stop the conflicts, for the Indonesian government to uphold the law, and for Indonesians to hold those in power accountable for their performance.

- U.S. influence has declined dramatically, starting with the invasion of Afghanistan and snowballing after the invasion of Iraq. U.S. credibility is at its lowest point. Many Indonesians believe America is "engaged in a hostile imperial experiment." Indonesia is engaging in a brutal and counterproductive strategy, and respected scholars contend that current U.S. policy provides tailor-made propaganda for the radical minority.

- With so few diplomatic cards to play, the United States will have a very difficult time ahead. The day may come, say, in 15 years, when the United States needs to establish a major military presence in the region.

- The question is: What will the reception be like?

Steve LeVine, The Wall Street Journal

• The challenge for U.S. policy in the "Stans" of Central Asia—Kazakhstan, Uzbekistan, Tajikistan, Kyrgyzstan and Turkmenistan, as well as Azerbaijan—is more one of developing a steady, predictable long-term policy than of putting out the fires of war, according to Steve LeVine. The United States stands to benefit significantly if the situation turns around in the different states of the region. Pakistan's General Pervez Musharraf has to put an end to "home-grown jihadism." Kazakhstan's President Nursultan Nazarbayev has to establish a stable government. Many signs are negative: Azerbaijan has now established a ruling post-Communist dynasty, and Uzbekistan's President Islam Karimov, resisting all reform, seems to be taking the country with him down a slippery slope.

• One thing is certain: The Stans will either succeed or fail by themselves. The various presidents sneer at what they regard as U.S. nannying. Threats, pleas, and persuasion do not have a great record of success.

• The tool the United States should use is straight quid pro quo trading, using the cards it has to play: the European Bank for Reconstruction and Development loans, the International Monetary Fund's economic support and other multilateral finance. That said, if the Pentagon turns temporary military bases permanent and prolongs other military relationships, "What will you get for that from, say, Karimov, or from Kyrgyzstan's Askar Akaev?" LeVine asked.

• Today the region is at a crossroads. Two of the region's presidents, in Kazakhstan and Azerbaijan, are unindicted co-conspirators in U.S. criminal cases for receiving payments from U.S. companies. Azerbaijan, despite the opening of the new Baku–Ceyhan oil pipeline in 18 months, has done nothing to prepare its economy for the likely decline of its oil income flow in about 12 years, and the talk on the street is of going back to war with Armenia over Nagorno-Karabakh. Pakistan continues to host some of the world's most dangerous radicals, including fugitives who killed Wall Street Journal reporter Daniel Pearl.

• U.S. policy, however, has been inconsistent. Can Washington lecture Azerbaijan and Kazakhstan on the need for transparent bidding when it awards Halliburton an enormous, no-bid contract? The presidents of the Stans "realize that the dog is almost all bark."

• The United States gained little in exchange for its aid buildup in Uzbekistan except for a military payoff; though Karimov has little threat at home, he continues to crack down against opposition, while the standard of living continues to plummet and anger is growing in the country. U.S. and UN officials think they have made a connection with Karimov, but, in fact, "no one ever got through to Islam Karimov." Pakistan, by comparison, is on the way to real economic growth and has made small steps toward elected government.

• What the United States should do is require a quid pro quo. In Kyrgyzstan, this means that in exchange for opening a military base, the United States would require the release of opposition leader Felix Kulov. In Uzbekistan, there should be a concrete IMF (International Monetary Fund) program and amnesty for thousands who were imprisoned merely for being pious Muslims. In Pakistan, the United States should require a complete dismantling of the jihadi apparatus.

Douglas C. Farah, The Washington Post

• Douglas Farah began by taking issue with the comment columnist Charles Krauthammer made at the opening panel of the conference, stating that Liberia and other countries in West Africa do not matter because they are not and will not pose a threat to U.S. interests. Liberia, even before Charles Taylor came to power, was a "functioning criminal enterprise," and Taylor has set about gaining control over the diamond fields of Sierra Leone, Farah said. Taylor's instrument is war—war at home and war in Sierra Leone. As the situation in the region has deteriorated, it has become an attractive location for al Qaeda to take advantage.

• West Africa exemplifies Gutman's observation that so-called peripheral states are not peripheral at all because they are the breeding grounds for war and terror. In the mistaken belief that there are no strategic interests at stake, the U.S. government has all but abandoned the region in terms of intelligence gathering, despite the fact it is in such situations that terrorists best flourish. Following al Qaeda's attacks on two U.S. embassies in East Africa during August 1998, the U.S. government froze some $220 million in Taliban and al Qaeda assets in the United States. That was when al Qaeda sent a high-level envoy to Liberia buying diamonds and other commodities, and Taylor wanted weapons, which he was able to import with the help of Russian businessman Victor Bout. The other example of a failed state presumably being used by terrorists is the Democratic Republic of Congo, formerly Zaire. All the major commodities flow abroad without control—diamonds to Zimbabwe and South Africa, timber to Uganda, and other, presumably valuable commodities, on direct flights from an obscure airport in the south of the country to the United Arab Emirates. North Korea is looking for uranium in southern Congo. "There are a host of things that are going on that we simply have no idea of their magnitude," Farah said.

• What can be done about regions that turn into economic activity zones for criminals and terrorists? The best sanctions are the targeted travel bans and freezing of bank accounts, not general sanctions. "Name and shame" can work. What is most important is to begin to pay attention to these places. More and more, criminal organizations, allied with terrorist organizations, do not just traffic in weapons and commodities, but in people, drugs, and "everything else." When the pressure builds up in one place, "they're going to be moving to these countries that we consider peripheral and where they know we don't have much interest and that we think are at the edge of our interests."

Question–and–Answer Period

• Gutman asked whether other panelists agreed there should be a new focus on the so-called periphery. LeVine responded that it would be wrong to focus exclusively on the periphery "because you don't know where your big risks are going to come from." However, Krauthammer's comment that there are parts of the world that can be safely written off because they don't matter today, never mattered in the past, and never will matter in the future "is, from my experience out in the world, foolish." Terrorists in this era of globalization can develop through small cells in these states that are over the horizon or on the periphery. Areas that are not under the control of a central government become breeding grounds for terrorist groups. "If we ignore them, they will not ignore us, and they will come to visit, as we have seen on 9/11."

• Most questions from the audience related to the war in Iraq. The first questioner asked for a critique of al-Jazeera from a peer perspective. Melhem was quite critical, comparing the satellite television channel to Dubai, where it is located. "Just as Dubai is a virtual city … at al-Jazeera, you have a people who live in a compound and who have absolutely no contact with the people." Some of the programs are shouting matches like the "Jerry Springer Show." The problem is that journalism in the Arab world seems geared to the lowest common denominator and rarely challenges the powers-that-be, and their news judgment on occasion is outrageous. They have given a platform to "a bunch of masked men" inciting violence against the Iraqi people, and they have aired audiotape or videotape that someone has tossed in their laps with no editorial judgment and with no thought on the incendiary message it has. "Every time Osama opens his mouth, he curses the Jews, curses the Christians—and, by the way, there are about 14 million Arab Christians," Melhem said.

• On the question of what the United States should do about it, Gutman said, without wanting to advise the government on how to handle the press, it is important that when the media err or distort the facts, that those with knowledge of the facts write a letter of complaint. "Use that as your tool," he said. But the idea of banning a satellite network from covering the governing council in Baghdad was a "knee-jerk" reaction. "Get them when they're wrong. Make it known. Make it public. Shame them. And on the whole, the media will have to try to come back to doing serious professional work."

• A member of the audience asked if the media self-censored during the combat phase in Iraq and now was withholding positive news stories. Gutman replied that the deal for embedded reporters was not to reveal anything about future operations or specific locations. From the Pentagon's perspective, there was "a lot of very positive reporting" coming out, but it isn't clear that reporters were withholding critical or negative stories. Farah noted that "a lot of the negative" reports originate with American sources. "I think if we weren't reporting on people being killed and such, it would have been gross negligence." Right now, "there isn't a lot of time to have happy news stories when you see people getting shot at and people dying and troops unhappy."

• Gutman added that as the situation settles down and gets less chaotic, cultural and other stories would creep into the mix; however, at present, reporters note that things have gone wrong and could get much, much worse and feel a compulsion to uncover why things are going wrong. "How could there have been this lack of planning? How could the civilian leadership have made the assumptions they did about the rosy outcome, the crowds cheering in the streets?" Reporters "are all really worried." They are trying to figure out "how do we sound the alarm bell to the extent that it has to be sounded that things are as serious as they are?"

• Murphy said he was traveling to Baghdad in four days and if things are getting dramatically better, he would report it; but if they are getting worse or stagnating, he would report that as well.

• Another audience member asked what the United States could do to turn Iraq into a model for the entire Islamic community. Melhem replied that the United States rarely makes sufficient use of what Harvard scholar Joseph Nye called "soft power"—culture, education, and its own example of observing the rule of law and the rights granted in the American Constitution and the Bill of Rights. He urged the United States to support Arab and Muslim reformers. The United States did not do enough to demand release of an Egyptian-American scholar arrested on trumped-up charges. "How come you didn't even save the man with American citizenship who is known internationally?" he asked. In general, the U.S. attitude on the reformers is to help them but not try to lead them. "You are not going to change the Arabs or the Muslim world," but they must change themselves. "We have done it before and we should be able to do it again," he said. But the reformers have to do the work. "They have to empower themselves and do it. The only thing you can do is help them and . . . don't compound the challenge and make it more difficult." To assume the United States can do the job is a case of naivete. Iraq is a hodgepodge of minorities and groups, and it is extremely difficult to replicate the U.S. success in Germany and Japan after World War II. In this instance it is not clear that the neighborhood wants the United States to succeed.

• Melhem said his main objection to the war was what would happen the day after. Militarily, the United States has the most lethal military machine that the world has ever known. But the challenge to the United States is the day after.

Analysis

Because its participants are current or former journalists, one is not surprised by Panel 2's charter description of journalism as a mirror on contemporary events and an early-warning system that provides fresh and independent views of items that are high on the national agenda. This potential structural bias notwithstand-

ing, the panelists offered often candid assessments of the ability of the profession
to provide balanced reporting.

Panel moderator Roy Gutman offered two thoughts for further development
by the ensuing presentations. First, he opined that the states that were once considered on the "periphery" as far as U.S. national security interests were concerned are now at the "center." He also suggested that use of the term "failed
state" has become counterproductive since its use induces one to conclude that
failed states are "geostrategically" insignificant. He argued that placing countries
in the failed state category results in the United States turning its interest away at
a time when failed states pose serious global security challenges. He argued further that the focus of U.S. national security policy should be on states at war,
either internal or external, because those wars provide a cover for far worse things,
such as international terrorism.

Gutman's propositions are intriguing. Has what used to be called the periphery become the center and the center the periphery? Should the United States
adjust its national security policy and public diplomacy away from the great powers and toward the disenfranchised states that are not serious prospects for membership in the global community of nations?

Clearly, great power politics should remain the centerpiece of U.S. national
security policy and diplomacy, but the United States should not let the opportunities presented by this era of relative great power comity slip through its fingers. The
center remains the center and the periphery the periphery, but, metaphorically, the
United States has ascended a level or two up Maslow's hierarchy. Consequently, the
United States now has the opportunity to meaningfully address peripheral security
issues that were once much lower priorities. However, one should not discount the
national trauma occasioned by the attacks of September 11. If, indeed, inattention
to peripheral states such as Afghanistan leads to their becoming breeding grounds
for a form of international terrorism that threatens the very core of American values
and aspirations, then the strategic significance of those states surely must factor into
any U.S. intervention or other engagement calculus.

Hisham Melhem reminded conference participants that an ample reservoir
of Arab and Muslim goodwill toward Americans once existed. It derived mostly
from an awareness that the United States was the sole Western power without a
colonial legacy in the Arab and Muslim worlds. He observed that very little goodwill toward America can be found in those regions today. He stated that the dislike of America is not rooted in religion. It is rooted in the disdain for American
foreign policy vis-à-vis the Israeli and the Palestinian issue; support, in general,
for what he views as an expansionist Israel; support for autocratic and repressive
regimes in the Arab and Muslim worlds over the past 50 years to assure access to
oil; and, most recently, signs of American imperialism in the invasions of Afghanistan and Iraq and the spread of American culture.

The fruit of such nearsighted policies is the suffering of millions, such as that
which occurred in Iraq for decades while the United States supported, or at least

tolerated, the Hussein regime. Some might even argue that radical Islam is not compatible with democracy and that a state such as Afghanistan under the Taliban offered no hope for transition to a republic founded upon representative government in which all adult individuals participate. Others would argue further that Islamic fundamentalism impedes economic progress and prevents theocratic states from entering the global community on an economically competitive basis. Evidence to the contrary does not abound.

According to Melhem, as the spread of American culture—or, more appropriately, the spread of Western civilization—continues to expand, prosper, and flourish, the Islamic world is not experiencing such prosperity. While Samuel Huntington's claim of a "clash of civilizations" may be an exaggeration for effect, clearly, many Islamic states are struggling in this age of globalization. As the world becomes smaller and smaller through improved transportation and communications systems, cultural interchange and hybridization are becoming inescapable, except for the most closed societies. The Arab and Islamic states might be better served by viewing the situation as the globalization of cultures rather than a huge invasion, as Melhem characterized it.

Melhem compared terrorism to crime, stating that society will never be able to eradicate either completely. He also noted that the tactic of suicide bombing was developed by secularists, not Islamics. He observed that terrorist groups differ in their methods and purposes, and, therefore, each must be handled through unique, tailored strategies. Political engagement may be appropriate for terrorism born of legitimate political causes; however, for the "metaphysical, unrelenting, irrational" groups, there can be no political compromise.

In the global war on terror, Melhem appeared to believe the ends justify the means. From a Western perspective, the focus of the "war" is not on competing political aspirations. It is a concerted effort to stop a method of conflict resolution that is seen as barbaric—that is, the intentional killing and terrorizing of innocent nonbelligerents in order to terrorize a population. The focus is on stopping the inhumane method employed, not on prevailing politically. The legitimacy of the underlying political objective, if any, cannot justify the method employed. One man's terrorist is not another man's freedom fighter, as some have claimed. A terrorist is a terrorist.

Melhem's remarks concerning Iraq agreed with those of the most respected Middle Eastern experts. If the U.S.-led stabilization and reconstruction project in Iraq fails, the consequences surely will be disastrous. However, the United States cannot reasonably expect Iraq to become like Sweden, Switzerland, or Germany. The most the international community, including Iraq, should hope to achieve is a somewhat representative government that is not a threat to its neighbors and respects the rights of its citizens. The longer the United States delays in adjusting its expectations and those of the Iraqi people, the more difficult its task becomes.

Dan Murphy observed that the war on terror has severely damaged the stature of the United States throughout Southeast Asia, and particularly in Indonesia.

He assessed the terrorist movement in Indonesia to be an adjunct to al Qaeda. He believed that without U.S. help Indonesia has little chance of becoming a functioning democracy and lamented that, at this juncture, when Indonesia so desperately needs American help, America's ability to help is the weakest it has ever been. This is partially a result of Muslim reaction to America's declared war on terror, which is perceived to be directed mostly against Muslims. The American invasion and occupation of Afghanistan and Iraq also have turned many Indonesians against the United States, as has the swing in U.S.–Middle East policy toward Israel. Murphy feared that Indonesia will become a breeding ground for terrorists who will threaten U.S. national security in serious ways.

Murphy described a serious state of affairs in Indonesia but offered no policy initiatives as potential remedies. His often-graphic description based on personal involvement in the Indonesian society should be a clarion call to action. Many strategists have suggested that the center of gravity of the war on terror is moderate Islam. Were the Islamic population of Indonesia to slide from moderation into radicalism, the consequences would be incalculable.

It is possible that Murphy erred by suggesting that because Indonesians hold America in less esteem than in the past that U.S. policies are wrongheaded and offensive to Indonesians and legitimately increased attraction to terrorism. Could it be that the Indonesian government has a responsibility to educate the people of Indonesia that terrorism is anathema to the rules by which the civilized world functions? Is it not the duty of Indonesians to act as responsible world citizens and follow the rule of law, while seeking to change those portions of the international order with which they disagree through means considered legitimate by the international community? It may not be logical to suggest that since Indonesian discontent is based on U.S. foreign policy and leads Indonesian citizens to turn to terrorism, then U.S. policies are illegitimate because they indirectly foster terrorism.

Steve LeVine, commenting on Central Asia, Pakistan, and Azerbaijan, stated that the region is at a "[geopolitical] intersection and so is U.S. policy toward it." He assessed that the states within the region will "succeed or fail by themselves," but, in a seemingly contradictory way, stated that the United States has hard cards to play to influence the region's development. He proposed that the United States rely on a strict quid pro quo approach to affect regional governments. His rationale is that regional leaders are so intent on preserving their positions of power that they will act only in narrow self-interest when the cost-benefit calculation is sufficiently favorable.

LeVine's prescription for U.S. security policy for the region seems to place insufficient emphasis on a crucial factor: U.S. policy is not based on the narrow self-interest of its political leaders but on broad, enduring national values and the interests derived from them. Consequently, U.S. leaders are not predisposed to making deals with regional leaders who oppress their peoples, thrive on graft and corruption, and are involved in other criminal activity.

Sadly, LeVine's assessment that democracy in the region is generations away probably is on the mark. A key issue for U.S. policy toward the region is the degree of toleration of autocratic and exploitative regional leaders the United States is willing to trade for near-term regional stability and the promise of future democratization of some unknown extent. Granted, that is a familiar choice. But, perhaps events beginning with the September 11 attacks on the World Trade Center have established a new context within which the choice must be made.

Commenting on the failed states of West Africa, Doug Farah noted that failed states provide anonymity and other benefits to terrorists because of the predominance of the criminal element within the state. Goods and services that terrorists value are readily available in most failed states: passports, ship and aircraft registry absent the normal safeguards, weapons markets, drug and human trafficking bases and routes, money laundering through the purchase and sale of commodities, and the like. He also observed that rogue states like North Korea may seek raw materials, such as uranium, from failed states to pursue clandestine nuclear weapons programs. He remarked that U.S. intelligence-gathering capabilities in the failed states of West Africa are almost nonexistent.

If Farah's assessment of the region is accurate, it is alarming. If the United States is to prosecute a war against terrorists with global reach, it ignores West Africa at its peril. Farah astutely suggested that "name and shame" campaigns, such as that used against former Liberia ruler Charles Taylor, potentially can erode the power bases of criminal state leaders and force their abdication, if not removal, from within.

The name and shame campaign should be complemented by all manner of sanctions directed specifically at the targeted leaders and not their victimized populations.

A member of the audience asked if al-Jazeera has an agenda and, if so, how the United States could influence it so that U.S. policies and actions are reported more objectively. A panelist observed that the Arab world is rediscovering the rest of the world through al-Jazeera and that, unfortunately, al-Jazeera does not abide by the journalistic standards we have come to expect of the U.S. news media. The panelist opined that the best way to overcome the bias in al-Jazeera's reporting is to expose its inaccuracies. Over time, the panelist believed, al-Jazeera will be forced to become more objective or will lose influence within the Arab world.

The problem with this simplistic approach is the tendency for people to believe in what creates the least cognitive dissonance. To the extent al-Jazeera reports stories that ring true with Arab populations, the more difficult it will be to discredit al-Jazeera by pointing out apparent inaccuracies. Even if the Western press were to show that al-Jazeera never criticizes its financial backers, its spokesman is the son of a Lebanese journalist who used to publish an Iraqi weekly under Saddam's watchful eye. Similarly, if the West were to show that stories are based on fundamental inaccuracies, the tendency may well be for much of the Arab population to interpret those actions as efforts to discredit the leading Arab news media in order to keep the Arab masses from learning the truth.

Another question focused on the ability of the news media to censor itself responsibly in order not to thwart U.S. war aims. Not surprisingly, the panelists praised the media for the self-censorship practiced during Operation IRAQI FREE-DOM. However, another aspect of self-censorship has to do with balance in reporting or reporting good news as well as bad, and vice versa. Clearly, the reporting done by embedded media who had formed close relationships with the soldiers and unit leaders with whom they traveled and upon whom they depended for personal security was overwhelmingly positive. On the other hand, the reporting coming out of Central Command Headquarters, Combined Force Land Component Command Headquarters, and even from aircraft carriers tended to be less positive. This is evidence of journalistic bias brought on by the environment within which the reporting occurred.

Another plausible explanation for the preponderance of negative reporting is that journalists intentionally point out problem areas to draw attention to them in the hope of prompting corrective action. This is the argument forwarded to explain the dearth of reporting of the many accomplishments the coalition has achieved in postwar Iraq. This school of thought, perhaps, attributes too much altruism and not enough self-interest to journalists. It seems intuitively clear that some journalists can be expected to be politically motivated during this pre-presidential election period. One panelist offered, "No news is good news; bad news is news."

Although the panel did not cover the breadth of topics suggested by its title, it did provide conference participants much to consider and debate. Additionally, it provided glimpses into what motivates national security journalists to report what they do and what possible biases may find their way into their stories. Moreover, the presentations clearly demonstrated the thorough grasp regional journalists have on the issues most important to regional governments and populations.

Transcript

JANNE E. NOLAN, Ph.D.: Good afternoon, ladies and gentlemen. Welcome back to our afternoon session.

We have, as you can tell I'm sure from the video, an extremely interesting topic. This is the portion of the program that was sponsored by the Medill School of Journalism at Northwestern on "U.S. Power and New World Disorder: An Analysis by the News Media." And as the video highlights, we really are in a brave new world in which it is journalists on the ground, who are often not only breaking the news, but involved in the news, and acting as the leading edge of our information sources. This has become highly politically controversial this year and in recent months. It's definitely a new era for international correspondents, investigations, and so forth. We couldn't have a more distinguished panel, and I'm going to introduce the chairman, Roy Gutman, who has assembled this group of people.

I think again to say, in praise of the U.S. Army in sponsoring this event, it is really a precedent-setting approach to have these kinds of investigative reporters involved in a debate about international security and the role of the media.

It's very hard to introduce Roy Gutman, not least because his bio is justifiably very long. He has won multiple awards for his reporting, for his writing, for his authorship of several books. He is truly a cutting-edge journalist. He has been out in all the war zones of the recent past and is truly an innovator, both in terms of how to cover the news as well as the news that he has gotten access to, not least of which is the Balkans, being involved in that topic well before it was a headline-grabbing issue in the mainstream media. He has reported for multiple news agencies, including Newsday. He was posted for Reuters in several countries. He's been in Bonn, Vienna, Belgrade, London, and in Washington, D.C. I can't attempt to summarize his bio. I hope you'll look at it carefully. But please join me in welcoming Roy Gutman. Thank you very much.

ROY GUTMAN: Thank you very much, Janne, and thank you for having me this afternoon. Let me ask my colleagues to come out. Hisham Melhem, Dan Murphy, Steve LeVine and Doug Farah. Join me here at the table. Thanks.

Well, on behalf of the Medill School of Journalism, on behalf of our news organizations and our wives, kids, and mothers-in-law, thank you for having us. When I was asked to assemble this panel, my first reaction as a reporter was one of skepticism. You really want to have journalists here, at this conference? And I did my best to talk the organizers out of the whole notion. Capt. George Pivik was then the man in charge. And I said to him, "George, the only panel I'd want to assemble is one that has practitioners from the field. The sort that work in the worst of the weed patches of the world, as they dig out their stories. The sort who get their fingernails dirty. In other words, no columnists, no anchors, no speechmakers, but practicing journalists." And George said to me, "That's exactly what we want." Now, that was very refreshing. I decided, well, this is a thinking person's Army. About a week later, George Pivik got reassigned. Actually, he was named a White House Fellow and was promoted. I took the mandate and stuck with it. His successor Jim Craig agreed that we should go for investigative reporters, people who come straight from the field. But interestingly enough, when I went to each of my colleagues and asked them to join the panel, they gave me the same question that I had at the very start. They really want journalists? Do they want to hear it straight? Or are we supposed to tell them something we want to hear? So I gave my colleagues one admonition. I said, "Tell the audience what they probably don't want to hear until they hear it." And then yesterday when I told this story to Hisham Melhem, he commented to me. He said, "Roy, I don't think they're going to invite us back, but at least I'll be able to sleep at night."

Roy Gutman

Assembling this panel has actually been a very educational experience for me. I do have—and Janne, I appreciate your introduction—I have the background covering the Balkan wars of the 1990s. I'm currently researching a book about Afghanistan's civil war during the Taliban period. Everybody else at this podium, at the table, is an expert in a different part of the world. And over the last month or so, as we batted ideas back and forth about what we were going to say and what the themes ought to be, I reached a couple of conclusions. You know, broad conclusions or let's say tentative broad conclusions, which I want to offer to you now just to start us off because perhaps in a way we'll see whether these conclusions stand up as we go through the panel, as we discuss different parts of the world.

One conclusion is this: Since the end of the Cold War, the states on what used to be called the "periphery" of the east-west contest have become the center of the new world disorder. There is no periphery anymore. The periphery is the center. The second idea is that—it comes out of our discussions, out of the experience of the last four to six weeks—I'm not sure whether the term "failed state" is the one that we should be using as we describe these states that are formerly on the periphery and now in the center.

I realize I'm swimming upstream in making this suggestion. But it's partly from my own experience. I've covered several so-called failed states and it seems to me the rubric does not tell us a great deal that is meaningful about those states. Instead, my experience is, and I think this goes for both the Balkan states as well as Afghanistan and other places, that on the whole when you describe a place as a failed state it seems to be forced off the radar screen. Oh, it's one of those failed states. And I'm just not sure whether it's the term that's going to get our interest going, which is what really needs to happen with these states that fall under that rubric.

I should also mention, I am surprised it didn't come up in this morning's panel, something of the etymology of the term "failed state." Now, I can't pin it down precisely who is the first to use it. I know that Robert Kaplan, in his famous article in the *Atlantic Monthly* about West Africa, was one of the first people to use that term. And the State Failure Task Force set up at the CIA was, in many ways, around before Kaplan's article. But Kaplan's article helped give it a good impetus and led to the creation of that task force.

So, since a journalist helped to promote this term in the first place, it seemed to me that as a group of journalists, we can call it into question today. And we should, of course—if you're going to call a definition or a rubric into question, then you have to sort of offer some alternative. And of course there I don't have anything really definitive to offer. But one thing that has occurred to me as I've been talking to my colleagues and thinking of the work I've been doing over the last 10 or 15 years is that the focus that I think we really need is on states where there is a war going on—it can be an internal conflict, it can be an international conflict—or states that are on the edge of war because they have a power vacuum, which often leads to a civil war, or a security vacuum, which leads to an international war.

And it isn't just because these states get in the news by virtue of just having an armed conflict. But as my experience over the last decade that war, small wars, small obscure wars in faraway places on what, as I say, used to be called a periphery, these wars provide a cover for far worse things than just the war itself. They provide a cover for the drug trade. They provide a cover for criminality. They provide a cover for war crimes. They provide a cover for genocide. Now, of course, as Mr. Gordon pointed out this morning, some of these things will occur outside of war, and so it may be that war is not the only rubric. But in any case, it seems to me that war is the focus. And of course I'm thinking journalistically. And that's how we in journalism are able to focus people's attention.

Anyway, what I want to do is just offer those two thoughts to you to see whether they stand the test of the discussion we're now about to have. I've asked Hisham to start the discussion. And his bio is in the packet. But I'll just say this one thing: Besides going to Villanova, studying philosophy there and at Georgetown, working for some of the really best news outlets in the Middle East, what he's been doing over the years is both interpreting the United States to the Arab world and the Arab world to the United States. So he's one of these real messengers and cultural conveyors of information and interpretation. And he arrived here a little bit late because he was on deadline, as usual, this morning. Hisham is going to start by providing an overview of how the United States is dealing with the Arab and Islamic world. I turn it over to you.

HISHAM MELHEM: Thank you, Roy, for a well-deserved introduction. I feel I have to make some eye contact with the audience. I'm not standing the lights. Somehow I can't help but feel I know what went through the heads of those poor Christians when they were thrown to the lions in the coliseum of the early Christian era.

Let me tell you a story. Once upon a time in a galaxy far away called the Arab and Muslim world, there existed a huge reservoir of goodwill toward the young American republic. America, in the minds of many Arabs and Muslims,

Hisham Melhem

was a benign, progressive, enlightened power. It was the country that built the American University in Beirut in the 1860s, which became one of the finest American educational institutions in the world. A few decades later, the American University of Cairo. It was the country that proposed, through President Wilson, the principle of self-determination for colonized people. America was the country that received, with open arms, thousands upon thousands of Lebanese and Syrian immigrants in the second half of the 19th century—people who came to these shores and excelled in every field and wrote glowingly about the new homeland. And as a young lad growing up in Beirut, I read their accounts—I'm talking about people like Kahlil Gibran, Emile Habiby. And one of them was a feisty young man, in the 1930s, who came from Syria. And because he loved America so much, he ended up writing a book called *A Syrian Yankee*.

However, the most important fact that stood out in the minds of Arabs and Muslims in the 18th and 19th centuries and most of the 20th century was the fact that the United States was the sole, great Western power without a colonial legacy in the Arab and Muslim world. Americans did not rule over Arabs and Muslims the way the Brits, the Spaniards, the Portuguese, the French, and the Italians did. That is extremely important. This was what I would term the age of innocence in U.S.-Arab relationship or in the relationship between the United States and the Muslim world. That was the end of this kind of age of innocence, if you will. If you tell the story to your average person in Milwaukee or Kentucky or Idaho today, they will shake their heads because today we have a completely different situation. Today, when Arabs and Americans talk to each other, they talk at each other. There is no dialogue, serious dialogue. Americans complain they are being maligned in the Arab and the Muslim world. And the Arabs and the Muslims complain that they're being demonized in the United States. Both sides are correct but only partially correct. Observing the political discourse in the Arab and Muslim world, as well as the United States, since 9/11 and the war on terror and the war in Iraq, one could safely conclude that Arabs don't do enough introspection when they discuss their sorry state of affairs. And Americans don't do enough self-criticism when they discuss their own sorry state of affairs with more than a billion Arabs and Muslims.

Now, what happened? I mean, what went wrong? I mean, many things went wrong. And although now the debate in the Arab world, to a lesser extent in this country, takes on the aura of metaphysics and extremism and absolute truth. The differences and the problems between the Arab states and many in the Arab and Muslim world are not metaphysical, are not religious, they are political and they are rooted in history. That is extremely important, notwithstanding the crazy rhetoric from this side or the other side. Now, if you ask Arabs in the last few years and decades what are their problems with the United States? What are the reasons for their complaints or even their resentment? Or even, unfortunately, these days in some parts of the Arab and the Muslim world, anti-Americanism is becoming a religion. They usually recite a number of reasons. They are, as I said, mostly political. They start with Palestine. Or what they see as America's almost unqualified support of Israel—not only Israel's right to exist, but since 1967, Israel's conquest of more Arab territory; and, in fact, since the Johnson administration, that issue of Palestine resonated with Arabs and Muslims from Casablanca to Cairo, from Khartoum to Karachi. Honest people and dishonest politicians in the Arab and Muslim world used it to support their own, at many times, parochial agendas, but essentially they used it because they are smart and they know that issue resonates with the secularist Arabs—there are 15 or 16 of us left in the Arab world—or with the Muslims or with nationalists or whatnot. So Palestine is the real first issue.

The other thing, which is extremely important also—and it's very relevant today because of what's happening in Iraq, or is likely to happen in Iraq—is America's support for autocratic, repressive, and downright totalitarian regimes in the Arab and Muslim world for the last 50 years, especially during the height of the Cold War. The United States supported governments that rigged elections in Iran, as was the infamous case of 1953 against Mohammad Mossadegh. And you go back to 1990 in Algeria, when the United States and France supported the military regime in Algeria essentially, when they annulled an open, fair election, only because Islamists won. That is why it is extremely important today because when Arabs and Muslims hear the president of the United States or Dr. Condi Rice talk about the values of democracy, transparency, accountability, or when they talk about this concept of transforming the Middle East, which is extremely ambitious, many Arabs look with cynicism or even worse than cynicism. And again, you cannot blame them because they will tell you when we hear this talk from Washington, we think that the United States is now running against its 50-year legacy in the Arab world. In those years, people used to refer, in Washington among academics and politicians, to something they still refer to as "Islamic exceptionalism"—whatever that means. Well, it means Islam is incompatible with democracy. Therefore, let's not bother with reform and democracy and whatnot, and let's sleep in beds with those regimes that are willing to give us access to oil or maintain security and stability in the region.

Again, this is an extremely important issue. In the last 10 years, during the 1990s, because of the sanctions against Iraq, in the eyes of many Arabs and Muslims, the suffering of the Iraqi people was caused by the sanctioned regime. Now, obviously Arabs and Muslims did not want to admit also the reality in Iraq. And the reality has to be—the suffering of the Iraqi people should be laid at the brutality of a political regime in Baghdad, Saddam Hussein's regime, as well as an economic sanction regime that was supported mainly by the United States. That's, by the way, one of the reasons many people of Iraq do not believe in the United Nations and still have doubts of what the United Nations initiatives will do in collaboration with the United States. They also have a fourth reason, if you will. Which is sometimes explained and expressed by intellectuals in the Arab world—mostly Islamic intellectuals but also Arab nationalists—which is this incredible new, unfounded, almost irrational fear of globalization. For most of these people, and by the way in parentheses, this is how most of the French intellectuals look at globalization—they see it as the latest manifestation of an ongoing American hegemonic project, if you will. Americans have this incredible economy, incredible military power, and now they are invading us culturally—from the Internet to Hollywood to the information revolution. And they are threatening our very sense of identity. There's a great deal of exaggeration there, but at least this is one issue, especially among the intellectuals.

Now, let me say a few words about the war on terror. Because I see a great deal of conceptual and analytical problems in the way the issues are being framed in Washington, whether by the administration in the political domain or whether by people in our profession in the media or academia—just a few observations. I started—I wasted seven years of my life studying philosophy and European culture and Arab culture. And I don't know why I ended up in journalism, although my mother used to tell me, "Son, study something useful, not philosophy."

Terror. Terror is ubiquitous, is as old as organized human society. The tiny Greek city-state suffered from it as well as the mighty Roman Empire and every subsequent culture or empire or state. You could contain terrorism, but you could never eradicate it. It's like criminal acts, like criminality. You can contain it but not eradicate it completely. And incidentally, terrorism in its uglier form today in the Middle East and many parts of the Muslim world, i.e., suicide bombings, was not at least in the Middle East, was not created by Islamists, it was created by secularists. People talk about Hezbollah and how Hezbollah's suicide attacks elevated this thing into an art, if you will. Hezbollah learned its lessons from a group of small secularists in Lebanon, who began their attacks against Israeli troops in South Lebanon following the '82 invasion. And if you go to Beirut and ask about a woman named [inaudible], a 22-year-old woman who belonged to a secularist, pro-Syrian political party. She is the first one who inaugurated this kind of attack on the Israelis, in which she blew up a bus and took with her 13 Israeli soldiers. This was the beginning. Later this tactic was adopted and developed further by

Hezbollah. Incidentally, suicide attacks in Palestine and Israel are a recent development, only in the 1990s. In fact, if anything, in the late '60s in Israel in parts, West Bank and Gaza, in the '70s and '80s, no acts such as these were carried out against the Israelis. So again, it is a recent phenomenon.

Now, I'm going to say something that will probably sound like heresy in this town—my point is all terrorism is ugly, but not all terrorists are alike, and therefore there is no one way and one sure way to deal with terrorism. There is something throughout the history of terror and political violence that we call, in our business, a hollistic terror or millenarian terror, especially that kind of terror that is laced with religious symbolism. And there's a long line of that kind of terror, in many cultures, not only Muslim cultures. You can start, if you will, in medieval times by the so-called assassins of medieval Persia and medieval and western Syria, those who terrorized the crusaders in greater Syria at that time. And in fact, *assassins* is from the Arabic word *hashashin*, which is from *hashish*. Hashish is hash you and I, when we were in college, used to engage in and smoke once in a while. And some of us, I'm sure, did inhale. Those people were led by charismatic leaders, who used to send them on suicide missions to kill either other Muslim potentates or the crusaders. Hence, the crusaders—the French took with them the word *hashashin*, turned it into *assassin* and brought it with them when they went back to Europe. Folks, we gave you many great words like—words like *algebra* and *admiral*, *chemistry* and *cipher*, *zero* and [inaudible]. But you get the assassin story. If you jump, fast-forward, to the 19th century again, assassins were operating in a Muslim culture. You fast-forward to 19th century Europe, to the phenomena of the radical violent anarchists, and I'm talking about a group of secularist, highly educated, upper middle class, who waged a war of terror, unrelenting war of terror against every political order in Europe in the 19th century and up to the first part of the 20th century from Madrid to Moscow. And they were waging this existential struggle against state—*l'etat* as the French would call it. And you jump forward to 9/11, to Osama and his killers in New York and in Washington. What is in common here is that sense of atavistic, metaphysical, unrelenting, irrational kind of impulses behind all these groups, although they did operate in different cultures and different societies. There is no middle ground with this kind of terror. There is no political compromise with this kind of terror. And the only way you can deal with this kind of terror is through coercion.

Now, the problem is, there's another kind of terror, a kind of terror that is born out of—albeit in a deviant way—from legitimate political causes. The era of decolonization in the '50s and '60s in the Third World or developing world, whatever you want to call it, is full of examples of such terror. From the FLN, front for the liberation of Algeria in the war of independence against the French, to the ANC [African National Congress] in South Africa, to the struggle of apartheid there, to Palestine to Chechnya to Kashmir to Northern Ireland. If you want to add Israel to it in 1947 and '48, they did their own version of terror against the Palestinians as well as against the British military power at that time. So when the president of the United States tells us he doesn't want Palestine, this is again in parentheses, to be born out of violence, I would say, "Hurray for you, Mr. President." I wish it could happen and I admire your intentions, but even this great country of ours was born out of violence. And the Israeli state itself was born out of violence. The problem in all these examples and during the era of decolonization is that you cannot reduce those causes into a core issue of terrorism. You cannot reduce the struggle of the people of Chechnya or Kashmir or Palestine or Northern Ireland, notwithstanding the fact that many of them under the rubric of that legitimate struggle did carry out acts that you and I would in all honesty have to say are sheer terror—the violence against people with the intention to just intimidate the hell out of them. The problem is you're not going to reduce Palestine or Kashmir to an issue of terror that is going to be dealt with through coercive means. Therefore, you have to provide a political horizon. What was lacking in the discourse on terror since 9/11 was this kind of unpleasant but real distinction.

So that's why conceptually we have a problem. One word on Iraq because we have to go back now to Iraq. Because Iraq now—we are told the issue is Iraq, in the words of the president of the United States—is the central front on the war on terror. Now, obviously the reasons that led the United States to war in Iraq are evolving, they are in flux, and they will continue to be in flux. But that's another issue. The problem is, as someone who had deep, deep reservations about the war, and as someone who did publicly support regime change in Iraq in the 1980s when this great country and the Arab world and the French and the Russians and the Brits and everybody else was supporting that monstrous regime in Baghdad, I used to go on Arab television, on CNN, denouncing him, and calling him in Arabic and in English the Pol Pot of the Arab world. That's another issue. As someone who had objections to the war or trepidations or reservations, whatever, I would be dishonest with you if I tell you today that I am terrified, when I think of the consequences of an American debacle or failure in Iraq today, notwithstanding my objections, notwithstanding the ways—sometimes the silly way—in which the war has been framed here. If the United States project in Iraq collapses, for one reason or another, this would be truly a historic disaster because 24 million Iraqis will be victimized by an American failure. The United States will suffer a great deal in terms of stature, in terms of treasure and human life and material treasure. Also, who will claim victory? Osama will claim victory. Saddam will claim victory. The radicals in Iran will claim victory. Those who believe throughout the Muslim world that they can cower the United States by means of terror will claim victory. And the United States' relationship with a billion people will be jeopardized for a generation to come. And that is why Iraq is important. But let's not be naive about Iraq. Five years from now, 10 years from now, Iraq is not going to be Sweden or Switzerland or the United States. So let's not talk about democracy flourishing in Iraq the way it flourished in Germany. These are two totally different, alien situations. You cannot compare them. I can give you examples if you want later on. Let's not be naive about Iraq right now and let's lower the ceiling and talk about realistic plans.

I will be extremely happy with a regime in Iraq that empowers women and the minorities, that does not snatch people from their homes at 3:00 in the morning. That is somewhat representative. But let's not chase after Jeffersonian democrats in the Arab and Muslim world. They do not exist. They do not even exist in Europe. This is a unique democracy. Let's not be naive and think we can go and export this great system and implant it and make Baghdad on the Euphrates similar to Washington on the Potomac. It ain't going to happen. Therefore, let's focus on what can be done. Let's focus on those Arab reformers, Muslim reformers, democrats with a small "d," who do share in many of the values that you and I treasure in this country; but they are not going to necessarily be naive enough to think that they can import the American model and put it in Iraq so that Iraq, in turn, becomes—as President Bush and Condoleezza Rice would tell us—models for the rest of the Muslim world. This is not going to happen. Thank you.

GUTMAN: Well, thank you. I think that your note of realism is always a welcome thing, Hisham. And I hope—I'm sure you'll be able to sleep well at night having said that. Now, I wanted to go now from the general and overview, with some vital history thrown in, to the specific. Dan Murphy, who has just arrived on the red eye from Jakarta, works with the *Christian Science Monitor*, has been in the region, specifically Indonesia, but also covering the Philippines, Malaysia, and to some extent Thailand, for the last 10 years, also having worked for the *Far Eastern Economic Review*, for Bloomberg, and other publications. But what—the reason I wanted to have him here today was that he has been focusing on the small wars of Indonesia and the rise of al Qaeda in the context of those small wars. And he is a guy who has been out in the field and he probably is the most expert journalist on this subject. So, Dan, over to you.

DAN MURPHY: Thank you for having me, as well. My talk has two broad objectives. Number one is to explain how the war on terror has damaged our stature and influence in Southeast Asia, particularly in Indonesia, its largest country; and two, to illustrate how that loss of stature may allow a number of southeast nuisance conflicts to fester, which in turn could have long-term negative consequences for U.S. strategic interests.

I'd like to focus my comments and notes on Indonesia. And this isn't only because this is the country in which I am most familiar and therefore the easiest for me to talk about. It is also, as I'm sure you've heard many times before, the world's largest country with a Muslim majority. Though secular, and with the vast majority still disinterested in Islamic politics, it also has a small core of Saudi-influenced preachers in the terrorist movement, the Jemaah Islamiya, that is an adjunct of al Qaeda.

Dan Murphy

Indonesia is desperately in need of U.S. help as it tries to be a stable, flourishing democracy. Without American help, there is the very real risk that its government will continue to weaken, and if the conflicts within its borders will proliferate, negative security implications for all of us. Unfortunately, at a time when our help is most needed, our ability to lend a helping hand is at the weakest it has been in my almost 10 years there. I don't have a single Indonesian Muslim friend anymore who believes that America is a force for good in the world. Our weakness is a direct consequence of our foreign policy, the invasion of Iraq at the top of the list. Although increasingly in Indonesia, Palestine and the issue of Palestine has become important to people there, even though it's so very far away from the Middle East.

Let me start by explaining why Indonesia's conflicts matter. Here's a story of what went wrong in Indonesia at a time when we were well liked and had more influence, not so very long ago. Indonesia's dictator, Suharto, fell from power in 1998. Despite U.S. backing for his regime, America was well liked in the country and seen as having a powerful role to play in democratization. I remember attending July 4 parties at the ambassador's house in the mid '90s at which dissident authors and democracy activists, including the then-democratic icon Megawati Sukarnoputri, were invited to send a message to Suharto. Dreams of the country's scrappy young democracy activists, many of whom were jailed and tortured in 1996 and 1997, was to make Indonesia more like America. The activists at the time spoke glowingly of America's rule of law, it's criticism of human rights abuses inside the country, and the support we provided for many by helping to arrange their educations overseas. When Suharto was finally pushed from power in 1998, there was, of course, much euphoria that was quickly followed by chaos in many provinces. Fear of the regime had covered up ethnic and political grievances around the country, and when it fell, a number of small ethnic wars was sparked. As a nation of islands, Indonesia has dozens of ethnic groups. Migration and central government meddling in the Suharto years had seen some ethnic groups prosper at the expense of others, leaving pent up grievances all over the country like so much tinder.

One of the conflicts was in the two tiny Maluku provinces, known under the Dutch as the Spice Islands for the cloves and nutmeg that flourish there. The islands are home to just 1 percent of Indonesia's population, but they matter. Colonial Dutch association with the inhabitants had left a substantial number of Christians in the provinces, including a traditional Christian ruling class. But under Suharto, there was a substantial migration of Muslims from other parts of the country, some successful traders who outcompeted the locals. These migrants not only had a different religion but were ethnically distinct as well. For every migrant winner in the local political and economic stakes, there was a local loser. In other words, plenty of dry tinder. Brawling broke out in early 1999, quickly deteriorating into full-fledged warfare with the help of various police and military units who picked sides. The early fighting was evenly balanced, with Christian massacres of Muslim and vice versa, since the biases of the various police and military units there seemed to be canceling each other out. To the outside world, this was a regrettable situation, but one that would likely burn itself out eventually. The U.S. and other governments were alarmed, but there was little they realistically could do. And bottom, the conflict was made possible by the deep corruption and incompetence of the military and police, one of the poorest criminal justice systems in Asia, and an abiding distrust of the state by fighters on all sides. Fairly quickly, though, the demographics in Indonesia reached out and grabbed the conflict by the throat. Millions of incensed Indonesian Muslims blamed the government for the ongoing fighting—and they had a point—and supported the dispatch of Muslim militias to the province. At the height of the fighting, more than half-a-million people were displaced from their homes. In the turmoil, one of the groups that set up shop in the Malukus was Jemaah Islamiya, an organization that has received al Qaeda training and funding. At that time, the JI was completely unknown to outsiders. The covert and disciplined group devoted to creating a theocracy uniting the Islamic parts of Southeast Asia, from southern Thailand to the southern Philippines. They were just one of the handful of jihad groups in the province, most entirely Indonesian in origin, that participated in that conflict, and they were one of the smaller ones at that. Nobody really noticed them. The conventional wisdom at the time, and one that I have to admit I subscribed to, was that true Islamic militancy wouldn't take root in Indonesia and that the religious overtones of the conflict were less important than the social and economic grievances that had started it.

Boy, was I wrong. For the Jemaah Islamiya, the conflict was fertile ground for recruiting and training operatives, who remain at large and will continue to have an impact on Indonesian and regional security for years to come. As a consequence of Maluku, the genie of internationally networked terrorism is out of bottle in Indonesia, something that we all thought impossible a few years ago. Maluku served, in effect, as the Afghanistan for younger generations of Southeast Asian men, much as it works for the Afghan Arabs.

I remember meeting with the Muslim militia leader in the north Maluku capital of Ternate at the time—this was back in about 2000—who told me that the only real solution to the fighting in that often forgotten province was the conversion of everyone in the region to Islam and the eventual foundation of an Islamic state. He called himself a mujahedeen, the word of the Muslim fighters against the Soviet occupation of Afghanistan used to describe themselves. He told me Osama bin Laden was a personal hero and that the war in Maluku was the opening salvo in an effort to transform Indonesia and bring it "to the true path of Islam." My personal reaction was "you're dreaming, mate. Not in the Indonesia I know." I reported his comments but couched them in such a way as to emphasize that he was a member of a lunatic fringe—sort of an Indonesian-Michigan militia—and predicted along with most every other analyst that, if the government improved the conduct of its military, such men would lose their political platform and wouldn't have a meaningful long-term role anymore. Al Qaeda and its allies knew better. The JI's leaders, most of whom had fought against the Soviet invasion of Afghanistan in the 1980s, or at the very least received training at camps in the Afghan border region in the 1990s, understood the power of a radicalizing experience. With funding from a resolutely anti-Western and intolerant Indonesian organization, which had close ties to Saudi Arabian charities, JI members produced propaganda videos stressing the nobility of the jihadis and the depravity of the Christians. And they arranged for the screenings of these videos all over Southeast Asia. This was powerful stuff. Indonesian, Thai, Malaysian, and Filipino men who saw these videos answered the call. The Maluku conflict may now long be over and JI has moved on, but the men who served in the organization of Maluku are still out there. And veterans of Maluku have participated in every major terrorist attack attributed to the JI, which began with the bombing of almost 20 churches in Indonesia on Christmas Eve 2000.

Since then, with al Qaeda assistance, JI has gone on to bomb train stations in Manila, an airport in Mindanao, killed 202 people in an attack on two Bali nightclubs in October of last year, and arranged for the bombing of the J.W. Marriott Hotel in Jakarta this August. Some of the members of the JI cell in Singapore who were attempting to destroy U.S. and other embassies with a truck bombing campaign—they were stopped—were also Maluku veterans. In addition to the men directly recruited into the JI, there were thousands of other young Indonesians who fought in Maluku, acquired military skills there, and felt a powerful sense of purpose while participating in the conflict—the feeling that they were engaged in a struggle, literally, between good and evil. These young men with their bomb-making and other abilities are now back on Java, on other islands, engaged in farming, petty trading, and the like. Average Joes again. The experience of the countries that had large returning numbers of mujahedeen in the 1980s and early 1990s argues that not all of these men will be happy with the return to the quiet life. The megaphone the conflict gave to radical preachers helped them to reach millions more in the region, who had never dreamed of being involved in violence themselves, but who believed in the conspiracy theories being spun. To whit, that the U.S. and its allies had started the conflict in Maluku as part of a strategy of creeping Christianization for Indonesia. I know this sounds bizarre, but this is deeply believed.

What could America have done about the Maluku conflict? It's a tough question. What is an established fact is that Muslim radicals didn't invent the grievances that led to the outbreak of fighting in Maluku or even kick-start that fighting. Instead they were opportunists, moving in after the conflict had spiraled out of control and shaping it to their own ends. It was the failure of the Indonesian state that gave them their opening. When the war started and was still small, it was worsened by the corruption and incompetence in the Indonesian security forces that seemed to want to encourage the fighting to rage since that created economic opportunities for them.

Indonesia is going to need to build the political and legal means to stop these sources of conflicts before they get out of hand in the future. That means building a system in which elections are used as a means of holding those in power accountable for their performance rather than as an exercise in vote buying, a judiciary and police that fairly and accurately enforce the country's laws and a citizenry that feels they have a stake in their government. Helping Indonesia with all of this and much more has been a crucial component of ours and other countries' aid budget since the fall of Suharto. But these issues are famously thorny to deal with and slow to improve. Indeed, it's hard to argue that we were having much impact, as the case of Maluku points out, in the years immediately following Suharto's fall when we were still well liked there. But we were at least engaged in a productive dialogue. Starting with the invasion of Afghanistan, but really snowballing after the invasion of Iraq, I would argue that our ability to make a difference has been severely curtailed. Most of the democracy activists that were so enamored with American democracy, who I spoke of at the beginning of my remarks, are now scornful of America. Most see us now as hypocrites and many believe America is engaged in a hostile imperial experiment. One acquaintance of mine, a journalist who is educated on scholarship here in the United States, is one of many people I know who says he thinks it's possible that some of the terrorist incidents in Indonesia were engineered by the U.S. to make Islam look bad.

Our military and economic might is irrelevant in messy transitional states that aren't strong enough to either be good friends or dangerous foes. And here I'll say something briefly about the Philippines while we're engaged in an extensive amount of training and military aid at the moment. We're doing that because we're concerned about Muslim insurgency in Mindanao—specifically, the Abu Sayah, but more broadly about the security environment there. But you may have seen, there was a coup attempt in Manila last month and some of the officers that participated in that were the recipients of the recent U.S. training. While I don't think their training had anything to do with their involvement, I think what it does say is that when we begin to get involved with the militaries in some of these weak and very corrupt states, it makes it very difficult for us to then go to them and talk about the needs for improved democracies. Interestingly, a lot of Filipinos believe the reason that things have raged on in Mindanao for so long is because of the corruption of their own security forces who, like the Indonesians, seemed to like to encourage conflict in the south because of the opportunities it provides.

Let me just recatch my thread.

What we need now in the region is diplomatic clout and credibility to help places like Indonesia and the Philippines make the right choices as they try to build stable and just societies. Unfortunately, our credibility is at the lowest ebb I've ever seen it in my decade in Southeast Asia. When our diplomats urge Indonesia to deal fairly and justly with [inaudible] rebels in the troubled province of Aceh, where Indonesia is pursuing a brutal and counterproductive strategy, the generals throw back in their faces our treatment of alleged al Qaeda members at Guantanamo Bay. When we caution that negotiation provides the best solution to Indonesia's separatist conflicts, the generals point to our invasion of Iraq. Current president and former democracy icon, Megawati, who since she came to power has proved to be something of a reactionary, has lashed out at America as a bully and threat to poor countries, most recently at the UN this week. Azyumardi Azra, a moderate Muslim scholar in Jakarta, who I deeply respect, recently lamented to me that the U.S. has provided tailor-made propaganda for the country's radical minority. The students at the university he teaches at in Jakarta routinely describe America as an enemy of Islam. They didn't use to do this. Another Indonesian friend who I had lunch with the other day, a nonreligious Muslim and intellectual, tells how, since the invasion of Afghanistan, her 15-year-old daughter who used to love Starbucks and McDonald's, has become intensely anti-American and has given up all U.S. products. She spends time surfing new sites on the web and dinner table conversation now revolves around her anger at the U.S. Could this anger someday cause us problems? Who is to say that tiny Singapore won't someday feel it has to reduce its extensive military ties with us because of the hostility of its massive neighbors in Indonesia and Malaysia? How can we know what our loss of regional prestige will do to our efforts to press Burma to open up to democracy, particularly since in that case, we have so few diplomatic cards left to play on our own. Fifteen years from now, when we need a major military presence in the region, for whatever reason, what will our reception be like? Without improved democracies in Indonesia and neighbors like the Philippines, their internal conflicts will simmer for years to come. Each one a potential Maluku, or potential tiny Afghanistan, that could hide surprising negative consequences for us all.

Thank you.

GUTMAN: Thank you, Dan. And I just think that your example is so specific and so rich and, unfortunately, so true that—and the most interesting thing to me is the admission, and this is, you know, what I think any good journalist is going to do—that we—at the time this is happening in Maluku, on the whole we journalists miss the story. It's not just the government that did. We want to look back at these conflicts and see what really happened in them. To learn the lessons, which I think you've now sketched out.

Steve LeVine from the *Wall Street Journal* is maybe one of the best examples of a person who toils in the toughest of places. He, too, has had the experience Dan has and I think probably all of us have at some point of writing stories that we are convinced are truly momentous or at least really important. And that went largely unnoticed. My recollection of one of Steve's best stories was—I think it was around '97 or so—when he was writing [about] bin Laden's role in Afghanistan and bank-rolling the war on behalf of the Taliban. And the legend of the region is that he turned in a file to a major news magazine—which I have a certain association with—of 10,000 words, that was definitive and was stunning. Well, you can imagine, the space being what it is, how many words they ran—I think it was about 900. But he was there—and he wrote it first. And he got it the hard way. He's now got a unique beat with the *Wall Street Journal*. I guess you could say it is one that didn't exist until the end of the Cold War. He has central and south Asia. He is based in Almaty, Kazakhstan. I dare say he keeps his ear as close to the ground as you can without tripping. He's now working on a book. He comes to us from Almaty, by way of Stanford, where he has a fellowship. He is working on a book. The title will be *Players*—it will be published by Random House. It will be on the history of the Caspian Sea and its oil. I suppose if you dialed up Amazon maybe you can put an order in already. In any case, it won't be out for I think a good year. But Steve is going to talk about several countries that he's concerned with on his beat. Steve?

STEVE LEVINE: The "Stans" as my region is called, continues to cause confusion, even though it's been several years since it attracted attention because of big oil and the war on terror. They seemingly ought to, but don't include Tartarstan, for example. On the other hand, lots of people, including my bosses, incorporate places that strictly speaking have no business in the group, such as Georgia and Azerbaijan. For purposes of today's talk, I'm also including Pakistan in the group, which, despite its name, almost no one includes on a list of legitimate "Stans." I hope that's all clear now.

The region has seen a range of U.S. involvement. On one extreme was the short-sighted ostracizing of Pakistan and Afghanistan after the 1989 Soviet withdrawal from Kabul. On the other has been what I regard as a momentously successful oil pipeline in the Caucasus. Today, the region is at an intersection. And so is U.S. policy toward it. In Pakistan, General Musharraf still hasn't put an end to homegrown jihadism. In Kazakhstan, they're on the horizon of a flood of an oil wells, but President Nazarbayev still hasn't established many of the markers of stable democracy. Neither has Azerbaijan, where President Aliyev appears to be about to be succeeded by his son, Ilham. Uzbekistan's President Karimov, stubborn to make almost any reform, keeps sliding down a slippery slope to trouble, taking his country with him.

There is a strong U.S. policy advantage to all of these situations being turned around. You all know the reasons, so I won't bother enumerating them. One thing that the 11 years since the Soviet collapsed have taught is that the "Stans" are going to succeed or fail by themselves. No one can force Karimov, for example, to lighten up and stop provoking his people. The presidents sneer at what they regard as U.S. "nannying." Incidentally, elegant persuasion, threats and pleas also don't have a superb record of success. What do you do in a situation in which the

Steve LeVine

country's leader has no personal interest or is even hostile toward making changes that would or could reduce his own power? In my view, the only method that will work in my region is straight quid pro quo trading. Meaning you give something and you get something straight in return. And alone and through its influence, the U.S. has hard cards to play—EBRD [European Bank for Reconstruction and Development] loans, IMF economic support, and the doors that open to other multilateral finance, and the U.S. military. There is talk that the Pentagon either already has or is about to finalize decisions on when and where to make some temporary military bases permanent and perhaps to prolong other such relationships in the region. What will you get for that from, say, Islam Karimov or from Kyrgyzstan's Askar Akayev? I'm not a doomsday scenarist. I generally go along with the muddle-along rule. I think that countries tend to muddle along, even under terrible circumstances and not plummet into the abyss. The "Stans" conform to this rule. And there are clear success stories—the Bakujahan pipeline, which put the U.S. on a previously imperial Russian map before the American Army and Air Force showed up; and Kazakhstan's macroeconomic stability, which gives it a very strong platform from which to move forward.

Why do I say the region is at an intersection? Look at these events that are on the horizon. Two presidents of the region and one probable future one are unindicted co-conspirators in U.S. criminal cases for allegedly receiving payments from American companies. They are Kazakhstan's Nazarbayev and Azerbaijan's Aliyev and son Ilham. If the actual American and European defendants are convicted, it won't mean anything criminally for these political leaders. They're unlikely to face prosecution, either at home or abroad. But if there are trials, the evidence presented in court could alter the political and economic atmosphere, and possibly stigmatize these leaders. Nazarbayev has his own press under control so he isn't likely to face a problem that way. But I hear genuine angst from Kazak officials who say that Nazarbayev's local authority could erode, especially to the degree that his name comes out in court in an unflattering way. As for the Aliyevs, I don't expect much trouble at home over anything that is heard in court, bad or good. The Azeris have heard it all. But abroad is another matter. For example, what political calculations would President Bush be forced to make before publicly congratulating Ilham Aliyev on a future election victory, as he did recently when Aliyev was made prime minister, or inviting him to the White House? What calculations would you have to make as you continue your emerging role in the Caucasus? We are less than 18 months away from the scheduled inauguration of the Bakujahan pipeline. In about three weeks, however, Azerbaijan, the source of the oil and the hub of the transportation system, is probably going to have a new president. And the likely winner, despite his anointment by the U.S. policy and political establishment, is untested in a tough job.

How long will Ilham Aliyev last? That's anyone's guess. What I do know is about the talk on the street. The talk on the street in Baku is of renewed war in Armenia over Nagorno-Karabakh—something that Ilham Aliyev, himself, has encouraged with threats about capturing lost territory. He's no doubt posturing. But the richer that Azerbaijan becomes, the likelier it is that such talk could become serious. I won't be surprised if Armenia and Azerbaijan go back to war in the next five years. And that would destabilize the whole Caucasus, including the main oil and gas route. Moreover, Azerbaijan's oil income flow is projected to start declining about 12 years from now. Yet, the Aliyevs have done almost nothing to diversify the economy. Twelve years. That's not a lot of time to get one's population to work in jobs that will endure once the boom wanes. Not a lot of time to stabilize one's country in an enduring way.

At the other end of the region, the Taliban, not surprisingly, is reconstituting itself. And Pakistan continues to play host to some of the world's most dangerous radicals, including fugitives who killed *Wall Street Journal* reporter Daniel Pearl. I personally think that General Musharraf is sincere. I believe he really is challenging some of Pakistan's greatest demons. But he and the rest of the world will continue to be at risk until he excises his homegrown jihadi groups entirely. These are some of the reasons why I don't see stability or democracy in a form that Americans would recognize for some time in much of the Stans, perhaps a couple of generations. That's a problem because a stable Stans encompassing volatile Afghanistan and Pakistan, south of historically expansionist Russia, west of China, north of Iran, the site of much oil and gas, is manifestly in U.S. interests. One key trouble spot is that U.S. policy in the Stans is inconsistent. It's no good to lecture the Kazaks and the Azeris about holding transparent oil tenders and then award

Halliburton a $1 million no-bid contract. It's no good to lecture Uzbekistan on human rights and then deal with China, Syria, and Saudi based on no such concessions. With 11 years on the job now, the presidents of the Stans realize that the dog is almost all bark. They also recognize a traditionally short U.S. attention span.

The main practical problem, in my view, is that the U.S. makes few quid pro quo demands. There are almost no consequences to defiance. What did the U.S. receive in exchange for its aid bill in the region? Pakistan and Uzbekistan are good comparisons—Musharraf, with a real threat at home, and Karimov, with, in my view, little. The U.S. backed both after September 11 economically and militarily. It got a military payoff in both countries. But what did it get in terms of developing stable states that aren't embarrassments to U.S. ideals? Pakistan paid a price for its assistance. It was on its way arguably to real economic growth after meeting IMF targets year after year. It also has made elemental, if somewhat flawed, steps toward elected government. As for Uzbekistan, the U.S. got very little indeed. President Karimov is yet again promising to meet IMF standards. I'll be the first to cheer if he really does, but the record does not build confidence. Uzbekistan's standard of living continues to plummet. And Karimov continues to crack down against a supposed opposition threat that the U.S. already all but destroyed. I don't think the Uzbeks tend toward radicalism. Indeed, they're mostly apathetic. But I think anger is growing. Over the years, I've heard numerous times U.S. officials emerge from meetings with Karimov saying roughly the same thing. We really had a connection. I really got through to him. We really understand each other. Ladies and gentlemen, no one ever got through to Islam Karimov. He is a master of making powerful people feel they did. When base discussions are finalized with Kyrgyzstan, I think one of the issues on the table ought to be the release from prison of opposition leader Felix Kulov, and amnesty for all of his alleged past acts as an official and the right to run in the 2005 presidential elections. In Uzbekistan, there should be a concretely enacted IMF program and general amnesty for those imprisoned thousands who are in prison simply because they are pious Muslims. And in Pakistan, the U.S. should live up to its military and economic promises and in turn gets Musharraf to completely dismantle the jihadi apparatus.

Thank you.

GUTMAN: Thank you, Steve. I think journalists are, by our nature, observers. And we don't have that much inside information, unless you're really lucky. And you have to rely on your wit. And it seems to me, nevertheless, what you were just saying sounds pretty definitive to me.

I've asked Doug Farah from the *Washington Post* to give our final presentation. He's, you know, one of these reporters who has covered various regions, always with great competence. I think of his coverage from Central America, from South America, the drugs, the cocaine traffic in Colombia, and then finally, West Africa.

One of the unique things about his reporting in the *Washington Post* is—I think there's no tougher beat for reporters, quite honestly, than to cover terrorism because it just is an area where we have so little access to information. And we can be so easily manipulated. But what Doug has done, what he did in his time in West Africa, was to actually uncover a whole aspect of the financing of the al Qaeda network through precious stones there that was really path-breaking coverage. And I think it showed all of us in journalism that there really are stories we can still break in this area and vital ones. He's completing a book now as well. It's called *Blood From Stones*. I hope it will be out soon. I'm sure it will be a dramatic read. Doug.

DOUGLAS C. FARAH: Thank you, Roy. And thank you for having me here, too.

I thought I would pick up a little on what Roy said at the opening and the definition of failed states which I also find a little mushy; and I'd like to concentrate on perhaps the subset of the failed states which are criminal states which I have fairly extensive dealings with in West Africa, and try to point out why I think they matter. I was a little surprised in the vehemence of one of the panelists in the first panel that these countries don't matter if you can't see a particular threat. I'd like to maybe try to show you why the issues in Liberia and Sierra Leone in fact pose a major threat to the United States or have posed a major threat.

In 1991, a small group of Libyan-trained rebels carried out an attack in Sierra Leone for the first time. It was the coming of age of the Revolutionary United Front [RUF], an event that nobody paid particular attention to, even the government of Sierra Leone. And nobody could understand and nobody could see at the time why it mattered. Over the course of the next 10 years, on a very human level, it did matter. The RUF became internationally known for its signature atrocity, which is hacking off the arms and legs of women and children and noncombatants, the use of mass rape as a weapon of control, and the ability to completely destroy countries in ways I've never seen in covering many different wars in many different continents. And on a human level, that became apparent. What didn't become apparent until recently, until after 9/11, was that the RUF and its sponsor, Charles Taylor, the former president of Liberia, had a direct tie to terrorism. And what do terrorists look for in failed and collapsed criminal states? I think first you have to understand that Liberia, since before Taylor became a formal president, was in fact a functioning criminal enterprise. He controlled the money, he controlled the investments, and the goals of both the RUF war and his own personal war were the diamond fields of Sierra Leone. They're particularly lucrative or desirable because you don't need much investment to mine them. This is alluvial mining so you can take a little shake-shake, wash the stones and gravel that come out of the rivers in eastern Sierra Leone, and get diamonds with probably a $15 investment. Taylor made hundreds of millions of dollars by controlling the sale of those weapons. But why are criminal states attractive, why would al Qaeda and Hezbollah set up shop in West Africa? Largely because of the anonymity these states offer. And also largely because of the benefits you can get. In a criminal state, like Liberia, what could international criminals and terrorists get? Diplomatic passports, which Mr. Taylor issued to a wide range of international criminals including some of the most notorious Russian organized crime figures. Victor Bout, probably the largest illegal weapons dealer in the world, registered all his aircraft in Liberia because you could do it online—probably cost him about $15 an airplane. There were no inspections and no corporate records required. He didn't have to base his airplanes there. He based them in the UAE [United Arab Emirates] instead. When the Belgians figured out that there was something sort of funny about Victor Bout's

Douglas C. Farah

operations, he simply moved his registration first to Equatorial Guinea, another bastion of democracy and transparency, where you could also register your airplanes online.

When that got a little uncomfortable, he moved on to the Central African Republic, another well-known democratic society with transparency. You can get numerous things from states like Liberia. But states like Liberia don't function—and I'd like to try to make a little distinction between failed states and criminal states in this sense—they don't function on their own. They need legitimate states also to survive. Taylor couldn't have operated completely in a vacuum. So he co-opted his neighbors, partly through threat of invasion and physical harm to their countries and partly through sharing some of the wealth that he acquired. Most notorious was Burkina Faso, the neighbor to the north where President Blaise Compaoré came to office by assassinating his best friend and then-President Thomas Sankara and then assumed the presidency himself and has been there ever since. What could Blaise Compaoré offer Charles Taylor? Well, Taylor was under an economic embargo and an arms embargo ever since he took office in 1997. What could Burkina Faso do but provide end-user certificates? End-user certificates, as you know probably better than I do, are necessary supposedly for the purchases of weapons of war. So Burkina Faso imported close to 250 tons of weapons in the course of just the ones we tracked from 1999 to 2000 for Mr. Taylor. Most of them went straight to the RUF and Taylor's own oppressive regime.

But there's a symbiotic relationship here. And that's how criminal states like this operate. And that's why I think they're so important to focus on in analyzing the security interest of the United States in areas that, as Roy said at the beginning, are considered peripheral. They're not peripheral. They're the breeding grounds and they give the lifeblood to organizations that need that kind of access and also need that kind of anonymity to operate in impunity. In Liberia, specifically what happened is that following the 1998 bombings in East Africa by al Qaeda, the United States froze about $220 million worth of Taliban and al Qaeda assets that were, incredibly enough, kept in gold deposits in the United States. They figured out that that was not a smart thing to have done, as they constantly analyze and reevaluate their own operations and they decided that would never happen again. Starting in 1998, they sent a very high-level envoy to Liberia to negotiate diamonds, both as a business and as a way of putting their finances into diamonds. There were intermittent business deals until early 2001, when you saw this sudden buying surge of diamonds by unknown buyers. Legitimate buyers couldn't buy in Sierra Leone in the summer of 2001 and then right after September 11, of course, it dropped off and the money is gone.

Al Qaeda, I think, made a conscious decision over this period, not only in diamonds. Best I can calculate, they probably put $20 million to $30 million into diamonds at this time, which is not a huge amount of money. They also went into tanzanite, as the *Wall Street Journal* reported extensively, sapphires out of Madagascar, emeralds out of Afghanistan, and a host of other commodities. But they're able to work because of their ability to function in these states. Who supplied Charles Taylor with his weapons? Who flew his weapons in, in the latter part of his regime? Victor Bout, the Russian arms merchant. Who supplied the Taliban in the mid-1990s? Victor Bout. Where did he register his airplanes? As I said, in Liberia. Where did he get his weapons? Out of what one would call the criminal states of the former Soviet Union, particularly Bulgaria. Taylor also bought massive amounts of weapons through another Russian named Leonid Minin, who is also one of the major organized crime figures out of the former Soviet republic. He brought in notorious South African mercenaries.

And these people formed over time a series of alliances and mostly economic alliances that allowed them to function in a world where one would think they shouldn't be able to function. It was stunning to me being on the ground in West Africa, both before and after 9/11, that the U.S. had almost completely abandoned the region in terms of intelligence gathering. To its credit, I'll say the DIA [Defense Intelligence Agency] had a stronger and much better sense of what's going on than the CIA and other intelligence agencies. And it's not because people are stupid or didn't want to do their jobs. But in West Africa, the CIA literally had a station chief running two or three stations. Maybe one other person would be helping him out. And they were lucky to do basic political reporting. The explanation to me was that during the Cold War largely the African embassies were used—by the station and others—to recruit Russians and other people of interest to their companion embassies. When the Cold War was ended, those stations were cut way back because there was perceived to be no strategic interest. I think that is exactly the type of thinking that leads to the ability of terrorist groups to continue to flourish.

I think as a final example, one could look at the Democratic Republic of the Congo, where no one knows what goes on outside of Kinshasa in any reasonable way, except the people who live out there. It's a country that was divided up among seven neighbors for economic reasons. Kabila has wanted to retain his power. The U.S. has nobody, at least what they tell me, and I think it's probably true because it's dangerous to be out there, very few people outside of Kinshasa. Diamonds flow to Zimbabwe. Diamonds flow to South Africa. Timber flows to Uganda. Timber flows around to all its neighbors. All of the major commodities of the Congo go elsewhere. And nothing is known what goes on. There are direct flights from the little town called Mbuji-Mayi in the southern part of the country to the United Arab Emirates. Why are there direct flights there? Well, nobody knows because nobody goes down to Mbuji-Mayi and nobody's actually figured out what these flights are. It's a little alarming given the fact that the financial capital of al Qaeda has been traditionally Dubai and flights go back and forth to there, and Mbuji-Mayi is not exactly a booming commercial center in the jungles of Africa.

North Korea has been known to be looking for uranium there. There are a host of things that are going on that we have simply no idea of their magnitude. I think one of the values that journalists play or correspondents play is being out in the field and trying to see some of these things—like I say, it's not because intelligence services don't want to do their job or because people are stupid. They simply don't have the resources any longer to go out there. And these are not things that will be detected through satellite imagery; they're not things that are going to be picked up through telephone intercepts. They're not going to be picked up through any of the ways we now gather so much of our intelligence. You have to have people on the ground to see it. And often we're not seeing it.

In talking with Roy about this a little bit before, I was trying to think of some of the policy recommendations. And I'm not very good at that. But the things that I have seen that worked to a degree and which have now seemed largely to have been abandoned—principally, as Steve was saying—I think a "name and shame" campaign is incredibly effective. When people started saying that Charles Taylor was a mass murderer and a criminal and was raping his own country and put a travel ban on him, that was devastating for him. It was the beginning, I think, of the end of his iron grip in Liberia and sort of slipped away from there for a lot of other reasons as well.

I think that when you target your economic sanctions at people or leaders of criminal enterprises that you know to be heads of state or in government it's much more effective than general sanctions that go after the general population—travel bans, freezing of accounts, if you can find them. Most people are far too smart to put their money anywhere you could easily find them. But it's also not that difficult to figure out where some of the money goes. Liberia registered for Taylor—for Liberia registered $3 billion in Swiss bank accounts just from Liberia. There aren't many Liberians who can put $3 billion in a Swiss bank account. So I think there are ways to get at this. But I think it's also just incredibly important to begin to pay attention to these places because as pressure grows in the developed world on financial structures, on banking systems, on weapons flows, more and more of these criminal organizations, allied with terrorist organizations, allied with a host of other terrorist organizations—don't just do weapons and illicit commodities. They do people trafficking, they do drug trafficking. They do everything else sort of in tandem. And as the pressure increases here, they're going to be moving to these countries that we consider peripheral and we don't have much interest in and that we think are sort of at the edge of the world and don't affect us, and they do.

Thank you.

GUTMAN: Well, thank you very much, Doug. I guess I should ask other members of the panel just before we go to questions from the audience. Is this thesis plausible that—what we should all be doing as journalists and probably even maybe the government might want to consider the same thing is to start taking a look at the so-called periphery as the center of all things that are going to go wrong?

Is that a fair thesis to advocate? Because I think Doug basically has endorsed it. And of course he's talking about West Africa. But the point that seems to me you made is that Liberia should not be written off as a place of marginal interest. And that Charles Krauthammer's argument this morning, which was, essentially, it is dispensable, that you can ignore it, that this is a—his argument is not based on an understanding of what really goes on in a place like Liberia when it's abandoned.

But let me ask the other panelists if they want to take up that basic question. Steve? No? Okay.

MURPHY: The whole point with, you know, what might happen in the future is you don't know where your big risks are going to come from. So I wouldn't only focus on the periphery. I think there are people that are pretty central where threats to us come from as well. But the comment this morning that there are parts of the world that can be safely written off because they don't matter today, never mattered in the past, and never will matter in the future—from experience out in the world—would seem foolish.

MELHEM: It's not possible to ignore the periphery in a globalized world. Doug talked about Hezbollah in Liberia. One of the reasons why Liberia is important probably for Hezbollah or why South America is important for Hezbollah, and I'm Lebanese, I know, is the fact that there are Lebanese communities in Liberia. At one time, there was a very influential Lebanese community in Monrovia that was influential economically, to the point where on Lebanese Independence Day the commercial sector of Monrovia would be closed down. And recently we read stories about how Hezbollah has been generating funds in Africa because of the Lebanese community, some in the Lebanese community, as well as in Latin America. And that's why it's extremely important these days, because of globalization, because of the information revolution, that small groups of people can employ Western technology and technical skills to do some tremendous harm. I mean, the only difference really between Osama bin Laden, and what he did on 9/11, and the anarchists of the 19th century, or the assassins of medieval times, is the advancement of technology. I have no doubt that if Osama had access to a small nuclear device or anthrax or whatever, instead of killing 3,000, he would have been able and willing to kill 30,000. And that's why 9/11, in an incredibly scary way, is the marriage between atavistic sense of beliefs and modern technology. That's terror in the year of globalization. And that terror can develop through small cells in areas of our—over the horizon or in the periphery or call them whatever you wish. And that's why you cannot ignore, and I think people like Colin Powell and others in this government can understand this, so-called failed states of Africa or the Muslim world or that area of no-man's-land between Afghanistan and Pakistan and parts of central Asia that are not under the control of any centralized government [because they] can be breeding grounds for groups. If we ignore them, they will not ignore us. And they will come visit with terror as we have seen on 9/11.

GUTMAN: Let me go to questions from the audience. We'll start right down here. Sir? Thank you.

AUDIENCE MEMBER: My name is Stacy [inaudible]. I'd like to ask a question about the Middle East with al-Jazeera. As journalists, what is, in your opinion, al-Jazeera's agenda? Not at a super institutional level, but on the part of your peers, the reporters, editors, the presenters, who are shaping the news as it is presented the to the Arab world? What is their agenda? And secondly, with that as a reality, how best does the United States deal with that? And how do we best present or use that as a vehicle to get our message across effectively? And to communicate effectively with that world?

GUTMAN: I think I know whom this falls to first.

MELHEM: I don't want to monopolize this. I'd be interested in what my colleagues would say.
You have to keep in mind that historically, with few exceptions, in the Arab world like Lebanon before the civil war and, to a lesser extent, Egypt, we did not have a long tradition of free press because of the nature of the political

regimes in the region. What happened with the proliferation of satellite technology in the 1990s—and these are, by the way, stations that are either sponsored by the powers that be, like in the case of al-Jazeera, it is essentially financed by the foreign minister and the sheik of Qatar. And al-Jazeera actually is like Dubai. I always refer to Dubai as a virtual city—I hope this is off the record, by the way. I want to be able to go back to the Arab world. Just as Dubai is a virtual city, really. I mean, to talk about thousands and thousands of Russians and people from the former Soviet republics that have been visiting Dubai by the thousands. I mean, there are three, four flights from those republics to Dubai in the 1990s and that's why I'm not at all surprised by what we heard from Doug. But just as Dubai is a virtual city, al-Jazeera is a virtual station. Practically 99.9 percent of those who work in al-Jazeera are not Qataris. In other words, you have a group of people who live in a compound who have absolutely no contact with the locals. And yet they are producing news about the rest of the Arab world. At times they are very critical. At times they are downright nasty. Many times they will not even get the story. Many times in their talk shows—I call them political "Jerry Springer" shows—you have two people shouting at each other, and people mistake that for democracy. We have that in this country, too, unfortunately, with the influence of FOX. I don't care if this is on the record, by the way. I don't care if that's on the record. I call FOX "al-Jazeera-lite."

I have an aristocratic sense of American television, folks. My first appearance on American television was on the "News Hour" 21 years ago, so I can afford it. I do a weekly program show for Al-Arabiya, which is a new satellite, which is supposed to be the alternative for al-Jazeera, although in the recent few months and weeks, they are making some of the same—that competing with al-Jazeera by trying to outdo al-Jazeera, unfortunately, and in that it is not obviously very encouraging.

But, to be fair, this new phenomenon, this proliferation of satellite television in the Arab world, had some positive benefits in the sense that for the first time, Arabs are rediscovering the rest of the Arab world through Arab eyes and Arab language and whatnot. Some of the artificial barriers are being brought down and some of them did discuss topics that have been hitherto some sort of taboo. So there is a positive sign to it. On the other hand, what is very disturbing about this is that they did not elevate the level of journalism the way we know it in this country. Instead, they appealed to the most common denominator. And instead of challenging the powers that be, instead of, for instance, as in the case of al-Jazeera—al-Jazeera criticizes other Arab states, but it does not criticize the emir or the sheik of Qatar. Other Arab satellites, they don't criticize their financial backers, whether they are governments, as the case of Egypt, or even powerful, wealthy donors, as is the case in Lebanon and other places. So you have this strange phenomenon in which one satellite challenges or criticizes other countries but does not or will not criticize the country from which it operates. They did not, as I said, challenge the powers that be or elevate the level or standard of journalism. In fact, I have a big problem even with the network that I—and, you know, that's one reason, actually, I'm a freelance journalist. I would never put my neck on the scaffold of one Arab editor.

For instance, just one thing. Recently, the United States, from Donald Rumsfeld to Paul Wolfowitz, whom I interviewed—and I interviewed George Bush, by the way, before he went to the Middle East—they did something that was outrageous. I mean, totally outrageous. They gave platform to a bunch of masked men, leaving statements, inciting violence against members of the Iraqi Council. Now, no matter what you think about the Iraqi Council, you cannot allow a bunch of masked men who may be thugs and killers, Saddam's people, foreign terrorists, or whatever, to read a statement like that and then complain, as they did with the United States, complained officially, that they represent the Iraqi resistance. I mean, what kind of Iraqi resistance is this?

Again, when they show Osama bin Laden's tapes—I mean, the joke in the Arab world, even among us journalists, is that al-Jazeera now is Osama's network and Al-Arabiya is Saddam's network. And when these guys sit down and somebody throws in their lap, literally, a tape or audiotape or videotape, and then they air it in toto, with no editorial judgment. And every time Osama opens his mouth, he talks about the Jews. He curses the Jews. He curses the Christians, and by the way, there are about 14 million Arab Christians, and then he curses the crusaders. And these guys show it on and on, practically every hour, with no sense of judgment as to what this kind of incendiary message is doing to people there.

And while I criticize the American media's coverage of the war because everyone focused on shock and awe, and there was a sense of American triumphantism, especially by our friends at Fox and some of the other cable stations, although print media in America did a wonderful job and the folks from the *Washington Post* and the *Christian Science Monitor*, in particular, and a few people like John Burns and others at the *New York Times* did a superb job. I mean, thank God for print media in this country because, if it was left to the cable and FOX, we'd be in deep trouble.

But just as the American media focused on that sense of triumphantism, at least early on in the war, in the Arab world, they focused only on the civilian victims. And they did not want to believe that the Iraqi Army is going to fall apart in a few days. And I got into trouble because I appeared on Arab television and said the war, the conclusion is known, the regime will collapse, this is the house of cards, and whatnot. People did not want to believe it. And now they are extremely anti–the Iraqi Council just because it was appointed by the United States. And that is the sad part. Many people in the Arab world don't want to admit that the United States is capable of doing something good. Even when the Americans saved the Kosovars and the Bosnians, Muslims—from the slaughter at the hands of Milosevic—denounced the attack as a violation of the sanctity of Yugoslavia, as if Milosevic left anything of the sanctity of Yugoslavia. This is why there's a negative impact of these satellite stations in the Arab world, unfortunately.

GUTMAN: But the second part of the question was what should the United States' attitude be toward it? And I wanted to throw in another one. What is the state of accuracy of al-Jazeera, Al-Arabiya, and the others? How good are they on technical reporting and getting things right?

MELHEM: I mean, take the war in Afghanistan. The fellow who is now—and I really hate to talk about a colleague—I've been on the record saying this—he covered the war from Kabul essentially saying the Americans were bombing civilians on purpose. He went on record in saying 9/11 could not have been carried out by a bunch of people from the Third World, which I call a reverse-sense racism. As if we, in the developing world and in the Arab world, are a bunch of idiots. We can't coordinate the hijacking of four airplanes. And I remind everybody that in 1970, a group of Palestinians coordinated a hijacking of three airplanes and took them to a remote place in Jordan. He was believable. Many people believed him.

In fact, talk about accuracy, the editor of *Al-Ahram*, the largest Arab newspaper in Cairo, accused the United States of throwing tainted, poisoned food to the Afghans when the war began—and this guy was appointed by the Ministry of Information in Egypt. So we have sometimes inaccurate reporting. There is no one level; there's no one standard. And depending on the background of the journalist—some of those who worked for the BBC at one time did a relatively good job because of their training. Others follow the flow. And today, the spokesperson of al-Jazeera is the son who used to work for the Iraqi news agency when Saddam was in power. His father was a Lebanese editor who used to publish the weekly sponsored by the Iraqi government. And now he criticized the Americans when they showed the bodies, which, by the way, was a silly decision on the part of the United States, to show the bodies of Uday and Qusay, especially the second batch of bodies. The first one, fine. But the second one, when they cleaned them up and cut them up or whatever, that was totally uncalled for and silly and disgusting. But, you know, he said we were vindicated. Why? Because we showed the bodies of American soldiers, the dead bodies of the American soldiers or because we showed the Ansar al-Islam types who were killed in the north. And at that time you know what they did, they focused the cameras on these mutilated bodies and faces and ran it in slow motion.

GUTMAN: I was going to say one answer to your question—and I don't think any of us wants to start advising the U.S. government on how to handle the press, we have a hard enough time getting information from the U.S. government on our own—is when you spot an inaccuracy, and there are quite a few of them, some of them are a genuine mistakes, accidents, they happen. And some of them are exaggerations and hypes and deliberate distortions. I always say write a letter to my editor. Or complain. We in the press say that we're the watchdogs. Well, who's going to watch the watchdogs? Somebody has to complain and make it very clear if there are errors and use that as your tool. I think the whole idea of banning reporters from covering the Governing Council in Iraq, I don't know that that's a great idea. I think a lot of it is knee-jerk reaction. I think, get them when they're wrong, let them know, make it public, shame them. And on the whole, the media will have to try to come back to doing serious professional work.

Next question. Up there, sir.

AUDIENCE MEMBER: Thank you. Hello? I'm from Azerbaijan. My question actually goes to Mr. LeVine. You spoke about central Asia and Caucasus and you gave us very good examples, and there's a lot of examples of instability and potential instability in the region. But you didn't actually touch or touched just a little on regional intrastate and interstate conflicts. Actually, these conflicts brought to the vacuum in the region a lot of trafficking and other criminal activities. Don't you really see these as a threat for security and stability of the region? Thank you.

LEVINE: When you say interstate, do you mean Armenia, Azerbaijan? What do you mean?

AUDIENCE MEMBER: Interstate.

LEVINE: All right. And you mean specifically Azerbaijan?

AUDIENCE MEMBER: I mean Nagorno-Karabakh. I mean all the states where you have lots of criminal activities.

LEVINE: This was a phenomenon in the late 1980s and throughout the '90s. Georgia, at one time, I think I counted, had five civil wars going on at the same time. Five different civil wars involving different groups. You know, frankly if you present something that you think concretely is a current danger—I don't know what you mean specifically.

AUDIENCE MEMBER: [inaudible]

LEVINE: Okay. I think I know what you're getting at. I mean, are you getting at this rumor that nuclear stuff goes through there?

AUDIENCE MEMBER: I'm not getting at any rumors. Because you're talking about veritable instability, right? If you're speaking of instability, you said about some issues, which I can't agree or not. But you didn't mention this issue, which I consider as the biggest threat to security and stability.

LEVINE: Okay I guess we can agree to disagree on that. Nagorno-Karabakh is a live and raw issue right now. And as I said, I do think it's going to lead to renewed war between Armenia and Azerbaijan. There is an open border between Armenia and Iran. This is how Armenia keeps alive to a large degree. I don't know if this rumor is true that I mentioned, that nuclear material somehow passes through from Nagorno-Karabakh into Iran or not. But my own focus is, I think, on regarding the kind of hard conflict involving war and instability, I think it is a conventional war between Armenia and Azerbaijan.

GUTMAN: Next question, sir, standing in the back.

AUDIENCE MEMBER: Yes. It's twofold. Several weeks ago, Christianne Amanpour—I believed I pronounced her name correctly there—she talked about self-censorship. And I was wondering if we could get some insights from the panel on just media and the whole self-censorship prior to and during the war. And the fact that this statement was made after or in a postwar environment. And then, personally, my own perception and what I see as a seemingly negative outlook from the media. You know, a soldier died today. Two soldiers died today. Rather than any talk—and I know this is a problematic question—of the positive things that are going on inside Iraq, and I know that's a specific question to Iraq. But maybe you can speak across.

GUTMAN: Was the point by Christianne Amanpour regarding coverage of Iraq during the war?

AUDIENCE MEMBER: Right. That the media had, and she was speaking for an awful lot of media, I know, exercised self-censorship.

GUTMAN: Just to give a top of the head response, I know, I was not an embedded journalist, but that was the deal. That was the agreement that you had to self-censor in order to be part of an operation. You could not reveal anything about future operations or specific locations. And I think journalists accepted that. And I think if that's the point she was making [that that was] a reasonable restriction in order to be able to give the fullest possible account of what happened after it happened.

AUDIENCE MEMBER: I thought she was speaking more on the sense of being positive versus being negative. Not so much in the security aspect of it, but from being optimistic versus being pessimistic, if I gathered that correctly. That was my impression.

GUTMAN: There was a lot of very positive reporting coming out. Certainly on the tactical level during the conflict. I know the American government, I think the DOD, I think the Pentagon, I think the uniformed military was very happy with [it] because it was just straightforward reporting of what people were seeing. You really have to give examples of where reporters withheld stories that would be at the time, critical or negative. I mean, you recall the example of the story of the killing of civilians at a roadblock, where it was witnessed by a reporter from the *Washington Post* and some others, and it was a hard one to read and hard to swallow because it was such a terrible tragedy that these people were killed. And he just sort of deconstructed it and reported what happened. And I thought that was a great example of, you know, warts and all. It's a good idea to have the media along because you can report those things right away in the fullest possible way. Another example is the shooting of the Reuters journalist at the Palestine Hotel. There were reporters embedded in the unit, including one from FOX, I believe, who were able—within a very short time—to report what happened within the unit, even though there are still questions about it.

So I think, on the whole, things went wrong, they got reported. As for the problem you have now with reports on things going wrong, well, as you very well know, no news is good news. Bad news is news. And mistakes, things happening that shouldn't be happening are, almost by definition, what news is. You know, on the whole, reporting, I'm just saying as a consumer, is pretty serious from the region. I wish there were more reporters embedded now because I'd like to know what the feeling is within the units. I'd like to know just how tense it is, how concerned they are, how they avoid being targets. Now is the moment I would really like to see embedded reporting. And unfortunately, the news organizations have, on the whole, withdrawn most of their staff.

GUTMAN: Does anybody else want to comment on this? Doug?

FARAH: Well, I would just say on the issue of the negative reporting, too, what I've seen is a lot of the negative stuff is coming from the Americans on the ground there, too, especially the troops. And I think if we weren't reporting the people being killed and stuff, it would be gross negligence. I think, and it's not because he writes for our paper, but we have a guy named Anthony Shadid there who may be the only native Arab speaker there. And he does, I think, fantastic work. And you can tell he speaks the language. And I think that he's done an extraordinary job of conveying the reality on the ground there far above any reporter at the [Washington] Post or any other publications that I've read. So I think that people make a real effort—I've been through a lot of war coverage, and I think you know, it's hard—there isn't a lot of time, a lot of times, to do the happy stories, too, when you're getting shot at and you see people dying and troops are unhappy and things come out, I don't think it's deliberately negative. And I think as the situation settles down and is less chaotic, I think you'll see probably a lot of types of other stories. Maybe not happy stories, but certainly stories like culture and other things that should be out there.

GUTMAN: I'd like also to pick up on the point Hisham made earlier. I think we're all really scared in our boots that things—while things are going wrong now on a certain level, they could get much, much worse. And I think everybody feels a compulsion to try to uncover why things are going wrong. How could there have been this lack of planning? How could the civilian leadership have made the assumptions they did about the rosy outcome, you know, the crowds cheering in the streets, and so on, and have had so little real planning? I think we're all really worried as citizens, but certainly as reporters, and so you'll probably see a lot more reporting on this very thing because there's an irresponsible set of decisions made at a certain point before the conflict began, basically not to plan. So, you know, now the chickens are coming home to roost, and it could be the beginning of something far worse. So we're all really worried. And I think our colleagues on the ground are sensing that and are trying to figure out how do we report this to the American people? How do we sound the alarm bell to the extent that it has to be sounded, that things are as serious as they are?

Dan?

MURPHY: I'm going to Baghdad on Monday. I've never been there. And if I get there and it seems like things are getting dramatically better or in certain areas there are fewer troops being killed, I hope to God that I'll notice that and report it. Conversely, if it seems to me that things are getting worse or stagnating and I'll report it that way. I think that's what we try to do. We believe in getting it objectively right and sometimes we get it wrong. But I think that's probably the issue.

GUTMAN: Another question? Yes. Good afternoon.

AUDIENCE MEMBER: Good afternoon. My name is Katherine [inaudible]. First of all, I want to give you kudos, which for me, this has been a great bit of insight and great dialogue back and forth. I can't not make a couple of comments before my question. I'm just compelled in that direction.

Roy, I would recommend not hatching our chickens before they're counted, in terms of just counting the good news stories. We don't want to fall into the same mindset perhaps of our al-Jazeera counterparts, to only focus on the bad news story using the propaganda methodology of not bringing out whether there are miscalculations on whatever side of the equation. I think being able to be that fair and balanced set of professional journalists is to tell the good news story so that everybody sees the favorable outcomes that are happening, alongside of the bad news stories, so that the people who might want to, you know, take full opportunity and exploit bad things—they are seeing the positive things that go on as well. I just felt compelled to throw that in there.

The biggest question that I have, I heard it said that within the last week, that President Bush perhaps was very optimistic in taking on this Herculean task and this endeavor. And then the retort was, who but an optimist would take on this Herculean task? And then to hear Hisham's comment regarding the Baghdad on the Euphrates is not going to be the Washington on the Potomac. My question would be, as Iraq—if we want to try to model this program, so to speak, for the entire Islamic community, if we're not going to be able to do it in this setting, what would your recommendation be, perhaps either Hisham or anyone else on the panel, how can we closely approximate that? What would it look like, perhaps? And, more importantly, what are the impediments out there in making that happen? And what can this community perhaps do to make that happen?

The other observation I wanted to make is the comment about the media perhaps not getting access to information from the government. I've had the good fortune to be able to both purvey and get information from all sides, both when in uniform, as a contractor and in the private sector, and I think that in my 11-plus years of doing that, it's come a long way. And I think it's a great two-way street. It has a lot to do with the approach and the relationship building side. I think it's come a long way. I think that we do a great job on the DOD side. And on the panel's side of the fence, I think it's just all in how we portray the objective and how we execute the mission. For my uniformed brethren and government brethren, I just want to kind of put that out there. But I do think this is a wonderful opportunity. I think it's great. But there are no women up there. I just can't help but notice that. I just wondered if you might be able to comment on that? Because women seem to have a big stake on war.

GUTMAN: You are absolutely right. If I could just say on that, a terrific journalist was invited to come from Kandahar. But frankly—a woman journalist—but unfortunately, the logistics were so difficult she couldn't make it. So—I tried. Blame it on whoever runs Kandahar Airport. I think it's the U.S. Air Force. And literally, travel there from Afghanistan is exceptionally challenging and just couldn't do it. I think on your other point, though, Hisham really ought to respond on this.

MELHEM: Look. I mean, this country is a great country, can influence events in the Arab and Muslim world, but the United States cannot be the agent of positive change in the Arab world on its own. And that is my problem with the whole notion of transformation in the Middle East.

Now, we are in Iraq. And you tried to make the best out of it, obviously. But there are other assets that the United States has, which is beyond the military power and beyond the economic power, which is what Joseph Nye refers to as "soft power." I'll give you my example, of my own childhood in Lebanon. I grew up admiring—the first time I saw "Citizen Kane" was in an American cultural center. The first time I read Steinbeck and Faulkner was in Arabic, translated by the same center. In Beirut, I used to watch the best of Hollywood and the trash of Hollywood. And I fell in love with the American blues. And I know so much about the blues I can even write a book, and I'm not exaggerating. So that aspect of popular culture, that aspect of the soft side of America is extremely important and it is rarely used. It is rarely employed in a creative way in other cultures.

During the Cold War, I used to argue that there is no way the Soviet Union will win the war for a variety of reasons. One of them is the appeal of the popular culture of America. This is incredibly vital, you know—transformative—it has its crazy side, too, but it is extremely important. Many people in the world don't know much about why someone like me would love this country. Which is, you know, in my case, I can do well in Canada and Western Europe. But, consciously at one time, although I came here as a student not to live here, I used to be extremely radical but now I am mellowed because of what I refer to as my secular bible, which is the American Constitution, the Bill of Rights, the Federalist Papers, and whatnot. That aspect of America is not known. And when I criticized the United States during the Cold War years [it was because] these great values of this country and in those days would stop at the water's edge, and the other side would see nothing but a hypocritical America. And to me, there is a lot the United States can do, culturally and economically, to help those reformers in the Arab and Muslim world—and there are reformers in the Arab and Muslim world. They would have to change their own societies. You can help them, but you cannot lead them. And that is the problem. I'll give you an example. Egypt. Egypt is a country that you and I, as good taxpayers, provide every year with $2 billion. I am Arab and I say publicly I don't want that $2 billion to go to Egypt, and by the way, I don't want that $4 billion to go to Israel, but that's another issue. But last year the United States didn't do much to save a social scientist, a man who was involved in human rights issues, Saad Ibrahim, 68 years old, who happens to be a dual citizen, who has an American citizenship in addition to his Egyptian citizenship, and is married to an American woman. And he was in jail on trumped up charges for six months. Talk about not being able to influence.

GUTMAN: There were protests—

MELHEM: Later on. I mean, later on, after six months. Then, when the president of the United States, after six months and every human rights organization was raising hell in this country and we were signing petitions on his behalf, he threatened to withhold some financial aid.

I mean, when you tell me, through the president of the United States or Condoleezza Rice, that you want to support the reformers in the Arab world, I will tell you how come you didn't even save the man who has an American citizenship and who has incredible stature in the Arab world and is known internationally? These are some of the problems that we face.

You are not going to change the Arabs or the Muslim world. And I'm not saying that those societies, that maybe seem exotic or alien to some of us here, cannot have genuine representation and viable societies. All you have to do is just read the history of medieval Spain and Cairo and Damascus and Baghdad and see a great deal of vitality, culture, creativity, and whatever. We have done it before and we should be able to do it again. But they have to do it. They have to empower themselves and do it. The only thing you can do is to help them and don't compound the challenge and make it more difficult. And that's why there is the sense of, you know, forgive me for saying, naiveté, that we can go there and get rid of the big dictator and rebuild everything from scratch. Germany, at the end of the Second World War, was a very developed society culturally and politically. Japan was like that. Iraq is a hodgepodge of minorities and groups. And it's not even a homogenous society. It is extremely difficult to do in Iraq today what the United States did in 1945 in Germany or in Japan. I mean, at that time at least, the neighborhood wanted you to succeed. I'm not sure today that the neighborhood wants you to succeed in Iraq. At that time, with Germany and Japan, we had a common enemy called the Soviet Union, which scared the hell out of all of us. And that was another incentive for people to collaborate with the Americans. And when Condoleezza Rice and Secretary Rumsfeld—forgive me again folks for saying it—dredge up what happened in 1945 and talk about Nazi opposition to the Americans, that didn't happen. There was very little of that. I mean, the Americans in Kosovo and Bosnia and other places, when they were embarked on nation building, they are not being attacked like they are being attacked in Iraq.

That's why the story—all the negative parts of what is taking place in Iraq—has to be reported. Because the context is, we might not be great at nation building in America, but at least people don't shoot at us. And they didn't in Bosnia, they didn't in Kosovo and other places or in Germany and in Japan. In seven years of American occupation in Japan, did anybody get killed? That's why it is disturbing what's taking place in Iraq. That's why it's incumbent on people who want the Americans not to fail in Iraq to report the negative side and try to raise the questions as to what happened. What Roy was saying, what happened? One of my main objections to the war was what is likely to happen in the day after? Militarily, I know this is the most lethal military machine that history has ever known. And I mean, that ragtag army of Saddam's is supposed to stand up to them? That's nonsense—but the day after—and these are the challenges that you are dealing with. I mean, I'm sorry.

GUTMAN: Hisham, thank you. I think that's the right note to end on. It's a provocative, controversial note, maybe in this audience. But I think it is telling it as you see it. And I thank you very much, the panel. And I thank the audience; I think it was a good discussion. Thanks a lot.

KEYNOTE ADDRESS

Donald H. Rumsfeld, Secretary of Defense

Introduction by: General Peter J. Schoomaker, Chief of Staff, United
States Army

Summary

- Although most people are familiar with the innovative war plan that General
Tommy Franks and his superb team of joint warfighters put together to defeat the
Iraqi regime, less familiar is the equally innovative and impressive plan to win the
peace. It is important to discuss the strategy being employed to secure the peace in
Iraq and in Afghanistan—the philosophy behind the American approach, why it is
different, and, indeed, it is different from some of the so-called nation-building efforts
of the past; and why this new approach is important not just for Iraq and Afghanistan,
but potentially for international efforts to help struggling nations recover.

- There have been suggestions that the Iraq plan is flawed, that the United
States is going at it alone, that the United States did not anticipate the level of
resistance the coalition would face, and that the United States failed to send enough
forces to do the job. Today there are suggestions declaring that the postwar effort
is on the brink of failure—that it will take longer than 21 days. But when all is
said and done, the Iraq plan to win the peace will succeed just as the war plan to
win the war succeeded.

- Why did some predict failure in the first days and weeks of the Iraq war?
One reason is that Franks' plan was different and unfamiliar. Because it did not fit
into the template of general expectations, many assumed at the first setback that
the underlying strategy had been flawed. But it was not flawed.

- In the postwar effort in Iraq today, once again, what the coalition is doing
is different. It is unfamiliar to many, so when the coalition faces the inevitable
setbacks—and it will—the assumption being widely expressed is that the underlying strategy is failing. That is not the case. The United States is on track.

- Today, in Iraq, the United States is operating on the guiding principle that has
brought success to its effort in Afghanistan. The United States does not aspire to own
Iraq or Afghanistan or to occupy or run them. During the war in Afghanistan, this
philosophy shaped how the United States approached the military campaign.

1. Instead of sending a massive invasion force, this country adopted a strategy of teaming with local Afghan forces that opposed the Taliban. After the major fighting, the United States did not flood Afghanistan with Americans. Instead, the United States worked with the Afghans to establish an interim government and an Afghan national army.

2. In Iraq, no force of Iraqi fighters could have toppled Saddam Hussein without significant numbers of coalition forces. Even so, the United States did not flood the country with a half million U.S. troops—the United States kept its footprint modest. When the major combat ended, the United States immediately began working to enlist Iraqis to take responsibility for governance and security. And the United States has made significant progress.

• There is no comparable experience in history, even in postwar Germany, postwar Japan, Kosovo, and Bosnia, where things have moved so rapidly.

1. Within two months, all major Iraqi cities and most towns had municipal councils. This took eight months to accomplish in postwar Germany.

2. Within four months, the Iraqi Governing Council had been appointed and a cabinet had been named. This took 14 months in postwar Germany.

3. In just two months, an independent Iraqi central bank was established and a new currency was announced. This took three years in postwar Germany.

4. Within three months, the United States began training a new Iraqi army and within two months, a new Iraqi police force was conducting joint patrols with coalition forces. It took 14 months to establish a police force in Germany and 10 years to begin training a German army.

• It is important to enlist Iraqis in security and governance at the early stages because it is their country. The United States is not in Iraq to engage in nation building. The U.S. mission is to help the Iraqis build their own nation. This is something the Iraqi people have to do for themselves, something that cannot be handed to a people.

1. This is an important distinction. A foreign presence in any country is unnatural. It is a lot like a broken bone. If a broken bone is not set properly in a relatively short period of time, the tendons and the muscle and the skin grow around the break. The break then becomes natural, and eventually the body adjusts to what is an abnormal situation. If one tries to refix it, or extract it to mend that break after it has already healed incorrectly, then there is a problem.

2. This is what has happened in some past nation-building exercises. Well-intentioned foreigners arrive on the scene, look at the problem and say, "Let's go fix it for them." Despite good intentions, there can be unintended, adverse side effects. Also, when foreigners come in with their international solutions to local problems, it can create a dependency.

• The U.S. objective is to encourage Iraqi independence by giving Iraqis more and more responsibility over time for security and governance of their country.

1. Long-term stability will come not from the presence of foreign forces—American or any other—but from the development of functioning local institu-

tions. The sooner the Iraqis can take responsibility for their affairs, the sooner the United States and coalition forces may leave.

2. With the money the president has requested, the goal is not for the United States to rebuild Iraq, but rather it is to help the Iraqis get on a path where they can pay to rebuild their own country. The money is a crucial element in the coalition's exit strategy: the sooner the United States helps Iraqis defend their own people, the faster foreign forces may leave. Then the Iraqis can move forward with the task of fashioning truly Iraqi solutions for their future.

• The United States cannot underestimate the challenges in Iraq today, which include foreign terrorist and Ba'athist remnants and criminals. The work is difficult, costly, and dangerous, but it is worth the risk and cost because, if the coalition succeeds, terrorism will be dealt a significant blow. A democratic Iraq in the heart of the Middle East would be a defeat for the ideology of terror that is seeking to take control of that area of the world.

• America needs to proceed with some humility to help Iraqis succeed. American and coalition forces cannot provide permanent stability or create an Iraqi democracy. In the last analysis, that has to be up to the Iraqi people. And it will take patience, but if the United States is steadfast, Iraq could become a model for a successful transition from tyranny to democracy and self-reliance.

Analysis

The secretary of defense, of all the speakers at the Eisenhower Conference, was the only one heckled by a couple of protesters at the start of his speech. As the hecklers were being led away, Donald Rumsfeld reminisced about the Berrigans protesting decades earlier about the Vietnam War. For someone who continues to state that we are not headed for another "Vietnam quagmire," the use of a Vietnam analogy was perhaps unfortunate. For the rest of his speech and in his response to questions, the secretary remained much more on theme. He touted the joint force that won the war so quickly, contrasted gloomy media reports about casualties and lack of progress with the amazing successes that have transpired in the five months since the end of major combat operations, emphasized that the current force in Iraq is about right in quantity and international makeup, and restated his position that the U.S. military is not overstretched. Good arguments all, but each can be challenged.

At one time during April of this year, it looked as if victory would be slower in coming and would be more costly, both in terms of casualties on both sides and damage to Iraq. The media predictions at that time proved to be incorrect and the operational objectives were rapidly achieved at perhaps the lowest possible cost. The danger now is that a victorious force will succumb to what Commander, Joint Forces Command Admiral Edmund P. Giambastiani, Jr., calls "victor's disease." The victor in battle frequently is unable to analyze his performance critically to make the force adjustments necessary to ensure success in future campaigns. That is especially important when the foe is one who was as technologically overmatched and as inept as the Iraqi Army. The leadership points to knowledge, precision fires, speed, and increased lethality, along with improved jointness, as key to victory. All of those are valuable characteristics of the armed forces, but the Defense Department needs to discern fairly precisely which were key and which were not so decisions can be made about where to invest limited resources and how to apply them in future conflicts against more capable enemies.

The military itself, though, may own part of the blame for the wrong messages being sent to the public. It is useful to point out, as the secretary did, that major combat operations only ceased some five months ago, but comparisons to progress in post–World War II Japan and Germany may not be particularly helpful. The devastation in those countries was far more extensive than the combat damage in Iraq. Positive news from Iraq—of which there is plenty—needs to be exploited better to garner international support, sustain domestic support, and convince Muslims in Iraq and around the Middle East and the world that the United States is not at war with Islam. The continuing combat operations must be complemented by civic action and diplomatic initiatives if the war of ideas is to be won. The coalition may be killing lots of terrorists every day, but if their actions are creating resentment that produces more breeding grounds for terrorists, they will lose in the strategic context.

Secretary Rumsfeld's comments about the size of the force in Iraq may have focused too much on the numbers of countries that are contributing to the war and reconstruction effort. The fact that dozens of nations are contributing troops is important, but size really does matter. The small contributions of countries like Latvia are important in the information war, but they do not make up for the absence of countries like Germany, France, and Russia, nor do they make up for the lack of UN resolutions. The force is an international one, but the U.S. contribution continues to overwhelm the others. Until a UN resolution is passed, the imbalance between U.S. forces and the rest of the coalition will remain. Secretary Rumsfeld did not talk as much about the total numbers of military personnel on the ground. The operational success was achieved with a minimum number of troops on the ground, but that smaller number left the coalition somewhat unprepared for the manpower-intensive occupation tasks in the post-hostilities phase of the war. That remains true today. More international support is needed, but if that comes, it does not necessarily follow that a corresponding number of American service members will be coming home. They will need to be routed instead to the parts of Iraq where economy of force measures are required now. The growth of the Iraqi security forces will compensate somewhat in the long run, but that effort remains behind schedule because of overly optimistic predictions of security forces surviving the war intact. This was complicated, of course, by the decision to disband the military.

Finally, it is becoming more difficult to accept the statement that the U.S. military is not stretched thin. On September 11, 2001, the U.S. military—particularly the Army—was already challenged in meeting its global commitments. Just over two years later, the nation is embarked on a major war and none of the previous commitments have been eliminated—but the size of the force remains unchanged.

This weight of the added commitments has been carried on the backs of the soldiers, sailors, airmen, and marines who constitute the force today. In the fairly near term, that added weight may result in retention and recruiting problems.

Transcript

The Army Chief of Chaplains, Maj. Gen. David Hicks

HICKS: Let us pray. Almighty God, we live in an unpredictable world where the nature of human power continues to change and evolve. Institutions and issues once thought to be stable have been under assault from within and without. All of us in leadership are endeavoring to find solutions to these perplexing problems. As the 34th president of the United States, a man known for the courage of his vision and the stability of his spirituality once said, "We must come together to help promote a common knowledge and understanding of the critical issues of our time." Lord, your holy scripture reminds us that if any lacked wisdom, let us ask God, who gives generously to all, and it shall be given to us. We come to you today with full hearts and empty hands, as we stand at the crossroads of complexity. We offer ourselves to you, maker of heaven and earth. I implore you, oh Lord, to renew our minds, restore our souls, protect our nation, and bless this gathering and the food that we are about to eat. For it is in your holy name that I do pray. Amen.

JANNE E. NOLAN, Ph.D.: Thank you very much. It's a great honor to be here to, once again, introduce General Schoomaker and to say welcome to all of you—those of you who were here during this very, very interesting day and those of you who have just joined us. Again, it is a huge tribute the U.S. Army to have put together this marvelous eclectic, very forward-looking, and very original set of presentations that we heard today.

If you look at the list of participants for tomorrow, as well, you see the sponsorship of the U.S. Army and its co-sponsors with a serious vision for the future security of this country. For those of us who live in the civilian world mostly and operate out of places that are academic and think tanks and you look at the kind of organization that's been brought to bear just this evening, and all you can say is, wow. Thank you for including us.

General Schoomaker is known to, I think, most of you. And as I introduced him this morning, he is a great leader, a great visionary; we are all very lucky to have him back in Washington I think perhaps the only person who doesn't share that view, maybe, his wife, who I'm sure supports him fully, but was also part of private life. What a great thing to have him back. Please join me in welcoming him to introduce Secretary Rumsfeld.

GENERAL PETER J. SCHOOMAKER: Well, good evening everyone. It is my great pleasure to introduce our keynote speaker, the Honorable Donald H. Rumsfeld.

He is a distinguished public servant, a steadfast patriot who has dedicated his adult life to the service of this great nation. A graduate of Princeton University, Secretary Rumsfeld has a wealth of experience gained over half a century in service in both the public and private sectors.

He served the nation as a naval aviator, a congressman, a counselor to the president, ambassador to NATO, White House chief of staff, and he was our youngest secretary of defense the first time he held this position. In the private sector, he served as the chief executive officer of two Fortune 500 companies. As our 21st secretary of defense, he has used his experience and talent to confront an array of national security challenges.

He directed the actions of the Defense Department in response to the terrorist attacks on September 11, 2001, he led us through two wars in Afghanistan and Iraq, and he continues to lead us in the global war on terror.

He has led the most profound change in the Department of Defense since it was organized in the late 1940s, from a new national security strategy to a joint CONOPS [contingency operations], to restructuring missile defense, to a new global posture, and a new investment strategy. These changes are remarkable and far-reaching. To lead change of this magnitude takes vision, perseverance, and courage and our secretary of defense embodies all these key attributes.

Ladies and gentlemen, please welcome our secretary of defense, the Honorable Donald H. Rumsfeld.

DONALD H. RUMSFELD: Thank you very much. Thank you.

Thank you all and good evening. And General Pete Schoomaker, thank you so much for your willingness to come back and serve your country. Some people said that it was an unusual selection to have somebody come back in after being gone. I said that's not unusual at all. In fact I thought it was a terrific idea, so we really appreciate it Pete, and we're so pleased you're willing to take on these big responsibilities.

General Sullivan, ladies and gentlemen. It is a pleasure to be here. It's appropriate that this conference be co-hosted by the United States Army and that it bear the name of one of the Army's greatest leaders, Dwight David Eisenhower. As we all know, in the last century he led the Allied forces that liberated Europe from tyranny and terror. Today, in the 21st century, the armed forces he once led are now doing the dangerous work of liberation, this time in Iraq and in Afghanistan. It's a little embarrassing, but I've been around so long that I had the benefit of having former President Dwight Eisenhower help me in my first campaign for Congress, back in 1962. And I tell you as a 29 year old running for Congress for the first time, having someone like former President Eisenhower come in and give you a boost—it was an impressive and memorable thing.

I recently had the opportunity to visit with several of the Army's divisions now in Iraq. I met the troops of the 4th ID [Infantry Division] whose forces went under

Donald H. Rumsfeld

Eisenhower's command—were among the first to assault the Normandy coast and the first American troops to enter Paris. This year, a half century later, they were the first coalition forces to enter Tikrit and Kirkuk. In Mosul, I visited the 101st Airborne, same division that in World War II fought its way from Normandy to Hitler's mountain hideout—the Eagle's Nest—and in Iraq, the 101st stormed another regime hideout, the Mosul mansion, where Uday and Qusay Hussein had taken refuge, and dealt with those two dangerous individuals. In Baghdad, I met with the troops of the 1st Armored Division, a division that defeated Rommel's *Africa Corps* in the deserts of North Africa. Today, in Iraq, this division is once again dealing with deadly adversaries working to bring freedom to a long oppressed people. These Army divisions that helped bring freedom and democracy to Europe half a century ago are now helping the Iraqi people get on a path for democracy and self-government alongside their comrades from the Air Force, the Navy, the Marines, and the Coast Guard; and I should add alongside the troops from 32 separate coalition countries.

I know some of you folks here, certainly General Schoomaker and others, have had the opportunity to visit these troops; they're doing so many things that are so innovative and so constructive and so different from each other. This "facts on the ground" in different portions of that country vary dramatically, and these leaders and their terrific troops are fitting in and adopting approaches that are distinctive, are innovative, are unique, so too are our coalition forces; and it is a truly impressive thing to see. So much of what's been done, they have contributed to in a fundamental way.

By now, all of you are familiar with the innovative war plan that General Tom Franks and his superb team of joint warfighters, General McKiernan and General Mosley and Admiral Keating, General Daly, put together to defeat the Iraqi regime. Less familiar is the equally innovative and impressive plan to win the peace. So I want to discuss the strategy being employed to secure the peace in Iraq and in Afghanistan, the philosophy behind our approach, why it's different, and indeed it is different from some of the so-called nation-building efforts of the past, and why this new approach we believe is important not just for Iraq and Afghanistan, but potentially for international efforts to help struggling nations recover.

My goodness gracious.

Twenty-five years ago, when I was secretary of defense, we used to have the Berrigan brothers come in and dig graves in our front yard. So I guess everything changes and nothing changes.

I'm sure you've heard suggestions that the Iraq plan is flawed, that the U.S. is going it alone, that the U.S. didn't anticipate the level of resistance the coalition would face, and that the U.S. failed to send enough forces to do the job. I'm speaking of course about the suggestions that were offered two weeks into the Iraq war when some prognosticators were declaring that Operation IRAQI FREEDOM was a failure. The coalition forces then took Baghdad in 21 days. Today we're this time declaring that the postwar effort is on the brink of failure, that it will take longer than 21 days, but I believe that when all is said and done the Iraq plan to win the peace will, in fact, succeed just as the war plan to win the war succeeded.

Why did some predict failure in the first days and weeks of the Iraq war? One reason, I suspect, is that General Franks' plan was different and it was unfamiliar to the people who were commenting. And because it didn't fit into the template of general expectations, many assumed at the first setback that the underlying strategy had been flawed. It wasn't. In the postwar effort in Iraq today, once again, what the coalition is doing is different; it's unfamiliar to many. So when the coalition faces the inevitable setbacks, and it will, the assumptions being widely expressed are that the underlying strategy is failing. Now, I don't believe that's the case. Nor does our combatant commander General John Abizaid, nor does Ambassador Jerry Bremer, the head of the Coalition Provisional Authority, nor do General (Richard) Myers or (General) Pete Pace, the chairman and vice chairman of the Joint Chiefs of Staff. They all believe that we are on track.

Today, in Iraq, we're operating on the guiding principle that has brought success to our effort in Afghanistan. Iraq and Afghanistan belong to the Iraqi and to the Afghan people. The United States does not aspire to own those countries or to occupy them or to run them. During the war in Afghanistan, this philosophy shaped how we approached the military campaign. Instead of sending a massive invasion force, we adopted a strategy of teaming with local Afghan forces that opposed the Taliban, and after the major fighting ended, we did not flood Afghanistan with Americans, despite the many who urged us to do so. Instead, we worked with the Afghans to establish an interim government and an Afghan National Army. You may remember that the Soviet Union had 300,000 troops in Afghanistan and lost. So the numbers of forces, it seems to me, do not necessarily determine an outcome.

In Iraq, no force of Iraqi fighters could have toppled Saddam Hussein without significant numbers of coalition forces, though in the North, Special Operations Forces and Kurdish Peshmerga fighters not only tied down Saddam Hussein's northern units, but also captured Mosul and helped to unravel the northern front with dispatch. Even so, we did not flood the country with a half-million U.S. troops. We kept our footprint modest, liberating Iraq with something slightly over 100,000 forces in the country. And when major combat ended, we began working immediately to enlist Iraqis to take responsibility for governance and security of their own country, and we've made solid progress. Within two months, all major Iraqi cities and most towns had municipal councils—this is something that took eight months to accomplish in postwar Germany—and I should add that a great many of those councils—representative councils were encouraged by the Army forces and the Marine forces on the ground in that country and the coalition forces through their fine work. Within four months, the Iraqi Governing Council had been appointed and a cabinet had been named—something that took 14 months in postwar Germany. In just two months an independent Iraqi central bank was established and a new currency announced, accomplishments that took three years in postwar Germany. Within three months we have begun training a new Iraqi army and within two months a new Iraqi police force was conducting joint patrols with coalition forces. By contrast, it took 14 months to establish a police force in Germany and 10 years to begin training a German army. All this and more has taken place in Iraq in less than five months. I know of no comparable experience in history—whether postwar Germany, postwar Japan, Kosovo, and Bosnia—I know of no example where things have moved as rapidly.

Now why is enlisting Iraqis in security and governance early so important? My view is it's important because it is their country; we are not in Iraq to engage in nation building. Our mission is to help the Iraqis so that they can build their own nation. It's something that a people have to do for themselves; it cannot be handed to a people, and I think it's an important distinction. The foreign presence in any country is, in my view, unnatural. It's a lot like a broken bone; if a broken bone is not set properly in a relatively short period of time the tendons and the muscle and the skin grow around the break and the break becomes natural, and eventually the body adjusts to what is an abnormal situation. If one then tries to refix it, to extract it, to mend that break after it's already healed wrong, there's a problem. And this is what's happened in some past nation-building exercises in my view. Well-intentioned foreigners arrive on the scene, look at the problem, say, "Let's go fix it for them" and, despite good intensions, there can be unintended adverse side effects.

When foreigners come in with their international solutions to local problems, it can create a dependency. For example, East Timor is one of the poorest countries in Asia, yet the capital is now one of the most expensive cities in Asia. Local restaurants are out of reach for most the Timorese and cater to international workers who are paid probably something like 200 times the average local wage. At the city's main supermarket, prices are reportedly on a par with London and New York. Or take Kosovo—a driver shuttling international workers around the capital earns 10 times the salary of the university professor. Four years after the war the United Nations still runs Kosovo by executive fiat. Decisions made by the elected local parliament are invalid without the signature of a UN administrator. And still to this day, Kosovo ministers have UN overseers with the power to approve or disapprove their decisions. Now that's just a different approach—I'm not saying that may be okay for Kosovo, but my interest is to see if we can't do it in a somewhat different way. Our objective is to encourage Iraqi independence by giving Iraqis more and more responsibility over time for the security and governance of their country.

Long-term stability will come, not from the presence of foreign forces—ours or any other countries, but from the development of functioning local institutions, and the sooner the Iraqis can take responsibility for their affairs, the sooner U.S. and coalition forces can leave. That is why the president has asked for $20 billion to help the Iraqis get on a path to self-government and self-reliance. He's requested $15 billion to speed repairs to Iraq's starved and dilapidated infrastructure, so Iraq can begin generating income through oil production and foreign investments. He's requested another $5 billion to help the Iraqis assume the responsibility for the security of their own country. So the goal is not for the U.S. to rebuild Iraq, rather it's to help the Iraqis get on a path where they can pay to rebuild their own country. The money the president is requesting is a critical element in the coalition's exit strategy because the sooner we help Iraqis to defend their own people, the faster foreign forces can leave their country, and they can get about the task of fashioning truly Iraqi solutions to their future.

This is not to underestimate the challenges in Iraq today. Foreign terrorist and Ba'athist remnants and criminals are doing a variety of things to try to stop the Iraqi people's transition to democracy, and we can expect that they'll continue to attack our successes and that the brave Iraqis who work with us will be attacked as well, but coalition forces are dealing with the threat. The work is difficult, costly, and dangerous, but it's worth the risk and it's worth the cost because if the coalition succeeds we will deal terrorism a powerful blow. A democratic Iraq, in the heart of the Middle East, would be a defeat for the ideology of terror that is seeking to take control of that area of the world. But to help Iraqis succeed, we need to proceed with some humility. American forces and coalition forces can do remarkable things, but they cannot provide permanent stability or create an Iraqi democracy that, in a last analysis, has to be up to the Iraqi people. It will take patience, but, if we are steadfast, Iraq could become a model for a successful transition from tyranny to democracy and self-reliance.

A few months ago, that statement would have seemed fanciful to many. If you think about it, it's been less than five months since the end of major combat operations in that country, and yet today, given the progress taking place and the support from 32 countries on the ground and additional countries providing financial assistance and humanitarian aid, that goal seems at least possible. But only if we help the Iraqis build their nation, instead of trying to do it for them and if we have the wisdom to know the difference.

Thank you very much.

Now, I'm told there are some microphones, and I see one there and one over here, and maybe there are some others. If people would like to go stand up by the microphone and ask a question, I'd be delighted to try to respond to some questions, and if they're too tough, I'll get Pete Schoomaker up here to answer them.

AUDIENCE MEMBER: Thank you, Secretary Rumsfeld, first of all for coming. My name is Don Courtney. I'm a student at American University. Now recently President Bush met with Prime Minister Schroeder to mend relations and to discuss postwar Iraq.

RUMSFELD: You're going to have to talk slowly there's an echo that makes it hard for me to follow your words.

AUDIENCE MEMBER: Got you. It's been reported that President Bush and Schroeder agreed to mend relations and get on with the rebuilding of Iraq. Can you lend a little bit of insight into the agreement they made, be it troops or financially, that Germany will help us, and the significance of that agreement?

RUMSFELD: I cannot. I have not seen the president since he got back from New York and met with Mr. Schroeder. I plan to see him tomorrow morning about 8 or 9 o'clock and if you check in with me later, why maybe I can give you some insight.

I would say this about the Federal Republic of Germany. They have very recently taken over responsibility for the International Security Assistance Force in Kabul, Afghanistan. If I'm not mistaken, it's the first time that German forces have assumed a military responsibility outside of the Federal Republic since World War II, and it is a big responsibility. I met with the German general, they're tackling the job in a very orderly way and discussing at the present time ways that NATO may expand their responsibility in Afghanistan, which we believe would be a good thing, and we're delighted they're doing what they're doing there.

Yes, sir, no I'm going to go over here. Yes, ma'am.

AUDIENCE MEMBER: Can you hear me? My name is Lorelei Kelly. I work in Congress in the House of Representatives and my question for you is, I've been noticing with the discussion of the supplemental on the Hill that whether or not people agreed with the Iraq war, it's become obvious that our budget for foreign affairs in general and defense is out of balance and our interagency planning process is inadequate for not only the prevention of state failure, but for interventions and for post-conflict challenges. My question is: do we need a reform initiative equivalent to Goldwater-Nichols for our civilian policy agencies, and what can we learn from the military's experience with jointness?

RUMSFELD: The last part of the question, what can we learn about what?

AUDIENCE MEMBER: What can we learn about jointness, working jointly from the military's experience since Goldwater-Nichols?

RUMSFELD: Well, let me first take the jointness and then I'll come back to the Goldwater-Nichols for the government as a whole. We've learned a lot about jointness. I think that the historians, some of whom are in this room, will very likely look at the Iraq war and conclude that in earlier conflicts individual services—land, sea, and air—tended to work very hard to de-conflict, but did not get the true benefit of jointness and the leverage and the lethality and the power that that provided. And in this Iraq war, my guess is that historians will look at that and say, there, more than ever before, they did in fact achieve a leverage through jointness because of the unique personalities and the time they had to think about it and work together and their recognition that they could in fact achieve a great deal more by forgetting whether or not some capability came from land, sea, or air. It didn't matter—they wanted to have the ability to put power on a target, and they worked exceedingly well together. So I think that one of the lessons learned out of this is that there's an enormous advantage to having a truly joint warfighting capability. We're taking those people—with the exception of General Franks, who unfortunately made a decision to retire, which it was certainly his right but we would have loved to keep him around—who are involved in that warfight at the next level down and engaging them in various key spots in the Department of Defense so that they can bring that joint warfighting knowledge and experience, and indeed I would say conviction, which is so important.

Your other question, or the part of your question, is an important one and I would say this: I'm not an expert on the rest of the government, but I know that the Department of Defense still is organized in a way that is a bit related to the industrial age rather than the 21st century; and all of us know that, all of us see that, all of us recognize that we've got to see the procedures and the processes we use are modernized and shortened, abbreviated, because if we're going to be agile and capable of responding in days or weeks instead of months or years we're going to have to fix these systems in our department.

The point you raised is every bit as valid for the government as a whole. The problems we face in the world are not problems that come and fit neatly into one department or agency. They're problems that inevitably require the involvement and engagement of more than one department or agency. And we end up spending incredible amounts of time that just kind of suck the life out of you at the end of the day spending four, five, six hours in interagency meetings; and the reason is, is because the organization of the government fit the last century instead of this century and frankly the organization of the Congress—it's a mirror—and the jurisdictions of the committees and the subcommittees clearly are something that people are comfortable with and know about. But let me give you an example. We've got wonderful people in the Department of Treasury trying to deal with the finances of terrorists, we've got great people in the Department of Justice working on it, we've got terrific people in Homeland Security and in the Department of Defense and in every department, the Department of State working, trying to put pressure on terrorist networks, trying to find ways that we can share intelligence and capture or kill people who are determined to go out and kill innocent men, women, or children. While that's all going on, there are a number of locations in the world where new terrorists are being trained, people are not being taught math or science or language or something that would enable them to contribute to the world and make a livelihood for themselves. They're being taught how to kill people and being told that that's a good thing to do. Now do you suppose we're capturing or killing or incarcerating more than are being made in that process? No one knows. Are we winning the battle of ideas in the world? Are the things that we can contribute to the folks in that part of the world that are fearful that their religion has been hijacked by a small minority and turned into a terrorist force? Are we doing the kinds of things that can reduce the intake in that process, that can reduce the flow of funds to the small number of Madrasas schools that are training people to kill?

Here's this country of ours that's got the best advertising, the best marketing, the best communication of any country on the face of the earth, enormous skill sets, and we're not doing a very good job at that. Why is that? There are a lot of reasons—there's our organization, which I personally think we need to address and ask how can we better bring together all the skills that exist. We've got laws that inhibit certain types of things; we have traditions that we have to be careful about, and sensitivities, but by the same token we've got a problem in the world and the battle of ideas is taking place out there, and we need to engage it in a much more thoughtful, innovative, constructive way than we're doing it; or we're going to find that while we're working the problem over here, more people are growing up over there. So we've got to do something for the government in that field. It's not easy, goodness knows, it's not easy to make the kinds of changes that General Schoomaker listed, that we're working on in the Department of Defense, but it's worth doing.

Thank you. Yes.

AUDIENCE MEMBER: First of all, Mr. Secretary, I'd like to thank you for coming. My name is R. J. Cloon. I'm from American University. I was just wondering, if you could please comment on the morale of the troops in Iraq right now?

RUMSFELD: Well I guess it's been three or four weeks since I've been there, but General Schoomaker's been there. I've talked to John Abizaid today and our military leadership is persuaded that the morale of the troops there is high. I see the troops that are wounded at Walter Reed and Bethesda and at Brooke Army Hospital, and I know from those recent visits in the last weeks that their morale is high, as badly wounded as some of them are. I am convinced that they know why they're there, they know that the global war on terror is important; they believe in what they're doing and they're proud of what they're doing. They also have to be rewarded by feeling the response they're getting from the Iraqi people for the work they're doing. For every incident you read in the newspaper about an attack on Iraqis or on us, around coalition forces, there are probably a hundred, two hundred instances where our forces are assisting people with schools or soccer teams or forming city councils or training policemen or training the army or training different aspects of the security forces. We've gone from zero Iraqis providing for their own security to 56,000 Iraqis in four and a half months with another 14,000 recruits that are in training and within a matter of weeks will make it 70,000 Iraqis providing for their own security. So when you hear people running around wringing their hands saying there's no plan, there's a plan; we don't know what we're doing, the sky is falling—how in the world do you go from zero to 56,000 Iraqis trained, armed, equipped, and out contributing to the security of the Iraqi people? Our goal is not to add more American troops; our goal is to keep increasing the number of Iraqis involved in their own security so that they can take over that responsibility.

Thank you. Yes

AUDIENCE MEMBER: Good evening, Mr. Secretary. Larry Porter, U.S. Army. My question is, are there concerns about Syrian or Iranian influence and, if there are, how are they being addressed?

RUMSFELD: There is concern; we're getting cooperation from most of Iraq's neighbors—Kuwait, Saudi Arabia, Jordan, Turkey. We've scooped up, I don't know, something between 200, 250 foreign fighters who've come across the border into the country, and when you look at their nationality a very large fraction—more than half—are Syrians and another cluster are Lebanese, which Syria occupies. So we are concerned about that border, and we're not getting the kind of cooperation that we would hope to get. The situation in Iran—a large number of Ansar al-Islam terrorists moved from Iran back into Iraq and are there now and are undoubtedly involved in a number of attacks that are taking place. So we're working on it; we're talking to those folks and allowing as how we have a minimum of regard for what they're doing and we'll just have to see how it all works out.

Yes.

AUDIENCE MEMBER: Evening Mr. Secretary, Lt. Conrad Thoreau, U.S. Coast Guard. I wanted to also thank you for coming out tonight. I wanted to thank you and the Bush administration as well for the excellent job you're doing and for your guidance.

RUMSFELD: Thank you, sir.

AUDIENCE MEMBER: Quick comment and question. My wife and I talk about how our country as a whole, we feel, needs to embark on a better advertising campaign and I think that you kind of hit on that a little bit already, so that was kind of my suggestion and I would use the example that you put out, I believe you said, we have 32 countries involved with us in Iraq, is that correct?

RUMSFELD: With troops, and we have some additional countries helping financially and with humanitarian assistance.

AUDIENCE MEMBER: Until I heard that, I probably could have named about three myself, and I guess I would suggest that would be a great piece of media along with everything else you've shared with us tonight, to help us at home and those abroad see what's truly going on. And my quick question for you is, could you give us a few of the names of some of those countries because I'm really quite interested?

RUMSFELD: I can. I'm going to have to sift out the ones that are public and the ones that are not public, but the United Kingdom, Denmark, Norway, Poland, Honduras, El Salvador, I believe Mongolia; there are 32 of them and they're from all parts of the world. I'm not surprised you weren't aware of that. I am absolutely dumbfounded that the people keep saying you shouldn't go it alone. The president of the United States, after September 11, put together a coalition of 90 nations in the global war on terror—possibly one of the biggest coalitions in the history of mankind. He has put together, starting from day one of the Iraq war, a coalition now that's up to 32 with troops in that country. And people say, why are you going it alone, why don't you turn it over to the UN or why don't you turn it over to NATO? I'll tell you there are not a lot of volunteers, and it's easy for someone to say that, but Colin Powell has gone out to something in excess of 75 countries to get additional countries to participate and a lot of countries have participated. I've heard people be dismissive; they say, oh another country was Latvia, someone the other day said Latvia, you know like that, doggone it, those people showed political courage. Those people showed personal courage to send their troops there and almost all the troops that are in there are volunteers, like ours are; and I'm grateful for that; and, as a proportion of their population, some of those countries are making contributions of troops that are truly significant, and I think it's important for us to be appreciative of what those countries are doing.

I'm sorry I didn't realize there wasn't a mic there, my apologies.

AUDIENCE MEMBER: That's all right. Nick Fraser of BBC. You're the author of the most famous and notorious remark, for Europeans at least, that you divided Europe into old Europe and new Europe. I wonder, since some months have passed, if you'd like to say if you stick by this remark or if you'd like to modify it or you'd like to retract it?

RUMSFELD: None of the above.

What I will do is tell you how it happened. I was at the Foreign Press Club one day, just good old Don minding my own business. I went over there and they started asking me a whole bunch of questions. And one question after another was, Europe is against you, Europe this, Europe's not doing that, Europe is not cooperating in the UN, Europe—and I started listing the European countries that were supporting us and there was an overwhelming majority of the European countries that were supporting us. France wasn't, Germany wasn't, Belgium wasn't, but country after country after country was supporting us, and I was getting a little tired of people casting their questions with the premise being that France, Belgium, and Germany constituted all of Europe. Now I was ambassador of NATO back in 1973 and '74—I see Arnaud de Borchgrave sitting over here somewhere I think, where are you Arnaud? There you are. You were over in Belgium and Switzerland during those days. My recollection is NATO had 15 countries at the time in it, today it's got 19 going to 26 invitees, most of those countries that won their freedom very recently and they value it very highly. And out of my mouth in response to this repeated statement that Europe is against you, I allowed as how Europe wasn't against us, that the overwhelming majority of the countries in Europe were supportive and friendly and helpful. And I was mentally thinking about the NATO I knew—the old NATO at 15 and the new NATO at 26, which is a different NATO. The center of gravity of NATO has shifted; it's moved toward the east and out of my mouth, instead of saying old NATO and new NATO, I said what you said I said and I've never said it since. (Laughter.)

Sir.

AUDIENCE MEMBER: Nick Berry, Foreign Policy Forum. If you'll indulge me, Mr. Secretary, with more humor. You seem to think that the media must ask you bad questions because you tend to ask yourself your own questions.

RUMSFELD: I do. I like them better.

AUDIENCE MEMBER: Thank you very much.

RUMSFELD: Yes, sir.

AUDIENCE MEMBER: Mr. Secretary, David Georgie. You spoke earlier about the war of ideas and with the 20/20 vision of hindsight, what preconception, assumption, belief would you now change that you held say prior to the action in Iraq? And what action would you take proactively to enhance our stature in the world in this war of ideas?

RUMSFELD: You know there are certain things a country can do alone and there are a lot of things a country can't do alone. One of the things a country can't do alone is deal with the problem of proliferation. It just doesn't work to try to think you can do it yourself; we simply have to have cooperation to deal with that problem. That means that the linkages that our nation, or any other nation, has with other nations are enormously important, and we are sensitive to that, the president is, Secretary Powell is; and they spend a great deal of time worrying about that and thinking through how they can engage people.

The problem that we've gone through is there was a conviction on the part of the president and Prime Minister Blair and other countries that what was done in Iraq had to be done; and there was a conviction on the part of some countries that it should not be done. The UN passed a resolution; a few countries opposed an additional resolution. The coalition went forward. It created the issues that we're now seeing, and I think that what one has to do is exactly what the president and all of his administration are doing and that is recognize that we have to continue to try and engage the international community in the projects we believe are important and the tasks we believe are critical to a stable and peaceful world. I don't know that I can—that I would go back and try to second guess the decisions that were made by the president. I think he was right, and I believe that he will be demonstrated to have been right by history.

Yes, sir.

AUDIENCE MEMBER: Secretary Rumsfeld, I'm Chaplain Lt. Col. William Lee and honored to see you this evening, sir. If I might make one note, the last time I saw you was September 17, when you took time to come out during shift change while I was at the north parking lot at the "wash" site; and somebody said, "Look up, it's the SecDef," and I thought, "what?" and you were there early in the morning. If a measure of a man [is not] what he says but what he does, I might forget that and so thanks for letting me ask you a quick question.

RUMSFELD: Thank you.

AUDIENCE MEMBER: I'm usually the state area command chaplain for the Maryland Guard. This year I'm privileged to be at the Kennedy Center doing a year of research as a national security fellow. When you mentioned the Muslim world or at least from your read on Iraq as people who feel that their faith has been hijacked by a small radical element, how successful do you feel we are at bringing local faith leaders or indigenous religious people to the table as part of our stability operations' planning and implementation? As a way to perhaps close that door of suspicion about us being, if you will, a western occupying country rather than a people there to help them and to build their own country?

RUMSFELD: I think that if one looks worldwide, we would have to say we're not—we do not have a very good approach to that worldwide. If one looks in Iraq, I would give very high marks to General Petraeus and General Odierno and General Dempsey and the Marine leadership, as well as Jerry Bremer. I think they're spending a good deal of time—they recognize the importance of faith in that country and they recognize the role that's played and believe that through their actions and their activities, they can gain greater support for the kind of Iraq that would be a country that is at peace with neighbors and respectful of all the diverse elements and religions and ethnic groups in the country.

I'm told that I'm going to get the hook in a few minutes. Why don't I take these two and these two and then I will let you have your dessert or whatever it is that comes next. Yes, sir.

AUDIENCE MEMBER: Thank you, Mr. Secretary, for coming out. My name is Capt. James Saddler. I'm currently a SAIS student here in Washington, D.C., and as a husband and a father of four, you hear a lot these days about overstretch and the ability of our Army to meet all of the demands in this new global war on terrorism. I'd like your thoughts, sir, on the concept of overstretch especially with Congress talking about more divisions, the need for more troops. What are your concerns about overstretch and are we able to do what we can with what we have knowing that transformation is a priority?

RUMSFELD: The Joint Chiefs of Staff have done a number of tabletop exercises and analyses that indicate to me and to the president that we have the capability to fulfill our strategy the way it's written. Second, there is no question but that there is stress on the force. We're in a major spike in activity in Iraq with 130,000 troops there; that is not the norm. Third, we have been imperfect in drawing down forces in other countries. We need to do it better, faster, smarter, and to do that you've got to see that the civil side is built up and that those countries do what we're talking about trying to do in Iraq—see that they have the civil side developed and the police and the security capability, so that we can in fact continue to draw down forces. It's working pretty well in Bosnia—those forces probably will continue to be drawn down. Kosovo is still at a higher level. We still have troops in the Sinai that have been there 22 years, not a lot but some. We have a footprint that better fits the last century than the current century, and we're addressing that. What we have to do is make sure we recognize that the single-most important thing we've got in the Department of Defense are the people, and we have to make sure we manage that force—the total force the active component and the reserve component, in a way that's respectful of them. And to do that, you've got to be very sensitive about the risk of back-to-back deployment for active service; you've got to be very careful about short call-up periods for the reserve, you've got to give them as much certainty as possible, you have to use volunteers to the extent possible; and you have to, in addition it seems to me, undertake a project which Pete and other folks in the department and I spent a lot of time talking about today about rebalancing the Guard and the reserve with the active force. We have a number of skill sets that are only in the reserves—the result of that, of course, is you end up calling those people up over and over and over again and you simply can't do that. If they wanted to be on active duty, they'd be on active duty, and it's not fair to their families; it's not fair to their employers. So we have to fix that and we're working on it.

Yes.

AUDIENCE MEMBER: Good evening, Mr. Secretary. Brook Weiss from the Medill School of Journalism.

RUMSFELD: In Evanston?

AUDIENCE MEMBER: Yes, but we have an office in D.C.

RUMSFELD: Ahh, that's too bad. You should be there, back in my hometown.

AUDIENCE MEMBER: Since the end of combat operations, how do you feel the soldiers in psychological operations and civil affairs are doing with getting U.S. policy to the Iraqi people, and how is the press with bringing it back to the American people?

RUMSFELD: I would give the folks in civil affairs an A+; and I wish we had four or five times as many as we have and I wish we had many more on active duty than we have—we have so many of them in the reserve force. Now that said, the ones in the reserve force tend to be people who are doing things that particularly equip them to do civil affairs, and you don't want to have it all on the active force because the value you get by bringing those folks in from time to time is significant—but I would certainly give them an A+. What was the second part?

AUDIENCE MEMBER: How is the press doing with bringing the information back?

RUMSFELD: I thought that's what it was. (Laughter.)

Ahh, we're going to be back to that earlier question in the center aisle that caused such a stir about old NATO and new NATO.

I continue to hope it will be better. (Laughter.) I am so young and optimistic that I have conviction that it will get better, and I think we ought to try to help them get better every chance we have.

Question.

AUDIENCE MEMBER: Good evening, Mr. Secretary. My name is Maj. Mark Recardi. I'm with the Colorado National Guard. One point and one question. I just returned from Afghanistan, and I wanted to thank you for giving me an opportunity to, in a small part, change a nation. I will tell you from the ground point of view that the soldier morale there is excellent, the Afghan people welcomed us, and we did change a nation, and we have you to thank for that and the president obviously.

RUMSFELD: Well thank you for what you've done and—something like 46 million people have been liberated in the last two years and that is something important.

AUDIENCE MEMBER: My question, sir, dovetails on the previous question. Is there a plan to transform or increase the size of the National Guard so that we can address both our state and our federal mission with the amount of overseas deployments that we're currently seeing?
Thanks, sir.

RUMSFELD: Thank you. The answer to that is that there are people who are thinking about that. At least it has not come to my level that there is a demonstrated shortage of people to contribute to the homeland security task as well as the normal rotations that we may be likely to see with respect to the regular force. I was asked a lot of questions by the press recently about whether or not, given the hurricane and the fact that some Guard forces were serving, and we counted up the number of Guard forces that exists in the United States that was not activated in that moment, and it was obvious that it was a large, large, large number. So at least, at the moment, we have not seen a competition or a conflict between the needs. On the other hand, you can't look at the active force without looking at the Guard and reserve because they're so intimately connected. And as a result, the study that the senior officials in the department are engaged in are in fact looking at that as well as the balance.

RUMSFELD: Next to the last question. And there's the last.

AUDIENCE MEMBER: Good evening, Mr. Secretary. My name is Becky Bowman. I'm also with the Medill School of Journalism, here in D.C.

RUMSFELD: Good.

AUDIENCE MEMBER: And I want to thank you for letting me ask you a question this evening. I understand that members of Congress have been making their way, group by group, to Iraq to get a firsthand look at the country and to visit with troops there and visit with the Iraqi civilians.

RUMSFELD: With my encouragement, we're hoping the more of them that go there the more they'll see what's actually taking place and come back and talk to their constituents and give them a straight talk about it.

AUDIENCE MEMBER: I understand that this had quite an impact on the Democrats especially who have become critical of the media since their return from their trips. How critical do you think it is for the U.S. people that members of Congress make their way over there in larger numbers?

RUMSFELD: I think it's important. I think it's important that people, not just people from the Congress but others. There are a lot of knowledgeable people around who are experts, and to the extent they are physically [active] and they talk to people, not just in Baghdad where a lot of people go and just stay, but out. It's very different in the north; it's different in the south; it's different in the west; the central area of Baghdad and in that central area is where most of the difficulties are, obviously—it's a city of six million people.

I was with a president of a country the other day that have six million people, and he said by actual count last year they had 3,500 homicides, assassinations, and murders in a country of six million people. Baghdad is about five-and-a-half to six million people. Here's a country with 3,500; I don't know what the number is for the United States, and of course I'm sufficiently prudent that I wouldn't ask. But I do think it's important for members of the House and the Senate—they serve such an important function of representing; they're the human link between their people and their government; they have to vote on these matters, and over and over again, the ones that go over come back with an impression that is distinctly different from what they have as an impression. I think part of it's because of 24-hour news; we see the same thing over and over and over again, you think it happened 15 times and if it's something bad, then something bad happened 15 times in the 24-hour cycle. Goodness knows, it's not going to be something good that's going to get repeated 24 times in 24 hours.

Yes, sir.

AUDIENCE MEMBER: Good evening, Secretary Rumsfeld. First, I'd like to thank you for coming and taking my question this evening. My name is David Houlihan. I'm representing American University this evening. I was wondering if you could tell us a little bit about your perspective about the soft power and its role that Mr. Nye discussed with us earlier today?

RUMSFELD: I wasn't here to hear Mr. Nye. I know who he is and he's a thoughtful person, but—what was his subject?

AUDIENCE MEMBER: He discussed like a difference between a hard and soft power. I was interested—I was kind of wondering what you thought about the role of soft power, being the secretary of defense?

RUMSFELD: I don't know what it means. I learned to say I don't know when I was very young. What is the difference between soft power and hard power?

AUDIENCE MEMBER: I'm afraid of slightly over simplifying, but he discussed hard power as more military and forceful power and soft power being more politically influenced and cultural.

RUMSFELD: Diplomacy.

AUDIENCE MEMBER: Diplomacy.

RUMSFELD: Oh, they're linked. I mean the last choice in the world is to have to use military power, to have to use kinetics; you don't want to do that. You want to do everything humanly possible through persuasion and diplomacy and economic activity and coalition building to try—I mean think what President Bush went through. There were 17 UN resolutions on Iraq and Saddam Hussein defied them. He then went to the UN; there was patience and then before he did anything with the coalition, he gave one last chance for Saddam Hussein to respond to the United Nations or leave. So, it is your absolute last choice. And on the other hand, simply passing resolutions, 17 resolutions, didn't do it. There needs to be sometimes a consequence and we were hopeful that we could through the build up of forces over a period of some five or six months, affect diplomacy favorably, that is to say support diplomacy and not have to use force. That was what the design was and that was the hope and indeed the prayer.

So I think that it's not easy to separate the two. I think that your last choice always is the use of force, and we need to always try to find ways to be persuasive and help countries. And people who wish ill of others or intend to invade their neighbors, find ways to persuade them short of the use of force, if it's humanly possible.

Thank you all—nice to see you.

NOLAN: Thank you very much to Secretary Rumsfeld. It is perhaps fitting that we have no further discussion except one very important addition to this evening, which is the United States Army Band, which you will hear over your dessert. We will see you all tomorrow.

Morning Address

How the Changing Role of National Power Affects International Corporations

David M. Cote, Chairman and Chief Executive Officer, Honeywell

Introduction by: Frances Hesselbein, Chairman, Board of Governors, Leader to Leader Institute

Summary

- Not only does a strong economy strengthen national power, it also creates stability within a nation and between nations.
- Honeywell is a good example of how to run an organization.

1. Honeywell is one of the 30 companies in the Dow Jones Industrial Average. It operates in four major, diverse business areas: aerospace, automation control solutions, specialty materials, and transportation systems.

2. Honeywell does many different things and that generally leads to the question of how one manages an enterprise as large and complex as Honeywell. The challenge is to figure out which decisions should be made locally and which should be driven centrally. Too much local is anarchy. Too much central is paralysis. Neither works.

3. Leadership and ownership of three essential company processes—strategy, operations, and people—need to be centralized. These three processes, common to most companies, need to be robust.

4. The key is how well a company performs these processes. The intensity of and commitment to each process is more important than the written policy covering them. The idea that a business leader can just be a big picture guy is a mistake.

5. Simultaneously, it is important to drive decision making as close to the action as possible. A potent combination for decision making includes overall direction from the top that also is rapidly responsive to local conditions.

6. Honeywell has five initiatives that include growth, productivity, cash, people, and enablers. They apply across all business segments, and, even though they may apply to varying degrees, everyone has to embrace them.

• Growth is essential because organizations that stand still become stagnant. Driving growth is a great stimulus for thoughtful customer focus.

• Productivity is a shorter way of saying, "How do we do more with less everyday?" Honeywell believes growth is compatible with productivity and that success consists of being able to do two seemingly mutually exclusive or opposite activities at the same time. Honeywell also believes that as it grows it becomes more productive, and as it becomes more productive, it grows because it can be even more price competitive.

• Cash is especially important because as much as people focus on income and accounting, it is not cash. Although measurements are done through accounting using income as the bottom line, cash is what one actually spends. Everyone is paid with cash. Cash is used to purchase new equipment. It is essential!

• People are the ultimate differentiator. The best people, organized correctly and motivated, generally overcome bad processes and sometimes even bad strategies.

• Enablers include two major sets of tools for improving the other four initiatives. Digital Works makes it easier for people to get their jobs done and done well. Six Sigma provides quality-oriented tools that ensure products, services, and processes are robust and work every time.

• Business is part of a well-functioning society. It is important to consider the role of business, its contributions, and how business and government work together to accomplish the mutual objective of enhancing U.S. national security. There are several important concepts to consider when thinking about the role of business.

1. Economics is not a zero-sum game. Someone else's gain is not Honeywell's loss, and both sides benefit. A crucial implication of this concept is that productivity, or the ability to do more with less every day, is a good thing. Another implication is that globalization, provided companies and countries compete fairly, is a good thing for everyone.

2. "Creative destruction," as described by economist Joseph Schumpeter, is a reality. For the world to advance, old technologies and old ways of doing things have to die as new technologies and new ways of doing things come into existence. An implication of this concept is that companies have to be allowed to fail if they do not do well. Another important implication is the importance of free flow of information, capital, goods and services, people, and entrepreneurship. Freedom counts.

3. Trust in the entire system is important. There must be trust in our institutions, in government, in how business is conducted, and in the court system. Although there has been a price for America's principled stand, it is overshadowed by the standard it sets for all nations.

• It is helpful to look at how various parts of the world are evolving in their ability to support business and productivity as they project the element of national power.

1. Japan is still the number two economy in the world but has been relatively stagnant for a decade. Japan must acquire the ability to allow companies and people fail, that is, to encourage creative destruction, which is necessary for advancement.

2. China is a formidable economic force and has made huge strides in the last decade. Although it is doing many things correctly, China needs to enforce more strictly intellectual property protection. The development of a middle class also will have a profound impact on China.

3. India has much potential and some incredibly well-educated people; but at the same time, it has a stultifying bureaucracy with its attendant regulation that stops progress in its tracks. India provides a lesson: When one gives up power—in this case, regulation, one gets power—here, innovation and growth.

4. Much of Africa suffers from a lack of credibility in its institutions and government stability. There is much to do.

5. Europe is in a fascinating transition with the evolution of the European Union. Overall, there is good trust in the system, but the region would benefit from greater freedom of movement and from a greater commitment to creative destruction.

6. Brazil has to address its cost-prohibitive social system, and Mexico would benefit from a greater commitment to technical education.

• Business plays a crucial role in the development of living standards around the world. Business should not go unbridled, but government should be the most ardent supporter in creating an environment where business can flourish. A robust economy provides a strong base to project national image and exercise national power. As business prospers so do people, and prosperous people increase stability. Stability contributes to our national security and helps to keep our troops out of harm's way. Business and government need each other; smart nations support productivity and business.

Analysis

In his opening remarks, David Cote discussed three topics: the management of his corporation; the relationship between national businesses practices, a stable and prosperous society, and national security; and the evolution of worldwide business. He intimated that each topic would provide some information of value for military leaders, but generally avoided offering direct comparisons with or lessons for the military.

Cote's management principles sounded very much like those proposed by the Department of Defense for the transformed force. Centralized senior managers must be responsible for intensely prosecuting overall strategy, operations, and personnel policies. On the other hand, local execution and decision making are the responsibility of local leaders, who must be rapidly responsive to local conditions. Though material products and measures of success for his company are different from those of the military, effectively managing and leading similar processes, using many of the same techniques, is equally important to both endeavors. Especially cogent for the military are Cote's comments about the importance of investing in "good people," the ultimate differentiator, as a means to "overcome bad processes and sometimes bad strategies."

The need to manage changing technologies is faced by both business and military communities. Cote's comments on the benefits and costs of "creative destruction" once again reinforced what the Department of Defense and the services are facing in transformation. He and most military leaders recognize that their respective enterprises must adopt new technologies if they are to advance and stay competitive. The potential cost is to people, those whose knowledge and training are in danger of becoming obsolete in ever-compressing cycles of innovation. His solution was to facilitate required shifts in skills and individual flexibility through continuous quality education and lifelong learning.

At a different level, Cote offered some support for John F. Kennedy School of Government Dean Joseph Nye's concept of soft power. He said that the Foreign Practices Act of 1997 and other reasonable regulation, though they may have lost some business, have resulted in standards of business practice that make the United States admired, respected, and trusted by the world. This positive outcome is ultimately good for business, diplomacy, and U.S. interests.

Finally, Cote's assessment of regional strengths and weaknesses can be valuable to regional combatant commanders in their Theater Security Cooperation Plans (TSCPs). Though TSCPs are primarily for application of military assets, those assets address a number of regional issues that go beyond application of military power. As Nye pointed out in his opening address, the soft power aspects of military-to-military relationships have great impact on other countries. The TSCPs and their predecessor theater engagement plans have a tradition of addressing a variety of "good governance" issues.

Transcript

JANNE E. NOLAN, Ph.D.: Good morning to all of you, ladies and gentlemen, distinguished guests. We have today, this second day of the 2003 National Security Series, sponsored by the U.S. Army, along with its co-sponsors. For those of you who were with us yesterday, you know that we had an extremely vivid, provocative, and I think really unprecedentedly eclectic program of speakers, culminating with a speech and quite an act of dialogue with Secretary Rumsfeld last night.

It's really again a tribute to the U.S. Army, to General Schoomaker, and to all of those associated with him who have pulled together this really wonderful event. We have another very special day today, beginning with this session. And my job here for the initial introduction is, once more, to give a couple of administrative announcements, to remind you to turn off your cell phones,

which I forgot to do last night, actually,
and mine went off during the speech. I
shouldn't have to confess that, but I just
did. Also, when we do take questions
and answers, if you would wait for the
microphone to come to you and stand
and identify yourself. Hopefully today,
unlike yesterday, it will be a little easier
to see the audience, so that it is actually
possible to moderate.

Let me proceed with the
introduction of our first speaker today.
It's a great, great pleasure to have
Frances Hesselbein with us. She is the
chairman of the Board of Governors of
the Leader to Leader Institute. But you
all have a copy of her biography. She is
a formidable woman. A woman who
has been a corporate leader, a pioneer
in every sense in the business world,
as a management consultant, as an

Frances Hesselbein

expert on that subject, as an educator, as an author, as a recipient of so many
honors, including the Presidential Medal of Freedom, which is the highest civilian
honor that a person can receive. She also is the first recipient of the Dwight D.
Eisenhower National Security Series Award, which is notable. I am particularly
humbled by her 16 Ph.Ds. I only have one. But you can see from her bio and
from her speech to come that this is a woman to reckon with in the best possible
sense. Please join me in welcoming her today.

FRANCES HESSELBEIN: Thank you, Janne. Good morning.

At 8:00 Friday morning, one year ago, I stood at this lectern, about to
speak on managing change to our country's great military and civilian leaders.
And it was our first Dwight D. Eisenhower Conference on National Security.
And I knew at that moment that it was one of the great moments of my life as
well as one of the most intimidating moments of my life. And that 2002
Eisenhower Conference obtained a level of excellence and commitment of
performance and results that is rarely experienced in our world. So this week, I
wondered if our second Eisenhower National Security Conference could reach
that incredible level. I think you will agree with me that yesterday, from the
moment that Janne Nolan and General Schoomaker and Susan Eisenhower
welcomed us, that all day through all of those open and powerful and provocative
speeches and panels, that it was five stars all the way. And today, promises to be
its equal.

Our opening speaker this morning is profoundly well qualified to address the topic, "How the Changing Role of National Power Affects International Corporations." Born in Manchester, New Hampshire, David Cote graduated from the University of New Hampshire in 1976. He went to school during the day and worked at night as an hourly punch-press operator for the local GE aircraft factory. And after graduation, he continued with General Electric, progressing through a series of positions of manufacturing and strategy planning and marketing, finance, and general management, and then rising to corporate senior vice president, CEO, and president of the $6 billion GE appliances business. After leaving General Electric, he joined TRW, serving as that $16 billion company's chairman and CEO prior to assuming his current position in 2002. No one could address this topic with greater experience, greater understanding.

So ladies and gentlemen, it is a great honor for me to introduce the chairman and chief executive officer of Honeywell International, David Cote. Dave?

DAVID M. COTE: Thank you, Frances. Both your kind introduction and the opportunity to participate in the prestigious Eisenhower National Security Series are appreciated. This is an impressive conference and a compelling topic.

When first invited to share my views on national power in an unpredictable world, I was impressed to see that business had been accorded a significant role in the agenda. Not only does a strong economy strengthen national power, it also creates stability within a nation and between nations. It's great to see business considered along with diplomacy, culture, and the military as a key contributor to the nation's power. I hope to accomplish three things in this discussion. The first focuses on Honeywell and how we run the company. And I expect you'll draw from that whatever you would like, in terms of running your own organizations. The second is my perspective on business as part of a well-functioning society— what's the role of business, how it contributes, how to help it; how business and government, when working together, accomplish our mutual objective by enhancing our national security. The third concerns my views on how various parts of the world are evolving from a business standpoint.

Now let's begin with something I am very familiar with and that is Honeywell. Honeywell is one of the 30 companies in the Dow Jones Industrials Average. We have over 100,000 employees working in 95 countries. Our sales in 2002 totaled $23 billion, with $8 billion of that outside the United States. Of that $8 billion, $6 billion was in Europe, and $2 billion in Asia, with $500 million in China. We operate in four major diverse business segments: aerospace, automation control solutions, specialty materials and transportation systems. Our largest business is aerospace with $9 billion in sales, $5 billion commercial, and $4 billion in defense. We make jet engines, auxiliary power units or APUs, engine controls, very sophisticated avionics, like digitally integrated cockpits for the space shuttle, and for business jets, allowing pilots to fly with easy-to-use point-and-click methods. We make precision guidance mechanisms for the most advanced weaponry such as JDAMs [Joint Direct Attack Munitions]. High-level systems integration for complex applications like satellite tracking and collision avoidance avionics for aircraft. Our collision avoidance product called EGPWS or Enhanced Ground Proximity Warning System has a database of the world's terrain, and it actually tells pilots when they are on a collision path with terrain or structures that they aren't aware of. It's a problem that occurs more often than you might think, an example being the crash of Secretary Ron Brown's plane in Croatia. We also recently announced an additional application of this technology—the runway collision avoidance, another issue that occurs more often than you might think. Even more importantly, we are now testing

David M. Cote

a further development of EGPWS that will preclude a pilot from being able to fly into a nuclear plant, a chemical plant, or even over a no-fly zone like Washington.

So, as you can see in our aerospace business, we make some pretty technically advanced and very relevant stuff. Our automation control solutions business has $7 billion in sales. Major business areas include integrated and distributed process control systems for complex process operations like refineries and pharmaceutical manufacturers. We make energy-efficiency products, from the very simple like that Honeywell thermostat found in 100 million homes and five million buildings around the world—and hopefully there is a little round yellow dial in all of your homes also—to the complex, energy management systems for entire complexes like military bases, government buildings, and campuses with multiple buildings. We have fire and security systems for homes and commercial buildings that will see significant growth with the world's commitment to homeland security. If you were to go to the Sydney International Airport in Australia, for example, you would be protected by a state-of-the-art, totally integrated Honeywell security system that includes fire, barrier, access control, HVAC [heating, ventilating, and air conditioning], all tied into a single, simple central control system. And there is nothing like it in the United States today. Our controls business, part of ACS [Automation and Control Solutions], is also the world's biggest player in sensing and control devises that measures things like temperature, pressure, position, and increasing presence of gases, people, anything. Sensors usage will increase substantially as semiconductor costs decrease and applications become interconnected. From computers to cars to medical equipment, sensors will proliferate. They'll be connected and they'll act as small information systems. Our sensing technologies, combined with our ability to make microminiature machines, known as MEMS (Micro ElectroMechanical Systems), gives us a worldwide leading position here.

We also have a chemicals business called Specialty Materials with about $3 billion in sales. We arrange for more prosaic products like nylon and polyester to the complex, like non-ozone depleting HFCs (hydrofluorocarbons). We are especially excited about some of our new products like Spectra and Lumilux. Spectra, a product 10 times stronger than steel, floats. It's used in bulletproof vests, including those used by our soldiers in Iraq and Afghanistan, blast-containing cargo containers, rope and protective barrier nets being [used] by the Coast Guard. Lumilux, a nontoxic phosphorescent material used in paint, to provide emergency pathway lighting without electricity. The light is bright enough that you can read by it. Lumilux is also used as a luminescent anti-counterfeiting thread in Euro currency.

Our fourth business is transportation products. We make automobile brakes and we're in the retail auto after-market with well-recognized brands like Fram filters, Autolite spark plugs, and Prestone antifreeze. We also have a magnificent turbo charger business for both automotive and large engine applications that's growing at a double-digit rate. The significance of a turbo charger, and it's really just a small jet engine, is that it allows an internal combustion engine, be it gas or diesel, that is a third to one-half smaller in size to deliver the same power at the same total cost to the consumer—in effect, the 4-cylinder engine that can perform like a 6-cylinder. That means the consumer gets the same power and performance that they always did, but because the engine is smaller, both fuel usage and emissions can be cut by a third. We call it responsible power.

Now, as you can see, we do a lot of different things. And that generally leads to the question of how do you manage an enterprise as large and complex and diverse as Honeywell? The challenge, in my view, is to figure out what decisions should be made locally and what should be driven centrally. Too much local is anarchy. Too much central is paralysis. Neither works. What does need to be centralized is leadership and ownership of three essential company processes: strategy, operations, and people. These three processes need to be robust, and almost all companies have them. The key is how well you do them. The intensity of and commitment to each process is more important than the written policy covering them. In each of the three, I can assure you, without direct CEO and operating management involvement, they will not be robust processes. The idea that a business leader can be a big picture guy is a mistake.

Simultaneously, it's important to drive decision making as close to the action as possible. Decision making that is consistent with overall direction from the top, but is also rapidly responsive to local conditions, provides a potent combination. So with these core processes in place and decision making combined, it's then possible to drive broad themes across a company. In Honeywell, we have out five initiatives: growth, productivity, cash, people, and our enablers, Digital Works and Six Sigma. They apply across all business segments and may apply to varying degrees, but everyone has to embrace them. Growth is essential because organizations that stand still get stagnant with all the unpleasantness that word implies. Driving growth causes people to think about what's right for the customer, what needs aren't fulfilled, what technologies can be applied; it's a great stimulus for thoughtful customer focus. We concentrate on several areas: having a robust process in every business to generate, select, develop, and then kiss or kill ideas. Doing a great job for our customers every day in quality, delivery, value, and technology. Actually it's amazing how often businesses forget the importance of doing a great job for their customers. Developing superior sales and marketing so we really understand customer needs. Globalization is critical. And finally, having robust, funded technology roadmaps for new products and services, all supported with design for Six Sigma. The strength of our company for 100 years has been technology, and we always need to excel.

Our productivity initiative is one we talk about along with growth. Productivity is a shorter way of saying how to do more with less every day. Some consider growth to be incompatible with productivity, thinking you either have a growth focus or cost focus as a company. We reject that notion and instead say that success consists of being able to do two seemingly mutually exclusive or opposite activities at the same time, finding the root cause or the balance that allows you to do both. We believe that as we grow, we become more productive. There are more units to spread costs over. And as we become more productive, we grow because we can be more cost competitive. In business and in life, it seems, you're always trying to accomplish or balance two competing goals. Some examples: you want low inventories, meaning not much cash is used, or do you want good customer service? Do you want the speed of local decision making or the control of central command? Do you want high quality or low cost? Do you want foreign policy to be multilateral or unilateral? Do you want a smaller force or a more lethal force? Focusing on just one and not recognizing the need to accomplish the seemingly repeating goals is a failure mode. The trick is to find a way to do both. The cash initiative is especially important because as much as people will focus on income and accounting, it's not cash. Although related, cash is different. The significance is that although measurements are done through accounting, using income as the bottom line, cash is what you actually spend. That's what all of us get paid with. That's how you buy new equipment. It's essential.

Our fourth initiative is to focus on people. People are the ultimate differentiator. People make all the difference. The best people organized correctly and motivated generally overcome bad processes and sometimes even bad strategies. We pay a lot of attention to having the very best. So what does that actually mean? It means providing a stimulating place to work, where you feel challenged all day.

compensation and benefit plans at the top end of the range; truly paying for performance, meaning top performers get high-end rewards while low-end performers get zero raises and sometimes have to leave; having corporate learning centers and a company committed to learning; and an environment where people can fulfill their natural human desire to get ahead if they perform. It means focusing more on the 90 percent of the people who come to work everyday wanting to do a good job and go home at night feeling good about what they did, rather than on the 10 percent who don't. And most importantly, being a company where people can be proud of where they work. That means a worldwide focus on integrity, which we accomplish through our code of conduct, a commitment made public on our web site. We commit to obey all laws in all countries and when standards are higher, for example in the United States, on safety or environmental matters, we follow the strictest standard no matter where we are in the world. It means having a foundation. In this case, Honeywell Hometown solutions where we donate $10 million annually to causes like the USO [United Service Organizations], Rebuilding Together, the National Center for Missing and Exploited Children, and NASA-sponsored education programs for children. Supporting employees in the communities where they work through Dollars for Doers, providing $500 grants when they volunteer 50 hours. Allocating nearly 50 percent of our foundation budget to education, supporting 33 American universities and doubling our commitment outside the United States to $500,000 for 27 schools. In India, we are supporting 2,400 students with scholarships, employee mentoring, and, in many cases, the clothes they wear to school.

For our servicemen and women called to duty, we continue to pay their annual salary on top of their government pay. We value the dedication of these men and women and want to support them as best we can. People are critical to success. And it really is ironic that, as important people are, it seldom gets discussed in the analysis of any company.

In our enablers, we have two sets of tools for improving the initiatives just discussed. They are Digital Works and Six Sigma. Digital Works, meaning a focus on information systems to make it easier for people to get their job done and done well. Six Sigma provides quality-oriented tools that ensure products, services, and processes are robust and work the way they're supposed to every time.

You've probably gathered by now that I'm pretty proud of where I work. And while it can seem to be a pretty complicated portfolio of unrelated businesses, by focusing on broad themes and having terrific people, leading an enterprise like Honeywell is made significantly easier.

Let's turn now to the next topic for discussion. That is, what is the role of a business in a well-functioning society? And what needs to be in place for business to function well? There are several important concepts to consider when thinking about the role of business. First is that economics is not a zero-sum gain. Second, the creative destruction, as described by the economist Joseph Schumpeter, is a reality. And third, the importance of trust in the entire system. Economics is not a zero-sum gain. That means that someone else's gain is not my loss. In economics, both sides benefit from a trade. When someone buys something, both the buyer and the seller are enriched. One is not enriched at the expense of the other. One side receives the money. The other gets goods or services they deemed worth paying that money to receive. Both benefit. Now, it sounds simple, but it's extremely important. It's incredible how often people still view economics as zero-sum. One of the critical implications of this concept is that productivity, that ability to do more with less every day, is a good thing. To the extent you can get more output per dollar of input, the nation and the world become richer and more able to provide for an expanding population. It still sounds simple.

Let's bring the issue a little closer to home. Consider a plant in the United States that's closing because operations are being moved to a developing country, say the Czech Republic, for cost savings. If you view economics as zero-sum, you would say the United States lost and the Czech Republic won. If, however, you view it as a mutually beneficial transaction and, assuming the other nation is competing fairly, you would say both nations benefited. The developing country gains jobs and will help to create wealth and the United States gains lower cost goods or services that enhances the buying power of the country's citizens. In addition, the company has more money to invest in R&D [research and development] and other things. The difficulty here lies in that it is easy for anyone to see the job losses because it's focused and visible, while the purchasing power benefit is diffused among the population of an entire nation. And it's tough to see that it's a net gain for the country. It's also why Honeywell, and many other companies for that matter, provide transition benefits for employees in this situation because it's a little more than unreasonable to expect an employee being laid off to ask them to feel good about their job loss directly contributing to the productivity of the country. Nonetheless, it is important to recognize that productivity is a tremendous source of the wealth for nations. Another implication of the concept that economics is not a zero-sum gain is that globalization, again provided companies and countries compete fairly, is a good thing for everyone. All nations win as globalization expands. Countries that impede productivity and impede trade hurt the standard of living of their own citizens. The prosperity of other nations increases our own prosperity and our national security. Economic security directly contributes to national security for all nations involved. Increased trade between nations promotes peace because ties become closer.

The next concept, and you could say it's a corollary to the first one, is the importance of creative destruction. For the world to advance, old technologies and old ways of doing things have to die as new technologies and new ways of doing things come into existence. Buggy whip manufacturers were not excited about the automobile. Retailers felt threatened by the Internet. Typewriters and typesetters are nearly extinct. Staff organizations in every company have been reduced because of information systems advancements. In each case, the old way of doing something declines or disappears. Resources are redeployed. Companies and people adapt. The new way grows and society benefits. The problem with creative destruction is that it's painful for anyone who's involved in the old way. Quality education and lifelong learning for all is essential to facilitate these shifts and provide that needed flexibility. While we may want to smooth some of the rough edges, it is important that, as a country, we support the constant transition that creative destruction generates. An implication of creative destruction is that companies have to be allowed to fail if they don't do well. The specter of liquidated bankruptcy must be real. Risk is an important part of human nature and essential for a thriving economy. It applies to people, companies, and militaries. It causes you to think differently about deployment of resources so you don't waste them, helps to ensure the prize is worth the risk of failure, and causes everyone to adapt faster. But risk is not real if it has no teeth. If people and companies know you always get a second chance.

Another important implication is the importance of free flow of information, of capital, of goods and services; of people, of entrepreneurship; free markets, freedom counts. Just like a business where people need the freedom to make decisions at a local level, it's important for countries to allow freedom as well. In countries where it's difficult to let people go during difficult times, it causes companies to be extremely cautious about adding during good times. The result? Resource redeployment is delayed and so is economic recovery and growth. Bad times happen and can't be avoided. They can be minimized, though, through our ability to react. Being open to the movement of people, for example, immigration in the United States, particularly those with skills, is good for our economy and shouldn't be restricted. In a simple example, the NBA [National Basketball Association] and major league baseball are made significantly better because the world's best players want to come here and we let them. I like sports and I can tell you it's exciting to know that I'm watching the world's best. When it comes to technical talent, we can't have enough. At a time when many would agree we don't graduate enough of our own technical talent, we should be very open to others. Freedom of entrepreneurship means making it easy for people to start companies with the hope that their idea will make them $1 million or in some cases today, even $1 billion. It harnesses, to the benefit of society, human nature's desire to get ahead. It is a powerful catalyst for innovation and hard work. We should want to open up America to the best ideas and people in the entire world. That's a good thing.

Now, for the final concept, the importance of trust in the entire system—trust in our institutions. That means trust in the government, trust in how business is conducted, and trust in the court system. This is why corruption is such a killer of commerce. A few people benefit and the nation suffers. Some might say the Foreign Corrupt Practices Act of 1977 that precluded bribes by American companies operating anywhere in the world was overreaching. In other words, who are we to say what rules an American company must follow in another country? Instead, it's been the absolute right thing to do. There is no doubt

American companies have lost business because they weren't allowed to make payments. So there has been a price for our principle stand. But it's overshadowed by the stand that it sets for all nations. And it's widely understood we won't do it, and as the global leader in business, it was the right thing for the United States to do. Trust in the government also applies when it comes to regulation. Now I'll be the first to agree that some regulation is always needed because unbridled business is as bad as any other unbridled force, whether it's government, military, or even torte lawyers. It's a question of degree and consistency. The balance question discussed in the beginning comes into play here. Too much and you have central control, no freedom in movement, and resulting stagnation; too little or inconsistency in application and you have chaos. There has to be certainty of how things work, how regulation is implemented. Business and people need to know regulation is thoughtful and considered, not arbitrary or capricious. As an aside, all that being said, I can say as a businessman, I felt no shortage of regulation to date. Trust in how business is conducted is important and clearly was damaged in the United States with revelations of corporate scandals over the last couple of years. Unfortunately, there will always be criminals in business, just like we have murderers and muggers. There still needs to be faith, though, that when business people do something criminal, they will be treated like criminals. Trust in the court system is essential, so everyone knows disputes will be handled fairly, peacefully, and reasonably expeditiously. Disputants need to know the system can't be unfairly influenced. There can't be a fear of violence or fear of ridiculous outcomes. This is a big deal.

Let's consider now the third question teed up at the beginning. How are various parts of the world evolving in their ability to support business and productivity as they project this element of national power? We'll start in the Far East and move westward. And please recognize I'm only recognizing my views and undoubtedly oversimplifying to make a point, but hopefully it will be helpful. Japan is still the number two economy in the world but has stopped moving for a decade. They need to acquire the ability to let companies and people fail, to encourage that creative destruction so necessary for advancement. China, clearly a formidable economic force, has made huge strides, particularly in the last 10 years. They are doing a lot of things right. Certainly, we would like to see stronger enforcement of intellectual property protection. That has to get solved to build trust. But with every visit there, I am astounded by the progress since my previous visit. It's easy to predict an onward and upward path that [was] once internalized as China taking over the entire globe. Now, all of us know deep down that that's not the way things work. Something will happen. One consideration is what happens as a true middle class develops? The middle class in any country acquires a power and influence all its own as it becomes more wealthy. This phenomenon will undoubtedly have a profound impact of some kind on China. Although it's tough to predict what it will be, certainly we should be thinking about it. India has all kinds of potential and some incredibly well-educated people, many of whom have fueled technical and economic growth in the United States. At the same time, it has an incredibly stultifying bureaucracy with its attentive regulation that stops progress in its tracks. Interestingly, that is not true for software, back office operations or call taking, where the Indian "cognizantee" would say success came because these areas were new and unregulated, they moved faster than the bureaucracy could catch up to them and then grew at an incredible rate. Clearly there is a lesson here for all of us. In this case, when you give up power, regulation, you get power, innovation, and growth. Much of Africa suffers from a lack of credibility in its institutions and government instability. Anti-corruption drives, peaceful and fair settlement of disputes, freedom of movement, and entrepreneurship all have to be addressed. There's a lot of work to do. Europe is in a fascinating transition. Evolution of the European Union [EU] could take decades, but it is inevitable. City-states [that] become nation-states will someday become a Euro state. Not without considerable "Sturm und Drang," of course. Overall, there is good trust in the system, but the region would benefit from greater freedom of movement, for example the ability to lay off workers during tough times, and from a greater commitment to creative destruction, allowing poorly performing companies to fail. Inclusion of Eastern European countries will benefit the EU overall because of their increased competitiveness. It is important for all of us to pay attention to Euro developments, not just when they make balance of power comments and alarm all of us who think that we should instead be all working together, but also to the daily activities. We've all noticed the impact of EU anti-trust authorities, of course. But Euro activity is becoming pervasive.

A good example is their effort to establish a single sky policy where all Euro flights will be coordinated on a regional basis rather than separately by each nation—a very good idea. In the United States, it's been said that this effort merely allows them to catch up to where we are today because the U.S. already has a single sky. However, given that many would say our air traffic control system is antiquated, with bottlenecks that will become very evident when air traffic returns to previous levels, that seems a naive position. As we all know, Europeans are smart people, too. You have to expect that they would also upgrade their entire system at the same time. They would involve European companies in the process. And they would set the standards. If the United States doesn't engage in the process or doesn't start to upgrade our own system, American companies could very well be left out in the cold, and we would eventually have to adapt to whatever standards are established in Europe. Europe is a big trading partner and all of us need to pay attention to what the European Union is doing and engage them.

Looking at the biggest countries in the Americas, Brazil has to address their cost-prohibitive social system. And Mexico would benefit from a much greater commitment to technical education. In the United States, we have faith generally in the strength of our institutions. Despite the constant concerns and occasional trauma, generally there is trust in the system. Creative destruction works. And I think it's absolutely magnificent that many of the smartest people in the world want to come here with their ideas so they can make $1 million or $1 billion. There is good freedom of movement in all areas.

The biggest concern now is that companies are losing trust in an out-of-control tort system, our court process. No company advocates the abolition of the tort system. We all recognize its importance in a system of checks and balances. However, as we discussed in the beginning, where competing goals have to be balanced, we have gotten way out of whack here. It sucks the life out of companies frequently for unjustifiable reasons. There has to be a better way that allows all people for redress for legitimate issues and grievances while providing a consistency and fairness for all participants in the process. Asbestos is a perfect example. Even the Supreme Court has said the current court system resolving asbestos claims is broken and needs to be resolved legislatively to compensate the sick expeditiously and fairly. We need to restore trust in our court system.

As you probably have already determined, I believe business plays a critical role in the development of living standards around the world. That doesn't mean business should go unbridled. But it does mean government should be the most ardent supporter in creating an environment where business can flourish. A robust economy provides a magnet for the world and generates resources needed to support a strong military and to soften the harsher aspects of economic transitions. It also provides a strong base to project national image and exercise national power. As business prospers, so do people. A prosperous people tend to be stable. Stability contributes to our national security, helps to keep our troops out of harm's way and focuses people on a better world rather than their fears. Business and government need each other, and when working supportively can accomplish objectives that serve everyone. Smart nations support productivity in business. Our company, Honeywell, succeeds because the United States is a strong and vibrant nation. And I want to thank all of you, the United States government, and our military, for establishing and protecting those freedoms that are so necessary for our company to succeed. Thanks for listening.

Thank you. And I believe Janne will be moderating for any questions.

NOLAN: Thank you very, very much for the excellent, excellent presentation. It really kicks off the morning in a great way. Now the lights are way better today, so it will be easier to see those of you who have your hands up. If you, it could please raise your hand, someone with a microphone will come to you. Stand up and identify yourselves.

Over here, we're going to take this question here. And is this someone else? Let's start.

AUDIENCE MEMBER: Thank you, sir. My name is Sarah Trout. And I'm a student at American University. My question was regarding Brazil and where you see our trade relations going with Brazil under its new government since Lula assumed presidency?

COTE: Yeah. I'd have to say I'm cautious—and I can only speak as a businessperson myself, and how I end up viewing the country. Is it one where I'm cautious about putting money in? As somebody who made a big investment when the real was pegged at a $1, one for one, and now it's around $3.50 or $3.96, you understand the pain of the devaluation when you've made that kind of investment. So it tends to make you very cautious. And the social system, I think people know it needs to be changed. It's just the political will needs to be there to make that happen. But you have people retiring in their 40s from government jobs in the system that can't afford to support it. It's an area that I tend to be cautious.

NOLAN: Question?

AUDIENCE MEMBER: Grant Hammond, Air War College. Would you give us a business perspective on concerns about both the half-a-trillion-dollar foreign trade imbalance and half-a-trillion-dollar budget deficit and what that may do to business, not only at home, but more importantly abroad and the entire international community in terms of investment to pay off the interest on that?

COTE: Well, that's a loaded question. First of all, I should say there are people much more qualified than me to answer that one, but I'll certainly give you my perspective on it. From a trade deficit, in general, you know, you'd like to have a better balance there. But at the end of the day, all that's really happened is we got all the goods and services and our money is overseas. One of the things that I'm encouraged to see is that there is discussion about cash repatriation. I'll give you a good example. If I take a look at Honeywell, out of our $3 billion in cash on the balance sheet, a huge chunk of it, in fact, a big majority of it, is outside the United States. It is not here. And one of the reasons is, as we pay dividends, for example, we have to pay them out of U.S. banks. So any cash generated in the U.S. has to get used to pay our dividend, meaning all the cash outside the United States has to stay there. If I try to bring that cash in the United States, I have to pay a tax of about 20 percent. So if I have a $100 in France, when I bring it back here, now I only have $80. I'm not bringing it back. Nobody is. You wouldn't. Right? It makes no sense. So all this tax that everybody thinks is worth something is worth nothing because unless you're absolutely pressed to do it, you don't. And I'm not alone. Now this discussion in Congress about reducing that to something more like 5 percent, which I think would be a nice revenue enhancement and bring more cash back into the U.S. because right now it makes no sense. If I have to borrow here, it is cheaper for me to borrow than to pay the taxes. Silly. When it comes to the budget deficit itself, I have to say maybe it's just my conservative growing up in New Hampshire, but I tend to like to have a balanced budget on anything. By the same token, we've made some huge mistakes in the past as a country when we have been too afraid to spend our way out of a problem. I think there have been times, and I do believe this has been one of them, where it's been a smart thing for us to do. I don't like deficits more than anyone else does, because I do think it ends up creating an issue that you have to address down the road. I do also believe, though, that things will be even worse today if we hadn't done the tax cuts that we had, for example. Having low interest rates and having more money in the hands of consumers who represent two-thirds of the economy has just been extremely important to keeping us going the way we have. Signs are becoming increasingly bullish. You know, if you talk to most bankers, most Wall Street types, they would say economic indicators are looking better than they have in years. I would tell you, though, that it still hasn't quite flowed to the manufacturing or industrial sector. And most of us would say we don't see order rates picking up yet. But certainly, all the signs are there that things are going to become much better.

AUDIENCE MEMBER: Sir, Capt. Mike Jason, U.S. Army. Yesterday, we got a lot of news and briefings and talks on anti-Americanism throughout the world. How have those feelings affected your corporation, both in terms of economic principles, but also maybe practically, such as security for your facilities, buildings, and workers overseas?

COTE: Addressing that last one first. All of us have had to pay a lot more attention to security for everything. We think about things that we never did before and that's true around the world, whether our facilities are in France or Russia or here. We just have to pay more attention to it. In terms of how it's impacted business dealings, not that much, actually. It's been kind of funny that Europeans that you talk with in particular are very careful to point out that they like Americans; they just don't like what we're doing here, which, really kind of talking as an aside here, 20 years ago they were more than ready to tell you they didn't like Americans, too. So it's been, I think, kind of an interesting transition that we've seen over 20 years. This is one that you have to say we're going to work our way through. It's a painful one to work our way through. Sure would be easier if we didn't have this going on. But I have no doubt it will go through. And we still talk with customers the way we always did. I'm more concerned, quite honestly, about the economy in Europe today, with many of the countries having double-digit unemployment rates. And we're not seeing any big signs of improvement yet, that's more of a concern to me. I'd like to see their economies start moving.

AUDIENCE MEMBER: I'm Diana Feraga, with American University. In your talk, you had mentioned that globalization and those countries resisting it today could be stunting their own economic growth. There is a view, however, that globalization can be detrimental for developing countries because they lack stable financial, social, and political institutions that drive corporate and economic growth in the west. That is, in many ways, the western concept of globalization is not suitable to foster business growth in the fragile economies of many of today's developing countries. In addition, there are also concerns that economic globalization is detrimental to a country's heritage and culture, in what is seen as an invasion of American culture as a consequence of globalization. What is your view? And do you see any alternatives to minimize such negative perceptions?

COTE: I think if some of this ends up coming back to, if you don't have good institutions or trust in the institutions of your country in the first place, whether you globalize or don't globalize really isn't even an argument. Because the issue is if your own institutions aren't working, whether you globalize or don't isn't going to help or hurt in my view. You have to have a robust set of foundations or institutions in the first place. Globalization is an irrelevant question, I think, at that point. In terms of does globalization hurt or help? The world has been in flux since the beginning of time. There used to be little tribes and tribes had to learn how to get along together, and cultures meshed and changed as they learned from each other. If you take a look at Europe, they used to start with little towns and city-states and they ended up having to come together. As the world globalizes, you start to see the same thing. I think this is part of the creative destruction that we've always talked about that says you have to be able to work your way through that process. To say we have to stop it now is, I think, a sad attempt, really, at trying to stop the inevitable, trying to stop the tide. It's going to happen. It's the way people are. And as the six billion grows to 10 billion, you're just going to have more and more of that kind of discussion. You should try to preserve heritages. You know, we're all proud of wherever we came from. But to say, that's it, and I don't want to go further, I just don't think that's realistic. It's just not the way the world works, and we create more problems for ourselves than we solve.

NOLAN: Over here. I just want to make sure we get some people back in the balcony back there. If anyone is raising their hands, if there's a question there.

AUDIENCE MEMBER: Good morning, sir. Barbara Wolf with American University. I was wondering, how do you see the enlargement of the European Union affecting the international trade between the United States and the European countries?

COTE: First of all, I'm very much in favor of inclusion of the Eastern European countries in the EU. I think it's one of those things that can help the country become much more competitive as they start to bring in some of these developing countries, and quite honestly, in a lot of these developing countries, a real hunger to get ahead, a real ambition to make a difference. But I think it's good for everybody involved and will improve the mix. I would hope that what doesn't evolve is this idea of trading blocks, where we end up with something that's less interactive and, rather now, two poles as opposed to something that meshes together, which is why I strongly encouraged in my comments the idea that we need to constantly be engaging the EU. There is a difficult transition going on there now—you still run into, so who is in charge? Who makes the decision here? Whether it's the EU or one of the nations. You have to say, over time, though, and seeing the way the EU is operating, that EU presence is going to grow. The more we can engage with them on things, for example, like the air traffic control system, to create something where we create a global standard or at least a hemispheric standard, it's just we're all better off. So I'd like to see a lot more engagement and not let it grow up as a separate entity.

AUDIENCE MEMBER: Robert Berlin. School of Advanced Military Studies, Fort Leavenworth, Kansas. First, thank you for coming and sharing your thoughts with us today. In light of recent events at the New York Stock Exchange, what are your views on executive compensation?

COTE: Now, I don't know if you're aware, but I've taken some shots on that one myself. I've learned that it's an interesting reporting that goes along with compensation. The first thing that it needs to do, and I do believe this has been important—is making sure that everything is public, that there is nothing in there, there's nothing occurring in that institution when it comes to compensation that isn't visible and known to everybody, which was one of the issues with the stock exchange. You could argue it was a quasi-private, quasi-public, quasi-regulatory organization, so how exactly did reporting fit? And those are all legitimate arguments. But at the end of the day, if a lot of that had been public, I don't think it would have ever developed to the state it did. That being said, this is another one that's kind of gone overboard, and because of the difficult times and because of some of the revelations that have come up, it's attracted a lot more attention than was probably warranted—as long as it's fair. And I can tell you that I've been on the receiving end of some of that press and it is difficult to ever refute. Because quite honestly, people would rather read the headline than they would, and be titillated by whatever that says, rather than actually get to the facts. So some of this, you find executives just say, take the beating and move on because nobody wants to hear it.

NOLAN: Thank you. Yes...over here.

AUDIENCE MEMBER: Good morning. Comdr. Robert Burke, United States Navy. A question with regard to the export—I guess more of the export of jobs but more of the capability: As a worldwide business manager, do you see a risk in the continued export of the manufacturing capability worldwide? Not just out of the U.S., but from shifting from countries as it applies to how quickly things can change in the world, not only from a governmental standpoint, but economics. You know, you think you're making a good move by exporting those jobs to save costs, but in the long run—10, 15, 20 years down the road—what is the net gain then? Has it been worth it?

COTE: First of all, I would say generally yes. You can always point to an exception where it hasn't worked out that way. But I would say the world and U.S. would be a less prosperous place today if there wasn't trade between nations. And we didn't have a case, meaning the jobs are some place else producing something that we want. That's what trade ends up being. The idea of jobs moving back and forth to places where it makes the most sense, whether it's manufacturing or services, is not one that bothers me, except to the extent that you might be putting those jobs in a country where there could be a greater risk of instability. And I would tell you that is one that we are concerned about. And we're careful about where we put jobs. So you won't see us generally putting jobs in countries where there is a real instability or that the possibility of success doesn't far outweigh the potential costs. You look at a country like China, which usually comes to mind for everyone. The gains are potentially big, but everybody is scared to death when it comes to intellectual property protection. So you tend not put jobs or businesses in the country where you think there is any kind of risk. You put jobs in, assuming that whatever you're doing will get out. So you're very careful about what you do. But in the end, I just believe that, in general, the world is significantly better off than we would have been if we had never done this. If we had stayed as just an island nation or ocean-separated nation, we just wouldn't be as well off as we are today. And it's painful. And as I tried to say in my comments, everybody can see the plant that moves. And you see that plant and you think that's wrong, something right didn't happen here, somebody took our stuff. And it makes people feel badly. And for those people, we should feel badly. We should help them through that transition. But at the end of the day, the world is better off. Unless you believe economics is a zero-sum game, which I don't. And I think most people who have had a chance to really think about it a lot would say that it's not. You're better off.

AUDIENCE MEMBER: Avon Williams, United States Army. Up here on the balcony. Could you elaborate on your last comments in the context of the erosion of the defense industrial base; specifically, your general attitude toward free trade and free movement of capital among nations has to be qualified in the context of national security when you manufacture high-tech goods that are essential to military programs for our country.

COTE: Yes. I think it absolutely has to. And again, it's like anything else, where there's a balance that you have to maintain on anything. I would say when it comes to trade, there's a lot more we can do. And the recent collapse of the Doha or Cancun talks, I think, is sad and needs to be brought back. It will be better for the developing countries and for developed countries for that to happen. At the same time, we have to be careful about what we do put overseas. And sometimes the standards or strictures can be a little tight as we look at stuff that for us it's tough to see how this can be a compelling military or safeguarded technology. It's tough for us to understand it sometimes. But in general, the system seems to work pretty well. We have to be careful about anything we put overseas. We have to go through the State Department, DOD. The system seems to be able to work. I wish it would be a little easier sometimes, but in general, it works. And I think it's a smart thing for us to do. So I agree with you, that caveat is important.

NOLAN: Is there anyone in the balcony? It's very hard to see from here. Question over here.

AUDIENCE MEMBER: Sir, Jim Rye, U.S. Army. Getting back to some internal Honeywell processes and in particular your discussion about your people. Could you explain a little bit about how you do selection and development of leadership within Honeywell?

COTE: Yeah, actually a magnificent question because it's one of those things we're paying even more attention to than we have in the past. And actually I look to the military for some of the examples because I do believe that when it comes to leadership training, the military has done a better job at this than companies have in a long period of time. If you look at company training, it tends to focus more on how do you reduce cycle times? How do you do market segmentations? As opposed to a lot of important leadership training because as soon as you get your first managerial job, you're spending most of your time trying to get stuff done through other people. It's important to know, how do you motivate them? How do you make sure you have the best? And we're trying to develop a total talent management process that encompasses selection, making sure we have the absolute best, annual performance appraisals, a methodology that most of the military and the government do not get to do, and that's differentiate rewards, which in my view, when it comes to human nature, that's just the way human nature is. If somebody is doing a great job, I kind of go back to when I was an hourly employee. I can remember working on my machine with other people and working at over 100 percent of standard while other people next to me weren't. And I remember one of them saying, "Dave, why are you working so hard? You make as much money as I do." Good question. Good question. Not so bad. You find yourself thinking, "Geesh, he's not that far off." Being able to differentiate rewards, I think, makes a lot of difference. And we put a lot of attention to that. And I will actually look at screens and analyses for the entire company to make sure we are differentiating rewards in every single business and enterprise. We have training programs in place at various levels of the organization. One that we've just started, that I consider very important, is this training for new managers. The thing that we were just talking about. I found that with all the jobs I've had in my career, the most difficult one, transition wise, was when I went from being an individual contributor to having people work for me. Because all of a sudden, you can't just do it yourself and know that you're going to get the kind of product you're looking for. You have to start working through someone else. We're paying a lot more attention to that now. Good university recruiting, trying to get people from everywhere. We also pay a bonus to people who bring other good people from outside the company. So if somebody is opposed to paying recruiters all the time, what we'll do is tell an organization, we need 10 terrific engineers. Anyone who finds a terrific engineer to come in gets a bonus of $2,000. And it's amazing—you tend to find good people [who] tend to know other good people; and they'll bring them in. We have a training center in a corporate learning center in Morristown, New Jersey, that is constantly full, and we're always running people through there. And we'll tend to focus on different things at different times. Over the last couple of years, it's been designed for Six Sigma. Now we're starting to move more into marketing, market segmentation, reducing engineering cycle times, reducing manufacturing cycle times. And that tends to evolve. But the biggest one, and the one that concerns me the most, is being able to get this leadership training. To get people to learn how to work through others, with others, make sure that you have the best team members and that they are motivated as hell to make things happen.

NOLAN: David, thank you so much. I can't imagine a better contribution to start our second day. I think, as President Eisenhower's references to the military industrial complex, you give us a beacon of hope for the true synergy of business and the military, for the best possible outcomes. And thank you very, very much for this very informative and very interesting presentation.

COTE: Thanks, Janne. Thanks for the invitation.

NOLAN: We'll take a break now. The Army is very generous. We'll now take a break for 30 minutes and resume after that. Thank you.

PANEL 3

PREDICTING NUCLEAR PROLIFERATION:
RECENT CASES AND LESSONS

Co-sponsor: Center for International Security and Cooperation, Stanford
University

Moderator: Scott D. Sagan, Ph.D., Co-director, Center for International
Security and Cooperation, Stanford University

George Perkovich, Ph.D., Vice President for Studies, Carnegie
Endowment for International Peace

Polly (Mary) Nayak, Senior Advisor, Abraxas Corporation

Daniel B. Poneman, Principal, The Scowcroft Group

Panel Charter

There is perhaps no more important intelligence challenge for U.S. national security than to have an accurate understanding of the status of ongoing or potential nuclear weapons programs in other countries. Although much attention has focused recently on the accuracy—or lack thereof—of U.S. intelligence estimates concerning Iraqi nuclear weapons programs prior to the 2003 war, far less attention has been paid to the broader "proliferation prediction problem." How well have American intelligence agencies been able to predict the capabilities and intentions of a wider set of potential nuclear proliferators? How has this intelligence been used by policy makers? What can be done to improve intelligence estimates, avoid surprises, and enhance nonproliferation efforts?

The history of U.S. intelligence concerning nuclear proliferation has witnessed major success stories, major failures, and many cases of mixed success and failure. U.S. intelligence agencies accurately predicted the year that China was likely to develop nuclear weapons in 1964 and reportedly penetrated the nascent Taiwanese nuclear program in the 1980s, enhancing the ability of the U.S. government to pressure Taipei to shut it down. The U.S. government, however, was

Left to right: *Scott D. Sagan, George Perkovich, Polly (Mary) Nayak, and David B. Poneman.*

surprised by the first Soviet nuclear test in 1949 and only learned how close Saddam Hussein was to getting nuclear weapons in 1991 when Iraqi defectors, after the war, informed international inspectors about Baghdad's covert underground nuclear materials production facilities.

This panel examines three cases of current nuclear proliferation concern, focusing on how well or how poorly the U.S. government has understood the motives, capabilities, and likely outcomes of foreign governments' nuclear programs. The panel also will examine the reciprocal interaction between intelligence estimates and U.S. government policy making. Over the past decade, the U.S. government has sought to shape and change the nuclear policies of the governments of Iran, India, and North Korea. The ability of Washington to influence other governments' policies is not, of course, solely determined by the accuracy of intelligence about production capabilities and political debates and decisions going on inside foreign capitals. The regional threat environment, the position of friends and allies, international organizations and treaty regimes, domestic and bureaucratic politics in the foreign country, and the strengths of U.S. tools of persuasion and dissuasion will also impact the outcome of future proliferation crises. Still, accurate, tactical and strategic intelligence estimates are likely to be crucial factors determining the success or failure of U.S. nonproliferation and counterproliferation efforts in the decade to come.

Discussion Points

- How should the strengths and weaknesses of U.S. intelligence concerning the nuclear weapons programs and decisions in Iran, India, and North Korea be assessed?
- How have intelligence estimates influenced U.S. government policy toward these governments?
- Have U.S. intelligence estimates been informed sufficiently about likely U.S. policy shifts to take them into account when predicting the behavior of foreign governments?
- What lessons can be learned from comparing these cases to other recent proliferation assessment dilemmas?
- What could be done, if anything, to improve our ability to understand and predict future proliferation and nonproliferation decisions?

Summary

George Perkovich, Ph.D., Vice President for Studies, Carnegie Endowment for International Peace

- Since the 1980s, analysts inside and outside government clearly have provided U.S. leaders with strategic warning that Iran is seeking a nuclear weapons capability. The estimates of when Iran could acquire nuclear weapons, however, have varied, and there seems to be a certain amount of guesswork. In 1992, for example, the CIA estimated that Iran would have a nuclear weapon by 2000; in 1995, the Arms Control and Disarmament Agency's John Holum testified that Iran could have the bomb by 2003. More recent estimates are that Iran could have the bomb by 2005 to 2007.
- The media, Congress, and scholars may criticize the accuracy of details and timing in intelligence estimates, but these really concern tactical intelligence problems. When it comes to nuclear proliferation, however, if one waits for tactical intelligence, it is often too late to do much about the problem. Take, for example, India's nuclear tests in 1998. Afterward, commissions were established to study why the United States failed to anticipate the tests. One may wonder, "So what?" If somebody had gone in to the president, say, on May 9, and said, "Mr. President, in 48 hours India is going to test nuclear weapons," does anybody really think the Indians would have stopped? The focus on a tactical warning often leads to forgetting that the bigger problem was strategic and happened long ago.
- In Iran, the key issue now is whether it is too late to do anything. U.S. leaders have had at least 13 years of warning that Iran has been moving down this path and, thus far, really have not been able to develop policies that would prevent that.
- Intelligence and policy making must focus as intently on the motivation of proliferators as on their capabilities. Some argue that intelligence must focus

on capabilities because intentions are changeable. Yet intelligence agencies' focus on capabilities reflects their biases, not necessarily what is needed for better policy. We focus on the technical means of intelligence gathering because we have great technical assets to do that. We focus on capabilities because we can measure things, take pictures of them, and show them to policy makers as hard facts. Intentions and motivations, however, are subject to interpretation.

• Yet, to enhance nonproliferation, it is crucial to address both the supply side and the demand side of the equation. Do they want nuclear weapons? Who is the "they"? Why do they want them? What could change their minds?

• In the case of Iran, U.S. policy makers and the U.S. intelligence community have not devoted sufficient energy to understanding the motivations behind Iran's intentions to acquire nuclear weapons. What if Iran's need for a nuclear capability were seen within Iran largely as an energy requirement, not a security requirement? Then, could Iran give up this capability if presented with a more attractive energy option? What if some of Iran's top leaders insist they do not want nuclear weapons, that nuclear weapons would violate religious injunctions? If alternative means of protecting Iran's security interests were made available, would that change the whole question about reactions? Answering these questions ought to be in the front of what the intelligence community does.

• Another problem is the Heisenberg uncertainty principle or principle of intelligence. Heisenberg described how experiments actually affect the phenomena that scientists are trying to observe or measure. Like scientists, intelligence analysts also profoundly affect the phenomena they are trying to observe.

• Analysts privately express fear and trepidation about including considerations of U.S. policy as a variable that influences proliferation. There is often a perception of what policy makers want that limits one's capacity to present other interpretations. An example of this in the case of Iran is the whole question of the "Axis of Evil." It is doubtful that the intelligence community vetted the Bush speech that introduced this term because analysts who focus on Iran would have said that use of that phrase was counterproductive. But can you imagine any analyst walking to the White House and saying, "Excuse me, Mr. President and Dr. Rice. I know you like this 'Axis of Evil' phrase a lot, but it will make the Iranians more reluctant to give up nuclear weapons efforts."

• In Iran, the domestic nuclear debate has become more open, and the nuclear issue has become a proxy for the overall political struggle in Iran. This debate is about much more than whether to build a bomb. It is about which form of leadership is needed, which faction is truly nationalistic, which will defend the Islamic character of Iran, and which will protect the country against the "Zionist-American conspiracy."

• The U.S. invasion and occupation of Iraq along with the recent statement and demand by the International Atomic Energy Agency, in which the European Union was firmly tied with the United States, have deeply alarmed Iranian leaders. They do not want to be isolated nor considered pariahs. They are scrambling to figure out how to deal with this situation.

• Iran's fluid political dynamic confronts our analysts and predictors as well as policy makers with a challenge that is analogous to handling nitroglycerin. The United States must shape it without shaping so hard that Iranian nationalists would explode and say, "Yes, we withdraw and you cannot stop us." Pressure works, but it's only part of the strategy. The fact that we do not have a presence in Iran means that we do not have officials who engage with Iranians and come back and have a sense of who is on various sides of the debate.

• Washington needs to create space with inducements for the positive change we seek from Iran. Does the perceived threat of regime change make Iranian decision makers more or less likely to change the behavior we see? Do Iran's denials that it seeks nuclear weapons provide an opportunity, a way to save face?

• What interest do actors in Iran have in foreign trade, investment, and economic engagement? Iran needs tremendous investment in its oil fields. Do the people in Iran who want that investment play in the internal nuclear debate? Finally, if hard-liners in Iran know that the public does not want to be isolated but, rather, wants to improve relations with the American people, doesn't that mean we have to deal with hard-liners if we want to make the breakthrough? Does engagement with the antidemocratic elements in Iran undermine the future of reform as some people here alleged? Or does it actually create space within Iran for reform? These are the important questions that the intelligence community must ask and answer if we are to predict and shape the outcome of Iran's nuclear decisions.

Polly (Mary) Nayak, Senior Advisor, Abraxas Corporation

• On May 11 and May 13, 1998, India tested five nuclear weapons and caught the United States by surprise. Why? What can we learn from this failure?

• The failure was tactical and not strategic. For at least three years before the 1998 tests, discussions in Washington had centered mainly on when—not whether—India would test. Long before 1998, U.S. officials knew that India had the motive, the opportunity, and the means to test its largely indigenous weapons to ward off Pakistan, and to a lesser degree China, and to enhance India's international stature.

• During the 1990s, an added factor emerged. India was angered over the double standard it saw in the policy of the five nuclear powers to keep newcomers out of the club. In 1998, as the nationalistic Bharatiya Janata Party [BJP] moved up in the polls, Washington clearly understood that the BJP would abandon India's policy of nuclear ambiguity if it won the election. What was unclear was whether the BJP simply would declare India to be a nuclear state or whether it would test its nuclear weapons as a deterrent.

• So why were so many people in Washington surprised by the tests in May 1998?

1. First, U.S. policy makers were overconfident in believing they could keep India from crossing that red line to overt nuclear status. The Clinton admin-

istration had succeeded in late 1998 in dissuading the then–prime minister from testing. At that time, the economy seemed decisive, and BJP officials appeared equally concerned about the economy. In addition, in late 1997, the White House had decided to make India the lynchpin of its South Asia policy and to replace its nonproliferation focus, which India hated, with a multifaceted approach. President Clinton planned to visit India in the fall.

2. Second, the Indian government's deception plan was effective. Indian officials assured the United States that they would take no major nuclear steps before they stood up before a national security advisory board, which would then conduct an extensive review. The defense minister reiterated these assurances publicly in late March, soon after the BJP came to power. Diplomats repeated this position in meetings in New Delhi, New York, and Washington. There were also other Indian statements that downplayed the need and immediacy.

3. Indian technical measures aided this deception. In mid-December 1995, the *New York Times* and the *Washington Post* revealed that U.S. intelligence was closely watching Indian preparations to test, perhaps soon. Specifically, they noted that instrumentation at the test site pointed to test preparations and not maintenance. U.S. Ambassador Frank Wisner decided at this time to show photos of the test sites to senior Indian officials to convince them not to test. His sharing of that information widely has been blamed for teaching the Indians to bury their cabling in order to avoid detection. Actually, the same information was contained in the newspaper articles.

4. Third, there was insufficient priority within the U.S. government for intelligence collection on India. There was competition with other imagery targets. Iraq and the Balkans were given higher priority. In addition, deficient satellite imagery and photo interpretation were caused by budget-driven reductions of analysts and a reduced numbers of satellites.

• Was this an important intelligence failure? Yes, it was in a number of respects. Primarily, preventing the tests was important to U.S. policy because the tests ultimately torpedoed the efforts to stop the spread of nuclear weapons. Would the United States have done anything differently if there had been clear, tactical warnings? Probably, for the president would have brought almost the entire weight of U.S. pressure to bear on New Delhi. Without the final tactical warning, no diplomatic effort was started.

• Would such pressure have stopped the test? Perhaps, but the reasons would have been domestic in nature and not related to Indian foreign policy. U.S. concerns and pressure might have brought the test decision before some of the BJP's 14 coalition partners, and a long debate among 14 parties could have been a showstopper. This may explain why the New Delhi government went to such lengths to conceal the tests from the United States—to have its test decision free from getting tangled in India's domestic system and open to debate by other Indian parties.

• What are the lessons? It is clear that forecasting single events is very difficult. It is hard to determine when a lack of information signifies that nothing is happening and when it points to denial and deception. In this case, there was insufficient information to determine whether denial and deception was at play, and there also was no tie-breaking information to help decide when the Indian tests might occur.

- There always will be a tension between the perceived need to pressure a government and the need to keep secret the information that provided the tactical intelligence that such pressure is needed. In this case, it is clear that Indian denial and deception was influenced by earlier newspaper and diplomatic disclosures. Yet it sometimes may be necessary to present intelligence to convince an opponent that one really has the goods and is serious about preventing proliferation. But success in this effort may increase the risk of serious failures in the future.

Daniel B. Poneman, Principal, The Scowcroft Group

- North Korea is a notoriously difficult intelligence target. It is perhaps the most insular society in the world. It is a Stalinist police state, and its very backwardness and lack of economic development deprive us of many sources such as computer connections, telephone lines, and people traveling. But, ironically, while intelligence on North Korea is very, very hard to get, prediction about its behavior is less difficult. Why? North Korea, notwithstanding the popular rhetoric, is not a crazy state with crazy leaders. Indeed, the DPRK (Democratic People's Republic of Korea) leadership tends to be extraordinarily shrewd and calculating. They deal pretty well with a deuce-high hand.

- To say that North Koreans cannot "eat the bomb" and therefore must go in a direction we would favor really misses the point. The people making these decisions do not care about issues of feeding their people; they care about maintaining the security and viability of their own political control of their system. The ultimate goal is regime preservation.

- North Korean leaders view the best defense as a strong offense. History is replete with examples of how, when they feel completely cornered, they will lash out. They try to kick over the card table and hope the cards fall in a more favorable position. This falls into a fairly predictable pattern with a regular overplaying of their hand. For example, during the spring of 1994, unification talks were about to lead to a potential summit between then-leader Kim Il Sung and the South Korean president but broke up when the North Korean delegate threatened to engulf Seoul in a sea of fire. This led to a more coherent U.S.–South Korean strategy, which led to the framework that bottled up the North Korean plutonium program. Similarly, it appears that the series of provocative actions that the North Koreans started last December—breaking the seals on their nuclear facilities and turning off the cameras—was overplaying their hand and induced a level of Chinese involvement that has been very helpful to the United States and unwanted by the North Koreans.

• The United States should be careful not to overinterpret and attempt to conclude from this record what North Korea's ultimate objective is. The DPRK may want a weapon or it may not have decided yet. North Korea may have decided, and it may change its mind.

• We are all familiar with the self-reliance theory of the North Koreans. There is also a very keen sensitivity to save face, something that we ignore at our peril. We always need to leave them an escape hatch. If we want them to do something, we need to provide an avenue for them to do it in a way that they do not consider disgraceful. The most interesting manifestation of this strange combination that is so characteristic of the North Koreans is one of the first things that a senior analyst told me when I entered the government. The North Koreans do not respond to pressure, but without pressure, they do not respond. For example, when the Chinese suspend oil deliveries, they do so in a quiet way, and the DPRK responds.

• Unfortunately, the intelligence historical record for North Korea is not very good. Intelligence on October 12, 1950, stated that while full-scale Chinese intervention was to be regarded as a possibility barring a global war, such action was not probable. We all know what happened after that. The Chinese came pouring across the river.

• Similarly, in 1993 and 1994, it was assessed that there was a better-than-even chance that North Korea had one to two nuclear weapons. This is what one colleague calls an assessment with precision but not accuracy. It imputed a level of understanding that did not disclose the huge gaps in our understanding. We knew very little. Essentially, we knew that North Korea, if it had completed the plutonium reprocessing efforts on the spent fuel that we were aware existed, could have produced one to two nuclear weapons. What the DPRK had actually done was much less clear.

• There is a need to react more quickly to early strategic warnings. In 1985, North Korea was building a large research reactor that, in fact, is the source of the plutonium about which we now worry. At that time, there was pressure on North Korea to join the Treaty on the Nonproliferation of Nuclear Weapons (NPT), but no vigorous action was taken. Thus, by the time North Korea came onto the world stage with the completion of its plutonium reprocessing facility, all of our easy and cheap options were gone. We should have been much tougher in the mid-1980s. Although the NPT requires North Korea to negotiate a safeguards agreement with the International Atomic Energy Agency (IAEA) within 18 months, after 17 months North Korea said, "You sent us the wrong form." The IAEA then told North Korea it could take yet another 18 months. Another 18 months passed, and there was still no agreement. There was no penalty for such behavior, which was a big mistake.

• What are the lessons? First, if there is anything we could do now to improve the situation, it would be to get some of the safeguards back in so we could reassess and resecure that plutonium. Second, our intelligence collection should

be done with the most diverse sources possible, such as using unclassified literature, engaging North Korean diplomats wherever we can, and using third-party
countries. Finally, we need to have a wide range of analytical possibilities, not to
bury in footnotes, but to allow each analyst, within his or her organization and
outside the U.S. government, to have a fair chance at expressing his or her views.
Once that is done, let the policy makers decide. It is important to get this right
because the consequences of getting it wrong in North Korea could be catastrophic.

Scott D. Sagan, Ph.D., Co-director, Center for International Security and Cooperation, Stanford University

• Tactical warning that a government has decided to develop or test nuclear
weapons immediately is not only very difficult to get, but, once such decisions are
made, only highly unattractive options to stop such nuclear programs may be
available to the U.S. government. Strategic warning about a government's potential interest in getting nuclear weapons is therefore crucial. Yet it may also be
harder to get U.S. domestic agreement or international agreement on appropriate
next steps, based only on what is inevitably more ambiguous strategic warning
about potential nuclear weapons programs in the future.

• We should expect more from our intelligence officials and analysts in terms
of understanding our own behavior and how that behavior influences others.
This is partly a problem of intelligence officers and their focus on other countries.
Intelligence officers therefore need to learn more about their own country, not
just the countries they are professionally assigned to observe. There is also a problem of excessive compartmentalization: The intelligence shop does not talk enough
to the policy shop. But this is also a problem of political correctness and courage.
It is difficult—and sometimes dangerous—for intelligence officers to say things
to policy makers that they believe the policy makers may not want to hear. Professional responsibility sometimes requires a willingness to take such risks. That, in
turn, requires that policy makers have more willingness to listen, engage, and
actually encourage dissenting opinions. Ultimately, this is in everyone's best interest, since the U.S. government needs to avoid group thinking and blind spots that
may lead to intelligence and policy failures.

• Cases like Iran, India, and North Korea point to the importance of understanding the domestic politics inside potential proliferant countries. Domestic
disputes are muted, of course, in nondemocratic countries, but that does not
mean that conflicts of interest or differences of opinion on proliferation choices
do not exist. U.S. intelligence must not solely focus on technical capabilities, but
also should take into account political motives for proliferation, asking which
actors want nuclear weapons, which do not and, in each case, why.

• It is important not just to focus on other states' nuclear behavior, but on our
own as well. Under Article VI of the Nuclear Nonproliferation Treaty, the nuclear
weapons states agreed to work in good faith toward eventual elimination of nuclear
weapons. During the 1995 NPT negotiations, the United States specifically promised

that if nonnuclear states accepted a permanent extension of the treaty, the nuclear states would sign and ratify the Comprehensive Test Ban Treaty (CTBT) as a signal that we and they would work toward eventual elimination. We have not done that.

Reasonable people can disagree about the importance of Article VI, but what we do with respect to that part of the NPT is going to influence the domestic debate within proliferant countries. If the United States tests nuclear weapons again, it will open up many opportunities for hard-liners in potential proliferators to say that they need not follow the NPT since Washington has not followed it fully either.

• The intelligence officer and policy maker should never say that there is nothing we should do about a problem, therefore, we can stop discussing it. One may call this the "Columbia accident principle" because that is what happened during the Columbia space shuttle accident. A piece of foam hit the shuttle and the senior policy maker said there was not much anyone could do about it if that foam had caused a hole. Of course we now know they could have gotten satellite photographs, or told the shuttle crew to go outside and take photographs themselves, or they could have sent up another shuttle on a rescue mission.

All those creative potential solutions were thought about in the after action report, not in the situation room. One hopes in the next nuclear crisis, when we think there is not much we can do about this nuclear program now, the creative potential solutions are thought about then, rather than in the after action report about the major mistakes that we made.

Analysis

Two key themes emerged from the presentations and discussion in this panel: one, the challenge of intelligence "getting it right" on matters of proliferation; the other, the motivations of countries seeking to acquire nuclear weapons.

Panelists made several excellent points about the challenges confronting the intelligence community in its efforts to monitor, discover, and predict efforts by states to go nuclear.

Intelligence failures can also be policy failures. Although policy makers may not purposefully and explicitly set out to influence or politicize the processes of intelligence collection and intelligence analysis, they inevitably shape and influence both processes in ways that can skew or even sabotage the results. Intelligence collectors, for example, have limited resources and must make difficult choices about where and how they use these assets. Policy makers set priorities and hence make the choices about what is most important and what is not. In the case of the May 1998 Indian nuclear tests, policy makers in Washington were convinced that India was not going to test and hence had not directed the intelligence community to look for indications that such an event might be in the offing.

Intelligence failures in the proliferation field have tended to be tactical rather than strategic. We do discover which countries have nuclear programs and which of these are close to the testing stage. However, we are not as good at detecting or predicting exactly when a state will test. This also is likely to be true in the cases of Iran and North Korea.

Countries can be very good at deception and denial. India was very skillful in shielding preparations for its May 1998 tests from U.S. satellites and thoroughly convincing U.S. officials that it was not going to test anytime soon. There is every reason to believe that other states such as Iran and North Korea are similarly adept at deception and denial.

The consensus of the panelists was that the United States needs to focus greater attention on understanding the intentions of states seeking nuclear weapons than we do at present. Most panelists believed that the United States pays much more attention to discovering and tracking the capabilities being developed by a particular country than on identifying the motivations that are driving that country's effort.

Accurately discerning a country's motives is vital if the United States hopes to dissuade it from acquiring nuclear weapons. However, identifying motives is even more difficult than detecting capabilities and the progress of programs. The U.S. intelligence community is generally skillful at identifying enemy capabilities, but it has proved much less capable of discerning enemy intentions.

To discern motives, we must use a wide variety of intelligence options especially human intelligence. Relying on satellite and other high-tech means is simply inadequate or unsuitable for detecting motives. A U.S. diplomatic presence on the ground in capitals such as Tehran and Pyongyang can be extremely valuable. Other sources such as third-party countries can be very useful too. Careful analysis of official statements and pronouncements by prospective nuclear states can be very valuable. If used judiciously, these statements can provide significant insights about changes, continuity, and the evolution of a regime's strategic thinking over time.

States probably develop nuclear weapons for multiple reasons. Two of the most important motives are prestige and psychological security. Acquiring nuclear weapons is seen as an important means of attaining great power status. Moreover, possession is considered to give states a key deterrent in the face of perceived serious external threats.

The United States must recognize that what it says and does influences target countries and not always in ways that are desirable or in ways the United States intended. Profering both carrots and sticks is important in providing states with appropriate incentives. Identifying regimes as "rogues" or part of an "axis of evil" may be counterproductive by unnecessarily antagonizing or heightening the paranoia of a regime.

We should be aware of the lessons nuclear-aspirant states such as Iran and North Korea have drawn from various proliferation successes and failures. How have states such as Brazil and South Africa benefited from decisions to abandon their nuclear programs? Have India and Pakistan, on balance, suffered or benefited from acquiring nuclear weapons? What is the lesson of Operation Iraqi Freedom? Would Saddam still be in power today if he had demonstrated beyond a doubt that Iraq either did or did not possess nuclear weapons?

The preceding analysis suggests that it is very difficult to dissuade states with multiple motivations from developing nuclear weapons. This is especially true if the state believes its security is gravely at risk—that is, it perceives a direct, serious, external and proximate threat. If this logic is correct, then it may be quite possible for Iran to be dissuaded from going nuclear, but nearly impossible for North Korea to be put off.

Transcript

JANNE E. NOLAN, Ph.D.: Good morning. Hello to all of you returning and those of you who have just arrived.

This will be our first panel discussion of our second day of the Eisenhower National Security Studies Series. This is a particularly timely topic and, I think, potentially quite controversial subject. This subject of how we parse intelligence and use all of our information resources to predict a very unpredictable future. With a specific focus on nuclear proliferation, proliferation in general, you couldn't have a better group of people to address this topic, and most particularly, Scott Sagan, who is the director of the Center for International Security and Cooperation at Stanford University, known as CISAC.

CISAC is a pioneering institution that goes back, actually, in a variety of forms to the 1970s, whose main and most noted feature, in my mind, is its ability to draw on the vast resources of the many disciplines represented at Stanford and in Silicon Valley to put together groups of experts and very smart people to solve problems. This has always been a difficult thing for academic institutions to do. It is actually interesting that it's an innovation to have synergistic, multidisciplinary groups of people working to solve problems in an academic setting. Scott Sagan has been at the forefront of creating these kinds of groups, looking at issues to do with proliferation, looking at issues of bioterrorism, and in each case bringing together scientists, people from the law, people from ethics, various regional experts, and others to take on the very severe challenges that our country faces in our security. Scott Sagan himself is a gifted teacher. I have heard him lecture to both graduates and undergraduates. I think teaching undergraduates is probably the hardest thing you can do, except for second graders. He is an extremely well-liked and respected professor. He is a prolific author. He is even a championship Little League coach. I should just note that he is very much a renaissance man. And I will now stop gushing. And one of the reasons I am gushing is because I was lucky enough to have a fellowship at CISAC way back then. And it is one of the, I think, really foremost research places in this country.

So please join me in welcoming Scott Sagan. Thank you.

SCOTT D. SAGAN, Ph.D.: Well, thank you very much, Janne, for that kind and indeed, even mildly embarrassing introduction. It was so kind.

Scott D. Sagan

How well do American intelligence agencies and senior policy makers understand the status of current and of potential nuclear weapons programs in other states? As the video that began this panel noted, there is no more important and daunting question for our national security than that one. For the nuclear programs in other states will strongly influence the regional balances of power, the prospects for peace, and the risks of war. Those nuclear programs in the future will influence the likelihood of U.S. military intervention in those regions, the contours of combat operations, and the consequences of conflict, if it does occur. Future nuclear weapons programs, new proliferators will strongly impact the likelihood of what happens afterwards in the region. How will other states react to new nuclear powers emerging in their region? Will they, too, move forward with their nuclear programs? Or will they be restrained? Finally, the status and details of nuclear weapons programs in other countries will shape the probabilities that terrorists, through either sales or theft of nuclear materials or nuclear weapons, will someday be nuclear terrorist groups.

This panel today will address a profound and difficult set of proliferation prediction puzzles. First, how well have U.S. agencies been able to predict and understand the behavior of potential nuclear weapons states? Have we understood their capabilities and the trajectory of their technologies? How well have we understood their intentions? And because, in many states, there are debates, indeed, deep struggles and bureaucratic fights about what they should do, how well have you understood whose intentions matter? Which actors and which states really are the most powerful and will get their way? And which ones will not? Second, how well or poorly have U.S. policy makers used their intelligence inputs in this arena? Policy makers often publicly complain about the quality of the intelligence they are given. But intelligence officers often privately complain about how often the policy makers use or misuse the inputs that they are given. As one intelligence officer put it, if you read the newspapers, you would think that there are never policy failures, there are only intelligence failures. And yet, looking back and looking forward, we obviously have to look at both successes and failures, both on the input, the intelligence side, and equally important, successes and failures on the policy-making side. Third, what are the major factors that have determined the accuracy of our proliferation predictions? This is an interactive process. How well have states of concern masked their intentions and their capabilities? How well or how poorly have we perceived or misperceived what they are doing? That is, how often have we been fooled by others? And how often have we simply fooled ourselves?

We have three very distinguished and thought-provoking panelists today. Their biographies are in your programs, and so I will be exceedingly brief. The first speaker will be George Perkovich, vice president of the Carnegie Endowment, the author of what I consider the single best study of the Indian nuclear weapons program, who has now been focusing on Iran and U.S. understandings of their weapons

George Perkovich

program. He'll be speaking first. Polly Nayak will be speaking second. A long-time CIA official, she will lower our focus into a very specific case study of intelligence success or failure in understanding the May 1998 Indian nuclear weapons test. Is our failure to predict that an intelligence failure? A policy failure? Neither? Or both? Finally, Daniel Poneman, who served on the National Security Council from '93–'96 and is now a senior fellow for the Forum of International Policy, will speak about the North Korean nuclear weapons puzzle. How well did we understand the DPRK's behavior when we had our last crisis with them? How well do we understand their behavior, intentions, and capabilities today? And how well will we do tomorrow? Without further ado, I'll turn it directly over to George Perkovich.

GEORGE PERKOVICH, Ph.D.: Thanks, Scott. Good morning. I have the pleasure—feels like a pleasure—of being able to talk about Iran. But there's an obvious liability in it. Which is that between the time we entered this room after the break and when we leave, there could be two major changes in the Iranian proliferation problem. So consider this a snapshot.

The first point I want to make in keeping with the theme as Scott described today about predicting proliferation is that U.S. analysts in and out of government have clearly provided the Republic with strategic warning that Iran is seeking nuclear weapons capability. Since at least the 1980s, warnings have been sounded that Iran is moving forward in this quest. Now, the estimates of when Iran would or could acquire nuclear weapons have varied and there seems to be a certain amount of guesswork. But the warning is there. So in 1992, for example, the CIA estimated that Iran would have a nuclear weapon by 2000. In 1995, the Arms Control and Disarmament Agency director, John Holum, testified that Iran could have the bomb by 2003. In '97, Holum testified that Iran could have the bomb by 2005 to 2007. And this is a two- to four-year lag on the prior estimate, but the warnings are always there. Now the media, and especially the Congress and also people like me in think tanks, may criticize the accuracy of intelligence estimates, but the most important thing is whether we have been provided long-term warning of a particular proliferation threat. And in the case of Iran, we clearly have. By focusing on the time estimates and the precision, what we're really saying, what outside critics, especially, are really saying is that there is a tactical problem. What we need is tactical intelligence. But I would submit that when it comes to proliferation, if you wait for tactical intelligence, it's too late. By the time you get tactical intelligence, unless you're talking now about informing a very precise military operation to take out a certain capability, it's too late. And the great example of that was the Indian nuclear tests in 1998 that Polly is going to talk about. And I'll be brief. But there was a big uproar in those tests. Congressional leaders were in high dudgeon and commissions were established and everything else. Because we missed that it was going to happen on the morning of May 11. And having worked on this, I always wonder, well, so what? If somebody had gone into the president, let's say on May 9, and said, "Mr. President, in 48 hours, India is going to test nuclear weapons." Does anybody here think the Indians would have stopped? So the focus again on intelligence failure if its a tactical warning, I think, often leads us to chase the issue without recognizing the bigger problem was strategic and happened long ago. Now in Iran, it may not be too late. But it's also true that Democrats and Republicans alike in succeeding administrations have had at least 13 years of warning that Iran was moving down this path and thus far haven't really been able to develop policies that would prevent that.

This leads to the second big point that I want to make, which is that intelligence and policy making must focus at least as intently on the motivations of proliferators as on their capabilities. Now, to be sure, intentions are changeable, and so, therefore, the famous argument that intelligence and policy making must focus on capabilities. Yet our focus on capabilities reflects certain of our own characteristics and capabilities, not necessarily what it is that we need. So, for example, we focus on technical means of intelligence gathering because we have great assets to do that. We can try to pick out what the other guy's technical capabilities are. That bias is in many ways the system that you play to your strength and ignore what is your weakness. Another thing that drives us to focus on capabilities is that with capabilities that discussion is an empirical discussion. You can try to measure things, you can take pictures of them, you can show them to policy makers as hard facts. Whereas if you're dealing with intentions and motivations, they're rather subjective, they're political, they're interpretive. And the presenter of that kind of analysis then is subject potentially to criticism that you wouldn't be if you're presenting hard facts because the facts speak for themselves.

And I think the third reason that we focus on capabilities is that our policy focuses on supply denial. So you take a picture, you get an intercept of capability, and the policy is to try to stop people from shipping that capability. Or to impose sanctions on the people who ship the capability that you know about because you intercepted the communication.

And yet, just as important as supply side assessments and policy, the demand side of proliferation is key. Do they want nuclear weapons? Who is the "they"? Why do they want them? What could change their minds? In the case of Iran—at least as far as public sources go and for the last number of years—there is real doubt that U.S. policy makers, and to some extent the intelligence community, have devoted considerable energy to understanding the perceptions and motivating factors behind Iran's intention to acquire nuclear weapons. Now, I can presume only in terms of the classified domain, there is a lot of assessment of these motivations, but you don't see it come out, for example, in any of the congressional discussion, where a lot of this debate takes place, or in any of the kind of open-policy discussions that get reported in the press. One of the closest things you get to that kind of assessment of motivations was the Director of Central Intelligence's statement on February 11 of this year where he said, "No Iranian government, regardless of its ideological leanings, is likely to willingly abandon WMD programs that are seen as guaranteeing Iran's security." Now, this actually was a controversial statement because it suggested that even if you had regime change in Iran, you may get the same drive for proliferation. But even that statement, which is rather rare of its kind, deserves a lot of unpacking. And I think this is an intelligence and assessment challenge. What if Iran's need for nuclear capability were seen within Iran largely as an energy requirement, not a security requirement? Then, could Iran give up this capability if presented with a more attractive energy option? What if Iran's top leaders insist they do not want nuclear weapons, that nuclear weapons would violate religious injunctions, and that the capability is sought for energy purposes to protect against U.S.-led technology embargos? Would that change the whole question about whether this is seen as guaranteeing security and therefore you could affect it? What if alternative means of protecting Iran's security interests were potentially available? Would an Iranian government then be unwilling to do without nuclear weapons? In other words, how should U.S. policy makers shape Iranian perception that these weapons would be in their security interest or not? Seems to me this is a big challenge and ought to be in the front of what the intelligence community does, to kind of unpack the seemingly self-explanatory statement by the director.

Now, one of the problems historically and today, in Iran especially, is that we do shy away from dealing with questions of motivations. And I think there are reasons for that that are fairly obvious. Iran has been a politically too-hot-to-handle topic since the revolution in 1979. Jimmy Carter lost his presidency, in many ways, over the hostage crisis. Remember Ollie North and the cake? There's a parody in American political culture of officials in search of the everlasting Iranian moderate. All of this kind of dynamic in the political culture makes people very reluctant to try to get into the motivations and perceptions and dynamics within Iran. As one former special envoy to Iran put it to me, there is no Iran in our Iran policy. Our policy debate, the analysis about intentions and perceptions, is more about us than it is about what's really going on in Iran. And this tendency is all the worse because we don't have a presence in Iran. Now, there are reasons for that that have nothing to do with the United States, that have to do with Iran. But whatever the reasons, the fact that we don't have a presence there means that we don't have officials, whether the intelligence community or policy makers or Congress or otherwise, who engage with Iranians and come back and have a sense of flavor for what the dynamic is within the country, that there is a debate, who's on various sides of the debate. That kind of texture is missing and is a real liability for policy making and for intelligence gathering.

The third large point I want to make now is what I call the Heisenberg principle of intelligence. Now Heisenberg's uncertainty principle described that the experimenter actually affects the phenomena he's trying to observe or measure. In this case, the U.S., as an observer, as an intelligence analyst, also is an actor that profoundly affects the phenomena we're trying to observe. In recent years, the parameters of U.S. intelligence analysis have been broadened to allow some consideration of the U.S. as an independent variable that shapes the phenomenon being analyzed. Yet analysts privately express trepidation about doing that. This is even before the controversy over the WMD assessments in Iraq. The whole question about whether intelligence has been politicized or whether there's a certain perception of what people want in the policy community and how that limits your capacity to present other interpretations. An example of this would be having to do with Iran and the whole question of the axis of evil and of enshrining Iran in the term, in the club of the axis of evil, in the State of the Union address. I doubt that that was vetted by the intelligence community because, if it had been, I think analysts who focused on Iran would have said that the use of that phrase was actually very counterproductive in terms of affecting Iranian behavior the way we want to. But the problem is, can you imagine any intelligence analyst walking into the White House and saying, "Excuse me, Mr. President, Dr. Rice. I know you like this 'axis of evil' phrase a lot, but it will drive the Iranians nuts and may make them more resistant to the policies that we want." It's very hard to imagine that, and yet it's precisely that kind of question and formulation that's very important in shaping Iranian behavior. As the former finance minister of Iran put it in *Foreign Affairs*, many Iranians took the axis of evil phrase as a "deep insult to their national dignity." Any U.S. strategy that even remotely raises the specter of foreign interference in Iran is doomed to fail.

What we've seen in the past week in Iran has been lots of debate coming out more openly than before over the nuclear issue, but what's very apparent is the nuclear issue has now become a proxy for the overall political struggle in Iran. So it's about much more than whether to build a bomb. It's about whether, which form of leadership, which faction is truly nationalistic, truly will defend the Islamic character of Iran, truly will protect the revolution, truly will protect the country against the Zionist-American conspiracy. All of this is now being tied into the nuclear debate as a proxy.

Having said that, the administration has created some conditions that clearly are favorable to resolving the nuclear issue. And again, this is kind of the experiment of the analyst, the object that's doing the studying is affecting the behavior. The U.S. invasion and occupation of Iraq has alarmed Iranian leaders in potentially helpful ways. Moreover, the recent statement and demand by the IAEA, in which the European Union was firmly tied with the U.S., has deeply alarmed Iranian leaders. I mean, this was a profound shock to their system. They do not want to be isolated. They do not want to be pariahs. And they're scrambling now to figure out how to deal with this problem and avoid isolation. So Iran's fluid political dynamic confronts both our analysts and predictors, as well as policy makers, with a challenge that I'd say is analogous to handling nitroglycerin. The U.S. must squeeze Iran and its suppliers enough to block Iran's acquisition of nuclear weapons capabilities, without shaking so hard that Iranian nationalists explode and say essentially, "Yes, we withdraw from the NPT and you cannot stop us."

Pressure works, but it's only part of the strategy. You also need to create space with inducements for positive change in what we seek from Iran. So it seems to me that the big intelligence questions, the important questions, that have to be asked are the following: Does the perceived threat of regime change make Iranian decision makers more or less likely to change the behavior we see? Do Iran's denials that it seeks nuclear weapons provide an opportunity, a way, to save face? Or, should we somehow be trying to get them to admit they are liars? What do other cases of nonproliferation suggest about what we should do in Iran? I'm thinking of South Africa, Brazil, and North Korea as prime examples. Will Iran's calculations of security requirements be affected by the future security arrangements that may be coming in the Persian Gulf? How will various possibilities of U.S. military basing and presence in the region affect Iranian interests in having or not having nuclear weapons? What are the new rules in the region going to be? Who are the actors that are going to be there? What's the future of the Iraqi nuclear capability and intention toward Iran going to be? These are things that, if you're an Iranian, you have to figure out if you're trying to figure out how to deal with the pressure now on your nuclear weapons capability. And these are not things that, as far as I know, have been discussed, said, publicly at all in the U.S., whether on the Hill or elsewhere.

If regional dialogue is a good idea concerning North Korea, and I think it is, wouldn't a regional dialogue process in the Persian Gulf make sense too—to bring in Iran's neighbors who Iran is trying to woo into a better relationship? Get them into a room and say, "Hey look, we're concerned about what you're doing with your nuclear capability." And show it's not just the U.S., but people they care about are going to react in ways they may not like if Iran goes forward. How does Israel's possession of nuclear weapons affect the politics, if not the strategy, of Iran's decision to give up nuclear capabilities, as we and Israel demand? What interest do Iran's various business communities have in foreign trade, investment, and economic engagement? And how might these business interests and their political coalitions affect nuclear decision making? Just this past week, Japan had been given the lead option on a $2 billion development project of an Iranian oil field. Japan then joined tightly with the U.S. at the IAEA to issue a demand that Iran stop its enrichment work. Iran announced this week that they were denying now Japan's place as an opportunity to bid in this field. Well, Iran needs tremendous foreign investment in its oil fields. Do the people in Iran who want that investment—can they be made to play in the internal debate in Iranian politics? And how? That's a very important question.

Finally, if hard-liners in Iran know that the Iranian public wants not to be isolated and wants to improve relations with the American people, won't hard-liners keep anyone else in Iran from getting credit for that kind of breakthrough? And doesn't that mean that we need to deal with hard-liners if we want to make the breakthrough because they have the veto position otherwise? And then that leads to a further question, does engagement with the anti-democratic elements in Iran actually undermine the future of reform, as some people here allege? Or does it actually create space for reformers within Iran, for them too to engage with the U.S. because now the hard-liners have shown that it's okay to do that? If regime change is a good idea in Iran—and clearly the Iranian people think it is, they've voted for it, they've tried to do it through the ballot box for the last six years—can and should the U.S. play a role in bringing it about? Or will a U.S. role only distort the process negatively? These are the important questions in my view that we must ask and answer if we are to predict and shape the outcome of Iran's decisions, whether to acquire nuclear weapons or not.

. Thank you.

SAGAN: Thank you, George. Polly?

POLLY (MARY) NAYAK: Good morning.

On May 11 and May 13, 1998, India tested five nuclear weapons. The tests caught the Clinton administration by surprise and led to lengthy debate about the shortcomings of U.S. intelligence. What I'd like to do this morning is to parse that set of tests, what the failure looked like, and then pull out some implications for the future of intelligence. I want to draw your attention up front to two angles. One is the difficulty of single event tactical forecasting, especially on a friendly nation. And the second is to an aspect of U.S. policy intelligence interface that we rarely discuss. We often talk about how intelligence informs policy, but rarely about how policy shapes intelligence. And in fact, policy makers set the terms for collection and the standards of evidence for finished intelligence. I'll come back to that point shortly.

So to what extent were the tests a surprise to the U.S. government and why? The answer, I think, varied depending on the part of the government, but, wherever we're talking about, the failure was tactical and not strategic. For at least three years before the 1998 tests, discussions in Washington had centered mainly on when, not whether, India would test. And long before 1998, U.S. officials knew that India had the motive, the opportunity, and the means to test its largely indigenous weapons to warn off Pakistan and, to a lesser degree, China and to show India's international

Polly Nayak

stature. In the 1990s, an added factor emerged. India peaked over the double nuclear standard, the effort by the five nuclear powers to keep newcomers out of the club. In early 1998, as the nationalistic BJP moved up in the polls, U.S. observers focused closely on how the BJP might shape India's nuclear decisions if it won the election in March. Washington clearly understood that the BJP would abandon India's policy of nuclear ambiguity. What was unclear was what it meant by declaring India a nuclear state. There really were two ways it could do this. One was simply by declaring itself a nuclear state with a small number of untested weapons, the weapons of untested design. And the second way would have been to test its nuclear weapons as a deterrent. The BJP did come to power in March, on March 19, not alone as it had hoped, but as the anchor of a very disparate coalition, with 14 other parties. And in fact, the Prime Minister Vajpayee had won their reluctant support by moderating his position on a number of issues. Nevertheless, in late March, Vajpayee publicly stated again that the BJP would exercise all options, including the nuclear option, to protect India's sovereignty and territory. And in April, the army chief of staff urged the government to develop a strategic deterrence capability, which most people understood to mean a nuclear stockpile.

So why were so many people in Washington surprised, apparently, by the tests in 1998? I think the answers lie in three different areas: first, the policy context, including the convictions of U.S. policy makers in '98; second, Indian diplomacy, which successfully misled U.S. officials and played on U.S. uncertainty in the face of very limited information; and third, an incomplete intelligence picture, in which intermittent information was buried in a great deal of noise.

First, the U.S. policy context. For years, successive U.S. administrations have worried that India would break the global taboo on testing, shred international accords, and maybe set off a chain reaction and would trigger an Indo-Pakistani nuclear arms race. By May '98, though, U.S. policy makers were quite confident they could keep India from crossing that red line to overt nuclear status. They were confident really for three different reasons. First, the Clinton administration had succeeded in late '98 in dissuading the then–prime minister from testing. At that time, the economic carrot seemed decisive, and BJP officials now seemed equally concerned about the economy. Reason number two, in late 1997, the White House had decided to make India the lynchpin of its South Asia policy and to replace its nonproliferation focus, which the Indians hated, with a multifaceted approach in which they were sure the Indians would welcome under any government. President Clinton planned to go visit India in the fall. Note, the U.S. still saw relations with India as a means to influence its nuclear decisions. And a third reason, Clinton administration officials were very high on their initial context with the BJP camp, even before the elections; thought that they were compatible in perspective, and the U.S. could work with India to fulfill its economic and its foreign policy aspirations, consistent with U.S. concerns.

The White House tried to be clear and pleasant on the nuclear issue, but New Delhi very quickly in public reacted with a great deal of acerbity. Senior U.S. officials put out the word that an Indian nuclear test would trigger legally mandated sanctions. And Vajpayee stated, right after taking office, that India would exercise the nuclear option if need be, not further specified, regardless of others' annoyance. In private, however, Indian officials were very reassuring and appeared increasingly responsive to Clinton administration officials. They assured the Americans that they would take no major nuclear steps before they stood up a national security advisory board, which would then conduct an extensive review. And the defense minister reiterated these assurances publicly in late March, soon after they came to power. A delegation led by then–UN Ambassador Richardson saw the Indians as receptive to a nuclear restraint message. And on May 1, the U.S.-Indian strategic dialogue resumed. So, ten days before the test, U.S. policy makers believed the BJP was headed in their direction and would avoid anything precipitous that would derail U.S.-Indian talks and bring on sanctions.

Now, let me talk for a moment about the second strand of this '98 intel failure: India's diplomatic deception. In the spring of '98, Indian officials set out, very successfully, to assuage U.S. concerns in meeting after meeting. They communicated they were receptive to U.S. concerns, that there was still time to discuss India's nuclear plans, and that there were meetings in Delhi, as well as New York and Washington, in which this occurred. There were also other Indian statements, which played down the need and immediacy for Indian nuclear tests, including articles about India's ability to test nuclear weapons in computer simulations. In retrospect, it's clear that the U.S. side probably didn't give enough weight to Indian anger at the U.S. for ignoring the growing Pakistani threat to India, as well as Chinese assistance to Pakistanis. And the real sore point was Pakistan's firing, in early April, of the nuclear-capable Ghauri missile soon after the BJP came to power. The Ghauri gave the Pakistanis for the first time the ability to penetrate deep into India. But there is no question that the Indian officials had played the deception card with the U.S. After the tests, feeling betrayed, U.S. officials asked a Vajpayee aide about the broken promises and he said, "You cannot debate, discuss, and then do a nuclear test." While India's diplomacy was misleading Washington, the Indians also engaged in other efforts to blunt U.S. collection. An *India Today* article today noted that after each U.S. demarche, the Indians incorporated new security test measures at their test sites. For example, they used widely known satellite coverage gaps to hide movements of people and equipment. They used sandstorms and they timed the tests to hide test preparations and they relied on shifting sands to cover tire and track treads at the site.

The U.S. intelligence side: Was U.S. intelligence on the ball? Well, they had been monitoring test preparations, or activity at least, since the first test in 1974. And they repeatedly alerted policy makers to the possibility of tests. The India watchers understood that test decisions would be driven by political factors, and they tracked them closely. For example, Indian pressure to sign on to nonproliferation regimes. Analysts clearly understood that India's effort in the mid-'90s to keep the CTBT, the Comprehensive Test Ban Treaty, from going through, was linked to its desire to keep open the testing option. Analysts also tracked strategic developments in the region, for example India's reaction to China's nuclear test in '92 and Indian domestic politics. U.S. intelligence on Indian test preparations had hit the press in '95. In mid-December '95, the *New York Times* broke the story that the U.S. intelligence was closely watching Indian preparations to test, perhaps soon. And a day later, the *Washington Post* carried even more details. Specifically they noted that instrumentation at the test site pointed to test preparations and not maintenance. U.S. Ambassador Wizner decided, in the same time frame, to show the satellite imagery of the test site to senior Indian officials to convince them not to test. His sharing of that information has been widely blamed for teaching, in effect, the Indians to bury their cabling in '98 to avoid detection. But actually the same information was contained in the *Post* article. In the spring '98, the U.S. intelligence community again warned us policymakers that tests were possible. And in fact, they brought the test activity at the Pokhran test site so often to the attention of senior policy makers that they may have actually numbed them to its significance.

So what kind of intelligence failure did we have in '98? Well, the U.S. intelligence community did warn policy makers that India might test again. But it did not, along with the rest of the scholarly community and government observers, anticipate tests in May. So, strategic warning—yes, tactical warning—no.

Opinions varied on how much that mattered. Senator Shelby said it was a colossal intelligence failure. Admiral Jeremiah, who was heading up the investigation, the post-mortem on the tests, said yeah, it wasn't Beirut, wasn't Khobar Towers, but CIA had prematurely dismissed the BJP's public statements and failed to focus intelligence collection on India. The policy community was pretty steamed. There were a lot of different accounts about where the fault lay—resource shortfall because of budget cuts, analysis, human or sigint [signal intelligence] shortfalls, and the tasking of satellites. I'll briefly run through these very quickly.

First, intelligence analysis. Some claim that U.S. intelligence analysts hadn't even considered the possibility of a test. But DCI [Director of Central Intelligence] Tenant soon after the test stated that in fact the community had focused on the possibility of tests, particularly after the Ghauri missile test in Pakistan. Admiral Jeremiah conceded that, yeah, people in the IC [intelligence community] had indeed worried about a test, in spite of Indian assurances. The reality was that, for many reasons, including India's successful denial and deception, analysts had very little grist on which to forecast whether a test might really occur. And none of the information they had pointed directly to tests. They had two types of information: diplomatic reporting on India's stated intention not to test and imagery of ambiguous activity at the test site. The scarcity of intelligence on Indian intentions put the onus on analysts to take their best shots based on assumptions about how India calculated the pros and cons of a test. Some analysts thought the tests would occur sooner rather than later because India had a technical need to test and because BJP decision makers had a hard-line history on security issues. But without hard intelligence to back this up, even though it proved to be correct, the assurances—this argument won few converts. Others argued that the BJP in power was pragmatic, unlike the BJP on the campaign trail. The fact that India was a friendly country just confused the issue. Had the story been about North Korea, which Dan will talk about, no one would have quarreled with any doubts about this truth of government statements. Because India had a record with the U.S., a pretty straight shooting, in spite of the disagreements between the two. Much has been made about the fact that if the U.S. had looked to an open source, they would have known the truth. In fact, that's not so. Indian press and public statements were either misleading or they were ambiguous, and academic experts who were pulsed by the intelligence community before the tests, thought the BJP would avoid rocking the boat with the U.S. On the other hand, the IC's focus on the Ghauri missile test as a possible spark for tests was indicated afterwards. *India Today*, for example, describes the tests as the last straw in the BJP decision to produce a nuclear test.

Why did analysts have so little intelligence to work with? Well, first there was insufficient priority for intelligence collection on India. There was competition with other targets, particularly on imagery. Some of you will appreciate support for military operations took the lead—Iraq and the Balkans. There were also policy distractions and Senator Bob Kerry acknowledged that actually Washington had really taken its eyes off the nuclear threat. Inadequate human and sigint, that we had a new Indian government just weeks before the test—it was hard to get information on inner circle decision making. And in fact, we knew in retrospect that only a handful of Indian officials were present and knew of the decision to test. Even India's president was informed only a day before. Third, deficient satellite imagery and photo interpretation. There were reduced numbers of analysts and reduced numbers of satellites, budget-driven changes. And second, some U.S. satellites were pointed at nuclear—at missiles, rather than nuclear test sites. The nuclear test sites were imaged only three days, every third day.

Let me run through very quickly some implications and we can pick more up in the Q&A. It's clear that forecasting single events is very difficult. It's hard to determine when a lack of information signifies that nothing's happening and when it points to denial and deception [D&D]. In this case, there was insufficient information to determine that D&D was at play. There also was no tie-breaking information to help decide where the Indian tests might go. Was this an important intelligence failure? Yes, in a number of respects. First, preventing the test was very important to U.S. policy, not because of national survival, but because the Indian tests effectively torpedoed U.S. efforts over decades to cap the spread of nuclear weapons. If the IC had been able to tell policy makers India intended to test, would the U.S. have done anything differently? I think so. I think, given unambiguous evidence, the U.S. would have brought a very scarce resource to bear on the issue—presidential attention and persuasion. Perhaps more important, and George alluded to this in the case of Iran, the president would almost certainly have brought the entire G–8 to bear on India, including Japan, which mattered enormously. And that, in fact, is what happened after the tests. Would such pressure have stopped the tests? I'd like to suggest differing a little bit from George that it might have. For one thing, the reasons would have been domestic and not foreign policy reasons. I think concerted international pressure would have brought the test decision before some of the BJP's 14 coalition partners. And a debate among 14 parties would have been a showstopper. In fact, some people think the tests were timed to occur before the other 14 members could get their act together and take part in decisions.

This brings me back to why India went through such lengths to conceal the tests. Maybe it was to avoid having its test decision tangled up both in our preventive diplomacy and also opened up to domestic debate.

Thank you very much.

SAGAN: Dan Poneman.

DANIEL B. PONEMAN: Thank you, Scott. And I am honored to join such a distinguished panel before such a distinguished audience.

I would like to offer my remarks about the North Korean case in four sections: I'd first like to offer some preliminary observations about the nature of intelligence and prediction when it comes to North Korea; second, to briefly review the historical record of the role of intelligence and prediction, third, to offer some comments on the relationship between intelligence and policy, which will mirror some of my colleagues' remarks; and finally, fourth, to draw some lessons for the future.

First, the preliminary observations. North Korea is a notoriously difficult intelligence target. It is, perhaps, the most insular society in the world. It is still driven and controlled by a Stalinist police state. Its very backwardness and lack of economic development deprives us of many sources of intelligence. The computer connections, the telephone lines, people traveling, and so it is just a tough, tough nut to crack. And as limited as our resources are in the United States, the resources elsewhere are also quite limited. There are not so many countries in the world, as, for example, there are in the case of Iran, that have much more extensive access to information from

Daniel B. Poneman

North Korean sources. You have some additional contacts from obviously the Russians and the Chinese. You have the historical and familial ties between North and South Korea. But sometimes the South Koreans deep personal stake has an element that may color some of their analytical conclusions. And so to begin with, we're dealing with a very tough case. But ironically, I would note that, while intelligence is very, very hard, prediction, I think, is less so. Why? Because although you need intelligence to see objects, you don't need intelligence—at least in the classic sense—to understand human nature. And again, this will refer back to some analogies to the Iranian case that George made a few moments ago, and indeed, I would submit to you that a careful reading of Aristotle's Nicomachean Ethics would offer you some useful clues as to how the North Koreans might act in the future.

The premise of this observation is the thought that North Korea, notwithstanding a lot of the popular rhetoric, is not a crazy state, that its leaders are not crazy people, that they are not just rogues who are going in one way or another without any predictable patterns. But rather, and I think the history will support this view, that they tend to be and their leadership tends to be extraordinarily shrewd, extraordinarily calculating, and—it's not my image, but I think it's a good one—they deal pretty well with a deuce-high hand. So to say, as has been said, that North Koreans can't eat the bomb, and therefore they must go in a direction that we would favor, really misses the point because the people making these decisions don't care about issues of having to do with feeding their people, not because they're rogues, but because they're interested in other things like maintaining the security and viability of their own political control of their system. So—and I would say finally on that point—that the history of the last half century testified to the fact that the ultimate goal that they have is regime preservation. So if they are rational, I think we can then turn to several sources to assist us in prediction as to the North Korean proliferation profile. And I would look to their actions, to their words, and then finally, not exactly rational, but to their culture, which forms their rational decision making.

Their actions. If the North Koreans keep turning back to nuclear activities, I think it is reasonable to conclude that pursuing those nuclear activities is a major objective. And to predict that no matter what we do that they're likely, at least as long as this regime is in power, to keep going back to a nuclear program, notwithstanding our diplomatic efforts. I think that the historical record also provides a number of actions that provide good guides for the future as to the tactical decisions that the North Koreans will make. For example, it's quite clear going back to the negotiations at Panmunjom, and even before, that they view the best defense as a strong offense. I think the history is replete with examples that when North Koreans feel truly cornered, they will lash out and try to kick over the card table and hope the cards fall in a more favorable position from their perspective. This combination leads to a fairly predictable pattern, with what I would call a regular overplaying of their hand. Some people will recall, in spring of 1994, in March, that the unification talks that were about to lead to a potential summit between then-leader Kim Il Sung and South Korean President Kim Young Sam broke up as the North Korean delegate threatened to engulf the South—to engulf Seoul—in a sea of fire. Well, at that time, the analysts on our side, the U.S., Japan, and South Korea, had been having some difficulties in coordinating a position. That stopped. And led, in my view, directly to a much more coherent diplomatic strategy, which in turn finally led to the agreed framework which bottled up the North Korean plutonium program.

Similarly, I believe that the series of provocative actions that the North Koreans took last December—kicking out the IAEA inspectors, breaking the seals on their nuclear facilities, turning off the cameras—had the effect of overplaying their hand and inducing a level of Chinese involvement that's been very helpful and I don't think the North Koreans would have wished. But I would just note one caution: That we should be careful not to overinterpret. That is to say, I don't think we can conclude from this record what North Korea's ultimate objective is. They may want a weapon; they may want a weapons capability; they may not have decided yet; they may have decided; and they may change their mind. And if that remains true, then I think we need to be very careful from a policy perspective not to assume something that may not, in fact, be true. And I'll return to that in my third section.

Their words. As with actions, the words of the North Koreans can give rise to conflicting interpretations. Certainly they lie and dissemble when it is in their interest. They lie, but they don't lie about everything and so I think we should view their words as data and to note that there are some occasions in which there is a fairly linear relationship between what they say and what they mean. And this does go to the point of intentions. I don't think it's a coincidence that chronically the North Koreans emphasize security concerns over economic concerns: A—because they think they are most interested in regime survival; B—because I think they see economic reform as a Trojan Horse potentially that can lead them to the kind of end that Ceausescu and others who have opened up totalitarian states to some greater liberties have found. So I think it's useful to look at their words and to note there are some tried and true tactics and some guidelines to useful interpretation when they communicate with the Americans: often they will engage in very tortured prose, very propaganda-laden prose. But when they get very serious, you would notice it drops off, and they get down to sort of straight, simple declaratory sentences. When you see those, pay attention.

Secondly, nuances in languages sometimes may reflect conflicts within the elite. It is a totalitarian system to be sure. But there are, within the very highest levels, debates between the military and nonmilitary leadership. And I think you can look for clues there. And finally, watch for the second to last paragraph in any of their statements because that's usually where the hook that they may have some concession and they often will appear.

Finally, I think you need to look at their culture. We are all familiar with the Juche, the self-reliance theory of the North Koreans. It's not just the North Korean phenomena, however. I think it's a very keen sensitivity to "face"—something that we ignore at our peril and policy, and, specifically, this gets back to another one of George's remarks as well, we always need to leave them an escape hatch. If we want them to do something, we need to provide an avenue for them to do it in a way that they don't consider disgraceful. The most interesting manifestation of this combination, strange combination, that is so characteristic of the North Koreans in my view is one of the first things that a senior analyst told me when I entered government, which is the North Koreans do not respond to pressure, but without pressure, they do not respond. And that seemingly contradictory statement means, I think, that when the Chinese, for example, suspend oil deliveries, they do so in a quiet way. When the U.S. deploys more military assets to theater, but does so in a quiet way, that often is the most effective way to get the North Koreans to do what we want.

Secondly, the historical record. The historical record in North Korea of the role of intelligence and prediction unfortunately is not very good and it's venerably not very good. There have been declassified documents on October 12th, 1950. The CIA Office of Records and Estimates Paper 58-50 stated, "While full-scale Chinese communist intervention in Korea must be regarded as a continuing possibility, a consideration of all known factors leads to the conclusion that, barring a Soviet decision for global war, such action is not probable in 1950." Well, we all know what happened a few weeks after that. The Chinese came pouring across the Yalu River. I think that, if you look back at the mid-1990s, we had continuing difficulties. And I think it would be interesting for people in this group to discuss, perhaps in question and answer, how sometimes the military personnel on the ground end up with a better perspective on the real threats of war and warning of war than the people who are just studying it from a civilian intelligence community perspective. Part of the problem here is, of course, that the North Koreans are forward deployed to such an extent across the DMZ [Demilitarized Zone] that there are very few indicators of additional things they could do to prepare for war.

I would note a special case, not of prediction but of assessment, and some of the dangers that this includes in the same period in 1993 and 1994, where it was assessed that there was a better than even chance that North Korea had one to two nuclear weapons. This is what one of my colleagues at the time calls an assessment with precision but not accuracy. It imputed a level of understanding that did not at all disclose the huge gaps in our understanding. We knew very little. We knew essentially that North Korea, if they had completed the plutonium reprocessing campaigns on the spent fuel that we were aware existed in North Korea, could have produced one to two nuclear weapons. What they had actually done was much less clear. Unfortunately, that condition, that ambiguity, didn't get into the headlines and what happened was you had a very strong public response that unfortunately distorted the public policy discussion. And I think that what it reminds us now is that assumptions can be extraordinarily dangerous, and this is a lesson that's true today as it was a decade ago. Policy makers, in short, do not have the luxury to build a policy on such unproven assumptions. At that time, we could not assume that North Korea had the bomb, because such an assumption could breed a resignation that might not be required by the facts on the ground. Certainly, no one would suggest that they should have a free pass to nuclear weapons if they had not already gotten them. Secondly, we certainly could not assume they did not have the bomb, for that could lead to a complacent policy that could needlessly expose American troops, U.S. allies, and indeed the world to a risk of a nuclear attack. And therefore, as uncomfortable and unsatisfactory as it was, the answer is that we need to have a policy that is robust enough to be viable and effective, whether or not North Korea did, in fact, possess one to two nuclear weapons.

Let's take a brief excursion to examine the historical relationship between intelligence and policy in North Korea. In 1985, North Korea was building a large research reactor that, in fact, was the source of the plutonium that we now worry about in North Korea. It was a 5-megawatt reactor, if rated electrically, but much more powerful in terms of its thermal production. We saw it. We watched it getting built. There was pressure on North Korea at that time to join the nonproliferation treaty. But basically, no vigorous action was taken. And this is where I think we did not take advantage of the strategic warning that we had. Because what it meant was that, by the time North Korea came on to the world stage with the completion of their plutonium reprocessing facility, all our easy and cheap options were gone. We should have been much tougher in the mid-

'80s, but, in fact, although the nonproliferation treaty requires North Korea to negotiate a safeguards agreement with the International Atomic Energy Agency within 18 months, in 17 months, North Korea said, "You sent us the wrong form." The IAEA said take another 18 months. Another 18 months passed, still no agreement. No penalty. Big mistake.

That changed in 1989. There was—I would say from 1989 through '95—a rough equilibrium, starting with the first Bush administration, when the discovery of the plutonium reprocessing facility led to a very active round of diplomacy that is the subject of a different panel perhaps, but that led to, I think, an appropriate balance between the policy and intelligence. From 1996 to the present, I would say that the intelligence has been more a foil to policy than anything else. Almost before the ink was dry on the agreed framework, people were trying to basically unhorse the agreed framework, and they tried to use intelligence discussions and discovery of apparent cheating as a means to do so. Unfortunately, the North Koreans gave them too much cause for that not to succeed. And so I would say that put policy in some degree of quandary in the years since then. But the most regrettable aspect in that period since that time is that the lack of progress toward the completion of the agreed framework's objectives led to a breakdown that included the enrichment in a clandestine facility of uranium by the North Koreans, which, in turn, led to the events of last fall, which have left us blind essentially to what is going on with the 8,000 rods containing five to six bombs' worth of plutonium. And I think that if there's anything we could do now to improve our predictability it would be somehow to get the safeguards inspectors back in so that we can reassess and resecure that plutonium.

What are the lessons for the future? Number one, I think we need to focus on the critical. And right now, the critical in my view is less the uranium, which we don't know where it is or how close they are to its production. We do know about the five to six bombs' worth of plutonium. We need to get better control on that. In focusing on the critical, I think we need to beware of the siren's song of thinking that somehow the odd proclivities of Kim Jong Il will lead to some regime change in time to save us from the consequences of proliferation. I think that would be a vain hope. Secondly, our collection should be done with the most diverse sources possible. All forms of intelligence using unclassified literature as much as we can, engaging North Korean diplomats wherever they appear elsewhere, and using third countries that have better relations than we do. And finally, when it comes to analysis, I've given up, at least for now, on getting a complete divorce between policy and intelligence. We can discuss through Q&A perhaps, that I find that each has a corrupting [influence] on the other. But in the absence of a clear divorce between a policy approach and intelligence that keeps each somewhat pristine from the other, I think your best solution is to have a wide range of analytical capabilities, not to bury those in footnotes, but to allow each and every analyst through their organization in the U.S. government and outside the U.S. government to have a fair shot at expressing their views. Then let the policy makers decide. It's important to get this right because the consequences of getting the intelligence wrong in North Korea could be catastrophic, not only for the United States, not only for its allies, but indeed for the world.

Thank you.

SAGAN: Thank you, Dan. Before I open it up to Q&A, I wanted to just make three observations and state my own opinion about them.

First, these talks suggest strongly to me that, with respect to tactical intelligence especially, we should lower our expectations of success in the proliferation area. Perhaps it's because the major league play-offs are coming, but it occurs to me that there is a metaphor, a baseball metaphor here that is appropriate. We often think about intelligence as if intelligence agencies are fielders. And to get it right if they're really good, gold glove fielders [field] in the high 90 percentages. But when it comes to tactical intelligence, they will be like baseball batters. If they get a hit 33 percent of the time, they're doing a good job. If they hit 40 percent of the time, they're like Ted Williams and should be in the Hall of Fame. We should not expect on tactical decisions in this area the kind of intelligence that we sometimes have expected.

Second, that being said, I think we should expect a lot more with respect to intelligence officials and analysts, understanding our own behavior and how that behavior influences others. George Perkovich, I think made an important analogy to the Heisenberg principle. I noted that I received a briefing at the Los Alamos Laboratory some months back called "Proliferation Studies as an Observational Science," where it compared studying behavior of would-be proliferators to a paleontologist trying to understand dinosaurs. Somebody in a nuclear laboratory whose organization's behavior strongly influences what people are doing in other countries, to have that as their analogy seems to be utterly mistaken. This is partly a problem of intelligence officers and their focus on other countries. It's partly a problem of compartmentalization. Intel shop doesn't talk to the policy shop. It's partly a problem of political correctness and courage, as George suggested. It's hard for intelligence officers to say some things to policy makers that they don't want to hear.

It suggests to me three things. One is that intelligence officers need to learn more about their own country, not just about the country that they are professionally assigned to observe. Second, they have to be brave and responsible. That's not just doing good intelligence. It's telling your boss sometimes things that he or she does not want to hear. And that requires, from the bosses and the policy makers, a better willingness to listen, to engage, to actually encourage dissenting opinions, lest you get into your own mindset and not understand how your policy might influence others. Not that you have to agree with those, but that you should listen. Lastly, my last point is that we should avoid what I will call the Columbia accident principle, which is the idea that there is nothing we can do about our problem, therefore, we should not pay as much attention to it as we otherwise would. Both George and Dan, quite correctly, and Polly as well, quite correctly note, that you can do things about problems early on, much more easily than when a proliferation problem has become an imminent one right on your doorstep. And I think that's true. But it is also true that it is dangerous to assume that there's not much we can do about it, even at that last day, at the last moment.

I won't debate the issues between the disagreement between George and Polly about what would have happened had we actually had better tactical intelligence that the Indians were about to test in May 1998. Although they may want to discuss that in Q&A. But a bigger point, a broader point, is that the intelligence and policy makers should never say there is nothing we should do about it, and therefore, let's stop discussing it. I call this the Columbia accident principle because that's exactly what happened when the space shuttle, Columbia was discovered to have a potential damaging piece of foam debris hit it. And at the situation room at NASA, senior policymaker says there's not much we can do about it, let's go on to the next issue. But of course we now know they could have gotten photographs from satellites. They could have told the analysts to redo the data to show how dangerous that foam could have been. It could have the shuttle crew go outside and take photographs themselves to observe it. And they could have set up another shuttle on a rescue mission potentially. All those events, all those creative potential solutions, were thought about in the after action report, not in the situation room. I hope, in the next nuclear crisis, when we think, "Oh, there's not much we can do about this now," those creative potential solutions are thought about then, rather than in the after action report about the major mistakes that we've made.

I'll conclude there, and let's open it up for Q&A from the audience.

The gentleman here.

AUDIENCE MEMBER: Good morning. Petty Officer David Gault, graduate student Joint Military Intelligence College. The distinguished panel has used terms of intelligence estimates, assessments, ambiguities, strategic warnings, surprises, threat, intelligence failures, indicators, predictions, and forecast assumptions, as well as capabilities and intentions. At the Joint Military Intelligence College, students study, discuss, and struggle with these terms on a daily basis. I want to focus on capabilities and intentions, for they are the major ingredients that result in the understanding of a threat for intelligence warning. However, they are not equal. And to understand one is much more important than the other. Which of these two factors is the most important for effective warning?

SAGAN: Who wants to? Which is more important? George?

PERKOVICH: Well, it depends on what you want to do. In other words, if you're trying to figure out how to fundamentally change the behavior, dissuade, affect the decision making in the other location, I think your intentions are more important. If you're focusing primarily on operational questions, whether it's covert or overt actions to take out a capability, then obviously the capability is the most important. So I don't think there's an a priori way you can say one or the other is more important. And obviously the capabilities tell you about what the other guy's intentions are, and vice versa. So it's not avoiding the issue to say you have to do both. What I was trying to suggest is that we have focused too heavily on capabilities that haven't balanced sufficiently.

PONEMAN: Can I just make one additional comment, which is, I think there is sometimes a tipping point. And in the case of India, after 1974, there is really no question as to the capability. I focused a lot more on intentions then. Similarly, in the case of North Korea, no question that they've got the capability, let's focus on intention. In Iran, where they still have some distance to travel, I think that the capability is still more worthy of focus. As George said, it's not either-or, you don't have the luxury, you have to do both. But I think the prominence of which is more important actually depends on how far they've traveled down the road.

NAYAK: I'd just like to add I think the importance of intentions depends a lot on U.S. stakes in the issue. If we're talking about going to war, we're talking about an attack, understanding people's intentions is considerably more important than if we're talking about a nuclear test.

AUDIENCE MEMBER: Rob Litwak from the Woodrow Wilson Center. My question is for George Perkovich and Dan Poneman. We've just finished a war in Iraq, one member of the axis of evil, and an objective was to obtain our nonproliferation objectives through regime change. Now, since major combat operations ended in Iraq, the administration has subdued its regime change rhetoric with respect to both Iran and North Korea. And where preemption is not an attractive option, it is opting for negotiation and regime reassurance. And my question for you both is the mantra of American policy makers that we must integrate force and diplomacy. How do we manage this, given the nuclear issue, which is imminent and immediate, is embedded in the broader question of change in these two societies where we do aspire for regime change or at least profound regime revolution in the long term? How do we bring the military instrument to bolster our diplomacy in a context where we're also trying to reassure the target state of regime survival as part of a process of dealing with the immediate problem?

PERKOVICH: I mean, it's a great question, Rob. I'll just speak to Iran. On the one hand, not only do we want regime change, but Iranian people want regime change. And so one question is how. But there's another problem, which is in the process of kind of fighting out this issue over the last year, it becomes less clear whether if you had a different regime in Iran, you would get a different nuclear policy. So if the idea is of regime change as the way to solve the nuclear proliferation problem in Iran, that's based on a hypothesis that may or may not be true. And you have to ask yourself—if the people who now control the nuclear policy making, who also probably control, you know, are supporting Hezbollah and Hammas and the other things we don't like, but those people— if they're the ones who are going to have to induce to change their behavior and they conclude that we're going to change them, remove them, no matter what, then the question is why would they deal with us to change behavior. I mean, I've had this discussion with the Iranian officials who say, "Tell us your intention. Because if you're going to remove us anyway, why should we do anything that you're telling us to do now, and especially why should we give up a potential deterrent if you're coming after us anyway?" Now, if you're prepared to live with us, and the internal Iranian process of deciding who leads Iran, then we can talk about these other things. And so I don't think Washington is clear on that. I've had this discussion. You get a different answer, depending on whom you talk to in Washington about that. And I think that's one of the reasons why we're not very clear in our dealing with Iran. And so everybody is confused. We're trying to figure out what the hell is going on in Tehran and who is on what side. And the Iranians are trying to figure out what the hell is going on in Washington, who's on which side and which is the policy.

PONEMAN: I agree basically with what George said. We need to choose our remedies. And especially since it is true, usually, that you cannot be confident that a successor regime would be more pacific or less interested in nuclear weapons, especially since they tend to be driven by security interests. Then I think we need to be very clear about presenting them a choice. If you go down the road of compliance with international obligations and staying clear of plutonium and highly nourished uranium, you get one set of attractive options. If you take the other road toward nuclear weapons, your options are unattractive. My view is the appropriate role of military force is twofold. Number one, in reinforcing that distinction, that through the channel of defiance, you'll find only pressure, including military pressure. And secondly, to the extent that we need to, as we have in the past, go to such issues as the imposition of UN Security Council sanctions, as was contemplated in June '94 in Korea, to make sure that we have a sufficiently robust military presence, including the enhancements required, in theater, to deter, in that case the North Koreans, from taking any foolish steps, which even though they would ultimately lead to their military defeat, they would do so after loss of a tremendous amount of life and treasure. So I see it both as reinforcement, the distinction between the two futures, and as a critical deterrent against military folly by your adversary.

SAGAN: Polly, do you want to make a comment?

NAYAK: Yes. Actually on a slightly different issue. I wanted to come back to your comment, Scott, about the policy intelligence interface. I thought you made very good points about antidotes to having intelligence people clueless about their own government. Clearly that's vital knowledge.

I'd like to say that on the India test case, there was no lack of that knowledge. Neither was there any lack of contact. In fact, if anything, the problem was that analysts were excessively dependent on reporting by policy makers who were cast in conflicting roles. On one hand, they were reporters; on the other, they were consumers. On one hand, they were actors; on the other, they were evaluators. They were in effect tasked to evaluate the likelihood of a test when they believed their own diplomacy had made that highly improbable. So the real problem there was partly the conflicting roles the policy makers had. Another one was that the priorities were set by senior policy makers. As I mentioned before, very understandably, Iraq and the Balkans were getting a great deal of the only kind of intelligence that worked on the test sites and that was imagery. And the challenge for intelligence people in such cases is to get enough intelligence on something that is not the number one or two priority to give effective warning. So there's a little bit of a circular problem. Another element that I didn't mention before, that's worth at least touching on, is the difference in perspectives between intelligence people and policy people on demarches. There's no right answer to this. But as I mentioned in my talk, the demarche by Ambassador Wizner in '98 clearly blew, along with newspapers' disclosures, some important information that then fed back and, in a Heisenbergian fashion, changed the way the Indians went about their test preparations. They incorporated D&D. Should such demarches take place when the cost is clearly high, sometimes on the intelligence side? Policy people view intelligence as a currency, and rightfully so in important cases. You pull out the intelligence in order to make a point and convince your interlocutor that you're serious, that you really have the goods, or that they really should play ball in some other respects. And that's often true particularly on counterproliferation and counterterrorism, where we feel the need to show them what we know in order to get their cooperation. We can't stop using intelligence and demarches. It's not going to happen. But clearly this will remain an area of tension.

And I just want to highlight also that the intelligence failure in the India test case was a failure of both policy and intelligence. And it's impossible to disentangle the two.

SAGAN: We have time for one last question, I believe. The gentleman there. Is there a microphone?

AUDIENCE MEMBER: Sir, Lt. Col. Meter, Army fellow at Tufts University. Over the last couple of weeks, we've had the privilege of meeting with Ambassador Lee from South Korea and the UN ambassador from Hungary, who chaired the nonproliferation treaty. With U.S. existence on international treaties and agreements, I find it rather strange that you didn't mention on a strategic level that perhaps something was amiss when we have nations that do not sign the treaty, the nonproliferation treaty. Would that not be an indication of possibly, their possession or working toward a possession, of nuclear weapons? Does it not set a bad precedent for allowing nations to exist outside of the nonproliferation treaty? And how would you get them back into it?

PONEMAN: That's a very good question. I think you can, and for nuclear weapons intentions, if you haven't signed the treaty by now since I think there are 188 parties, and the only ones who are not are India, Pakistan, and Israel, about whom little need to be said about their proliferation profiles, other than to mention their names because it's obviously a source of serious concern. That is, your premise is correct. Strategically speaking, the whole nonproliferation treaty regime is the cornerstone of our efforts and has been a very useful mechanism first to corral countries into—and it's probably not the right term—to persuade countries their best interests are served by living without nuclear weapons. And then in the very critical moment of the 1995 extension conference when the treaty would have expired on its terms, it provided a very critical opportunity, one to marshal some of the last holdouts into the regime, and secondly, to give it more vitality and to extend indefinitely into the future. I think the critical danger now is you don't have the luxury of not dealing with those final three holdouts and to find some formula to embrace them into nonproliferation norms. That A, is effective; but B, does not unravel the regime by giving some special status to those holdouts that is not enjoyed by the countries that figured they have given up this option willingly.

NAYAK: I completely agree.

SAGAN: Let me make one comment that clearly states how it's—whether states join a particular treaty or not is some signal of some intent or at least some debate within that country. But clearly also how they behave within that regime, even if they have signed it, how well are they honoring that agreement? But to return to the theme we repeatedly noted here, one should also look at one's own behavior in that regard, not just other states' behavior. Because under the nonproliferation treaty, in Article VI, the nuclear weapons states agree to work in good faith toward eventual elimination of nuclear weapons. And during the 1995 negotiations, we specifically said, if you nonnuclear states extend this treaty and have a permanent extension of it, we the nuclear states will sign the CTBT, the Comprehensive Test Ban Treaty, and ratify it as a signal that we are working in good faith toward eventual elimination. And we have not done that. People will debate how important Article VI is. How important our intention is to individual cases of potential proliferation out there. Some think it's not all that important

They're going to make decisions based on their own regional situations. Others say no, that's an important issue. But minimally what we do, with respect to that, is going to influence the debate within those countries. And potentially, I would think, especially if we test nuclear weapons again, we are going to open up many opportunities for states to say that you have not done what you agreed to do, and therefore, why should we do what we agreed to do? We have to look not just at other state's intentions and capabilities, but our own as well.

I just wanted to end on that reminder. This has been an excellent panel. Thank you for great questions. I apologize for so many of you who were not able to ask your questions. I wanted to thank you for an excellent set of presentations.

Thank you.

PANEL 4

IRAQ: POLITICAL AND MILITARY CHALLENGES

Co-sponsor: International Crisis Group

Moderator: Ambassador Nancy E. Soderberg, Vice President, International
  Crisis Group

Barham Salih, Ph.D., Regional Administrator, Sulaimania, Iraq

Fareed Yasseen, Ph.D., Advisor to Adnan Pachachi, member of the
  Iraqi Governing Council

Rafeeuddin Ahmed, Former UN Undersecretary-General and Special
  Advisor to the UN Secretary-General on Iraq

Ambassador James Dobbins, Director, International Security and
  Defense Policy Center, RAND Corporation

Panel Charter

As the Eisenhower National Security Conference examines *National Power in an Unpredictable World*, the question of Iraq is central. While the ouster of the regime of Saddam Hussein was a military success, the challenge for the United States in Iraq is, in the words of the Civil Administrator of Iraq L. Paul Bremer, to hand the country "over to a democratically elected Iraqi government as soon as we can." To do so, the United States will need to wield its national power on several levels: military, political, economic, and international. Several key issues must be addressed: establishing a secure environment; ensuring a recognized, representative, and functioning Iraqi Governing Council (IGC); rebuilding key infrastructure facilities and ensuring the basic needs of the Iraqi people are met; and devising a democratic political process that will enable the international community to leave behind a stable, responsible Iraqi government.

The political and military challenges facing the U.S.-led Coalition Provisional Authority are daunting. Relief among the Iraqi people at the ouster of the Ba'athist regime is coupled with fear over foreign rule and a resistance to working with the coalition authorities. While the appointment of the IGC is an important first step

Left to right: *Nancy E. Soderberg, Barhim Salih,*
Fareed Yasseen, Rafeeuddin Ahmed, and James Dobbins.

toward self-government, the legitimacy of the group, handpicked by the United States, remains to be established. While the CPA has succeeded in restoring some sense of normalcy—rebuilding some institutions and establishing basic services at local levels—the difficulties in restoring general law and order and a functioning infrastructure fuel resentment against the coalition authority and undermine its goals.

The first task of the CPA is to establish security throughout the country. Key steps include establishing a more extensive international military presence and placing more Iraqi police on the street by speeding up training of credible, vetted elements of the old force. The question of a new authority by the UN Security Council for a multinational force in Iraq remains central. Senior officers untainted by corruption and regime-related criminality will need to be reappointed and the de-Ba'athification edict will need to be reconsidered. The capture or killing of Saddam Hussein remains an important task.

Second, the legitimacy of the IGC must be established and the division of authority with the CPA must be defined. A gathering of political leaders with mixed popular followings, very little in common, and an awkward nine-person rotating presidency will need strong international support to succeed. For the first time in Iraq's history, sectarian and ethnic criteria have become organizing principles of government. As a result, the balance of power in Iraq has shifted from Sunni Arabs in favor of Shiites and Kurds. In addition, the IGC does not include local, grassroots organizations and is perceived to tilt disproportionately toward the diaspora. While perhaps unfounded, resentment of the diaspora is intense among Iraqi Arabs.

Until national elections are held that will genuinely transfer power to the Iraqi people, coalition forces and the IGC risk facing continued resentment, violence, and increased religious radicalism. To empower the Iraqis, the CPA should hand over, as much as possible, the administration, day-to-day policy-making and planning powers at the various ministries. The CPA also should accelerate the holding of elections at the local, municipal, and institutional levels, ensuring that they are as transparent and as widely publicized as possible in order to maximize popular support and participation.

In addition, it is important that the process of decision making be transparent. While the IGC officially has the power to prepare a budget, represent Iraq in international bodies, appoint a constitutional preparatory committee, suspend old legislation, issue interim regulations, and nominate interim cabinet members, the CPA's ultimate "veto" power undermines that authority. Thus, a key challenge during this period will be providing legitimacy and openness to the process. As the process evolves, the United Nation's role may be expanded.

This panel will examine these political and military challenges faced by the United States and the international community in Iraq. Panel participants will include representatives from the Iraqi political spectrum, the international community, and its neighboring states.

Summary

Barham Salih, Ph.D., Regional Administrator, Sulaimania, Iraq

- Barham Salih began by commenting that press and television coverage of the situation in Iraq is very different from the actual situation on the ground. The media "overtelevises extremists or incidents," thus allowing for unfortunate incidents of terror to dominate the dialogue on Iraq. The actual situation is much better than what was predicted before the war. Major disasters hoped for by political pundits have been averted. There is "no major civil war, no major humanitarian crisis, no refugee exodus, no mass casualties."

- Salih said the label of "occupation force" is ironic as the Americans are seen as liberators. In fact, many Iraqis look upon their predicament as one of the failures of the UN system. As in Rwanda, the problems were not dealt with in time. "A larger coalition and the [UN] Security Council coming to help us overcome the previous regime would have been welcome. However, it never came, and now the Security Council should wonder whether it should have acted sooner, instead of questioning the legitimacy of the liberation of and intervention in Iraq."

- He noted that the present problems of Iraq must be viewed in light of its contemporary context. Iraq is a failed, dysfunctional state that was controlled by Saddam Hussein for many years. Its security problems have to be viewed in the context in which terrorism affects nations and societies both rich and poor. But the terrorism present in Iraq has not originated within Iraqi society. Rather, it is propagated by remnants of the Ba'athist regime—the individuals who have benefited from the rule of Saddam Hussein for the past 35 years. They are putting up resistance and disrupting the political process in Iraq, aided by al Qaeda and other fundamentalist and terrorist groups coming to Iraq. It is imperative to understand that Iraq is a defining issue for the future of the Middle East. The stakes are very high for the antidemocratic forces in the region, and they are determined not to let those who envision a democratic sector in Iraq, mainly the coalition, to succeed. Therefore, the antidemocratic and fundamentalist forces in the region will invest everything they have into Iraq to ensure the failure of the coalition. The terrorist issue is thus bound to get worse before it gets better.

• Salih emphasized that Iraq is not yet ready to assume the responsibility of ensuring security. However, he believed that the Iraqi Governing Council could assume security responsibilities for some cities and towns in Iraq. Some of these forces would surely not be well-trained or consistent with the ideals of human rights, but they would provide a better alternative to the current situation in which American forces are dispersed all over the country, thereby providing a convenient target. A specific approach should be adopted by which security responsibilities are turned over to Iraqis in a gradual manner. Despite the result of the recent polls, most Iraqis are working closely with the coalition and want it to succeed.

• He added that despite the many difficulties ahead, he hoped that Iraqis will be able to "draft a constitution that will support the fundamentals of democracy as a basis for governing Iraq for the future." No matter what is reported in the press, most Iraqis understand that they have no other way of going forward than by accepting some form of democratic structure that will maintain the stability of the country.

• Salih mentioned that a large number of foreign troops in the country complicates the political environment in Iraq. Perhaps some Arab forces should be invited by the IGC and Coalition Provisional Authority to assist the process. These forces would speak the language and know the culture, thus helping to overcome some of the security problems that exist.

• Salih proclaimed that the economy is another major challenge for Iraq, emphasizing the need for good governance and anticorruption measures that will provide the proper legal and political oversight necessary to ensure that the aid package is used for the people of Iraq. Building a new, democratic Iraq is a very difficult challenge with extremely high stakes, but, nonetheless, a challenge where a sustained commitment will be effective.

Fareed Yasseen, Ph.D., Advisor to Adnan Pachachi, member of the
        Iraqi Governing Council

• Fareed Yasseen stressed that success in Iraq is not an "on-off thing," but, rather, a progressive movement in which maintenance of law and order and the securing of borders are important milestones, as are the provision of basic services and the drafting and approval of a constitution. Unfortunately, southern Iraq is still lacking law, order, and security, and the departure of coalition forces from there should be gradual.

• Regarding the IGC, Yasseen noted that the entity has been functioning as a legislative body, appointing ministers and making decisions. If its expansion is well-chosen, it may even form a cabinet to serve as a provisional government. As more and more responsibilities are passed on to Iraqis, the United States should assume a lower profile. It will happen as a matter of course. The IGC's legitimacy will, in the end, depend on its ability to provide what the Iraqis want. "The fact that there are now Iraqi ministers in place ... should help speed this up," he said.

• Yasseen stated that what is needed right now in Iraq is a "force that can guard the borders and that can guard the countryside." The new UN resolution should call for other nations to provide Iraqis with military training, so that such forces become available.

• Addressing economic issues, Yasseen welcomed the use of labor-intensive budgets to take care of the soldiers who have been dismissed. He also brought up the idea of spinning off Iraqi army reengineering units as companies, which would generate revenue under private-sector ownership. He stressed this point as crucial, given that currently in Iraq private wealth is in the hands of profiteers and cronies of the former regime. Giving them free rein to enhance their power in the country would pose a grave threat to the fledgling democracy.

• Addressing the question of the role of players in ensuring a stable, postwar Iraq, Yasseen emphasized that they need to be good neighbors helping Iraqis combat terrorism and transnational crime. They should help Iraq reschedule its financial debts. In addition, each country may be able to assist Iraq in its own way. The Gulf Cooperation Council (GCC) countries could help stimulate investment. Iran could help in promoting religious tourism; Turkey could help restore Iraq's water rights. "All neighboring countries should help bring to the region open trade relationships, networks to the electrical grid, and so on and so forth."

• During the discussion it was mentioned that neighbors of Iraq should stay away from the domestic scene of the country, so as not to complicate the environment. A stable Iraq will ultimately benefit the entire region. This includes the idea of putting Turkish troops in the south of the country, especially given Kurdish sensitivities to Turkish involvement. Turkish or even Iranian troops do not speak the local language and will not contribute as much as people assume they would. The indigenous Iraqi capability to augment the coalition should be promoted instead. On the other hand, some Arab countries that do not have a historical involvement in Iraq should be welcome to help the country.

Rafeeuddin Ahmed, Former UN Undersecretary-General and Special
Advisor to the UN Secretary-General on Iraq

• Rafeeuddin Ahmed, speaking in his personal capacity, pointed to several
questions raised by the deadly attack on the UN headquarters in Baghdad. Is
the United Nations now considered indistinguishable from the U.S. forces, or is
it still regarded as independent in the minds of Iraqis but undermined by those
seeking to destabilize the country further? Was this attack on the United Nations due to its political role in supporting the IGC? Ahmed stressed that, in the
long run, questions must be addressed "regarding what needs to be done to
enable the United Nations to start and return the country to operating safely."
The improvement in the quality of life for Iraqis, through the provision of food,
water, and other necessities, needs to be matched with local, grassroots support
for a peaceful transitional process. The challenges of post-Saddam Iraq require
international cooperation and solidarity, especially within the immediate region. Security should be addressed by the creation of a local Iraqi militia. Also,
the act of the demobilization of the armed forces must be reconsidered and its
negative impacts analyzed.

• The new draft resolution circulated by the United States on September 3
introduced relatively modest changes. Ahmed emphasized that any new resolution
must enable nonparticipating countries, along with the United States, to be active
in a substantially meaningful and effective way. Allowing the United States to proceed alone would form the perception that the IGC and cabinet administrators are
not fully representative of the Iraqi people. A Bonn-like conference, organized by
the United Nations, the Arab League, and the Gulf Cooperation Council might be
helpful. It is important to focus on how Iraqis themselves can take the leadership of
establishing a commission that would be led by Iraqis but supported by the international community as a whole. The multinational force should be established by
the Security Council and be truly multinational from an Iraqi perspective. The United
States must accept that the occupation needs to end soon, within a reasonable timetable. The international community must come in and facilitate the legitimacy of
the process giving the Iraqis a lead and sovereign role in their security. Within this
context, Ahmed pointed out that a timetable for the holding of free elections should
be announced. Finally, the Iraqi people need to understand and be convinced that
the United States has accepted ending the occupation, and that the United Nations
is coming in to help the them regain their sovereignty.

• In terms of law and order, Ahmed noted that an Iraqi police force should
be bolstered. Coalition forces—or any other military forces—are not trained to
perform law and order functions, and, thus, cannot fill this void. A multinational
police force might also be a possibility, comprised of Arabic-speaking police officers. Such a force should be established under the auspices of the United Nations
or the Arab League and could provide training to Iraqi police. Addressing the
question of how to end the occupation as soon as possible could make this scenario viable.

Ambassador James Dobbins, Director, International Security and
Defense Policy Center, RAND Corporation

- James Dobbins pointed to two issues with which the U.S. administration is battling: first, how quickly and how substantially to share power with the rest of the international community; and, second, how quickly and how substantially to share and ultimately transfer power to the Iraqi people. The United States has two main objectives in addressing these issues: the United States wants to use its presence in Iraq to ensure a transition to a stable democracy, and it wants to accelerate the exit of U.S. armed forces with as few casualties as possible. Experience suggests this will be a long, manpower-intensive process, and, thus, there is a great need to bring in the rest of the international community as quickly as possible. The models used to address the issues are Japan and Germany from the 1940s on one hand and Afghanistan today on the other.

- Dobbins stressed that those focusing on the importance of an enduring democracy tend to emphasize the amount of money and time involved, as well as the slowness of the process. The Marshall Plan is consistent with this, mentioned in the contemporary context as a justification to the administration's most recent budget request. Afghanistan is mentioned as a model where power was transferred quickly to a sovereign government, and resources to sustain the situation were limited.

- During the discussion it was noted that the major obstacle to transferring power to an enduring democratic government is the lack of adequate institutional capacity to run both a political system and an economy. Building up that capacity will be the key. Dobbins also stated that he does not believe this to be the defining moment for the global terrorist movement. Terrorist leadership and sources of funds will remain in countries that cannot be easily invaded.

- Dobbins emphasized that there are now problems with both models that are utilized to guide reconstruction efforts in Iraq. The Afghan model is failing. There is a lack of resources and troops in Afghanistan, especially when contrasted with Iraq. Winning the war in Afghanistan consisted of the United States joining an existing coalition, not forming a new one. After the war, the United States and the United Nations facilitated the process by which an existing government gained more legitimacy through the addition of new institutions and personnel. Also, in Afghanistan the United States succeeded in forging a regional consensus. The support of the ruling regime there by other countries "is one of the reasons it's been able to maintain its tenuous hold on power in the country." In Iraq, however, there is no regional consensus in favor of the transformation of the country, and the United States is not even seeking one. The Japan and Germany models are not applicable to Iraq either because Iraq does not have a homogenous population that was defeated in years of war. Dobbins declared that Bosnia and Kosovo are the most applicable analogies to Iraq, to the extent that analogies should be looked at as a guide.

Analysis

The panelists agreed on many central issues, including the need for Iraqis to take responsibility for their own government and economic reconstruction, and the desirability of substituting Iraqis for foreign troops on Iraqi soil. However, less consensus existed on just how soon these responsibilities should be transferred. In general, Barham Salih, Fareed Yasseen and Rafeeuddin Ahmed argued for faster transfer; James Dobbins emphasized the difficulties facing acceleration. Among the principal differences of opinion were:

- How large a military force is needed to provide security, and can this force be provided without foreign troops any time soon? Salih, Yasseen, and Ahmed tended to see security conditions in Iraq as better than the media typically depict, which would permit a sufficient Iraqi security force to be raised sooner. Dobbins put greater emphasis on the country's interethnic tensions and unsettled security environment, drawing from this a need for a much larger security force of up to 500,000 troops, which would take much longer for Iraqis to provide without outside participation.

- How much political development is possible in the near term? Salih, Yasseen, and Ahmed advocated rapid restoration of Iraqi sovereignty and accelerated development of Iraqi political institutions, often by expanding the role of the Iraqi Governing Council. Dobbins, by contrast, saw in Afghanistan an example of a failed effort to transfer power immediately to a sovereign, indigenous government and argued for a longer transition facilitated by a larger, international military presence.

Among the many challenges in policy making for Iraq is the lack of systematic, reliable data by which to resolve substantive differences such as these. Many would agree that conditions in Iraq are better than often reported in anecdotal journalistic accounts, but how much better? And are conditions improving or getting worse? How should we weigh the differences in conditions and trajectories in the country's different regions? The Sunni triangle is apparently less secure than the Kurdish north or the Shiite south, but what does this mean for the pace of Iraqi political development or the proper rate of sovereignty transfer at the national level? Explicitly or implicitly, members of the panel reached very different answers to these questions, which in turn gave rise to divergent recommendations for policy. The panel highlighted many of the key issues and illuminated the relationship between policy choice and underlying assessment. But until the underlying assessments can be based on a stronger foundation of agreed facts, it may be difficult to reach a solid, analytical consensus on the way forward.

Transcript

JANNE E. NOLAN, Ph.D.: Good morning. Welcome back. This is our fourth and final panel of the second day of the 2003 Eisenhower National Security Series

We have covered a great deal of ground in the last two days, and a great deal of ground in I think extremely original and provocative ways. The last panel's discussion on intelligence is one great example.

Yesterday, we had extensive discussions of some of the newer, more complicated and inevitably more controversial security challenges facing this country and the global system discussion of failed states, the discussion of the transforming role of the media in conflict situations, and discussions of the challenges of the proliferation of weapons of mass destruction. We've had the involvement of media, business leaders, members of the military, members of the United States government, and now some of the leading people coming from the nongovernmental organization side of this policy debate under the aegis of the International Crisis Group.

The description of the International Crisis Group is in the documents that you have. It's a very interesting and innovative institution that was established not that long ago as an innovative way to try to respond to the new conflict contingencies which emerged in focus after the Cold War as one of the sources of information that could be delivered in real-time to report on emerging or potential crises of a kind that exceeded any of the known crisis management institutions that we have in our government. It's been a tremendously helpful, and tremendously successful institution, which you'll hear more about and should read more about. I am introducing now the person who will moderate and share this panel, Nancy Soderberg, whose biography is also included in your materials. Nancy Soderberg has had a great deal of experience in the last decade working on any number of very difficult international foreign policy and security challenges. She began her career as a foreign policy advisor to Senator Kennedy. She has evolved through a variety of positions in the political world to serve as the number three person in the White House during the last Democratic administration. She served as the alternate representative with the rank of Ambassador to the United Nations and she's now the vice president for the ICG and has assembled an extremely distinguished and interesting group of people to talk about, perhaps, the most challenging issue before us, Iraq.

So please join me in welcoming Nancy Soderberg.

AMBASSADOR NANCY E. SODERBERG: First of all, I want to thank Janne for that very nice introduction and the Eisenhower Series and particularly the Army for putting together a very interesting few days, and a very jazzy film. I hadn't seen that before, so thank you very much.

Actually, I began my career—Janne is hiding one fact about the two of us—as an intern in the Walter Mondale campaign in 1983, when Janne was working on the enemy side of the Hart campaign. Neither one of those campaigns went very well, but we've had a long friendship coming out from that.

Today we're going to speak about one of the key challenges facing the international community, and we're delighted to have a vast array of voices from various elements of the debate on Iraq with us today. And really, the key question that faces the international community, as Paul Bremer, the civil administrator of Iraq has suggested, is to hand over to a democratically elected Iraqi government full power as quickly as we can. And today we're going to look at some of those challenges on how to reach that debate.

We've had an exciting few days up in New York at the United Nations with the president speaking to delegates saying, we're going to stay the course; with the secretary-general of the United Nations challenging the preemptive doctrine but also challenging other nations to make the United Nations more effective; at a time when the administration is putting forward an $87 billion price tag on the war; and in

Nancy E. Soderberg

the security situation remaining very unstable, as I don't have to tell many of you in this room. So you have vast military, political, and economic challenges in moving forward things on Iraq and we have an interesting range of panelists for you this morning. Two individuals from the Iraqi political spectrum, Dr. Barham Salih. He is from Sulaimania, and I will introduce him shortly. We also have an advisor to the Interim Governing Council who was up in New York the last few days, Dr. Fareed Yasseen. And we have the secretary-general's special advisor on Iraq and the world's premiere nation-building expert, Professor Dobbins.

What I would like to do is begin by introducing Dr. Barham Salih to you. If he would come out. I feel like we're in a beauty pageant, where they have to come out one at a time to some music or something.

Dr. Barham Salih is a long-time friend of myself. We met each other over a decade ago while he was the Kurdish representative here in Washington, which he served as for 10 years, back when things were very different in Iraq. He's been part of the Kurdistan movement since he was quite young, arrested twice by the Iraqi secret police—actually, took his high school finals in prison, which I learned reading your bio. You never told me that part. But he is currently the prime minister of the Kurdish regional government in Sulaimania in northern Iraq, and he's held that position since January 21. He was very instrumental in working closely with the U.S. forces during Operation IRAQI FREEDOM, and provided key support to the U.S.-Kurdish operations against one of the most notorious terrorist groups in the region, Ansar al-Islam, which also had a very serious attempt made on his life last year, killing a number of his close colleagues there. So we're glad he's with us here today. And he is very close to the PUK [Patriotic Union of Kurdistan] leader, Jalal Talabani, and, as I mentioned, was born in Iraqi Kurdistan.

So, please join me in welcoming Dr. Salih.

BARHAM SALIH, Ph.D.: Thank you.

SODERBERG: Next we're joined by Dr. Fareed Yasseen, who, on cue, will step out as we just orchestrated. Entrance.

He's been involved in the Iraqi political human rights movement for the last decade. Based in the United States, but going back and forth now quite often to Iraq, he's a member of the Movement of Independent Iraqi Democrats, and a close advisor to Adnan Pachachi, who is a member of the presidency of the Iraqi Governing Council, and he's been following the events in Iraq. Adnan Pachachi and Ahmed Chalabi are the two main leaders of the current government in Iraq, who have spent most of the time at the United Nations pleading their case for recognition at the UN, trying to get control [by] the United Nations. He's trying to work with the international community to get support in terms of troops and money there. So he'll be able to give us insight into what they're thinking there. He's also the founder of an online memorial to the disappeared in Iraq and has worked in a wide range of academic institutions, research institutions, MIT [Massachusetts Institute of Technology], think tanks, and works closely with the UN agencies in a range of issues. And he's got a broad education in Iraq, Switzerland, and the United States. He can provide us with a truly international view of events in Iraq.

So please welcome Dr. Yasseen.

Next, I'd like to introduce Mr. Ahmed—we all call him Rafee Ahmed. His first name is really much longer than that. But we'll just call him Rafee Ahmed.

He's got one of the longest and most distinguished careers in both diplomacy and at the United Nations. Since last February, Secretary-General Kofi Annan called on Rafee Ahmed to be his special advisor on Iraq. So he was at the right and left hand of the secretary-general during some of the most difficult times, in the lead-up to the war and in the aftermath. He has stepped down in the last couple of weeks with that post but is still very involved in the United Nations as a representative of the World Tourism Organization and the United Nations Development Fund for Women, which is his current role. But he's here to give you a sense of what the UN can and cannot do in Iraq and offer his own views on what, to many people who don't know the UN system well, looks like a very arcane and complicated and incomprehensible process up in New York. He can shed light on that for you.

Rafee started his career as a Pakistani diplomat and quickly joined the UN in the 1970s, and he served in innumerable, very high-level posts as undersecretary-general for International Economic and Social Affairs, as well as for the UN Economic and Social Commission for Asia Pacific, and has one of the deepest and broadest experiences in the United Nations. So please welcome Mr. Rafee Ahmed.

Last, let me introduce James Dobbins. Jim Dobbins, who is—he probably would not agree to this phrase—but I would really call him the world's expert on nation building. There is no one I can think of that has more direct and more high-level experience in every key issue on the post–Cold War world. We worked together at the White House when he was our sort of sane voice on some of the toughest issues that we were looking at from Haiti and trying to muddle through the Balkans. Jim was always one of the sanest voices around the table, and said, "You know you really could just look at it this way," and everyone just says "Well, why didn't we think of that?"

He was really extraordinary. He's also been, most recently, in Afghanistan; he was the diplomat who raised the U.S. flag over our newly reopened embassy in Afghanistan. He has served under four presidents, both Democrat and Republican; he has served in the White House, in the State Department and was special envoy to—if you can believe—these four places—Kosovo, Bosnia, Haiti, and Somalia. And we often wondered about his sanity when he would accept the next phase, but we're lucky to have him.

Through the 1990s, he supervised peace operations in Kosovo and Bosnia, managing American relief and reconstruction efforts in the Balkans, which was in excess of over \$1 billion. And he was the Bush administration's representative after 9/11 to the Afghan opposition and was really the key individual who worked very closely to install the regime in Afghanistan following the fall of the Taliban. He is going to be filling us in on sort of recommendations from a broad perspective of the options for the international community in Iraq and really bring some extraordinary wealth of talent to that subject.

So please welcome Mr. Jim Dobbins, as well.

Now what we'll do is that I've asked each of the panelists to speak for about seven to 10 minutes each, so that we'll have time for questions. I want to give all of you a chance to interact with this distinguished panel directly.

I will ask Dr. Salih to start first.

BARHAM SALIH, Ph.D.: Thank you Nancy. It's a pleasure for me to be here and to address this distinguished gathering about the defining moments in history, Middle East in history, in particular.

I came from Iraq on Sunday. I have to tell you that the last few days watching the debate in the United States, reading the press, watching television, somehow I have to resist confusion about the situation inside Iraq. I was in Baghdad about 10 days ago, and I've been visiting Baghdad from my hometown of Sulaimania once or twice every month. I can tell you that things are largely different from what you hear about in the press and watch on television screens. Regrettably, this media world that we live in often over-televise extremists or incidents—

Barham Salih

unfortunate incidents of terrorism and so on—tend to cover many other aspects of life and politics in a situation like that in Iraq.

Nancy and I go back about 10 years and when she was in the Senate she was kind enough to visit Iraqi Kurdistan in 1991 after the Gulf War. Life has changed a lot since then. I can tell you in the case of Iraq, having lived through the last six months of preparing for the war of liberation and going through the war of liberation and partnership with the U.S. and UK military that were in our region. Things are a lot better than what was predicted. Things are a lot better than what was expected before the war. Every major disaster that was won by analyst and political pundits was averted. No major civil war, no major humanitarian crisis, no refugee exodus, no mass civilian casualties. And if anything, frankly, from my perspective as an Iraqi, I think things have gone better than what was expected.

Why? We have to view the present day problems of Iraq in the context of a contemporary history of Iraq. Iraq is a failed state. If it is not a failed state, it's certainly a highly dysfunctional one. In the words of Fareed Zakaria, who recently wrote, in *Newsweek* I believe, about this issue. This country was ruled by a tyranny, with an iron grip of Saddam Hussein, over the last 35 years. Suddenly that controlling factor, that iron grip, was removed. Imagine that situation repeated anywhere else in the world. I think the confusion, the turmoil, the disorder would have been probably greater. It's remarkable given the history of Iraq, the lack of civil society, the lack of political process, the lack of institutions and governments—with all that, I think it's remarkable that things went better than what could have been.

That is not to say that we do not have problems. We do have problems. Certainly security, and violence is a very serious problem and one we cannot underestimate. But the security problem has also to be viewed in context; we live in an interconnected world in which this phenomenon of international terrorism is one that afflicts developed nations like yours as well as societies like ours. But I can tell you that terrorism in Iraq is not something that has deep roots within the Iraqi communities or Iraqi society. Certainly, the remnants of the Ba'athist people who have benefited from the rule of Saddam Hussein for the last 35 years, some of them, not all, are putting up a resistance and are trying to disrupt the political process in Iraq. They are being aided by foreign terrorists, al Qaeda, Islamic fundamentalists, and other types of terrorist groups who have come into Iraq. In a way, it's important to understand that the terrorists, the antidemocratic forces in the Middle East, understand that Iraq is a defining issue for the future of the Middle East. The stakes are very high for them. It's imperative for them not to let Iraq develop toward a democratic system of government. Because if we succeed in that—and by the "we," I mean the United States, the United Kingdom, and the Iraqi coalition partners, those who aspire to a democratic system of government in Iraq—we would have changed politics and political discourse in the Middle East in a fundamental way. So do not be surprised, ladies and gentlemen, that the terrorists, the fundamentalists, the antidemocratic forces in that part of the world will throw all of what they have into Iraq to ensure that we fail. I want to tell you that in terms of the terrorist issue, terrorist problem, it will get worse before it gets better. Again, remembering the context, the stakes have been so high. Why I do say it will get worse before it gets better is because I think, again, in this interconnected world, every incident in Baghdad or Basra or Sulaimania or Arbil resonates in Washington and impacts the political environment in Washington.

Now, we're entering into the presidential campaign in Washington, in the United States. And I believe most of those who want to see a failure in Iraq—they know that this is the moment to push hard and ensure that they will impact the political debate here in the United States and policy making in the United States. In some ways they want to repeat what happened to President Carter in 1979 as we enter this. That's why we need to redouble our efforts and make sure the terrorists will not have the better of us in that situation.

How to go about doing that? I believe it's important that we forge a closer partnership between the Iraqis and the United States–led coalition in Iraq in terms of security. I can tell you that the Iraqi component is not yet ready to assume full responsibility for security. Some of my Iraqi colleagues will disagree with me on that because these things take a while to develop and evolve. But I believe, at the moment, the Iraqi Governing Council and the Ministry of Interior can assume security responsibilities for many cities and towns in Iraq. We should be given that responsibility. I know it will not be a perfect solution. Some of these forces will not be well trained, may not be consistent with the ideals of human rights and democracy that I would be very committed to. But in my opinion, that imperfect solution will be better than having the present situation, where American forces are disbursed all over the place and provide convenient targets for the terrorists. We Iraqis have a responsibility toward our own country and we should approach a modular approach, a gradual approach by which security responsibilities will be turned over to Iraqis in a swift manner. In my opinion that is a better solution also than inviting foreign troops into Iraq because that will complicate the security environment and will complicate the political environment of Iraq. By and large, U.S. forces and UK forces are welcomed in Iraq, and I think you've seen the results of some polls that were conducted in Iraq in recent times. Although I'm not very happy about those polls because once we get into the poll modes, then policy will be driven by polls, what Iraqis think. Five points up, five points down.

So I'm a bit concerned about that. But at the same time, I want to tell you that most Iraqis are working closely with the coalition forces and want the coalition forces to succeed because they see the success of the coalition as their success, if the investment should be made in indigenous Iraqi forces to assume responsibility. Perhaps we may contemplate inviting some countries—by the "we," I mean the Iraqi Governing Council, in partnership with the coalition, some Arab forces that speak the language, who know the culture and can help the Iraqis and the coalition overcome some of the security problems that we have. We have obviously the important challenge of drafting the consutution that is starting soon. We hope the statement of Secretary Powell yesterday was an encouraging one. I'm hopeful that, despite the many difficulties that we will face in that situation, Iraqis will be able to draft a constitution that will reflect the plurality of Iraq and will assert the fundamentals of democracy and federalism as a basis for governing Iraq for the future. It will not be an easy process for us because these are some intractable problems and latent problems, accumulated problems since the inception of the Iraqi state to date. But I'm hopeful that we can do it because, I believe, despite what you hear in the press, despite the sometimes tension and the activities that go on, most Iraqis understand that they have no choice, no way forward but to accept some form of democratic federal structure that will keep the country together but at the same time tolerate the plurality that is inherently in Iraqi society.

The other key challenge for us is the economy, and we are gratified that the president is asking for help for a budget to an economic aid package for Iraq. We certainly look for help in other members of the international community. Coupled with that aid—because we're talking about building a democratic society in Iraq—I believe it's also important to emphasize the need for good governance and anticorruption measures because that money will only be useful if it goes to the people of Iraq. And just money being spent in the country without the proper legal and political oversight by Iraq in the international community, it may not be the right thing.

Ladies and gentlemen, in my opinion, we have embarked on a very difficult challenge—building a new Iraq, building a democratic Iraq. I can tell you from my own experience in Iraqi Kurdistan, my own interaction with my compatriots in Iraq, it's a difficult challenge; the stakes are high. Those who do not wish us success are working very hard to derail this process. But I can tell you, it can be done, and the implications of success are far greater than people imagine in the debates that are taking place in certain circles of Washington or Europe, for that matter. It's a challenge worth continuing with, the omens so far are good. I believe if we sustain and commit ourselves, we will make it happen. And Iraqis are serious about that proposition.

Thank you.

NOLAN: Thank you very much. Now, Dr. Yasseen.

FAREED YASSEEN, Ph.D.: I was thinking, as Barham was speaking, when he was mentioning the polls in Iraq, what a wonderful idea, couldn't do it three months ago. Actually, a little longer than that. Anyway, I'm very happy to be here. I thank Nancy for inviting me. I would like to recall for you a meeting, my first meeting with Barham Salih which was on February 25, 1994, where we organized a workshop in Washington entitled "Sovereignty, State Power and Human Rights." And those who might be interested in his remarks, which provide actually an interesting snapshot of the early democratic experience in Iraqi Kurdistan, if you ask me for a link, I will be happy to provide it.

In her invitation, Nancy asked me to address a number of questions relative to the political and military challenges facing Iraq under three different headings: security, political legitimacy, and the end game. I would like to suggest a fourth heading, which is that of the economy, which I will address if I have a little time left.

Let me address the questions posed to us by Nancy in reverse order of their headings. I don't know if the audience has seen them. But I'll address first the end game and the political legitimacy and then security, which is really, as Barham pointed out, the subject most on the mind of Iraqis in Baghdad. And finally, word on the economy.

Is a democratic Iraq a realistic goal? One point to be said here is that a democratic Iraq goes beyond stability and security, which is the means of strategic requirements of superpowers. It is not even called for by Resolution 1483, which only talks about a representative government. But democracy is indeed an Iraqi aspiration, and it is a realistic goal. Anyone in doubt of that should visit Sulaimania; I'm sure Barham would be happy to arrange for that. He or she should also visit cities south of Baghdad like Karbala, which is run by its own population. Karbala is not often in the news and that really is a good sign. They could also go to Mosul, which is an interesting city because it's very multiethnic, and see how its city council works in a democratic fashion to solve the problems of their constituencies. So, yes, an Iraqi democracy is possible.

What is the second question? What is the role of regional players in ensuring stable post-CPA Iraq? Well, first they should be and mostly are—but we ought to verify that—good neighbors. They should help Iraq and collaborate with the Iraqis and with the coalition, at least for now. To combat terrorism and transnational crime, in part, smuggling and—which is a serious problem, as you know, and the import of terrorists in Iraq. All that Barham said on the subject I absolutely second. To the greatest extent possible, they should also forgo their calls for reparations, which Iraq is really in no position to pay. They should also help Iraq with its efforts to reschedule its huge debts. For example, I'll give a figure or two. The UN Compensation Commission is now considering a figure of $30 billion in claims of environmental damages. This is not something that Iraq can pay at all. And, in fact,

Fareed Yasseen

these claims are, as seen by the way—the UN Compensation Commission has lowered them—really inflated. But beyond that, each country can assist Iraq in its own way. For example, the GCC countries and their nationals, who include many high-wealth individuals, could invest in Iraq, as was pointed out by Ali Alawi, who is Iraq's new trade minister at the recent IMF-World Bank meetings in Dubai. Iran could help in promoting religious tourism, which is a source of serious revenue from the long-neglected region of around Karbala in the south. Turkey could help restore Iraq's water rights, which are determined by a treaty, which is binding under international law, signed I think in the 1950s. Beyond that, Iraq has been cut off from its surroundings, so all neighboring countries should help it reintegrate the greater regions through open trade routes, open trade relationships, transport networks to the electrical grid, and so on and so forth.

How does the U.S. and the international community declare success and depart? That's another question. I think the embedded question here is, what is success? Well, success in Iraq is not an on-off thing. It's progressive; its signatures are a series of milestones: maintenance of law and order and secure borders, which implies the standup of the sufficiently manned, trained, and equipped Iraqi police force; the restoration of basic services; the drafting and approval of the constitution and the election of a representative government; the reestablishment of the national and regional levels of instruments of state that can implement the policies and laws that are enacted. And unfortunately, the south of Iraq is not a situation where you find in northern Iraq where you do have such well-established governmental institutions that can implement policy and in fact ensure, as we know, law and order and security there. The departure, then, of the U.S. and the international community should be progressive and gradual. Of course, after the UN decision to remove its foreign staff, I think all this implies first the return of the international community, but we should be working on that.

I shall move on now to the issue of political legitimacy. All the questions that were posed to us by Nancy, centered on the Governing Council, and I'll read them and answer them. What, if any, changes ought to be sought to the Governing Council's structure? How can it secure the right balance amongst Iraq's disparate, sometimes desperate, political factions? Well, the Council itself has been functioning as a legislative body. It's making decisions, it is appointing ministers, and there are suggestions that are being made to increase, in fact, multiply the number of members, say, from 25 to maybe up to 100. If the process of expansion is well chosen, then this will allow the Governing Council to become even more representative. Note that the Governing Council is the most representative governing body we have had in years. The Governing Council could then elect a cabinet among its members, which could then function as a provisional government.

Next question. Should the U.S. take a lower profile? Should the UN endorse the body, that is to say, the Governing Council and provide it with the Iraqi seat at the United Nations? Well, the U.S. taking a lower profile will happen as a matter of course, as more and more responsibilities and duties are passed on to the Iraqis. I just came from New York, and I can assure you that it is the Governing Council's delegation that is occupying Iraq's UN seats. It was actually a real pleasure for me to see a Kurd serving as the foreign minister of Iraq. It's a good point to highlight the diversity of the Iraqi population. Plus, he's a very capable man, as you know.

How can the legitimacy of the Governing Council be established? I'll consider two aspects of that: internationally and nationally. Internationally of course, it is well on the way of being established. I think the breakthrough here was the Governing Council's acceptance at the Arab League, which was very much held by strong lobbying by the GCC and also by the United States. Note that at the UN, and I just came back from there—the Iraqi delegation is having a full schedule of bilateral meetings at the ministerial level. So there's a level of recognition that's there. Internally, of course, the Governing Council's legitimacy, in the end, will depend on its ability or rather on the perception by Iraqis of its ability to provide that which the people want: security, jobs, better quality of life, so on. The fact that there are now Iraqi ministers in place, who are now completing the staffing of their ministries, should help speed this up.

Just a little aside, I'm an advisor to Adnan Pachachi, one of the members of the Governing Council. And in my dealings with him, he only accepts concrete proposals. He doesn't want critiques of other members of the Council. He doesn't want critiques of others. He wants concrete proposals that will help alleviate the problems that we are facing today in Iraq. So they are in governance mode, if you will. Please do note that this is a very important point, that in many parts of Iraq, the legitimacy of the Council is ensured by its very membership. So for example, the Governing Council is represented by the leaders of the two major political parties in northern Iraq who are elected, so that's not an issue.

SODERBERG: [inaudible]

YASSEEN: Wrap up, I'm sorry. Well, I'll skip a couple points. I'll go to security.

I'm not a military expert, but I will not detail the questions asked by Nancy. I'll just say that the unsatisfactory secured situation we have in Iraq can be traced to two factors: the open borders we've had for a while, which allowed many terrorists to come in, and the dismissal of the army in the absence of social safety nets. I think what is needed right now in Iraq is a force that can guard the borders and that can guard the countryside, very similar to France's Gendarmerie Nationale, of Germany's Grenzen Schutzpolizei. The UN's resolution should, at the very least the new one, allow these countries to provide Iraqis with training, so that they come up with such forces.

This brings me to the final point I wanted to address, which is that of the economy. Now, labor-intensive projects are being put in place, and they'll take care of the soldiers that have been dismissed and that don't have work now. What do we do with the officer corps? There's an idea I'd like to offer which I've not seen proposed anywhere. The Iraqi army has a lot of reengineering units that are very, very capable. In fact the most technically competent entities in Iraq. Why not spin these off as companies, value revenue-generating companies with, for example, mixed private, state private sector ownership? They can then become the agents or representatives of international companies willing to do business in Iraq—companies like General Motors or Ford or whatever. And this is an important point, because in Iraq, right now, private wealth is in the hands of sanctioned profiteers and the cronies of the former regime. And if they become agents of such companies and if they have free rein, then they won't even enhance their power in the country. And that is a threat I think a fledgling democracy cannot risk.

Thank you.

SODERBERG: Thank you very much, and we can come back to the other points hopefully during the questions and answers. We turn now to Rafee Ahmed for a view from the United Nations.

RAFEEUDDIN AHMED: Thank you, Nancy. I should like to emphasize that this presentation is being made purely on a personal basis by me.

This is a defining moment for the United Nations, and it cannot proceed on a "business as usual" basis. After the attack on the UN headquarters and the recent subsequent attack earlier this week, we have to ask some questions. First, is the UN now considered to be indistinguishable from the U.S. occupation forces? Or does the UN retain an independent identity in the minds of the Iraqis at large but has been attacked nonetheless by those seeking to undermine the coalition and to make the country ungovernable? Or was this an attack on the new constellation of power, represented in the Governing Council in the UN's political role in supporting it? In fact the attack on the headquarters occurred just four days after the adoption of the Security Council Resolution 1500, which welcomed the establishment of the Governing Council. So in the immediate term, I think there is no alternative but for the UN to have a drastic retrenchment, if not complete withdrawal, and the secretary-general announced yesterday that there will be such a retrenchment. The current security framework does not permit us to do what we had intended to do under the Resolution 1483 and the report that the secretary-general had submitted to the Security Council on the 17th of July. So in the immediate term, in some areas, there will definitely be a reduction. Clearly humanitarian activities will be prioritized while there will be delays in certain recovery and reconstruction activities. Meanwhile the UN is trying to strengthen Iraqi institutions and the UN national staff to take over some of those responsibilities.

Rafeeuddin Ahmed

For the longer term, we need to also address some questions. First, what needs to be done to enable the UN staff to return and to operate in the country in safety? Second, are the tasks that UN personnel are being asked to perform of sufficient importance to risk their lives? And third, is the security threat that the UN and international personnel now face a symptom of a much deeper issue with serious implications for the future of the country and the region in general?

The overall quality of life for all the Iraqis is improving, as we have already heard, with regard to the provision of food, water, electricity, and other necessities. But this needs to proceed on a much faster basis to build local grassroots support for a peaceful transitional process. So, in short, security cannot just be a function of military and paramilitary instruments only. The political and economic environment is just as important. What are the options for the way forward? Now, some of the fundamental issues that were recently raised by the UN Secretariat for the consideration of the Security Council were first, Iraqi sovereignty may need to be restored at a much accelerated pace than originally planned. Is this possible under the currently prescribed sequence for political transition? Second, the challenges of post–Saddam Hussein Iraq are so formidable that genuine international solidarity and cooperation, including within the region, is required on all fronts. Are there ways in which the ongoing political process could be made more inclusive, both outside and inside Iraq? Third, while Iraqis themselves ultimately would need to assure the security of their country, is the creation of local Iraqi militia at this juncture the right way to fill security vacuum? And fourth, there will be a need to reconsider the current policy on de-Ba'athification, which raises human rights and due process concerns, as well as the demobilization of the armed forces, which suddenly disenfranchised more than a half-a-million Iraqis.

who were armed and were not offered any alternate means of livelihood nor any prospects of reintegration.

As you know on the 3rd of September, the United States circulated to other Security Council members a draft resolution. But the resolution introduces relatively modest changes in the arrangements and the division of labor authorized under the earlier Resolutions 1483 and 1500. And in forecasting how this Security Council debate will play out, it is my view that any new resolution put forward by the United States has to enable non-coalition countries and the UN to participate in a clear, substantially meaningful, and effective way. Frankly speaking, one of the reasons why the UN has been coming under attack is because there is no clear delineation of responsibilities between the secretary-general's special representative and the Coalition Provisional Authority under Resolution 1483.

The dominant perception of Iraqis, as well as the countries of the region, is that the UN is primarily there to support the occupying powers, rather than to empower the Iraqi people. Let us consider what might be a possible future scenario if we discard the option of just letting the U.S. go it alone. In the political process, given that the current bodies that have been declared to constitute the Iraqi interim administration, the Governing Council and the cabinet ministers, are not considered to have been democratically elected by the Iraqi people and are not regarded as being fully representative, there should be a Bonn-like conference, which was convened for Afghanistan as you might recall, organized to discuss what process-mechanisms would best lead to the establishment of an internationally recognized provisional representative government. The UN could approach the Arab League and perhaps the OIC [Organization of the Islamic Conference], the GCC, the countries of the region, to discuss the feasibility of sponsoring a Bonn-like conference in a neutral third country. The invitees would need to be discussed with the Arab League and the OIC apart from, of course, the institutions which exist already in Iraq. In planning these discussions between the UN and Arab League for such a conference, it would be important to focus on how the Iraqis themselves can take the leadership through establishment of thematic commissions which would be led by Iraqis, but which will be supported by the international community as a whole, the UN, the Arab League and so on.

For security arrangements, there are two aspects to consider. One is the general security of the country. A multinational force could be established with the endorsement of the Security Council. It should be truly multinational from the Iraqi perspective in terms of composition, size, and operational area of deployment. The issue of command of the multinational force is a nonissue because most members of Security Council have already accepted the idea that the United States, as the largest contributor, would be in the lead. The second aspect is the law and order functions. The obvious primary need is to develop and bolster the incipient Iraqi police force, which requires substantial assistance in terms of financial, logistical, and human resources. The coalition military forces or, for that matter any other military forces, are not trained to perform law and order functions and, therefore, should not be filling the gap left by the absence of an adequate Iraqi police force. Until sufficient national police forces are fully established and to accelerate that time frame, one possibility could be to propose the establishment of the multinational police force comprised of Arabic-speaking police officers, particularly from the region, to provide training to Iraqi police and to assist with law and order functions as required. Such a multinational police force could be established under the auspices of the UN, the Arab League, or a lead nation or a combination, with the endorsement of the Security Council. In order to expand the number of Arab countries which will be prepared to deploy police officers, it might be possible to explore with some of those countries as to whether they could partner with such potential contributors by offering assistance in terms of funding or equipment, a practice which has been followed for certain military contributors in a number of UN peacekeeping operations. Irrespective of whether you find this scenario viable or realistic, the main question to be addressed in making such an assessment is how to end the occupation in the soonest possible time, while getting certain clear results.

To do so under any viable scenario, there is essentially a need for a tripartite understanding to emerge. First, on the part of the United States, it must accept that the occupation will end and end soon and that they will have to leave within a reasonable timetable, and that they are willing to show their good intentions in this regard. Second, the international community will have to come in to help ensure the legitimacy of the process and to facilitate giving the Iraqis the lead role so they can eventually be put in charge and regain the full attributes of sovereignty. In this connection, it would be important to announce the timetable for the holding of free and fair elections within a reasonable period, regardless of whether living conditions have come to par. Elections in many countries have been held in post-country situations where the living conditions have not yet fully recovered. The third understanding would have to be by the Iraqi people. They have to be convinced that the United States has accepted to end the occupation and will leave, and that the UN is coming in to help them, the Iraqis, regain their sovereignty.

Thank you.

SODERBERG: Thank you, very much. We'll leave it to Mr. Dobbins to try to make sense of these very disparate and interesting approaches.

AMBASSADOR JAMES DOBBINS: Thank you, Nancy.

The U.S. administration is currently wrestling with two major issues, which you're seeing play out in your newspapers every morning. One is the issue of how quickly and how substantially to share power with the rest of the international community. And the second issue is how quickly and how substantially to share, and ultimately transfer, power to the Iraqi people and their representative. In wrestling with these two issues, the United States has two fundamental objectives, one is to use its presence in Iraq, it's military presence in Iraq, in order to underpin and facilitate a transition to an enduring democracy. And the second is to minimize casualties and accelerate the exit of our forces. To the extent one places the priority on facilitating and enduring transition of democracy, experience suggests that this is going to be a long, expensive manpower-intensive process. It's never been done successfully in less than seven years.

Alternatively, if one places an emphasis on minimizing casualties and facilitating an early exit of forces while retaining a stable situation in the aftermath, that suggests that one should be turning power over to Iraqis as quickly as possible, even if that, in the end, does not produce a democracy fully up to international standards. So in one

James Dobbins

sense, those who look to a long, difficult manpower-intensive, expensive experience have an incentive to bring in the rest of the international community as quickly and substantially as possible. Those who are looking to complete this operation as quickly as possible are emphasizing the need to move power into Iraqi hands as soon as possible.

In wrestling with these issues, there's a search for appropriate models, appropriate analogies, upon which to hinge both our decision making and our justification for the decision making. And the models that this administration has shown a preference for are either Japan and Germany in the 1940s on the one hand, or Afghanistan today on the other. If one is looking toward an enduring transformation to democracy, Japan and Germany are excellent analogies, but they do tend to emphasize the difficulty, the expense, and the amount of time involved, and the slow process in which power is turned over to democratic institutions. Power wasn't fully turned over to German or Japanese governments until 1952. And talk of a Marshall Plan, which the administration has used to justify its most recent budget request, is very consistent with the use of Japan and Germany as models. The other model is Afghanistan, a model where the United States was able to transfer power quickly, in fact, immediately, to a fully sovereign Afghan government to retain a very small American and foreign footprint in the country, and to limit the resources that were required to sustain the situation. And you see that model was also cited, for instance, most recently in the op-ed piece that Secretary Rumsfeld published a couple days ago.

Now, there are problems, however, with both of these models, or all of these models. The problem with the Afghan model in the first instance is, it's not working in Afghanistan. That's largely a problem of resources; if we were spending the kind of money in Afghanistan that we are spending in Iraq, and if we have the kind of force structure in Afghanistan that we have in Iraq, on the Afghan model, it probably would be working, because Afghanistan had some unique attributes that are not present yet in Iraq. You know, looking back on the events after 9/11, there is an impression that the United States formed a coalition and then won the war in Afghanistan. Not true. There was an existing coalition, which the United States joined. It was a coalition that consisted of Russia, India, Iran, and the Northern Alliance, and it had been fighting a war for a decade. And the United States joined that coalition, provided it air power and forward observers and gave it the decisive edge, which allowed it to win the war and occupy most of the country. At which point the United States and the United Nations facilitated a process by which an existing government—there was an Afghan government, it was a Northern Alliance government, it had a president, it had ministers, it had police, it had an army—by which that minister gained legitimacy, first of all, through the offices of the former king of Afghanistan, who retained a great deal of prestige, and, secondly, by adding a minority of ministers from other parties, mostly émigrés, to the existing Northern Alliance government. And that's how the existing Karzai regime was established. And we don't have those prerequisites yet in Iraq.

The second, of course, is that in Afghanistan, the United States succeeded in forging a regional consensus, a consensus in which the countries that had been tearing Afghanistan apart for 20 years—Russia, Iran, Pakistan, India, et cetera— agreed that the great game in Afghanistan didn't have to be a zero-sum game, that they had an interest in a moderate, modernizing nonthreatening Afghanistan, and that they would join to support the Karzai regime. And the fact that all those countries continue to support the Karzai regime is one of the main reasons that it's been able to maintain its tenuous hold on power in the country. And again, that situation doesn't exist with respect to Iraq yet. There is not a regional consensus in favor of the transformation that the United States is seeking to promote. And quite frankly, the United States is not yet seeking to forge such a consensus. In Afghanistan, we talked frequently and very constructively with Iran, for instance. We're refusing to talk to Iran with respect to the future of Iraq. That makes it difficult to forge the kind of regional consensus which underlies a lot of the relative stability that we see in Afghanistan.

Similarly, the Germany and Japan models are not exact either. Germany and Japan were homogeneous populations, they were highly developed societies, and they've been thoroughly defeated in years of war, which left their populations devastated and acquiescent. Iraq, if you're looking for the most apt model—and no model is perfect—is close in 2003, is a lot closer to Yugoslavia in 1996 or 1999, than it is to Germany or Japan in 1945. First of all, Iraq, like Yugoslavia, was carved out of the Ottoman Empire at the end of World War II. It, too, brings together a disparate group of ethnicities and religion and religious tendencies that among whom there are tensions. So far, happily, not tensions of the scale that one has seen in Yugoslavia. And, of course, like Bosnia and Kosovo, Iraq is a Muslim nation. So in many ways, the Bosnian and Kosovo operations are the most recent and probably the most apt analogies, to the extent there are any analogies. And one ought to be looking to them for some guidance as to how to move forward in Iraq.

Now, there's a debate in the United States as to what needs to be done in Iraq. There's a recognition, I think, that the security situation is not yet in hand, that it is not yet improving at a rate that suggests it will soon be in hand, and that more is needed. But we can't agree on more of what. The neoconservatives are arguing we need more American troops. Neoliberals are arguing we need more European and allied troops. And others, including the secretary of defense and others in the Pentagon, are arguing that we need more Iraqi troops, police, et cetera.

My own view is that, unfortunately, they're all right. If you look at previous situations in which you have conflicted societies which are facing internally and externally supported subversion and terrorism, history suggests that you need a security force of approximately 20 men per 1,000 inhabitants. Those are the numbers that were necessary in Malaya in the '50s, they're the numbers that continue to be applied in Northern Ireland to maintain security there. They're the numbers that were generated for both Bosnia and Kosovo. And in Iraq, they generate a requirement for a force of about 500,000. Now, I hasten to add that's not 500,000 Americans, it's not 500,000 foreigners, that would include a reliable Iraqi force. But the critical modifier there is reliable forces. It would include the 30,000 or so police that we currently have, Iraqi police. It would include, I don't know, the 40,000 border patrols, I read recently. It would include the Kurdish militias in the north. But even if you add all of those together, you don't get much more than around 250,000, including the American and allied forces that are there. So it does suggest that establishing security is going to be difficult and that we are going to have to move on a variety of fronts. When I say establishing security, incidentally, I don't simply mean mounting a counterinsurgency campaign on which we intended to focus our efforts. We're not going to win that campaign unless we secure the support of the Iraqi people, and we're not going to secure the support of the Iraqi people unless we are providing them security, not against insurgence and terrorists, but against car thieves, rapists, murderers, and house breakers. And we're not doing a good job of providing that level of security, and until that level of security is provided, we can't expect these people to give us their loyalty, their support, and help us to isolate and eventually eliminate the extremists who are circulating in their midst. And that's the reason that the challenge does require forces to be generated at the level that I've suggested.

Thanks.

SODERBERG: Thank you all very much for a lot of food for thought. We have about 20 minutes, a little less, available for questions, and be happy to take them at this time.

In the middle in the back row? If you can maybe identify yourselves as well, that would be helpful for the panelists.

AUDIENCE MEMBER: Yes, my name's Larry Porter, U.S. Army. And my question for the panel is that, looking at the first Gulf War and this one, there appears no Arab country has come forth to support the democratization of Iraq, and looking around Iraq, there seems that all the countries around them, except for Turkey, will have something to lose due to the fact that Iraq would end up being a purely elected country, or purely elected officials. Do you have any suggestion on, or comments on, why that's so? And the second part is, do you think there should be a time line, just set in place, since everybody's looking at time, and just tell the Iraqis, hey, look, at the end of this date, we're gone, we'll support you at that date, but until that time, you've got to work on it until that date? That's all I have. Thank you.

SODERBERG: Okay, Barham, do you want to try that one?

SALIH: Well, I think the question was asking about the prospects of the democratization given the fact that the region is not highly democratic. I think that makes life very difficult for those of us who want to build a democratic system of government in Iraq. My own take on this is, this is a conference that has to do with U.S. national security challenges, and I want to argue a point relating to that. Fifty years of American foreign policy toward the Middle East, relying on elites that were undemocratic, corrupt, and unaccountable to their own people, might have provided a degree of stability in the Cold War and the power gain that existed in that part of the world. And I believe that those fundamentals of U.S. foreign policy toward the Middle East are no longer valid after September 11. Stability in that region, long-term stability, requires better systems of government that will have to rely on a greater degree of legitimacy vis-à-vis their own populations. In that context, I want to relate to some of the arguments that my friend Ahmed and others might have referred to about the legitimacy of political process in Iraq. It's ironic that some Arab governments and Arab leagues question the legitimacy of the Governing Council. The reality is that this Governing Council is probably the most representative, the most legitimate of governing institutions, across the Islamic Middle East. And it's ironic that we would be criticized for the legitimacy of this institution, being questioned by those who have come through coups and have never had to go through elections, even though we are always saying that this Governing Council is an interim arrangement until we have properly elected governing institutions for Iraq.

SODERBERG: Anyone else want to take that one? Okay.

AUDIENCE MEMBER: Eric Briggs, Secretary of Defense Fellows Program. It has been repeatedly said that Iraqi oil is for the Iraqis. Yesterday, our luncheon speaker, the president of the Ex-Im Bank, made an interesting suggestion that said at least some of the revenue from that should go directly to the Iraqi people, and I think the model would be, a North Shore oil profits, going to the citizens of Alaska in direct payments. I think this is interesting on a couple of factors, one it forgoes trickle-down economics, getting the money to the citizens who are out of work—they need disposable income now. And I also think that it provides a counter to the cynics inside and outside Iraq that said this war was just about oil and getting the profits from that into the Western companies. So my question is, what do you think about it?

YASSEEN: I think it's a nutty idea. I'll tell you why. It might work in Alaska, but it won't work in Iraq. It won't work to distribute wealth in Iraq. Iraq is a highly patriarchic, clannish society. What you'll be doing if you do that, you'll enrich the sheiks and patriarchs of families. This money will go then into, you know, high-ticket acquisitions like air conditioners and cars, and things like that; it's a disincentive to work. Bear in mind that then, this money will be tithed in many parts of Iraq, and this tithing might go to people that you don't want to have a lot of resources. I think it's a nutty idea. I think what would be much better is to use that money to institute a public works program. Pay people for work.

DOBBINS: Well, and the main problem with the idea in the short term, there isn't any excess funds to distribute. In the longer term, the main problem with it is that the Iraqi oil revenues essentially pay for the functioning of the state because people don't pay taxes. There's no tax system. You would have to set up a tax system so that the state would have revenue from taxes so that it could distribute the oil revenues. That would mean you'd have to set up a bureaucracy to distribute the oil revenue and to collect taxes, both of which would be difficult and subject to a good deal of graft and corruption.

SODERBERG: Rafee, did you want to comment on that, or no?

DOBBINS: Other than that, we're all for it.

AUDIENCE MEMBER: Hi, my name is Rebecca DeRenado, I'm from American University, and my question is for Mr. Dobbins. I was just wondering, given the criticism that the U.S. entered Iraq without the approval of the UN Security Council, and given that, despite that the international community is now willing to support and help rebuild Iraq, why doesn't the U.S. want to accept their help as soon as possible?

DOBBINS: Well, it's not as if a lot of countries are rushing to offer large amounts of help. The administration is prepared to cede some or share some degree of control in exchange for some degree of external resources. The administration has been very cautious about how much it's prepared to share. And the rest of the world has been even more cautious about how much of the burden they're prepared to share, and the more the security situation in Iraq degenerates, the less likely it is that other countries are going to be lining up to seize the opportunity. I think if the administration had made a more generous offer earlier on when it wasn't being compelled to do so by a deteriorating situation and mounting costs, they would have received a much more positive response than they're getting now. So this is going to be a difficult process played out over a number of months in which we seek to get more partners and more burden sharing and others seek to get greater control.

There are good reasons to be cautious about sharing control because unity of command is important in a peace operation just as much as it is in a traditional military or combat operation. And that's true on the civil as well as the military side. At the same time, we did find ways of achieving adequate unity of command and broad participation in both Bosnia and Kosovo, and so there are mechanisms by which you can achieve this if you have a will to do so.

AUDIENCE MEMBER: John Delong from Kurdish Service, Voice of America. The neighboring country of Iran has for too long interfered in Iraq's internal affairs. They not only opposed the U.S. policy in Iraq, but also in the whole Middle East. How would you seek to invite those countries to take part in security matters in Iraq? Thank you.

SODERBERG: Do you want to take it?

SALIH: I think I said in my opening remarks that neighbors of Iraq should stay away from the domestic scene inside Iraq. And I mean any of the neighboring countries will complicate the security and the political environment in the country. It's better to keep them out. And I think they will benefit that way as well because a stable Iraq will ultimately be to the benefit of the entire region.

SODERBERG: Would that include putting Turkish troops in the south?

SALIH: Obviously, there are sensitivities, known sensitivities, from the Kurdish sites to Turkish involvement. I want to respond to that issue of Turkish military involvement in Iraq, from a larger Iraqi perspective, not necessarily a Kurdish perspective. I believe that the neighbors of Iraq, with the historical baggage that they have vis-a-vis this country will complicate the security task. Turkish troops or for that matter, Iranian troops, not speaking the language, will not be able to enhance and contribute as much as people make it out to be. Turkey, as a neighbor of Iraq, has an interest in stability in that country, and I think we should all focus on promoting the indigenous Iraqi capability to augment the coalition in that regard.

I do have an open mind, as an Iraqi, to some Arab countries that do not have designs on Iraq, who have had no involvement historically of the domestic affairs of Iraq, to help us develop the capabilities that we need to take a better handle on security.

YASSEEN. Yes, I've heard this discussed, and I think most of the people I've talked about this with, the consensus is to try to get Moroccan troops or Algerian troops, no neighboring countries.

AUDIENCE MEMBER: Joseph, formally with the ICG and many of the organizations in the Balkans, now with the Woodrow Wilson Center. Two questions, one on this question about the pace of transfer to Iraqis themselves and the second on security. On the pace, Ambassador Dobbins, you said that Yugoslavia was the best example, maybe the best model to—the most relevant model. And what I'm wondering is, as you well know, one of the problems in the Balkans is not only ethnic conflict, but the fact that it's been the legacy of a socialist government, the transition—two problems there. And I'm wondering, if you and your colleagues there in the panel would agree that maybe there are similar problems in Iraq, that inefficiencies, corruption, lack of judiciary, and so forth, and will those in fact be the real obstacles to transferring to the Iraqis? The second question on security—Dr. Salih, basically, if I can fairly encapsulate, you said we shouldn't believe our eyes, the situation is much better, but yet the security situation may get worse. And you also mentioned the importance of getting this reconstruction money, $20 billion. The other day I was listening on the radio and heard Ambassador Bremer testifying before Congress, and he answered a very interesting question. The question was, this $20 billion, does it include money for sabotage? If we rebuild a power plant and then it's blown up, does it get rebuilt? He had a very interesting answer. He said, first, we're going to combat this because these saboteurs, terrorists, are going to get shot; and the second thing he said is that, in time, we're going to have alternatives, for example, alternative power sources up. So there won't be as much sensational impact from the terrorists, and the term he used is "tipping point." We're going to get to the tipping point. Now, my question for you is, are we really going to get to that tipping point in Iraq? If, as you say, this is a defining moment for these terrorists, if they lose here, they're going to lose in other places, and I think as one of your colleagues mentioned, the border situation, we have neighboring countries who may not share at all our interests in success in Iraq. Thank you.

SODERBERG: That's one way of cheating, you get two questions. So maybe Rafee and Jim would want to touch on the first question, and then we'll go to Barham about the transfer of power for you all.

DOBBINS: Well, I do think that the lack of adequate institutional capacity, both to run a democratic political system and to run a market-oriented economy, is the major obstacle to a smooth and rapid transfer to an enduringly democratic government, and building up that capacity is the main leg—it's the main obstacle to moving quickly. It's not just a lack of adequate police—it's across the board. Although, Iraq does have, you know, a reasonably competent bureaucracy, but one that's accustomed to working within a very different framework. On the— I know I was only asked to answer the first question—but on the second, I'm not sure that for, you know, sort of the global terrorist movement, this is a defining moment. This is from their standpoint, a target of opportunity. But their headquarters, their sources of funds, their leadership, and their capacity to organize is not going to be put into Iraq. It's going to stay in places like Canada and Germany and Indonesia and Malaysia and other noninvadeable countries. And it's going to be the frontline fighters that go off and wreak havoc in Iraq. But having defeated them will not defeat the mainline capacity of these organizations to create problems.

AHMED: On the first question, I believe that sovereignty can be transferred, even if all the institutions have not yet come up to the best functioning position.

DOBBINS: Oh, I agree with that.

AHMED: We have had instances like that. For example, in the case of Cambodia, sovereignty was transferred immediately to a council, which was established, the Supreme National Council, as it was called, and when discussions on the Resolution 1483 were taking place, people had thought that there would probably be three stages. The first stage would be the interim Iraqi administration, which would essentially concentrate on getting Iraqis involved in the day-to-day running of the administrative machinery. But then there should be an intermediate stage where you transfer sovereignty to a provisional Iraqi government, which is regarded as truly representative of all the people of Iraq. Later, once the constitution has been drafted or the old constitution is revived, it's up to the Iraqis to decide that and elections are held. There would be then an emergence of a democratically elected representative government. But the second stage would involve the full transfer of sovereignty and then, of course, the sovereign Iraqi authority would be able to invite anybody to stay there to help them, to maintain security. As in Afghanistan today, as Professor Dobbins was mentioning, the sovereignty issue was never there from day one. There was a sovereign government and the presence of the U.S. forces or the international security force that is there because the government asked their assistance for maintaining security. So the sovereign provisional Iraqi government could ask for support from the United States and other coalition partners or from other countries, if it so wished.

SODERBERG. Last word—it's 1:00, and I know we're standing between you and lunch. Sorry. So, Barham, you are going to get the last word in and then we'll close.

SALIH. Terrorism is a unique phenomenon. It should not be the barometer that would define every aspect of life to observe in the situation inside Iraq. I live in Sulaimania, I believe we have a good, solid security situation, but every day, we have to contend with the possibility of a car bomb at this government building or at that institution. I was living in the United States before September 11, having come back here after September 11 is an entirely different situation. Is the United States insecure? Could I take what happened in New York, or wherever, as a broad brush and say the United States as a country, as a society, is unstable, insecure? Obviously, I don't want to say that the situation in Iraq and that of the United States are comparable. You're talking about fundamentally two different situations. But much of the country is doing fine, doing much better than what was expected given the context that we described. That controlling fact, or that iron grip, that was in control of everything vanished, yet this society, the turmoil, the confusion that it has gone through was a lot less than many other comparable situations, including some places in the former Soviet Union.

Transfer of power and sovereignty. I'm not the legal expert. To me, it's ironic, this label of occupation force. And that was one of the more unfortunate things that is associated with the present situation in Iraq and has confused some of the politics of this. And I wish that we could do away with that label as soon as possible.

Lawyers should not be the only people who decide on these things because of political connotations of that notion of occupation and passing on sovereignty: it confuses the issues that are involved.

I can tell you most Iraqis, and I think these were borne out by polls in a recent Gallop poll or whatever, do not want the American forces to leave. Because if they leave today, regional powers will intervene, will come in, and we could possibly have a civil war. Americans are seen as liberators.

In fact, responding to some of the notions, the legalistic and political UN perspective on these issues, many Iraqis look upon their fate, their predicament, as being one of the failures of the United Nations system. Like Rwanda, Iraq was also missed; the genocide in Iraq was not responded to in time. It's difficult for many of us to accept the revisionist logic—unilateralism should be avoided, preemptive action should have been avoided in favor of multilateralism. That logic for me, as an Iraqi, and I hope my colleague would share the same view, obviously we would have liked to have had a larger international coalition and the entire Security Council coming to our aid as Iraqis and helping us overcome the mass graves and get away from that regime. But in those notions, those luxuries of the debates within the chambers of the Security Council and elsewhere, and in world capitals [that] did not come to our aid, and I believe the world should say,

the Security Council included, having seen those mass graves, we should have
acted sooner and we should have joined with the coalition that moved into Iraq,
and instead of questioning the legitimacy of the liberation and the intervention of
Iraq, they should say we have missed many important years, let's now work with
these people and make sure that the transition is easier than what it can predict to
be.

SODERBERG: Thank you very much. I want to thank the Eisenhower National
Security Conference, and Captain Craig in particular, for putting this all together.

I will say, if you liked what Jim Dobbins had to say, he has a new book out on
nation building that you can get through RAND, *America's Role in Nation-Building:
From Germany to Iraq*. We've brought some crisis materials. They're also available
on our web site—crisisweb.org—and give you some international updates there.
And we've given you some food for thought, and I want to extend a warm thanks
to our panelists.

Thank you very much.

Closing Address

National Power in Its Entirety

Ambassador Richard L. Armitage, Deputy Secretary of State
Introduction by Janne E. Nolan, Ph.D., Adjunct Professor, Security
Studies Program, Georgetown University

Summary

- The Eisenhower Series has long provided a forum for some of this nation's most gifted strategic thinkers to come together to challenge the orthodoxy of the day on the nexus between political and military strategy.
- Defense Secretary Donald Rumsfeld deserves a great deal of credit. His commitment to the task of transformation to an information-age military that is flexible, light, agile, and hostile has helped set our country on the course to a more secure future. In Iraq, the coalition forces were linked together by webs of information, with air surveillance guiding ground troops and ground reconnaissance aiding air forces—all in real time. The military operation was efficient, responsive, and absolutely precise in its lethality.
- We have reached a remarkable junction in the history of our nation, where we are able to wield our force at arms in a way that is consistent with our goals as a society. American troops are well-trained and highly motivated with technologically sophisticated equipment. They can carry out any mission necessary to achieve American interests, while greatly minimizing the destruction to civilian lives, property, and infrastructure and maximizing the ability to protect American combat forces.
- Even with this most powerful military history has ever seen, there are certain variables that do not change much. Today, it is still a soldier on the field of battle, seizing and holding ground, who ultimately determines the outcome of a fight. A soldier standing on enemy territory bends an enemy to our will, and Iraq proves the importance of this point.
- Iraq also has underscored another durable truth: The power of a nation and all the persuasion that power can command never has resided and never will reside solely in military might.

1. As the soldier holds ground, like U.S. forces and those of other countries are doing right now in Iraq, the United States must hold a different kind of ground. Victory in Iraq just will not be when American soldiers can hold their place without fear of attack or ambush. It also will be when the lights go on across the country; when clean water flows from all the taps, when ordinary people can go about their business in the streets of Kirkuk, Baghdad and Karbala; and when Iraq is governed by Iraqis, chosen freely and fairly.

2. We owe it to our men and women in uniform to use every tool we have to forge ahead. The United States also must work with other nations and work as a partner, not a patron.

3. It is now time for the world to turn to the task of helping the people of Iraq. We must succeed. It is not just as matter of principle or obligation, and it is not even to alleviate the suffering of the people of Iraq. We must succeed in securing Iraq now that we have saved it because it is a matter of our own national interests, because it is in the American character to finish the job and to finish it right, and because it is in the vital international interests to see that this nation in the heart of the Middle East will not only cease to be a threat to the region and the world, but also become a source of stability and success on today's terms.

• The United States and a coalition of 46 countries is not an occupation of Iraq in the sense that the world is most familiar with, a term that makes our friends and allies understandably wary.

• Iraq is also about humanitarian relief, security, and self-interest. And the U.S. investment will be worth the cost. The hard truth is that the $20 billion that President Bush has requested for reconstruction costs may seem like a lot of money, but the United States has spent an even more considerable sum of money combating and containing Saddam Hussein over the last 13 years. The United States has to be prepared to expend its resources to achieve peace, not just to make war.

• The vast majority of Iraqis want to redeem their country. And even though they are anxious about the timetable, they are on their way to reclaiming their sovereignty. In the end, only the people of Iraq can overcome the terrible legacy left to them by Saddam Hussein.

1. A new legacy will require good governance in a civil society and improved security.

2. The vast majority of Iraqis are hungry to resume the normal rhythm of life, and that is the desire that, in the end, will win out.

3. One of the central challenges will continue to be patience because democracy is not a quick fix; rather, it is an interlocking system of citizens' groups, institutions, and businesses, which takes time to form and flourish. If the coalition leaves the country too soon, all that has been achieved to date, all of the sacrifice of the soldiers and millions of Iraqis who want a better life, could be rapidly undone.

• The actions today in Iraq will delineate what kind of world we want to see, and America's place in it.

1. It will take confident American leadership and a comprehensive effort, working in cooperation with many nations, to succeed in Iraq. This is what it also will take to meet the other great challenges of today.

2. For the United States, this will mean membership in multilateral organizations that are productive, including a growing NATO and World Trade Organization, which serve the interests of all of their members. It also means nurturing a network of relationships with our oldest allies in Europe and our newest friends around the world such as Russia and the People's Republic of China.

• Although the Pew poll on global attitudes tracked a strong current of anti-American sentiment in the world, it also tracked an equally strong current of admiration for American values.

1. A return to a great superpower competition with annihilation hanging in the balance is not in anyone's interests. There are certainly steps that the United States can take to allay some of the animosity, which include a more finely tuned public diplomacy.

2. The United States offers the world a flexible model of representative government, and it is a model based on values that everyone in the world wants and not enough people have.

• It is that basic desire to live free that forms the basis of President Bush's national security strategy.

• It is in the world's interests to see a strong America that succeeds, just as it is in the world's interests to see success in Iraq. The alternative would be an unacceptable failure—a victory for terror, chaos, and tyranny. It is in America's best interest to stand together with our partners and with the United Nations to help Iraq. In doing so, we help ourselves define our nation in a new century as an enduring force for prosperity in a peaceful world.

• At the end of the day, that American soldier standing there with tenure on the land has to stand for more than the power of a magnificent gun. The soldier also has to stand for the power of American ideals. This image of the young American standing resolute in the world ultimately speaks for the entirety of our national power.

Analysis

In his brief remarks, Deputy Secretary of State Richard L. Armitage made a policy statement in which he linked military transformation to success in Iraq and future conflict. Specifically, he addressed three things: military transformation as a foundation for the future; the need to secure Iraq now that we have saved it; and the requirement for good governance, socioeconomic development, and security for Iraq's new legacy. The creation and consolidation of this legacy will require all the instruments of power of the United States and other collaborating nations. Within that context, the deputy secretary brought us back to where we began: military transformation. He argued that strategic victory in Iraq—and elsewhere—will also require a military that can and will go beyond traditional warfighting to help consolidate battlefield success and turn military victory into strategic victory.

First, the task of transformation to an information-age military that is flexible, light, agile, and hostile has helped set the United States on a course to a more secure future. Armitage pointed out that in Iraq we saw coalition forces that were linked together by webs of information that gave us a military operation that was responsive to political direction, efficient, and absolutely precise in its lethality. He argued that we have reached a juncture in history in which the nexus of political and military capabilities and strategy allows us to wield our power in a way that is consistent with our goals as a society. In that connection, he underscored another point: The power of a nation and all the persuasion that power can command never has resided, and never will reside, solely in military might.

Second, Armitage emphasized that since the inhumane and murderous regime of Saddam Hussein is no longer a threat to the people of Iraq and the stability of the rest of the Middle East, we must make that country a model for the region and the future. Indeed, he argued that President Bush has invoked the idea of a new Marshall Plan for Iraq and the region and that the United States must again use its resources to reclaim peace, rebuild infrastructure, and ensure democratic processes. This is not just a matter of principle. It is a matter of our own national interest. As France and the rest of Western Europe were saved from political, economic, and military devastation by the first Marshall Plan, Iraq and much of the Middle East may also become sources of stability and success on today's terms. Armitage argued that, like our earlier investment in the European Marshall Plan, our investment in Iraq and the Middle East will be worth the cost, but will take time, effort, and patience. If the coalition leaves Iraq too soon, all we have achieved to date—all the sacrifice of our soldiers—will have been in vain. That would lead to victory for terror, victory for chaos, and victory for tyranny.

Third, the deputy secretary stated that Iraq is a critical test case for this new century. He reasoned that this case will delineate the kind of world we want to see, and America's place in it. A new legacy for Iraq and the region will require good governance, socioeconomic development, security, and peace. The achievement of such an ambitious and worthy objective will require several things. It will require confident American leadership and a comprehensive effort working in cooperation with our oldest allies in Europe and our newest friends around the world. Moreover, it will require the deliberate creation of legitimate Iraqi governance and a peaceful and prosperous civil society. It will require the socioeconomic reconstruction of Iraq and sustaining the great global coalition against terrorism. It will also require finely tuned public diplomacy to take our message of freedom to the region and the world. As important as anything else, a just, stable, and peaceful Iraq will require a strong and resolute America, using all the instruments of power at its disposal. In that connection, Armitage concluded that the image of the young American soldier ultimately speaks most for the entirety of U.S. national power.

Transcript

AMBASSADOR RICHARD L. ARMITAGE: I am honored to be here. I have participated in the past in the Eisenhower series. This series has long provided a forum for some of this nation's most gifted strategic thinkers to come together to challenge the orthodoxy of the day on the nexus between political and military strategy. Given that context, it comes as no surprise to me that General Schoomaker is one of the sponsors of this event. Whether he's on the fields of battle or in the halls of bureaucracy, Peter Schoomaker has never met a challenge he couldn't tackle and take down.

Richard L. Armitage

And speaking of challenges, I understand that I'm batting cleanup in this conference. After such heavy hitters as Don Rumsfeld and my friend, Joe Nye, it will be a challenge for me, I guess, just to get on base.

I think in such a gathering, Secretary Rumsfeld deserves a great deal of credit. His indefatigable commitment to the task of transformation to an information-age military that is flexible, light, agile, hostile has helped set our country on the course to a more secure future. Certainly, in Iraq, we saw coalition forces which were linked together by webs of information, with air surveillance guiding ground troops and ground reconnaissance aiding air forces, all in real time. And that gave us a military operation that was efficient, it was responsive, and it was absolutely precise in its lethality.

Indeed, you might say that we have reached a remarkable junction in the history of our nation—certainly, in that nexus of political and military strategy—where we are able to wield our force at arms in a way that is consistent with our goals as a society. We have well-trained and highly motivated troops with technologically sophisticated equipment. They can carry out any mission we might see as necessary to our interests, while greatly minimizing the destruction to civilian lives, property, and infrastructure and maximizing our ability to protect our own combat forces.

And yet, even with this most powerful military history has ever seen, we find that there are certain variables that don't change much. And so today, it is still a soldier on the field of battle, seizing and holding ground—tenure on the land—who ultimately determines the outcome of a fight. It is still the inescapable suasion of a soldier with a bayonet standing on enemy territory that bends an enemy to our will, and Iraq has proven to us all just how important that point is.

Iraq has also underscored another durable truth: The power of a nation and all the suasion that power can command never has resided and never will reside solely in military might. After all, even that essential soldier who takes and holds ground can only stand there defending territory for so long, particularly when he or she comes from an all-volunteer force of a democratic nation.

And so, as the soldier must hold ground, as our forces and those of 31 other countries are doing right now in Iraq, we must also hold a different kind of ground. Because victory in Iraq won't just be when our soldiers can hold their place without fear of attack or ambush, it will also be when the lights go on across the country, when clean water flows from all the taps. It will be when ordinary people can go about their business in the streets of Kirkuk, of Baghdad, and Karbala. It will be when Iraq is governed by Iraqis, chosen freely and fairly by their countrymen and women.

This is a noble and worthy goal, one for which the United States has accepted responsibility, and one that will not be achieved on the quick. After all, democracy means more than holding a vote. It means constituting an entire system, a system of laws, a system that guarantees the rights of all peoples, and all the necessary institutions of civil society and of a healthy economy.

Now, today in Iraq, the United States and our partners have cleared the way for this sort of development to take place. And now we owe it to our men and women in uniform to use every tool we have to forge ahead, not just our military force, but also our political and our economic clout, and the energy and the optimism of the American character.

We will also need to act in concert with other countries. We have never sought any gain of territory from the conquest of Iraq. And so for the sake of our credibility in this world, for the resources we will need to sustain this operation in the time it will take to succeed, we absolutely have to work with other nations and work as a partner, not a patron.

Saddam Hussein was murderous with unquenchable extraterritorial ambitions. He killed many hundreds of thousands of his people in wars against his neighbors and wars against his domestic opponents, and in his attempts to redraw the map of Iraq, the demographic map of Iraq. His control of the world's second largest reserves of oil not only kept him in place, giving him, in effect, a blank check for a military buildup of conventional and unconventional arms, it also gave him the ability to destabilize the region and threaten our vital interests out of all proportion to his real power.

All of the considerable pressure the international community brought to bear could not change that situation. Sanctions, however well meant, never stopped Saddam Hussein from spending billions whenever he wanted to. And so, regardless of disagreements over the actions we were compelled to take in March, every other country in the international community knew that where Iraq was concerned, a day of reckoning was inevitable.

Iraq has been a closed society for more than a generation, and so it was difficult to know the true conditions under which people lived. Oh, we knew conditions were bad, but they were worse than we could have known. I am talking about the people Hussein tortured, butchered, dumped into mass graves. I am talking about his criminal neglect of physical infrastructure. Bechtel performed a comprehensive assessment of Iraq back in April, and they found roads and bridges and sewage treatment plants, oil production equipment, and electric power stations had been left to rot for the better part of 20 years. And in many cases, those rotting structures were also bearing the scars of three successive wars. Ultimately, though, I am also talking about the terrible damage Saddam Hussein did to the psychological infrastructure of Iraqi society.

And so now it is time for the world to turn to the task of helping the people of Iraq, and we must succeed. It's not just as a matter of principle because we are somehow obligated to seeing this through, and not even because we want to alleviate the suffering of the people of Iraq, no matter how important that is. The sad truth is that there are suffering people all over the world, and the first obligation for any nation on that score is to its own people. We must succeed in securing Iraq now that we have saved it because it is a matter of our own national interests, because it is in the American character to finish the job and to finish it right, and because it is in the vital international interests to see that this nation in the heart of the Middle East, the very cradle of civilization and a mainstay of the modern economy, will not only cease to be a threat to the region and the world, but will become a source of stability and success on today's terms.

The United States and a coalition of 46 countries is working with determination to ensure that Iraq reaches that success and achieves stability. But I want to be clear that this is not an occupation in the sense that the world is most familiar with, a term that makes our friends and allies understandably wary. Certainly, France remembers all too well its own devastating and degrading experience in World War II. Indeed, it speaks to the unyielding spirit of France that the people of Paris liberated the city from within, even as the 2d Armored Division of Free French led American troops into the city. But the Third Reich had no intention of returning Paris to the French, certainly not intact.

What we see today in Iraq is the opposite. It was Saddam Hussein who turned his own country into a wasteland, and it's his remnant network of collaborators, along with their foreign recruits, who continue that dirty work today. These people offer their country nothing, just as the Taliban and its al Qaeda masters had nothing to offer to the people of Afghanistan, only a continued cycle of death, pillage, and destruction. And it's simply not an option to consign the 23 million-plus people of Iraq back to that fate, any more than it is an option in Afghanistan.

So Paris, in the end, was saved. Not just by the will of its inhabitants and allied forces at arms, but by ingenuity and by entrepreneurship, and by that massive investment in the future mentioned so many times in the course of your conference, the Marshall Plan. Indeed, President Bush invoked the Marshall Plan in his address to the United Nations. The vision of George Marshall, which met with skepticism at the time, was borne out. His intent was not just humanitarian, and it wasn't just security, even though he meant to make sure we were not drawn into another war. It was also about economic self-interest. And indeed, today, the European Union is this nation's largest single economic partner, accounting for some $376 billion in annual trade flows, and hundreds of billions more in investment.

And so Iraq is also about humanitarian relief, it's about security, and it's about self-interest. And here, too, our investment will be worth the cost. And I want to remind you all of a hard truth. The $20 billion that President Bush has requested for reconstruction costs may seem like a lot of money, but we have spent an even more considerable sum of money combating and containing Saddam Hussein over the last 13 years. At this point, we have to be prepared to expend our resources to achieve peace, not just to make war.

The vast majority of Iraqis want to redeem their country. And while they are understandably anxious about the timetable, they are on their way to reclaiming their sovereignty. The Coalition Provisional Authority and Jerry Bremer deserve a great deal of credit in my mind for the considerable progress we have seen to date and for laying out the steps it will take to support the development of a true democracy. But in the end, only the people of Iraq can overcome the terrible legacy left to them by Saddam Hussein.

A new legacy will require good governance, economic recovery, and a reconstituted civil society, and, of course, improved security. The Iraqi Governing Council has now been recognized as a legitimate interim representative of the people of Iraq by the Arab League, by OPEC, by the UN Security Council, and most recently by the United Nations General Assembly. The Council appointed 25 new ministers. And the tragic death yesterday of Minister Akila al-Hashemi has actually given her colleagues one more reason to carry on, one more reminder that they hold the future of Iraq in their hands. Of course, political developments won't succeed without tandem economic developments. So today, an array of projects are under way, including repairs that will make the country's infrastructure reliable for the first time in generations. Unfortunately, the repairs to the psychological infrastructure will be much more challenging. The economy has long been undermined by handouts, petty larcenies, and a significant black market. But Iraq has always had the natural and human resources it needed to feed the people and fuel the economy, and now Iraqis must find the willpower to do so. Our military forces have cleared the way, and now the Coalition Provisional Authority is helping constitute a healthy civil society that will be able to support a free market economy and a representative government, including better schools, local banks, hospitals, but also PTAs [Parent Teacher Associations] and local city councils, and paying work with reconstruction contracts.

Of course, for all of these fine efforts, security remains a challenge. And so we will continue to recruit and train Iraqi forces to police the streets and protect both peoples and facilities. And, indeed, the president's supplemental requests envision an additional $5 billion for that task alone.

It's my view that the vast majority of Iraqis are hungry to resume the normal rhythm of life. And I believe that is the desire that in the end will win out. In fact, I suspect that one of our central challenges will continue to be patience. Again, democracy is not a quick fix. It is an interlocking system of citizens groups, institutions, and indeed businesses, and they take some time to form where they have not been allowed to flourish. If the coalition leaves the country too soon, all we have achieved to date, all of the sacrifice of our soldiers and the millions of Iraqis who want a better life, could be rapidly undone.

Now, I realize that I was asked to speak to you today about "National Power in Its Entirety." It's a rather modest subject, I must say. And it may seem that I have driven off on a tangent from that magisterial topic by focusing so much on Iraq. Indeed, I'm sure Iraq has been the predominant theme of this conference, and that is as it should be. It may well be that Iraq is a critical test case for a new century. Indeed, I believe that our actions today in Iraq will delineate what kind of world we want to see, and America's place in it.

What it will take to succeed in Iraq—confident American leadership and a comprehensive effort, working in cooperation with many nations—is what it will take to meet the other great challenges of our day. This includes reconstructing Afghanistan and sustaining the great global coalition against terrorism, prevailing against the nuclear ambitions of North Korea and of Iran, and bringing peace to Israel and to Palestine. But it also includes dealing adequately with such sweeping challenges as HIV/AIDS, where there is no military solution at all, or for that matter, seizing on the tremendous opportunities of our day for expanding trade and for expanding investment, for sharing in intellectual property, agricultural productivity, and information technology. It all will take a world system of partnerships.

For the United States, that will mean membership in multilateral organizations that are productive, including a revitalized and growing NATO, a WTO [World Trade Organization] which serves the interests of all its members, and undertakings such as the Middle East Partnership Initiative. But it also means nurturing a network of relationships with our oldest allies in Europe and our newest friends around the world to include Russia and the People's Republic of China, which have increasingly acted as partners in a variety of common causes from trade and investment to the war on terrorism. Indeed, we expect that President Putin and President Bush will be able to extend the personal warmth between them into deeper relations between our countries in the course of their Camp David summit tonight and tomorrow.

Now, I believe we're all familiar with the Pew poll on global attitudes, which tracked a strong current of anti-American sentiment in the world. But you shouldn't forget that it also tracked an equally strong current of admiration for American values. And so while people around the world instinctively may not care for the concentration of power in American hands, the current state of affairs is far more in any nation's interest than the alternatives. The fact is that a return to a great superpower competition with annihilation hanging in the balance is not in anyone's interests, nor is forcing on the world a model of state power based on repression and selective deprivation. Now, there are certainly steps, including more graceful cooperation in worthwhile multilateral efforts and a more finely tuned public diplomacy, that we can take to allay some of the animosity and some of the built-up anxiety.

But the essential truth is that the United States offers the world a flexible model of representative government, one that thrives on free minds and on free markets. It is a model based on values that everyone in the world wants and not enough people have. Indeed, millions of people around the world aspire to these values in spite of their own governments. So it is no surprise that some governments try to distract attention with convenient anti-Americanism.

It is that basic desire to live free that forms the basis of President Bush's national security strategy, which is to prevail against terrorists, whether freelance or holding a state hostage, and to promote and support the development of democratic institutions across the Middle East and around the world.

And so it is in the world's interests to see a strong America that succeeds, just as it is in the world's interests to see success in Iraq. Not because other nations agree with every decision our government takes, but because the alternative would be an unacceptable failure—a victory for terror, a victory for chaos, and a victory for tyranny. It is in our interests to stand together with our partners and with the United Nations to help Iraq, and in so doing, to help ourselves to define our nation in a new century as an enduring force for prosperity in a peaceful world.

And so, at the end of the day, that American soldier standing there with tenure on the land has to stand for more than the power of a magnificent gun. The soldier also has to stand for the power of our ideals. It is the preeminence of these ideals that has given this nation such predominance at this junction of history. And it is that image of the young American standing resolute in the world that ultimately speaks most to the entirety of our national power.

Thank you very much. Good afternoon.

JANNE E. NOLAN, Ph.D.: This concludes our very successful meeting. I just want to extend, I think on behalf of everyone, profound thanks to Secretary Armitage for such inspiring remarks.

I have administrative remarks, which is such a downer after that. I'm so sorry.

I've been asked to please ask all of you who have participated in this conference to go to the web site for the National Security Series and fill in the questionnaire to give feedback to the Army organizers about what you liked and what you didn't like about the conference, so that, as we used to say in the interest of criticism and self-criticism, it can be improved next year.

And let me just conclude and, again, to thank the leadership of the U.S. Army, to thank General Schoomaker, to thank his predecessors, and to extend a very, very warm general thanks to all the people who worked so hard—all those wonderful young Army officers and their associates. And I have been told, by them specifically, I'm not allowed to name names, but you know who you are, for putting together such a really very, very brilliant, eclectic, fair-minded, and open dialogue for two days.

Thank you very much.

BIOGRAPHIES

Rafeeuddin Ahmed

Rafeeuddin Ahmed is the former UN undersecretary-general and special advisor to the UN secretary-general on Iraq.

Since June 2000, Ahmed has been special representative of the World Tourism Organization to the United Nations, as well as special advisor to the executive director of the United Nations Development Fund for Women.

Ahmed, a former Pakistani diplomat, joined the United Nations in May 1970 and since then has held numerous UN positions, including assistant secretary-general and executive assistant to the secretary-general; undersecretary-general and chef de cabinet of the secretary-general; undersecretary-general for political affairs, trusteeship, and decolonization; and undersecretary-general and special representative of the secretary-general for humanitarian affairs in Southeast Asia.

He also has held several economic and social development positions such as undersecretary-general for international economic and social affairs; undersecretary-general and executive secretary of the United Nations Economic and Social Commission for Asia and the Pacific; undersecretary-general and associate administrator of the United Nations Development Program; secretary of the Economic and Social Council; and director of the Resources and Program Planning Office, Department of Economic and Social Affairs.

From February 2003 to July 2003, Ahmed was undersecretary-general and special adviser to the secretary-general on Iraq. He also has had numerous special assignments at the United Nations including chairman, United Nations Appointment and Promotion Board; member, board of trustees, United Nations Institute for Training and Research; and principal aide to the secretary-general for the Iran hostage crisis.

Ahmed completed graduate studies in international economics and international law at the Fletcher School of Law and Diplomacy and earned his Bachelor of Arts with honors in economics and political science and Master of Arts in political science from the University of the Punjab, Lahore, Pakistan.

He jointly edited a book entitled, *Lessons Learned in Crises and Post-Conflict Situations*.

Ahmed speaks English, French, and Urdu.

Ambassador Richard L. Armitage

Ambassador Richard Lee Armitage's nomination as deputy secretary of state was confirmed by the Senate on March 23, 2001. He was sworn in on March 26, 2001.

Since May 1993, Armitage was president of Armitage Associates LC. He was engaged in worldwide business and public policy endeavors as well as frequent public speaking and writing.

He previously held senior troubleshooting and negotiating positions in the State Department, Department of Defense, and Congress. From 1992 to 1993, Armitage directed U.S. assistance to the Newly Independent States of the former Soviet Union. In January 1992, the Bush administration's desire to jump-start international assistance to the NIS resulted in his appointment as coordinator for emergency humanitarian assistance. During his tenure in these positions, he completed extensive international coordination projects with the European Community, Japan, and other donor countries.

From 1989 to 1992, he filled key diplomatic positions as presidential special negotiator for the Philippines Military Bases Agreement and special mediator for water in the Middle East. Former President Bush sent him as a special emissary to Jordan's King Hussein during the 1991 Gulf War.

From 1983 to 1989, Armitage served as assistant secretary of defense for international security affairs. He played a leading role in Middle East security policies.

From 1975 to 1976, he was posted as a Pentagon consultant in Tehran. After two years in the private sector, he became administrative assistant to Senator Robert Dole in 1978. In the 1980 Reagan campaign, he was senior advisor to the Interim Foreign Policy Advisory Board. From 1981 until June 1983, he was deputy assistant secretary of defense for East Asia and Pacific affairs in the Office of the Secretary of Defense.

Armitage graduated in 1967 from the U.S. Naval Academy. He served on a destroyer stationed on the Vietnam gunline and subsequently completed three combat tours in Vietnam. He left active duty in 1973 and joined the United States Defense Attaché Office, Saigon. Immediately prior to the fall of Saigon, he organized and led the removal of Vietnamese naval assets and personnel from the country. Armitage is fluent in Vietnamese.

He is a four-time recipient of the Department of Defense Medal for Distinguished Public Service. Other awards include the Secretary of Defense Medal for Outstanding Public Service, the Chairman of the Joint Chiefs Award for Outstanding Public Service, the Presidential Citizens Medal, and the Department of State Distinguished Honor Award.

David M. Cote

David M. Cote is chairman and chief executive officer of Honeywell. He was first elected president, CEO, and a member of the board of Honeywell in February 2002, and became chairman of the board of directors July 1, 2002. Previously, Cote served as chairman, president, and CEO of TRW, a $16 billion, Cleveland-based products and services provider for the automotive, aerospace, and information technology markets.

Before joining TRW in November 1999, he served for 25 years at General Electric, progressing through a series of top-level positions in manufacturing, finance, marketing, strategic planning, and general management. In 1996, he was appointed to his last position at GE as corporate senior vice president, president, and CEO of GE Appliances.

Cote is a 1976 graduate of the University of New Hampshire, where he earned a bachelor's degree in business administration. In April 2001, he was awarded Pepperdine University's highest honor, a Doctor of Laws, from the university's Graziadio School of Business and Management.

Chester A. Crocker, Ph.D.

Chester A. Crocker, Ph.D., is the James R. Schlesinger professor of strategic studies at Georgetown University's School of Foreign Service and serves on the board of its Institute for the Study of Diplomacy. Crocker's teaching and research focus is on international security, conflict management and mediation strategy.

From 1981 to 1989, Crocker served as assistant secretary of state for African affairs. He developed the strategy and led the diplomacy that produced the treaties signed by Angola, Cuba, and South Africa in New York in December 1988. These agreements resulted in Namibia's independence in March 1990 and the withdrawal of foreign forces from Namibia and Angola. As assistant secretary, he managed a regional bureau responsible for relations with 46 nations, supervising a budget of $116 million, 44 embassies, and a U.S. and foreign staff of 3,400.

Crocker serves as chairman of the board of the United States Institute of Peace. He also serves on the boards of ASA Ltd., Ashanti Goldfields Company Ltd., Modern Africa Growth and Investment Company LLC, and Boateng Baring and Partners Ltd. He is a founding member and director of the nonprofit Corporate Council on Africa and serves on the board of visitors of the National Defense University in Washington, D.C.

Crocker's previous professional experience includes service as news editor of *Africa Report* magazine, from 1968 to 1969, and staff officer at the National Security Council from 1970 to 1972, where he worked on Middle East, Indian Ocean, and Africa issues. He first joined Georgetown University as director of its Master of Science in Foreign Service program, serving concurrently as associate professor of international relations.

He has lectured and written on international politics, U.S. foreign policy, mediation and negotiation, African affairs, and post–Cold War security issues. He has appeared on numerous television shows; as a dinner or keynote speaker at conferences in the United States, Europe, and Africa; and as a witness in congressional hearings. His book, *High Noon in Southern Africa: Making Peace in a Rough Neighborhood*, was published by Norton in 1993.

Born in New York City in 1941, Crocker received his Bachelor of Arts from Ohio State University in 1963, graduating Phi Beta Kappa with distinction, in history. He received his Master of Arts and Doctor of Philosophy from Johns Hopkins University's School of Advanced International Studies. He and his wife, Saone, reside in Washington, D.C.

Ambassador James Dobbins

Ambassador James Dobbins is director of the International Security and Defense Policy Center at RAND, a nonprofit institution that helps improve policy and decision making through research and analysis.

He is a veteran diplomat who has held senior White House and Department of State positions under four presidents, having most recently served as the Bush administration's special envoy for Afghanistan. He previously served as a U.S. special envoy for Kosovo, Bosnia, Haiti, and Somalia.

He also has served as assistant secretary of state for Europe, special assistant to the president for the Western Hemisphere, special advisor to the president and secretary of state for the Balkans, and ambassador to the European Community.

Through the 1990s, he supervised peace operations in Kosovo and Bosnia, as he earlier had for Haiti and Somalia, managing American relief and reconstruction efforts in the Balkans in excess of $1 billion per annum.

In the wake of September 11, he served as the Bush administration's representative to the Afghan opposition. He worked to form and install a successor regime to the Taliban, represented the United States at the Bonn Conference, reopened the U.S. embassy in Kabul and represented the United States in the inauguration of Hamid Karzai as Afghanistan's new head of state.

Dobbins has expertise in Afghanistan, the Balkans, Iraq, and Europe and with U.S. foreign relations, NATO, and trends and issues in international security.

He received a bachelor's degree from the Georgetown University School of Foreign Service.

Dobbins has appeared on the BBC, the "CBS Evening News"; CNN's "American Morning"; CNN's "Larry King Live"; CNN FN; CNN International; "FOX News Sunday with Tony Snow"; PBS' "The NewsHour with Jim Lehrer"; ABC's News Radio; CNBC; ABC News Special, "The War in Iraq with Peter Jennings"; CBS' "60 Minutes"; NPR's "All Things Considered"; and NBC's "Saturday Today." He has appeared in articles by Cox News Service, Bloomberg, Knight Ridder News Service, the *Houston Chronicle*, Copley News Service, Reuters, and the *Financial Times*.

He is co-author of the book, *America's Role in Nation-Building: From Germany to Iraq*" (2003), with John G. McGinn, Keith Crane, Seth G. Jones, Rollie Lal, Andrew Rathmell, Rachel M. Swanger, and Anga Tamilsina.

Susan Eisenhower

Susan Eisenhower, president and chief executive officer of the Eisenhower Institute, is best known for her work in Russia and the former Soviet Union. Over the years, Eisenhower has testified before the Senate Armed Services and Senate Budget Committees on policy toward that region. She has been appointed to a third term to the National Academy of Sciences' standing Committee on International Security and Arms Control. In 2000, a year before the September 11 terrorist attacks, she co-edited a book, *Islam and Central Asia*, which carried the prescient subtitle, *An Enduring Legacy or an Evolving Threat?*

In the spring of 2000, the secretary of energy appointed Eisenhower to a blue ribbon task force, the Baker-Cutler Commission, to evaluate U.S.-funded nuclear nonproliferation programs in Russia, and since that time she has served as an advisor on another Department of Energy study. In the fall of 2001, she was appointed to serve on the International Space Station (ISS) Management and Cost Evaluation Task Force, which analyzed ISS management and cost overruns. She also serves as an academic fellow of the International Peace and Security program of the Carnegie Corporation of New York and is a director of the Carnegie Endowment for International Peace and the Nuclear Threat Initiative.

Eisenhower has spoken at diverse gatherings—universities, from Harvard to UCLA, World Affairs Councils; corporate gatherings; and to specialized audiences, such as the one assembled at the Army War College, where she gave the 1998 Commandant's Lecture. She also has spoken at the White House, as well as other prominent institutions.

Eisenhower's first professional experience was as a writer. Within the last 10 years, Eisenhower has authored three books, two of which—*Breaking Free* and *Mrs. Ike*—have appeared on bestseller lists. She also has edited three collected volumes on regional security issues and penned hundreds of op-eds and articles on foreign policy for publications such as the *Washington Post*, the *Los Angeles Times*, *USA Today*, the U.S. Naval Institute's *Proceedings*, the *Spectator* and Gannett newspapers. She has provided analysis for CNN International, MSNBC, "Nightline," "World News Tonight with Peter Jennings," "CBS Sunday Morning," "The NewsHour with Jim Lehrer," FOX News, and "Hardball," as well as National Public Radio and other nationwide television and radio programs.

Eisenhower also has consulted for major companies doing business overseas, such as IBM, American Express, and Loral Space Systems. She currently serves on the advisory board of Stonebridge International, a Washington-based international consulting firm chaired by former National Security Advisor Samuel "Sandy" Berger.

Douglas C. Farah

Douglas C. Farah recently joined the investigative staff of the *Washington Post*. For the previous 17 years, he worked as a foreign correspondent for the

Washington Post and other publications, covering Latin America and West Africa.

Born to missionary parents on July 22, 1957, he moved to the Amazon basin in Bolivia when he was 18 months old. When he was 7 years old, his family moved to La Paz. Following his graduation from the American Cooperative School in 1974, he spent several years working in rural development and traveling around Latin America and Europe.

In 1980, he enrolled at the University of Kansas, where he began working for United Press International. In 1985, after graduating with honors with a Bachelor of Arts in Latin American studies and a Bachelor of Science in journalism, he was named UPI bureau chief in El Salvador, covering the civil war there and the U.S.-backed Contra rebels in Honduras. In 1987, he left UPI to freelance for the *Washington Post*, the *Boston Globe* and *U.S. News & World Report*. In 1988, he won the Sigma Delta Chi Distinguished Service Award for Foreign Correspondence for a *Washington Post* series on right-wing death squads in El Salvador.

In 1990, he moved to Bogota, Colombia, to cover the exploding drug war in the Andean region. Working in Colombia, Venezuela, Ecuador, and Bolivia, he chronicled the rise and fall of the Medellin cartel and its leader, Pablo Escobar.

In 1992, he was hired by the *Washington Post* as staff correspondent for Central America and the Caribbean. In 1995, he was awarded the Maria Moor Cabot Prize by Columbia University for outstanding coverage of Latin America.

In 1997, Farah returned to Washington as the international investigative reporter covering drug trafficking and organized crime. He covered the emergence of Russian organized crime groups in Latin America and the Caribbean and the growth of Mexican drug cartels within the United States.

In March 2000, Farah was named West Africa bureau chief for the *Washington Post*. Based in Abidjan, Ivory Coast, he traveled and wrote extensively about the brutal civil wars in Sierra Leone and Liberia. In November 2001, Farah broke the story of al Qaeda's ties to those diamond and weapons networks. Later that month, because of threats against his life, Farah and his family were evacuated from West Africa.

He has just completed a book on terrorist financial structures, *Blood From Stones: The Secret Terrorist Financial Trail*, which will be published in May 2004 by Broadway Books of Random House.

David Gordon, Ph.D.

David Gordon, Ph.D., is the director of the Office of Transnational Issues at the Central Intelligence Agency. Analysts in this office provide direct intelligence on a broad array of crucial issues of national security, including global energy and economic security, corruption and illicit financial activity, foreign denial and deception programs, and societal and humanitarian conflicts.

Gordon joined the CIA in May 1998 when he was appointed national intelligence officer for economics and global issues on the National Intelligence Council (NIC). While on the NIC, he directed major analytical projects on country-level economic and financial crises, trends, and the changing geopolitics of energy and provided leadership for the NIC's seminal *Global Trends 2015* report.

Prior to his service on the NIC, Gordon was senior fellow and director of the U.S. Policy Program at the Overseas Development Council. Earlier, he served as a senior staff member on the International Relations Committee of the U.S. House of Representatives and as the regional economic policy advisor for the U.S. Agency for International Development, based in Nairobi, Kenya.

During the 1980s, Gordon pursued an academic career with a joint appointment at the University of Michigan and Michigan State University. Currently, he is an adjunct professor at the School of Foreign Service at Georgetown University. He also has taught at the College of William and Mary, Princeton University, and the University of Nairobi.

Gordon is a graduate of Bowdoin College and undertook graduate studies in both political science and economics at the University of Michigan, where he received his doctoral degree in 1981. He and his wife, Joan Parker, live in Washington, D.C., with their sons, Alexander and Charles.

Roy Gutman

Roy Gutman has reported on international affairs for more than three decades and is currently an adjunct professor at the Medill School of Journalism, a Jennings Randolph senior fellow at the U.S. Institute of Peace, and a Washington-based correspondent for *Newsweek*. From 1989 to 1994, he served as the *Newsday* European bureau chief, reporting on the fall of communism in Eastern Europe, the unification of Germany and the violent disintegration of Tito's Yugoslavia. His reports on "ethnic cleansing" in Bosnia-Herzegovina, including the first documented accounts of Serb-run concentration camps, won the Pulitzer Prize for international reporting in 1993, the George Polk Award for foreign reporting, the Selden Ring Award for investigative reporting, and other honors.

Gutman reported for Reuters in Bonn, Vienna, Belgrade, London, and Washington, D.C., including stints as the Belgrade bureau chief and State Department correspondent. His 19 years at *Newsday* included eight years as national security reporter in Washington.

He is the author of *Banana Diplomacy: The Making of American Policy in Nicaragua 1981–1987* (1988), named one of the 200 best books of 1988 by the *New York Times* and the best American book of the year by the *London Times* Literary Supplement. He also wrote *A Witness to Genocide: The 1993 Pulitzer Prize-Winning Dispatches on the "Ethnic Cleansing" of Bosnia* (1993). The latter was published in eight countries, including Bosnia-Herzegovina in the last year of the conflict.

Gutman and essayist David Rieff co-edited *Crimes of War: What the Public Should Know* (1999), which reduces the main precepts of international humanitarian law to a set of tools reporters can use in reporting conflict.

Born in New York City and a graduate of William Hall High School in West Hartford, Conn., he earned a Bachelor of Arts in history from Haverford College and a Master of Science in international relations from the London School of Economics. Gutman received an honorary Doctor of Letters from Haverford in 1995 and was the Marvin Weissberg Professor in International Relations at Beloit College in 2002. He was president of Overseas Writers, the oldest association of diplomatic correspondents in Washington.

Gutman is fluent in German and has a reading ability in French and Serbo-Croatian and a grounding in Russian. He lives with his wife and 16-year-old daughter in Herndon, Va.

Frances Hesselbein

Frances Hesselbein is the chairman of the board of governors of the Leader to Leader Institute, formerly the Peter F. Drucker Foundation for Nonprofit Management.

Hesselbein was awarded the Presidential Medal of Freedom, the United States' highest civilian honor, in 1998. The award recognized her leadership as the chief executive officer of the Girl Scouts of the U.S.A. from 1976 to 1990, as well as her role as the founding president of the Drucker Foundation. Her contributions were also recognized by former President George H. W. Bush, who appointed her to two presidential commissions on national and community service.

She serves on many nonprofit and private-sector corporate boards, including the board of the Mutual of America Life Insurance Company, New York; the Veterans Corporation advisory board; and the boards of the Center for Social Initiative at the Harvard Business School and the Hauser Center for Nonprofit Management at the Kennedy School. She is the chairman of the national board of directors for Volunteers of America.

She is the recipient of 16 honorary doctoral degrees. In 2001, Hesselbein was awarded the Henry A. Rosso Medal for Lifetime Achievement in Ethical Fund Raising from the Center on Philanthropy at Indiana University and the International ATHENA Award. In 2002, she was the first recipient of the Dwight D. Eisenhower National Security Series Award for her "outstanding contributions to America's national security."

Hesselbein is editor in chief of the quarterly journal *Leader to Leader* and a co-editor of a book of the same name. She also is a co-editor of the Drucker Foundation's three-volume Future series and *Leading Beyond the Walls* and *Leading for Innovation, Organizing for Results*, the first two books in the foundation's Wisdom to Action series. She was featured in a 2001 special issue of the *Harvard Business Review* as a member of a leadership round table of six leaders in an article entitled "All in a Day's Work." She is the author of *Hesselbein on Leadership*, published in August 2002.

Dr. Charles Krauthammer

Winner of the Pulitzer Prize for distinguished commentary, Dr. Charles Krauthammer writes a syndicated column for the *Washington Post* that appears in over 125 newspapers worldwide. He also writes a monthly essay for *Time* magazine, is a contributing editor to the *Weekly Standard* and the *New Republic*, serves on the editorial boards of the *National Interest* and the *Public Interest*, and is a weekly panelist on "Inside Washington" and a contributor to FOX News.

For two decades, his influential writings have helped shape American foreign policy. He coined the phrase and developed "The Reagan Doctrine" (*Time*, April 1985), defined the structure of the post–Cold War world in "The Unipolar Moment" (*Foreign Affairs*, 1990/1991), and outlined a radically new direction in American foreign policy months before September 11, in "The Bush Doctrine: ABM, Kyoto and the New American Unilateralism" (*Weekly Standard*, June 2001).

Born in New York City and raised in Montreal, Krauthammer received a Bachelor of Arts at McGill University in 1970, a Commonwealth Scholar in politics from Oxford University and a Doctor of Medicine at Harvard University in 1975. While serving as a resident and chief resident in psychiatry at Massachusetts General Hospital, he published scientific papers, including his co-discovery of a form of bipolar disease that continues to be cited in psychiatric literature.

In 1978, he left medical practice, moved to Washington, D.C., to direct planning in psychiatric research for the Carter administration and began contributing articles to the *New Republic*. During the presidential campaign of 1980, he served as a speechwriter to Vice President Walter Mondale. He joined the *New Republic* as a writer and editor in 1981. His *New Republic* writings won the 1984 National Magazine Award for Essays and Criticism, the highest award in magazine journalism.

In 2001, he was appointed to the President's Council on Bioethics. He is a founding board member of Washington's Shoresh Hebrew High School and president of the Krauthammer Foundation, a charitable organization principally dedicated to advancing Jewish culture and education.

Krauthammer lives in suburban Washington with his wife Robyn, an artist, and their son, Daniel.

Steve LeVine

Steve LeVine has been covering South and Central Asia for major U.S. publications for the past 15 years. Since early 2000, he has been the *Wall Street Journal's* correspondent for the Caucasus, Central Asia, Afghanistan, and Pakistan and is based in Almaty, Kazakhstan.

A graduate of California State University, Fresno, and the Columbia Journalism School, he began his reporting career with the Associated Press in Charleston, W.Va., in 1981. He started his overseas career as a *Newsday* special correspondent in the Philippines from 1985 to 1988, and then moved to Pakistan, where he worked for *Newsweek* from 1988 to 1991. He then moved to the former Soviet Union, where he wrote for the *Washington Post* from 1992 to 1995 and the *New York Times* from 1995 to 2000.

He researched and wrote the first lengthy account of the "Afghan Arabs," including Osama bin Laden, for *Newsweek* in 1991, and followed that with a *Washington Post* investigation into the 1993 World Trade Center bombing. Beginning in 1993, LeVine began writing perhaps the first lengthy articles in the U.S. or British press on Caspian Sea oil and Russia's attempts to foreclose the region's sovereignty through control of energy pipelines. Along the way, he covered almost all of the wars of successor states to the Soviet Union: Tajikistan, Nagorno-Karabakh, Abkhazia, Georgia, North Ossetia, and Chechnya. Currently a visiting fellow at Stanford University's Center on Democracy, Development and the Rule of Law, LeVine is writing a book on the history of the Caspian Sea and oil for Random House.

Robert S. Litwak, Ph.D.

Robert S. Litwak, Ph.D., is the director of the Division of International Studies at the Woodrow Wilson International Center for Scholars within the Smithsonian Institution in Washington, D.C., and an adjunct professor in the School of Foreign Service at Georgetown University.

Litwak is the author or editor of eight books, including *Detente and the Nixon Doctrine*, *Security in the Persian Gulf*, *Nuclear Proliferation after the Cold War*, and, most recently, *Rogue States and U.S. Foreign Policy*. He served on the National Security Council staff at the White House as director for nonproliferation and export controls from 1995 to 1996.

Litwak has held visiting fellowships at Harvard University, the International Institute for Strategic Studies, the Russian Academy of Sciences, and the United States Institute of Peace and is a member of the Council on Foreign Relations. He holds a doctoral degree in international relations from the London School of Economics.

Hisham Melhem

Hisham Melhem is the Washington-based correspondent for *As-Safir*, the Lebanese daily; *Al-Qabas*, the *Kuwaiti Daily*; and Radio Monte Carlo in France. He is currently the host of "Across the Ocean," a weekly show for Al-Arabiya, the Dubai-based satellite television station.

Born in Lebanon, Melhem received his Bachelor of Arts in philosophy from Villanova University in 1976; he was awarded the 1998 Alumni Medallion, an honor bestowed upon alumni of the university for exceptional professional and personal achievements. After receiving a Master of Arts in philosophy from Georgetown University, he became a Washington-based journalist and commentator.

Melhem's writings have appeared in publications ranging from the literary journal, *Al-Mawaqif*, to the *Los Angeles Times*, *Middle East Report*, *Middle East Insight* and *Middle East Policy*. He is the author of *Dual Containment: The Demise of a Fallacy*, published by the Center for Contemporary Arab Studies at Georgetown University. Melhem appears regularly on television programs such as "The NewsHour with Jim Lehrer," "Nightline," "Good Morning America," CNN, MSNBC, and "The Charlie Rose Show," as well as National Public Radio. He also speaks regularly at college campuses, think tanks, and interest groups on U.S.-Arab relations, intra-Arab relations, Arab-Israeli issues, the media in the Arab world, U.S. policies and the Arab world, and related topics.

Melhem has interviewed many national and international public figures, most recently President George W. Bush prior to his trip to the Middle East in May 2003.

Philip Merrill

Philip Merrill, president and chairman of the Export-Import Bank of the United States, is a publisher, diplomat, and investor with broad experience in both the public and private sectors. Before joining Ex-Im Bank in December 2002, Merrill was chairman of the board of Capital-Gazette Communications, Inc., which publishes *Washingtonian* magazine, the *Capital* newspaper in Annapolis, and four other Maryland newspapers, and has numerous other investments.

President George W. Bush nominated Merrill for the Ex-Im Bank position September 30, 2002, for a term expiring January 20, 2005. Merrill was confirmed by the U.S. Senate November 14, 2002, and sworn into office on December 4, 2002.

From 1990 to 1992, Merrill served in Brussels as assistant secretary-general of the North Atlantic Treaty Organization. From 1983 to 1990, he served on the Department of Defense Policy Board, and from 1981 to 1983, he was counselor to the under secretary of defense for policy. In 1988, the secretary of defense awarded him the Medal for Distinguished Service, the highest civilian honor given by the department.

Merrill has represented the United States in negotiations on the Law of the Sea Conference, the International Telecommunications Union, and various disarmament and exchange agreements with the former Soviet Union. He is a former special assistant to the deputy secretary of state and has worked in the White House on national security affairs. He has served in six previous administrations.

Merrill has served as a trustee of the Aspen Institute, the Chesapeake Bay Foundation, Johns Hopkins University, Cornell University, and the Corcoran Gallery of Art. He was vice chairman of the Center for Strategic and Budgetary Assessments and a U.S. director of the International Institute of Strategic Studies. He has served on the Defense Business Board. Among other organizations, Merrill served on the University of Maryland board of visitors and on the boards of the Johns Hopkins School of Advanced International Studies and the Advanced Physics Laboratories.

He is a member of the Council on Foreign Relations, the Chief Executives' Organization, and the World Presidents' Organization. For many years, he chaired the White House Fellow Commission regional panels.

Merrill graduated from Cornell University and the Harvard Business School's Program for Management Development. He and his wife Ellie have three children, Douglas, Cathy, and Nancy.

Dan Murphy

Dan Murphy has reported on Southeast Asia for the *Christian Science Monitor* for the past three years. His special focus has been on Indonesia, where he has lived for the past decade. Murphy produced some of the first stories linking al Qaeda to Indonesian militants; he also reported on the impeachment of President Abdurrahman Wahid, the failure to prosecute Indonesian troops for human rights abuses in East Timor, and the separatist war in Aceh. He also wrote a series on the impact that Indonesia's political turmoil is having on the environment.

From 1995 to 1998, Murphy founded and ran the Jakarta bureau for Bloomberg News, and, from 1998 to 2000, he was the lead economics and finance reporter in Indonesia for the *Far Eastern Economic Review*. He was the magazine's reporter on the ground during East Timor's independence referendum and wrote cover stories on the Suharto family's business dealings, on the battle for control of Indonesia's biggest car manufacturer, and on populist economic policies that were slowing Indonesia's recovery. Murphy is the author of a comprehensive report for the International Crisis Group on the religious war in Indonesia's two Maluku provinces and has contributed op-eds to the *International Herald Tribune*.

A graduate of Oberlin College, he is fluent in Bahasa Indonesia.

Polly (Mary) Nayak

Polly (Mary) Nayak is an independent consultant and a senior advisor at Abraxas Corporation, McLean, Va. She is currently consulting on issues ranging from nuclear weapons to terrorism. Nayak is a member of the Council on Foreign Relations, Asia Society Independent Task Force on India and South Asia, the Brookings' Islam Task Force, and working groups on South Asia and on nonproliferation at the Center for Strategic and International Studies and Henry L. Stimson Center. Nayak has lectured extensively on U.S. foreign policy and South Asia.

Nayak retired in October 2002 from the CIA after a 20-year career that began and ended with assignments on South Asia. As issue manager for South Asia from

1995 to 2001, she was the intelligence community's senior officer and expert on the region, shaping intelligence and crisis support for the White House and Congress. Nayak also ran the Directorate of Intelligence's South Asia Group, which produces multidisciplinary analysis of political, economic, military, and terrorism- and proliferation-related developments.

Nayak capped her CIA career with a Federal Executive Fellowship at the Brookings Institution in Washington during 2001–2002, which spotlighted her South Asia credentials after September 11. Brookings published her policy brief, "Reducing Collateral Damage to Indo-Pakistani Relations from the War on Terrorism," in September 2002.

Commendations received by Nayak for her work at CIA included an interagency award for developing and launching counterdenial/deception training for the intelligence community and a Career Intelligence Medal.

Before joining the CIA, Nayak served for four years on an Indian corporate team negotiating international turnkey projects. She lived in rural India from 1969 to 1974. She earlier worked at a Boston-based agency that helped resettle Mideastern Jewish refugees.

Nayak earned a Bachelor of Arts in the honors social studies program from Harvard University, a Master of Arts from the Fletcher School of Law and Diplomacy and completed coursework and examinations for a doctoral degree in political science at MIT. Her graduate fields include comparative politics, demography and political economy, with a South Asia focus. She is fluent in French and Spanish, and rusty in Hindustani.

Janne E. Nolan, Ph.D.

Janne E. Nolan, Ph.D., serves on the faculty of the security studies program at Georgetown University and is working on a book about dissent and national security for the Century Foundation of New York.

Nolan has held several senior positions in the private sector, including as foreign policy director at the Century Foundation of New York, senior fellow in foreign policy at the Brookings Institution and senior international security consultant at Science Applications International Corporation. Her public service includes positions as a foreign affairs officer in the Department of State, senior representative to the Senate Armed Services Committee for former Senator Gary Hart, and a member of the National Defense Panel and the Secretary of Defense's Policy Board.

Nolan chaired the Presidential Panel on U.S. Technology Transfer Policy in 1997 and was appointed to several blue ribbon commissions, including the 1998 Accountability Review Board investigating terrorism in East Africa and the Deutch Commission, examining government reorganization for nonproliferation.

Nolan is the author of six books and many articles on international security and foreign policy in publications such as *Foreign Affairs, Foreign Policy,* the *New*

York Times, Scientific American and the New Republic. She is a member of the Council on Foreign Relations, the Aspen Strategy Group, and the Cosmos Club and serves on the board of the Arms Control Association, the Chemical and Biological Arms Control Institute, the Executive Committee of the Institute for International and Strategic Studies, the Lawyers' Alliance for World Security, and the board of advisors for the Nixon Center.

Nolan earned a doctoral degree from the Fletcher School of Law and Diplomacy, Tufts University.

Joseph S. Nye, Jr., Ph.D.

Joseph S. Nye, Jr., Ph.D., became dean of the John F. Kennedy School of Government, Harvard University, in December 1995. He joined the Harvard faculty in 1964 and taught one of the largest core curriculum courses in the college.

From 1977 to 1979, Nye served as deputy to the under secretary of state for security assistance, science and technology, and chaired the National Security Council Group on Nonproliferation of Nuclear Weapons. In recognition of his service, he received the highest Department of State commendation, the Distinguished Honor Award. In 1993 and 1994, he was chairman of the National Intelligence Council, which coordinates intelligence estimates for the president. He was awarded the intelligence community's Distinguished Service Medal. In 1994 and 1995, he served as assistant secretary of defense for international security affairs.

A fellow of the American Academy of Arts and Sciences and of the Academy of Diplomacy, Nye has also been a senior fellow of the Aspen Institute, director of the Aspen Strategy Group and a member of the executive committee of the Trilateral Commission. He has been a trustee of Wells College and Radcliffe College.

A member of the editorial boards of Foreign Policy magazine and the Journal of International Security Affairs, he is the author of numerous books and more than 150 articles in professional journals. His most recent books are The Paradox of American Power (2002), Understanding International Conflicts, 4th edition (2002), and Power and Interdependence, 3d edition (2000). In addition, he has published policy articles in such venues as the New York Times, the Washington Post, the International Herald Tribune, the Wall Street Journal, and the Financial Times. He has appeared on numerous television news programs, as well as Australian, British, French, Swiss, Japanese, and Korean television.

In addition to teaching at Harvard, Nye has taught for brief periods in Geneva, Ottawa and London. He has lived for extended periods in Europe, East Africa, and Central America and traveled to more than 90 countries.

Nye received his bachelor's degree summa cum laude from Princeton University in 1958. He did postgraduate work at Oxford University on a Rhodes Scholarship and earned a doctoral degree in political science from Harvard University.

His hobbies include fly-fishing, hiking, squash, skiing, gardening, and working on his tree farm in New Hampshire. He is married to Molly Harding Nye, an art consultant and potter. They have three sons.

Sandra L. Pack

Sandra L. Pack became assistant secretary of the Army for financial management and comptroller November 12, 2001, following her nomination by President George W. Bush. Pack is the principal advisor to the secretary of the Army for all comptroller functions and all financial management activities and operations. Specifically, she is responsible for the planning, programming, budgeting, and execution system of the Department of the Army. She supervises Army finance and accounting policies, practices, and procedures. She also has oversight of the Army-wide cost and economic analysis functions and activities, and supervision, direction, and development of Army independent cost estimates.

Pack has served in a variety of financial management leadership positions to include director of planning and operations, MicroProse Division of Spectrum Holobyte Inc.; director, Small Business Consulting and Accounting Services; and director, Microcomputer Consulting and Accounting Services, Ernst and Young.

Previously, Pack served as the director of treasury for Bush for President, Inc., and for Bush-Cheney 2000, Inc. She also served as deputy director of treasury for Bob Dole for President, Inc., and director of treasury for Phil Gramm for President, Inc.

Pack is a certified public accountant with a business degree from Notre Dame College in Baltimore. She resides in Arnold, Md.

George Perkovich, Ph.D.

Until arriving at the Carnegie Endowment as vice president for studies in January 2002, George Perkovich, Ph.D., was deputy director for programs and director of the Secure World Program of the W. Alton Jones Foundation. He oversaw a total of $26 million in annual grants and also designed and implemented initiatives to further the board's mandate of reducing the risk of nuclear war. He was with the foundation from 1990 through 2001.

A prolific writer, Perkovich's work has appeared in a range of publications, including *Foreign Affairs* magazine, the *Atlantic Monthly*, the *Weekly Standard*, the *Wall Street Journal*, the *Washington Post*, and the *New York Times*. He wrote *India's Nuclear Bomb* (1999, updated paperback edition, 2001). The book received the Herbert Feis Award from the American Historical Association and the A. K. Coomaraswamy Prize from the Association for Asian Studies.

Before his work with the Jones Foundation, Perkovich served as a speechwriter and foreign policy advisor to Senator Joseph Biden. He is a member of the Council on Foreign Relations and the International Institute for Strategic Studies.

Perkovich speaks both French and Russian. He received his Bachelor of Arts from the University of California at Santa Cruz, his Master of Arts in Soviet studies from Harvard University, and his Doctor of Philosophy in foreign affairs from the University of Virginia.

Daniel B. Poneman

Daniel B. Poneman, principal, the Scowcroft Group, has extensive expertise in the defense, energy, and export control arenas. For nine years, he practiced law in Washington, D.C., assisting clients in a wide variety of regulatory and policy matters, including export controls, trade policy, and sanctions issues.

From 1993 to 1996, Poneman served as special assistant to the president and senior director for nonproliferation and export controls at the National Security Council, with responsibilities for the development and implementation of U.S. policy in such areas as peaceful nuclear cooperation, missile technology and space-launch activities, sanctions determinations, chemical and biological arms control efforts, and conventional arms transfer policy. Poneman joined the NSC staff in 1990 as director of defense policy and arms control, after service in the Department of Energy. He has served as a member of the Commission to Assess the Organization of the Federal Government to Combat the Proliferation of Weapons of Mass Destruction as well as other federal advisory panels.

He received his Bachelor of Arts and Doctor of Laws from Harvard University, and a Master of Letters in politics from Oxford University. Poneman is the author of books on nuclear energy policy and on Argentina and is a member of the Council of Foreign Relations.

Donald H. Rumsfeld

Donald H. Rumsfeld was sworn in as the 21st secretary of defense January 20, 2001.

Rumsfeld is responsible for directing the actions of the Department of Defense in response to the September 11, 2001, terrorist attacks. The department has developed a new defense strategy and replaced the old model for sizing forces with an approach more relevant to the 21st century. Rumsfeld proposed and the president approved a significant reorganization of the worldwide command structure, the Unified Command Plan, which resulted in the establishment of the U.S. Northern Command and the U.S. Strategic Command.

Rumsfeld attended Princeton University on academic and Navy ROTC scholarships and received a Bachelor of Arts in 1954. He served in the Navy from 1954 to 1957 as an aviator and flight instructor. He retired from the Navy Reserve in 1989 with the rank of captain.

In 1957, he came to Washington to serve as an administrative assistant to a congressman. He was elected to the House of Representatives from Illinois in 1962, and was re-elected in 1964, 1966, and 1968. Rumsfeld resigned from Congress in 1969 to join the Nixon cabinet. From 1973 to 1974, he served as the U.S. ambassador to NATO in Brussels.

He was recalled to Washington in 1974, to serve as chairman of the transition to the presidency of Gerald R. Ford. From 1974 to 1975, he served as the chief of staff of the White House and a member of the president's cabinet. He served as the 13th secretary of defense, the youngest in the country's history from 1975 to 1977. Rumsfeld was awarded the nation's highest civilian award, the Presidential Medal of Freedom, in 1977.

From 1977 to 1985, he served as chief executive officer, president, and then-chairman of G. D. Searle and Co. The successful turnaround there earned him awards as the Outstanding Chief Executive Officer in the Pharmaceutical Industry from the *Wall Street Transcript* (1980) and *Financial World* (1981). He served as chairman and chief executive officer of General Instrument Corporation from 1990 to 1993.

While in the private sector, Rumsfeld's civic activities have included service as a member of the National Academy of Public Administration. He has been a member of the boards of trustees of the Gerald R. Ford Foundation, the Hoover Institution at Stanford University, and the National Park Foundation, as well as chairman of the Eisenhower Exchange Fellowships, Inc.

In 1977, Rumsfeld was awarded the nation's highest civilian award, the Presidential Medal of Freedom.

Scott D. Sagan, Ph.D.

Scott D. Sagan, Ph.D., is a professor of political science and co-director of Stanford's Center for International Security and Cooperation. Before joining the Stanford faculty, Sagan was a lecturer in the department of government at Harvard University and served as a special assistant to the director of the organization of the Joint Chiefs of Staff in the Pentagon.

Sagan is the author of *Moving Targets: Nuclear Strategy and National Security* (1989); *The Limits of Safety: Organizations, Accidents, and Nuclear Weapons* (1993); and co-author with Kenneth N. Waltz of *The Spread of Nuclear Weapons: A Debate Renewed*, 2d edition (2002). Sagan received Stanford University's 1996 Hoagland Prize for Undergraduate Teaching and the 1998 Dean's Award for Distinguished Teaching.

Sagan's most recent articles are "The Madman Nuclear Alert: Secrecy, Signaling, and Safety in the October 1969 Crisis," co-authored with Jeremi Suri (*International Security*, Spring 2003) and "The Problem of Redundancy Problem: Why More Nuclear

Security Forces May Produce Less Nuclear Security" (*Risk Analysis*, Spring 2003). Sagan's redundancy article is also the 2003 winner of Columbia University's Institute of War and Peace Studies paper competition on political violence.

Currently, his main research interests are nuclear proliferation in South Asia, ethics and international relations, and accidents in complex organizations. He recently organized three CISAC-sponsored workshops on "Preventing Nuclear War in South Asia" in India, Pakistan, and Thailand. He has lectured on the dangers of nuclear weapons theft and accidents at Pakistan's National Defense College and India's Institute for Defense and Strategic Analysis in New Delhi and continues to collaborate with Indian and Pakistani officials and military officers on that project.

Barham Salih, Ph.D.

Barham Salih, Ph.D., regional administrator, Sulaimania, Iraq, was born in 1960 in Iraqi Kurdistan. He joined the Patriotic Union of Kurdistan in 1976 while it was still an underground movement. He was arrested twice by Iraqi secret police and was forced to take his high school finals while in prison. Nevertheless, he achieved the highest grade possible in all Iraq that year. He left Iraq in 1979.

In 1985, PUK leader Jalal Talabani called upon Salih to serve as the group's spokesman in London. In 1991, having been elected to the PUK leadership, he departed for Washington, D.C., and served there for 10 years as the PUK and Kurdistan Regional Government representative to the United States.

On January 21, 2001, he assumed the premiership of the Kurdistan Regional Government in Sulaimania. The main features of his platform are the need to revitalize the Kurdistan region to create an open, pluralistic society and develop civic culture; the empowerment of women; educational and social reforms; freedom of expression; and the creation of an environment in which a free media can exist. He is a leading advocate of a strong Kurdish role in shaping the new, democratic Iraq.

He was the target of an assassination attempt by an al Qaeda–affiliated terrorist group, Ansar al-Islam, in April 2002, during which five of his assistants and bodyguards lost their lives.

Salih and the PUK worked with the United States during preparations for Operation IRAQI FREEDOM and provided support for joint U.S.-Kurdish operations against Ansar al-Islam. PUK forces served under U.S. command and, with U.S. troops, helped liberate Iraq. PUK forces continue to work with the U.S.-led coalition in Iraq.

Salih received a Bachelor of Science in civil and structural engineering from the Cardiff University and earned a doctorate in statistics and computer modeling from the University of Liverpool.

Salih is married to Sarbagh Salih, Ph.D., a biologist, who is also a Kurdish women's rights activist. They have a daughter.

General Peter J. Schoomaker

General Peter J. Schoomaker became the 35th chief of staff of the United States Army August 1, 2003.

Prior to his current assignment, Schoomaker spent 31 years in a variety of command and staff assignments with both conventional and special operations forces. He participated in numerous deployment operations, including DESERT ONE in Iran, URGENT FURY in Grenada, JUST CAUSE in Panama, DESERT SHIELD/DESERT STORM in Southwest Asia, and UPHOLD DEMOCRACY in Haiti. He also supported various worldwide joint contingency operations, including those in the Balkans.

Early in his career, Schoomaker was a reconnaissance platoon leader and rifle company commander with the 2d Battalion, 4th Infantry Division, and a cavalry troop commander with the 2d Armored Cavalry. From 1978 to 1981, he commanded a squadron in the 1st Special Forces Operational Detachment–D. Later, Schoomaker served as the squadron executive officer, 2d Squadron, 2d Armored Cavalry. In 1983, he served as special operations officer, J–3, Joint Special Operations Command. From 1985 to 1988, Schoomaker commanded another squadron in the 1st Special Forces Operational Detachment–D. He returned as the commander, 1st Special Forces Operational Detachment–D from 1989 to 1992.

Schoomaker served as the commanding general of the Joint Special Operations Command from 1994 to 1996, followed by command of the United States Army Special Operations Command at Fort Bragg, N.C., through October 1997. His most recent assignment was as the commander for United States Special Operations Command at MacDill Air Force Base, Fla., from November 1997 to November 2000.

His awards and decorations include the Defense Distinguished Service Medal, two Army Distinguished Service Medals, four Defense Superior Service Medals, three Legions of Merit, two Bronze Star Medals, two Defense Meritorious Service Medals, three Meritorious Service Medals, Joint Service Commendation Medal, Joint Service Achievement Medal, Combat Infantryman Badge, Master Parachutist Badge and HALO (high-altitude, low-opening) Wings, the Special Forces Tab, and the Ranger Tab.

Schoomaker graduated from the University of Wyoming in 1969 with a Bachelor of Science degree. He also holds a Master of Arts in management from Central Michigan University and an honorary Doctorate of Laws from Hampden-Sydney College. His military education includes the Marine Corps Amphibious Warfare School, the United States Army Command and General Staff College, the National War College, and the John F. Kennedy School of Government Program for Senior Executives in National and International Security Management.

Ambassador Wendy R. Sherman

Ambassador Wendy R. Sherman is a principal of the Albright Group, an international advisory firm. Prior to forming the group, she was appointed by President Clinton to serve as the counselor of the Department of State from July 1997 through January 2001 with rank of ambassador. Sherman served then–Secretary of State Madeleine Albright as a special advisor and consultant on major issues of foreign policy, provided guidance to the State Department, and undertook special assignments. At the same time, she was the special advisor to the president and secretary of state and the North Korea policy coordinator.

Sherman has worked for over 25 years in both the public and private sectors—in national, state, and local organizations as well as in international arenas and neighborhoods. From April 1996 until July 1997, she was president and CEO of the Fannie Mae Foundation.

From 1993 to 1996, Sherman served Secretary of State Warren Christopher as assistant secretary for legislative affairs, where she directed the legislative efforts of the State Department with Congress. Among other issues, she led the successful efforts to obtain the funding for Russia and the Newly Independent States after the breakup of the Soviet Union and support for the Dayton Accords.

From 1991 to 1993, she specialized in strategic communications as a partner in the political and media consulting firm of Doak, Shrum, Harris and Sherman. Prior to that, she directed the political organization, EMILY's List. She is credited with the organization's strategic development that led to groundbreaking numbers of female candidates in 1992.

Sherman has worked in a variety of positions in both government and nonprofit organizations. She was chief of staff for three years for then-Congresswoman Barbara Mikulski; campaign manager for Mikulski's first successful Senate campaign; special secretary for children and youth in Maryland, a cabinet-level position; and director of Maryland's Office of Child Welfare, supervising protective services, foster care, adoptions, and group homes.

Sherman attended Smith College from 1967 to 1969, and completed her Bachelor of Arts cum laude from Boston University in 1971. In 1976, she earned a master's degree in social work, Phi Kappa Phi, from the University of Maryland.

Ambassador Nancy E. Soderberg

Ambassador Nancy E. Soderberg is Vice President of the International Crisis Group.

She has nearly 20 years of experience in the formation of U.S. foreign policy. Soderberg has a deep understanding of policy making and negotiations at the highest levels of government and the United Nations. Soderberg achieved international recognition for her efforts to promote peace in Northern Ireland, participated in a UN mission to Indonesia and East Timor, negotiated key UN resolutions regarding the Middle East and Africa, and advised President Clinton on policies toward many nations including China, Japan, and Russia.

In April 2001, Soderberg joined the New York office of the International Crisis Group as vice president. ICG, based in Brussels, is an international nonprofit organization that advocates policies to prevent and contain conflict.

From 1997 to 2001, Soderberg served as alternate representative to the United Nations as a presidential appointee, with the rank of ambassador. Her responsibilities included representing the United States at the Security Council on a wide range of current national security issues, including conflict resolution, promotion of democracy abroad, trade policy, and arms control. As a key participant in the development of U.S. foreign policy, she worked closely with Congress and key agencies of the U.S. government, including the White House, State Department, and Department of Defense.

From 1993 to 1997, Soderberg served as the third-ranking official of the National Security Council at the White House, as deputy assistant to the president for national security affairs. She was responsible for day-to-day crisis management, briefing the president, developing U.S. national security policy at the highest levels of government, and handling issues regarding the press and Congress. Soderberg served as deputy director of the Presidential Transition for National Security and as the foreign policy director for the Clinton-Gore 1992 campaign. Before joining the Clinton campaign, Soderberg worked as the senior foreign policy advisor to Senator Edward M. Kennedy.

In 1984, she received a Master of Science from Georgetown University's School of Foreign Service, concentrating on international economics and political risk analysis. She received her Bachelor of Arts in 1980 from Vanderbilt University. Soderberg speaks excellent French and intermediate Spanish. She is a member of the Council on Foreign Relations, a member of the board of Concern Worldwide, and an advisory board member for the National Committee on American Foreign Policy and the Tannenbaum Center. She publishes and speaks regularly on national security policy. She is a regular commentator on national and international television and radio.

Fareed Yasseen, Ph.D.

Fareed Yasseen, Ph.D., is an executive committee member of the Movement of Independent Iraqi Democrats and an advisor to Adnan Pachachi, member of the Iraqi Governing Council. He has been involved in Iraqi political activism and human rights advocacy for more than 10 years. Yasseen is the founder of Mafqud.org, an online memorial to those who have disappeared in Iraq. He has worked at leading research institutions, think tanks, and specialized United Nations agencies. Yasseen was educated in Iraq, Switzerland, and the United States.

GLOSSARY

ABM	Antiballistic missile
ACS	Automation and Control Solutions
AID	U.S. Agency for International Development
ANC	African National Congress
Arab League	The popular name for the League of Arab States, which was formed in 1945 in an attempt to give political expression to the Arab nations
Ba'athist	Ba'ath party, Arab political party, in Syria and in Iraq
BBC	British Broadcasting Corporation
BJP	Bharatiya Janata Party, an Indian political party that espouses Hindu nationalism
Cancun talks	World Trade Organization negotiations in Cancun, Mexico
CEO	Chief Executive Officer
CFR	Code of Federal Regulations
CIA	Central Intelligence Agency
CIS	Commonwealth of Independent States
CISAC	Center for International Security and Cooperation, Stanford University
CivPol	International Civilian Police program
CNN	Cable News Network
CONOPS	Contingency operations
CPA	Coalition Provisional Authority
CTBT	Comprehensive Test Ban Treaty
DCI	Director of central intelligence
D&D	Denial and deception
DIA	Defense Intelligence Agency
DMZ	Demilitarized Zone
DOD	Department of Defense

Doha talks	World Trade Organization negotiations in Doha, Qatar
DPRK	Democratic People's Republic of Korea (North Korea)
EBRD	European Bank for Reconstruction and Development
EGPWS	Enhanced Ground Proximity Warning System
EU	European Union
Ex-Im	Export-Import Bank of the United States
FLN	Front de Liberation Nationale
G–8	The countries of Canada, France, Germany, Italy, Japan, Russia, the United Kingdom, and the United States. Representatives from these countries meet to discuss economic concerns.
GCC	Gulf Cooperation Council
GDP	Gross domestic product
Goldwater-Nichols	Goldwater-Nichols Department of Defense Reorganization Act of 1986
Hart-Rudman Commission	U.S. Commission on National Security/21st Century
Heisenberg uncertainty principle or principle of intelligence	Uncertainty principle, physical principle, enunciated by Werner Heisenberg in 1927 that places an absolute, theoretical limit on the combined accuracy of certain pairs of simultaneous, related measurements.
HFCs	Hydrofluorocarbons
HIV/AIDS	Human Immunodeficiency Virus (HIV); Acquired Immunodeficiency Syndrome (AIDS)
HVAC	Heating, ventilating, and air conditioning
IAEA	International Atomic Energy Agency
IC	Intelligence community
ID	Infantry division
IGC	Iraqi Governing Council
IMET	International Military Education and Training
IMF	International Monetary Fund
ISS	International Space Station

JDAMs	Joint Direct Attack Munitions
JI	Jemaah Islamiya
League of Nations	A world organization established in 1920 to promote international cooperation and peace.
Marshall Plan	European recovery program
MEMS	Micro ElectroMechanical Systems
MIT	Massachusetts Institute of Technology
Mullah	A title of respect in Islamic countries for a person who is learned in, teaches, or expounds the sacred law
NAFTA	North American Free Trade Agreement
NASA	National Aeronautics and Space Administration
NATO	North Atlantic Treaty Organization
NBA	National Basketball Association
NIC	National Intelligence Council
Northern Alliance	The alliance is primarily composed of three non-Pashtun ethnic groups—Tajiks, Uzbeks, and Hazaras—and in the past relied on a core of some 15,000 troops to defend its territories against the predominantly Pashtun Taleban.
NPT	Treaty on the Nonproliferation of Nuclear Weapons
Nunn-Lugar program	Nunn-Lugar Cooperative Threat Reduction Program
OECD	Organisation for Economic Co-operation and Development
OIC	Organization of the Islamic Conference
OPEC	Organization of Petroleum Exporting Countries
Paris Club	The Paris Club is an informal group of official creditors whose role is to find coordinated and sustainable solutions to the payment difficulties experienced by debtor nations.
Pew polls	The Pew Research Center is an independent opinion research group that studies attitudes toward the press, politics, and public policy issues.

PTA	Parent Teacher Association
PUK	Patriotic Union of Kurdistan
Q&A	Question and answer
RAND Corporation	The RAND Corporation is a nonprofit research organization.
R&D	Research and development
Resolution 1483	UN Security Council Resolution 1483 lifts the sanctions on Iraq, and the international community pledges assistance for the people of Iraq.
RUF	Revolutionary United Front
Sigint	Signal intelligence
Soft power and hard power	Soft power is the ability to get what you want by attracting and persuading others to adopt your goals. Hard power is the ability to use the carrots and sticks of economic and military might to make others follow your will.
Sunni triangle	A roughly triangular area of Iraq to the northwest of Baghdad. It is inhabited mainly by Sunni Muslims. The usual definition of the triangle's three corners is Baghdad–Al-Ramadi–Tikrit.
Supreme National Council	Another name for the Supreme National Security Council. It is an institution founded in the course of the revision of the constitution of the Islamic Republic of Iran (IRI). It has been established with an aim to watch over the Islamic revolution and safeguard the IRI's national interests as well as its sovereignty and territorial integrity.
Taliban	A fundamentalist Islamic militia; in 1995 the Taliban militia took over Afghanistan and in 1996 took Kabul and set up an Islamic government.
TSCP	Theater Security Cooperation Plans—formerly Theater Engagement Plan (TEP)
UAE	United Arab Emirates, federation of sheikhdoms

UN	United Nations
UN Compensation Commission	It was created to process claims and pay compensation for losses and damage suffered as a direct result of Iraq's unlawful invasion and occupation of Kuwait.
UPI	United Press International
USO	United Service Organizations
WMD	Weapons of mass destruction
World Bank	The World Bank group provides loans and technical assistance to developing countries to reduce poverty and advance sustainable economic growth.
WTO	World Trade Organization